MacIntyre's *After Virtue* at 40

Since its publication in 1981, Alasdair MacIntyre's *After Virtue* has been recognised as a classic. Primarily a work of moral philosophy, it also draws on sociology, classics, political science and theology to effect a unique intellectual synthesis, and its combination of erudition and challenging, even provocative argument has made a significant impact throughout the humanities disciplines. This volume of new essays unpacks the influence of *After Virtue* on ethical and political theory, sociology and theology, and offers a multi-faceted exploration of its significance. The essays offer a way into MacIntyre's philosophy and demonstrate how, rather than waning in influence over the past forty years, his most seminal text has found an ever-wider audience and continues to inspire controversy and debate in the humanities.

Tom Angier is Associate Professor of Philosophy at the University of Cape Town. He is the editor of *The Cambridge Companion to Natural Law Ethics* (Cambridge, 2019) and the author of *Human Nature, Human Goods: A Theory of Natural Perfectionism* (Cambridge, forthcoming).

Cambridge Philosophical Anniversaries

The volumes in this series reflect on classic philosophy books from the second half of the twentieth century, assessing their achievements, their influence on the field, and their lasting significance.

Titles Published in This Series

MacIntyre's *After Virtue* at 40
Edited by Tom Angier
Rawls's *A Theory of Justice* at 50
Edited by Paul Weithman
Cavell's *Must We Mean What We Say?* at 50
Edited by Greg Chase, Juliet Floyd, and Sandra Laugier

This list can also be seen at www.cambridge.org/cpa

MacIntyre's *After Virtue* at 40

Edited by
Tom Angier
University of Cape Town

CAMBRIDGE
UNIVERSITY PRESS

Shaftesbury Road, Cambridge CB2 8EA, United Kingdom

One Liberty Plaza, 20th Floor, New York, NY 10006, USA

477 Williamstown Road, Port Melbourne, VIC 3207, Australia

314–321, 3rd Floor, Plot 3, Splendor Forum, Jasola District Centre, New Delhi – 110025, India

103 Penang Road, #05-06/07, Visioncrest Commercial, Singapore 238467

Cambridge University Press is part of Cambridge University Press & Assessment, a department of the University of Cambridge.

We share the University's mission to contribute to society through the pursuit of education, learning and research at the highest international levels of excellence.

www.cambridge.org
Information on this title: www.cambridge.org/9781316513781

DOI: 10.1017/9781009076036

© Cambridge University Press & Assessment 2024

This publication is in copyright. Subject to statutory exception and to the provisions of relevant collective licensing agreements, no reproduction of any part may take place without the written permission of Cambridge University Press & Assessment.

First published 2024

A catalogue record for this publication is available from the British Library.

Library of Congress Cataloging-in-Publication Data
Names: Angier, Tom P. S., editor.
Title: MacIntyre's After Virtue at 40 / edited by Tom Angier.
Description: Cambridge ; New York : Cambridge University Press, 2024. | Series: Cambridge philosophical anniversaries | Includes bibliographical references and index.
Identifiers: LCCN 2023019728 (print) | LCCN 2023019729 (ebook) | ISBN 9781316513781 (hardback) | ISBN 9781009074759 (paperback) | ISBN 9781009076036 (epub)
Subjects: LCSH: MacIntyre, Alasdair C. After virtue | MacIntyre, Alasdair C.–Criticism and interpretation. | Virtue. | Ethics.
Classification: LCC B1647.M124 M243 2024 (print) | LCC B1647.M124 (ebook) | DDC 170/.42–dc23/eng/20230523
LC record available at https://lccn.loc.gov/2023019728
LC ebook record available at https://lccn.loc.gov/2023019729

ISBN 978-1-316-51378-1 Hardback

Cambridge University Press & Assessment has no responsibility for the persistence or accuracy of URLs for external or third-party internet websites referred to in this publication and does not guarantee that any content on such websites is, or will remain, accurate or appropriate.

Contents

List of Contributors	*page* vii
Introduction	1

Part I *After Virtue* and Ethical Theory

1 *After Virtue* and Virtue Ethics TOM ANGIER	13
2 *After Virtue* and Happiness JENNIFER A. HERDT	31
3 *After Virtue*: Nietzsche *or* Aristotle, Institutions *and* Practices KELVIN KNIGHT	47

Part II *After Virtue* and Political Theory

4 *After Virtue*'s Critique of Liberalism DAVID RONDEL	69
5 *After Virtue* and the Rise of Postliberalism NATHAN PINKOSKI	85
6 *After Virtue* and Conservatism DAVID MCPHERSON	107
7 *After Virtue* as a Real Utopia JASON BLAKELY	125

Part III *After Virtue* and Narrative

8 Form, Style and Voice in *After Virtue* STEPHEN MULHALL	143

vi   Contents

9   *After Virtue*, Narrative and the Human Good   159
    MICAH LOTT

10 *After Virtue* as a Narrative of Revolutionary Practical Reason   179
    CHRISTOPHER STEPHEN LUTZ

Part IV   *After Virtue* beyond Philosophy

11 Theological Overtones in *After Virtue*   201
    CHARLES R. PINCHES

12 Law as Social Practice: *After Virtue* and Legal Theory   219
    MARK D. RETTER

13 *After Virtue*, Managers and Business Ethics   239
    PAUL BLACKLEDGE

    Bibliography   258
    Index   276

Contributors

TOM ANGIER is Associate Professor in Philosophy at the University of Cape Town.

PAUL BLACKLEDGE is Professor of Philosophy at Shanxi University.

JASON BLAKELY is Associate Professor of Political Science at Pepperdine University.

JENNIFER A. HERDT is Gilbert L. Stark Professor of Christian Ethics at Yale University.

KELVIN KNIGHT is Reader in Ethics and Politics at London Metropolitan University and Senior Researcher in Management and Political Science at Mykolas Romeris University, Vilnius, Lithuania.

MICAH LOTT is Associate Professor of Philosophy at Boston College.

CHRISTOPHER STEPHEN LUTZ is Professor of Philosophy at Saint Meinrad Seminary and School of Theology.

DAVID MCPHERSON is Professor of Philosophy at the Hamilton Center, University of Florida.

STEPHEN MULHALL is Professor of Philosophy at New College, Oxford.

CHARLES R. PINCHES is Professor of Theology at the University of Scranton.

NATHAN PINKOSKI is Visiting Faculty Fellow at the Hamilton Center, University of Florida.

MARK D. RETTER is Postdoctoral Researcher at the Lauterpacht Centre, University of Cambridge.

DAVID RONDEL is Associate Professor of Philosophy at the University of Nevada, Reno.

Introduction

After Virtue is, by common consent, Alasdair MacIntyre's most seminal work – and certainly the most cited. Compared to other books in late twentieth-century Anglophone moral philosophy, nothing can match its erudition, breadth of reference or the scope and ambition of its arguments. Its pungent advocacy of a resurrected Aristotelianism, in 'social teleological' mode – or what Kelvin Knight (Chapter 3) calls 'sociological Aristotelianism' – has challenged minds not only in philosophy, but also in political science, sociology, anthropology, theology and even beyond the academy. Late Chief Rabbi Lord Jonathan Sacks, for example, has referred to *After Virtue* as establishing MacIntyre as one of the intellectual *gedolim* ('greats'). It seems bizarre, therefore, that at the same time, and as Charles Pinches (Chapter 11) puts it, 'MacIntyre's work ... still lies somewhat off to the side; the bulk of modern moral philosophy goes on as if it had not been written'. Indeed, we find the same old utilitarian and deontological theories retailed in the philosophy journals, albeit with new qualifications and addenda. How is this state of affairs to be explained? Why has *After Virtue* gained more plaudits, if anything, outside philosophy than within it?

At least three immediate, compossible explanations suggest themselves. First, *After Virtue* constitutes a head-on critique of the dominant modes of Anglophone normative theory. Two of MacIntyre's favourite adjectives, 'rival' and 'incompatible', imply that the only proper mode of response to his critique is simply to cease fealty to Kant or Bentham and Mill altogether. It is not surprising, then, that this uncompromising approach to the *practice* of moral philosophy has met with little favour, especially given the *institutional* career paths that depend on its rejection. Second – and here institutions reinforce practice most strongly – *After Virtue* blurs disciplinary boundaries to an extent unprecedented in modern Anglophone moral philosophy. As I suggested above, it draws liberally on political science (e.g. Trotskyism), sociology (e.g. the work of Goffman), anthropology (e.g. studies of *taboo*) and theology (e.g. Aquinas). In the context of a highly, perhaps increasingly

2   Introduction

compartmentalised academy, this inter-disciplinary mode of moral enquiry cannot but inspire bewilderment, even hostility. Third, the argument of *After Virtue* is sometimes brusque and even dismissive, for example in its handling of the notion of rights. Although Stephen Mulhall (Chapter 8) provides a brilliant defence of this strategy, once again it is not surprising that many analytic philosophers – who pride themselves on their painstaking meticulousness – have found this a good excuse not to engage with the text more deeply.

While these three explanations have a role to play, they do not take us very far. In order to understand *After Virtue*'s seminality-cum-marginality more fully, we need to employ two concepts central to the text itself. This time the relevant concepts are not 'practice' or 'institution', however, but 'tradition' and 'narrative'. *After Virtue* partakes, in short, of a tradition of moral enquiry that is largely alien to the Anglophone world. That tradition takes its bearings partly from the Greeks, but no less – indeed, perhaps more – from Judaeo-Christianity and Marxism. That this is MacIntyre's *Gedankenwelt* is apparent from his first book, namely *Marxism: An Interpretation* (1953), later revised and republished as *Marxism and Christianity* (1968). Twenty-eight years later, moreover, the traces of this intellectual tradition are still visible in *After Virtue*, which takes Leon Trotsky as seriously as Saint Benedict. This bipolar movement between Christian moral reflection and Marxist critique has characterised much moral philosophy on the European continent. In Germany, one could cite, for example, Ernst Bloch, in France, Pierre Manent, in Italy, Augusto del Noce, and in Poland, Ryszard Legutko. For even if an individual thinker does not combine these two generic interests – Sartre, for instance, was interested only in Marxism – continental moral philosophy has, in general, treated both the Christian tradition and Marxism with great seriousness. By contrast, besides MacIntyre and Charles Taylor – both of whom moved from the 'New Left' to embrace Catholic Christianity – the same cannot be said of its Anglophone counterpart. This points to a deeper, underlying explanation of *After Virtue*'s strange and unwarranted marginality within Anglophone moral philosophy.

If *After Virtue* (or at least much of it) inhabits the 'wrong' tradition, this itself stands in need of explanation, since MacIntyre is himself an Anglophone. At an individual level, it can be explained by MacIntyre's unorthodox life-narrative as a philosopher. Rather than 'Greats' or 'Moral Sciences', he read Classics at Queen Mary College, London, and subsequently studied sociology at Manchester. This freed him, arguably, from the narrow disciplinary constraints then prevalent at Oxford or Cambridge. (Charles Taylor escaped such constraints through

Introduction

being educated in Québec, an intellectual milieu clearly open to French and other continental influences.) At a societal and cultural level, then, once MacIntyre had made his Christian and Marxist interests plain, his intellectual career could no longer fit within the narratological canons of Anglophone moral philosophy. He was bound to be cast as a philosophical maverick. For Anglophone philosophy as a whole was and is committed to a conception of itself as respecting 'Ni Marx, Ni Jésus' (Revel 1970) – neither Marx nor Jesus. Any work professing to take them seriously is, therefore, automatically at a disadvantage. And this is, I take it, exactly what *After Virtue* did: for having elaborated the Aristotelian origins of virtue theory, it then embeds such theory within the wider concept of a 'practice' (cf. Marxian 'praxis'), only to argue that Christian (and specifically Thomistic) virtue theory is in significant ways an improvement on its Greek predecessors. None of this suited a disciplinary narrative whose guardrails were firmly liberal and non-(even anti-)theistic.

After Virtue's conceptual scheme of practice, institution, tradition and narrative can thus throw light on its own character and reception. Although intellectually ground-breaking and a towering achievement in its own right, it was always going to struggle to enter the Anglophone philosophical mainstream, given the latter's entrenched liberalism and hence allergic response to both Marxism and religious tradition. Of course, much Anglophone commentary has dwelt on *After Virtue*'s supposed 'nostalgia' for the Greek *polis*, and hence its straightforward inapplicability to modern ethics or politics. But I have suggested that the real source of intellectual antipathy lay and lies elsewhere. If so, what are the prospects for *After Virtue* in the twenty-first century? To draw on a concept at the heart of MacIntyre's authorship, that of the 'common good', I suggest it will continue to contribute immensely to the intellectual common good. Its notion of 'goods internal to a practice', and the risks posed to such goods by institutions' focused on external goods, is alone sufficient to ensure its lasting significance. When it comes, however, to the hospitality of academic practitioners and institutions to *After Virtue* and its moral concerns, I think far more circumspection is in order. David Rondel (Chapter 4) may be right that these concerns will become only more pertinent and pressing in the years to come – but whether they are *recognised* as such is another matter. If anything, *After Virtue*'s own hospitality to both Marxist and Judaeo-Christian ideas and arguments will be taken as marks against it – and the story of this remarkable text will continue to be told mainly from the margins.

Let me now outline what lies ahead (i.e. the four parts of this volume and their constituent chapters). Part I tackles the relation between

4   Introduction

After Virtue and ethical theory. In Chapter 1, Tom Angier treats the relation between *After Virtue* and virtue ethics, arguing that the former should not be understood as supportive of, let alone a blueprint for, the latter. In fact, *After Virtue* subordinates the virtues to other notions, most saliently practices, traditions, narratives and the social goods that inform these. By contrast, virtue ethics hypostatises the virtues and tries to do 'everything with one thing' (viz. virtue). In order to show the misguidedness of this approach, Angier takes four different 'targets' for the virtue ethical agent – virtue itself, happiness, 'natural' ends and utility or duty – and argues that none of these, taken either singly or jointly, constitutes a genuinely virtuous end. In this way, virtue ethics is self-defeating. Indeed, if an ethic of virtue is to be sustained, it must adopt, explore and develop *After Virtue*'s structuring idea that the virtues are constitutively ordered to a panoply of social goods – goods that lie beyond the virtues themselves.

In Chapter 2, Jennifer Herdt focuses on the relation between virtue and happiness. *After Virtue*'s key foil here is the classical utilitarian conception of happiness, which reduces it to pleasure. This 'naturalistic teleology' belies the complex nature of happiness and thereby fails to supply a decision-procedure for action. Aristotelian *eudaimonia* fares better but is still found wanting, since it rests on a 'metaphysical biology' that MacIntyre (famously brusquely) rejects as no longer tenable. It reflects, moreover, a parochial conception of flourishing that is at home only in the Greek *polis*. MacIntyre proposes, by contrast, a revised eudaimonism that rests on a 'social teleology': viz. humans as essentially cultural and historical animals, who find their good only in and through particular social practices. While this may suggest a collapse into relativism, MacIntyre avoids this by casting social particularity not as a goal but as a necessary matrix within which to discover the universal good. Herdt ends on a more critical note, arguing that *After Virtue* never clarifies whether the eudaimonism it advocates is, as she puts it, 'welfare-prior' or 'goodness-prior'.

In Chapter 3, Kelvin Knight begins by noting *After Virtue*'s ambivalent relation to Nietzsche. On the one hand, Nietzsche pinpoints the failure of the 'Enlightenment project' to justify morality using either de-teleologised desire or de-teleologised reason. On the other hand, Nietzsche's own solution – that of the 'sovereign' individual who 'creates' his own values – falls into the very liberal individualism he seeks to reject. After erudite commentary on Weber and Marx, Knight then interrogates how far Nietzsche's own failure can, according to MacIntyre, be remedied by a return to Aristotle. Echoing Herdt, Knight highlights MacIntyre's rejection of Aristotle's aristocratic prejudices and 'metaphysical biology'.

Introduction 5

In place of these, MacIntyre elaborates the notion of goods internal to practices, practices that are sustained, in turn, by institutions. This 'sociological Aristotelianism' enables *After Virtue* to stand against both Nietzschean individualism and Weberian managerialism. Knight further articulates MacIntyre's 'historical sociology of the virtues' through the notion of 'tradition', and he ends by exploring the relation between ethics and politics in both *After Virtue* and MacIntyre's later works.

Knight's *entrée* into the political forms a nice prelude to Part II, which covers *After Virtue* and political theory. In Chapter 4, David Rondel explores *After Virtue*'s critique of liberalism. According to Rondel, MacIntyre criticises 'liberal individualism' for reducing the self to a radical chooser of values, while prescinding from any historical context in which such choice can be rationalised. This liberal conception of the self is commensurate with a 'neutral' conception of politics, with the State reduced to a facilitator of individual preferences, on the basis of purported managerial 'expertise' and its manifold procedures. In this way, the State comes increasingly to resemble a market. While we can discern some coherent and even valuable content to State neutrality, Rondel concludes that *After Virtue*'s critique of liberal individualism, though rhetorically powerful, needs to be more carefully calibrated. In particular, MacIntyre oscillates between liberalism as political theory and liberalism as social or cultural practice. With more precision, however, *After Virtue*'s critique will, Rondel judges, become increasingly pertinent as the twenty-first century unfolds.

In Chapter 5, Nathan Pinkoski places *After Virtue* in the context of the rise of 'postliberalism'. According to Pinkoski, MacIntyre locates the origins of liberalism not in the Enlightenment, but in late mediaeval voluntarism – thereby saddling liberal thought with an unworkable ideal of autonomous choice. Echoing Rondel, Pinkoski then unpacks the 'managerial State' as a political form reflective of this ideal. Since the latter is ultimately unworkable, however, the State cannot but become manipulative, presenting as 'just' what are merely powerful interests and dominant preferences. This pessimistic view of the modern State nevertheless does not spell a return to a baldly 'conservative', let alone 'communitarian' vision. Instead, true to his Marxist inheritance, MacIntyre thinks *any* modern, large-scale political order incapable of upholding the common good. And this stands in tension with the postliberal – yet far more State- and even State-Church-friendly – projects of Milbank, Pabst and Vermeule. Pinkoski ends on a rather disillusioned note: along with MacIntyre, he holds that liberal orders are likely to persist not because they can be justified philosophically, but merely because they have become institutionally entrenched.

6   Introduction

In Chapter 6, David McPherson takes up the theme of conservatism. Defining the latter as a 'life-orientation', he parses it along several dimensions. Conservatives are given to recognising human limits, particularly our epistemic and character limits. These suggest the wisdom of an anti-utopian politics, which embraces a 'prudent traditionalism' and constraints on capitalist economy, along with a suspicion of reductive moral theories. Particularly distasteful here is any utilitarian ethic, which treats all goods as commensurable and hence fungible, thereby riding roughshod over the conservative disposition to preserve things that are loved (not only people, but also places). This 'existential stance' guards against alienation and respects the human desire to be 'at home' in the world. McPherson then argues that *After Virtue* reflects these conservative traits in its advocacy of the virtues, which are embedded in practices, and thence also in traditions. Granted, MacIntyre criticises both Burkean and Thatcherite 'conservatism', but this is because he caricatures the former and the latter is merely a variation on liberal individualism. All in all, he is a brand of conservative – except, McPherson notes in closing, in his un-conservative repudiation of the present age. Here *After Virtue* remains Marxist-utopian and serves only to foster alienation.

In Chapter 7, Jason Blakely takes utopia up as a theme in its own right, rescuing *After Virtue*, as he sees it, from both right- ('reactionary') and left- (Marxist) utopianism. On a reactionary reading, MacIntyre sees liberalism as devolving into emotivism and its vices. But this ignores 'virtue liberalism': certain liberal polities' capacity to accommodate practices that foster virtue (as noted by de Tocqueville). Despite this possibility, right-utopians like Rod Dreher continue to advocate a retreat to virtuous enclaves, something inconsistent with MacIntyre's insistence on 'systematic debate' between rival traditions. For left-utopians, MacIntyre's hostility to the liberal market-State licenses the top-down imposition of socialistic equality. But this ignores MacIntyre's strictures on fantasies of social change in the absence of genuine human agency, viz. agency embedded in traditions. In contrast to both these interpretative dead ends, Blakely proposes *After Virtue* as a 'real utopia' (i.e. as advocating the bottom-up practice of the virtues in the context of local communities). This solidaristic vision avoids the Scylla of Dreher-like isolationism, yet also the Charybdis of neo-Marxist statism. It is the harbinger, indeed, Blakely claims, of a 'revived ethical socialism'.

Part III is on *After Virtue* and narrative. Stephen Mulhall (Chapter 8) begins with *After Virtue*'s opening portrayal of 'epistemic crisis', one in which we are unable to engage in scientific enquiry because we have been deprived of those historical narratives in light of which such enquiry is possible. Something similar applies, MacIntyre suggests, to the state of

Introduction

moral enquiry. And if so, this explains (in part) MacIntyre's willingness to dismiss large swathes of moral discourse, such as 'rights talk': such talk has been disembedded, he implies, from its proper narrative context and hence has become incoherent. In similar vein, MacIntyre turns Nietzsche's etymological enquiry against Nietzsche himself, showing how a *true* 'genealogy' of moral concepts discloses very un-Nietzschean conclusions. More widely, *After Virtue*'s turn to sociology, anthropology, psychoanalysis, etc., can be seen as affording more 'holistic registers' of narratological resource than those available within Anglo-analytic philosophy. Mulhall ends by highlighting *After Virtue*'s manifold uses of art, literary fiction and (most notably) social 'characters' in constructing its own, unprecedentedly 'non-compartmentalised' approach to moral enquiry.

In Chapter 9, Micah Lott starts by outlining Aristotle's conception of the human *telos* as a life well lived. Such a life must prioritise certain goods over others and arrange them into a coherent whole: in other words, a good life constitutes a unity. MacIntyre builds on this idea with his notion of life as a narrative, which needs to display its own unity. Without such unity, he argues, our lives lack intelligibility and our actions become unaccountable. So far, so good: life *qua* narrative points to the need for 'practical integration' among our ends. But can narrative as such supply those ends with substance or content? Not clearly so, Lott argues. Life narrated as a unified 'quest' is empty apart from a specification of its substantive objects. Equally, a unified narrative can recount a life that is itself disunified or fragmented. There seems, in point of fact, no way to infer from narrative unity *per se* to genuine goods, any more than we need tread a path from moral evils to narrative disunity. Lott rounds off his critique by exploring the several life-stories narrated in *Ethics in the Conflicts of Modernity* (2016). Here too, he maintains, narrative yields less than it promises – it fails, not least, to provide any determinate conception of a 'perfect' or 'complete' life.

In Chapter 10, Christopher Lutz engages with Jason Blakely's interpretation of MacIntyre's authorship as moving from historicism (*After Virtue*) to a 'tradition-free, ahistorical' naturalism (*Dependent Rational Animals*). In order to do this, he offers a narrative of MacIntyre's intellectual development. Ranging from Marxism to post-Moorean normative theory, MacIntyre, Lutz contends, became critical of both: the former could not sustain just regimes in practice, while the latter had no convincing account of communist injustices. Such an account requires, at root, an understanding of humans as social agents directed to various proper ends, ends that constitute their happiness or fulfilment. And it is this social teleological account of morality that, in effect,

8   Introduction

After Virtue embodies. Returning to Blakely, Lutz concludes that *After Virtue* is, despite Blakely's 'discontinuity narrative', perfectly continuous with *Dependent Rational Animals'* embrace of a 'naturalised teleology'. For the latter text simply expounds a naturalistic framework within which any social, traditioned moral enquiry must take place and whose constraints it must respect. Blakely's narrative of MacIntyre's intellectual development is thus ill-founded and should be rejected.

Part IV rounds the volume off by investigating *After Virtue*'s impact beyond philosophy. Charles Pinches (Chapter 11) casts MacIntyre's book as akin to Jewish prophecy. It opens with a 'disquieting', not to say apocalyptic 'suggestion', and it ends with a call for a 'another ... St. Benedict'. These are startling notes to strike, comprehensible only against a religious background. A difficulty with this interpretation is that MacIntyre strongly distinguishes between philosophy and theology, and he has explicitly disavowed being a theologian himself. *After Virtue* makes moves, nonetheless, that point towards theology. Crucially, its focus on narrative makes room for the idea that we are embedded in stories that we ourselves do not author. And this indicates the further idea that we have ends that are largely (or most deeply) not up to us to determine. Indeed, a specification of such ends is, in many ways, the task of those 'living traditions' we cannot but inhabit. Pinches concludes by sounding a note of caution about those who, like Rod Dreher, build on *After Virtue*'s prophetic voice to advocate a withdrawal from current liberal political orders. This 'strategy' goes against genuine prophecy, which engages its environment and inspires hope.

In Chapter 12, Mark Retter gives unprecedented attention to *After Virtue*'s relation to legal theory. According to Retter, MacIntyre's concepts of 'practice', 'institution' and 'tradition' all find illuminating application to such theory. Because 'practices' have internal goods, they can supply legal practice with good reasons, reasons that are lacking on Herbert Hart's narrow 'rule of recognition' view. The internal goods at stake form part, moreover, of the political common good, and thus cannot be disjoined from the cooperative virtues. What obscures the usefulness of MacIntyre's conceptual scheme for legal theory is basically threefold. First, MacIntyre over-emphasises the need for joint deliberation about the common good, which leads him to treat large-scale political and legal governance with an exaggerated scepticism-cum-pessimism. (It would have been more fruitful to emphasise the need for subsidiarity in the State.) Second, MacIntyre erects too strong a contrast between rule-following and the virtues. And third, he demonstrates a hostility to lawyers as 'the clergy of liberalism'. But *contra* MacIntyre, the ills plaguing liberal governance are always accompanied by an

Introduction

'admixture' of virtuous practice, and there is room within generically liberal polities for deliberative (not least legal) challenge to and debate about liberal norms.

In Chapter 13, Paul Blackledge turns his eye to *After Virtue* and business ethics. This conjunction seems untoward in light of MacIntyre's highly critical remarks about this burgeoning sub-discipline. Blackledge argues, however, that MacIntyre's work supplies a key critique of the alienating and exploitative essence of capitalist enterprise. Salient here is the generic 'character' of the manager, which is amoral and wedded to the manipulation of others, employees and customers alike. He or she professes an 'expertise' and unique form of effectiveness, but both are ideological fictions or mystifications. While business ethicists like Geoff Moore present business organisations as varied, and many of them as (at least potentially) virtuous, they ignore the deep structural barriers to *actual* virtuous business practice. Maybe the deepest barrier, Blackledge contends, is capitalism's commitment to the expansion of surplus value, which has inextricably alienating effects on the workforce. This essentially Marxist critique, which comes to fruition in *Ethics in the Conflicts of Modernity*, is blunted, admittedly, by *After Virtue*'s Weberian treatment of management in abstraction from its capitalist form. Blackledge concludes, nevertheless, that MacIntyre's more purely Marxist insights into managerialism help overcome this Weberian deviation.

Part I

After Virtue and Ethical Theory

1 *After Virtue* and Virtue Ethics

Tom Angier

1.1 Introduction

It has become something of a commonplace that *After Virtue* played a key role in the development of 'virtue ethics'. That development began with Elizabeth Anscombe's 'Modern Moral Philosophy' (Anscombe 1958), which expressed philosophical dissatisfaction with both Kantian deontology and 'consequentialism'. It then continued in and through the work of Peter Geach and Philippa Foot.[1] Finally, so the narrative goes, it was given a more historical and less Oxonian cast by Alasdair MacIntyre's seminal *After Virtue* (MacIntyre 1981). This intellectual genealogy has the air of plausibility, at least chronologically, since it was precisely in the 1980s that the modern literature on virtue ethics began its meteoric rise. Along with the development of sub-genres – such as agent-based, pluralist and exemplarist virtue ethics – there is by now a vast literature on the subject, not least in applied virtue ethics.[2] But is the above genealogy accurate? Can MacIntyre's most celebrated monograph really be cast as engendering a 'third method' of ethics?

In this chapter, I shall argue that it cannot, and that those who cast it in this light misunderstand it. For if we understand by 'virtue ethics' the view that virtue plays a foundational – or at least central and determinative – role in ethical theory, then *After Virtue* is not a virtue ethical work, nor is it meant to sponsor such work. Far from it. MacIntyre's core message is that virtue, although unduly neglected in the modern period, is not a self-standing notion and needs to be embedded in a wider, richer ethical framework in order regain its rightful place within moral deliberation and practice. As he himself puts matters, the virtues require a 'conceptual background' in order to be justified, a background derived from 'their traditional context in thought and practice' (MacIntyre 1981:

---

[1] See, for example, Geach 1977 and Foot 1978.
[2] The classic statement of agent-based virtue ethics is Slote 2001; of pluralism, Swanton 2003; and of exemplarism, Zagzebski 2017. For a selection of papers in applied virtue ethics, see Angier 2018a: vol. 4.

13

228). And that context should, on his view, be elaborated in terms of 'background concepts of the narrative unity of human life and of a practice with goods internal to it' (MacIntyre 1981: 228). These concepts, in turn, stand in need of further embedding, most saliently in the idea of a 'moral tradition' (MacIntyre 1981: 258). So virtue and the virtues are far from the all-important, relatively autonomous features of ethical theory that we encounter in the work of modern virtue ethicists. They are, instead, coordinate with other concepts – narrative unity, practice, goods and tradition – without which they lack sense and direction. Most importantly, the virtues operate within a horizon of 'shared goods' (MacIntyre 1981: 229), which constitute what MacIntyre calls 'the community's good' (MacIntyre 1981: 232), and thence 'the good for man' (MacIntyre 1981: 233). In other words, virtue is itself a *teleological* notion, which is ordered essentially to a panoply of social goods.[3]

In what follows, I will construct a 'negative determination' of MacIntyre's social teleological construal of the virtues (to borrow a Hegelian notion). That is, I will attempt to show that virtue ethics, by occluding the social and communal goods at which the virtues properly aim, effectively denatures them and renders them unintelligible as virtues. Put otherwise, my argument will be that virtue ethics systematically 'misses the mark', in the sense that – in all its various instantiations – it proposes aims for the virtuous agent that are inappropriate and ill-founded. The notion of an 'aim' here is recognisably Aristotelian, since Aristotle often refers to virtue as having a *telos* (end) or *skopos* (target).[4] While difficult to gloss in modern terms, these notions can be read as picking out an agent's motivation, or reason for action, or both. It will be my argument that virtue ethicists have proposed four types of practical aim: (1) virtue itself, either *qua* disposition or *qua* action; (2) *eudaimonia*, happiness or welfare; (3) 'natural' ends, such as individual or species survival; and (4) other, theoretically inflected values (typically, utility or duty). I shall describe the first two aims as 'involuted', or inwardly directed, and the second two as 'evoluted', or outwardly directed

---

[3] Goods such as marriage, the family, education, music-making and sport. One upshot of this is that Stoicism is viewed by MacIntyre as a degenerate moral tradition, since it pictures virtue as 'its own end, its own reward and its own motive' (MacIntyre 1981: 233). By contrast, Jane Austen, according to MacIntyre, 'restores a teleological perspective' on the virtues, understanding them correctly as ordered to manifold social goods (MacIntyre 1981: 240).

[4] NB in particular Aristotle's rhetorical question: 'Will not the knowledge of [the chief good] ... have a great influence on life? Shall we not, like archers who have a mark [*skopon*] to aim at, be more likely to hit upon what we should?' (*Nicomachean Ethics* [NE] 1094a22–4). Interestingly, the Greek for 'missing the mark' is *hamartia*, which in later, Christian authors is the term for 'sin'.

After Virtue and Virtue Ethics   15

(in senses that will be made clear). In either type of case, the kind of aim proposed is, I will argue, unsustainable, and ends up crippling the virtue ethical project.

1.2   Aiming at Virtue

The first view I want to investigate posits virtue itself as the proper aim of the moral agent. One possible, yet implausible, way of understanding this would be impersonally, so that agents are enjoined to promote virtue – either as a disposition, or kind of action, or both – simply because it constitutes a valuable state of affairs. We should see to it, in other words, that the world contain instances of courage, justice, temperance, etc., because the world would be better that way. The trouble with this construal is three-fold. First, it leaves unclear why one should be virtuous oneself, as opposed to fostering virtue in others – especially if they have a better chance of being virtuous. This would leave most agents aspiring, effectively, to the condition of Aristotle's legislators, who 'make the citizens good by forming habits in them ... those who do not effect this miss their mark [*hamartanousin*]' (NE 1103b3–5). But second, this opens the way to promoting virtue by vicious (or at least sub-virtuous) means, thereby posing for virtue ethics the kind of paradox that consequentialists have posed for deontologists: viz. why not contravene one's own values if doing so would bolster them elsewhere?[5] Supposing such bolstering were possible and not counterproductive, the loss of virtue in one's own case would seem justifiable. Yet third, this consequentialist spectre highlights how the impersonal approach just outlined undermines virtue ethics at its root. For virtue ethics developed historically precisely as a first-personal project, centring on the virtue of the self. To abandon this, adopting a third-personal (even maximising) approach, is essentially to abandon virtue ethics altogether.

A more plausible construal of the idea that one should aim at virtue is that one should aim at one's *own* virtue – even if this involves fostering virtue in others. In doing so, one will become – owing to the goodness of virtue – a good human being, or, as Daniel Russell puts it, 'a good specimen of one's kind' (Russell 2012: 47). This perfectionist conception of virtue has resonance in Aristotle, since although (as we shall explore in Section 1.3) Aristotle is a eudaimonist virtue ethicist, he incorporates within his eudaimonism the idea that virtue *per se* is a perfection – irrespective of its relation to our well-being. This is evident from his

---

[5] For the so-called paradox of deontology, see Scheffler 1994.

16   *Tom Angier*

claim that 'we choose [the virtues] indeed for themselves (for if nothing resulted from them we should still choose each of them)' (NE 1097b2–4). It is evident also from the fact that the Greek for virtue is *aretē*, which in its general acceptation means 'excellence' (i.e. that which brings to perfection or completion anything in which it inheres).[6] But this still leaves open the question of what, exactly, makes human beings good of their kind. Is virtue a sort of disposition or character trait? Or should it be understood rather as a form of action? If virtue were restricted to the former, then, as Aristotle adjures, being a good human being would be compatible with being asleep (NE 1095b32–3, 1098b33–9a3). And this seems highly implausible. Virtue is, rather, a disposition towards action, and in this sense it is properly an activity (*energeia*). Indeed, if this were not the case, the incentive to act well, as opposed to remaining simply well-disposed, would be absent. As Aristotle puts matters, 'as in the Olympic Games it is not the most beautiful and the strongest that are crowned but those who compete ... so those who act rightly win the noble and good things in life'.[7]

So the virtues are character traits directed essentially at virtuous action. But what *is* it to be so directed? For Aristotle, it is to aim at the 'mean' (*meson*) in both passion (*pathos*) and action (*praxis*).[8] The courageous person, for instance, feels spirited emotions at the right time, for the right reason and towards the right people, while acting (say) to defend the city from enemy attack. The temperate person demonstrates, *mutatis mutandis*, the same affective profile, while acting (say) to achieve their own health or fitness.[9] But crucially, if the courageous person fails to secure the city, or the temperate person to become healthy, they have not thereby failed in *action*. For 'action' here is an essentially self-related – or what I will call 'involuted' – end, which does not rest, fundamentally, on achieving certain results.[10] To rest it thus would, by Aristotle's lights, be to commit at least two fateful errors. First, it would be to assimilate

---

[6] Cf. 'every excellence both brings into good condition [*apotelei*] the thing of which it is the excellence and makes the function [*ergon*] of that thing be done well' (NE 1106a15–17).

[7] NE 1099a3–7. One should add that, on Aristotle's view, good dispositions arise only through practice (i.e. doing good actions; see NE II.1). So resting content with virtuous traits is not only implausible, but also incoherent.

[8] For references to virtue 'aiming at' (*stochastikē*) the mean in passion and action, see, for example, NE 1106b14–18, 1109a22–3, 28–30 and 1109b30.

[9] For the dimensions of 'rightness' within the mean, see, for example, NE 1106b21–2, 1109a28–9, b14–16 and 1115b18.

[10] These results or outcomes may lie beyond the agent, as in military victory, or occur within their body, as in health. But either way, Aristotle conceives of them as distinct *erga*, 'works', which contain their value intrinsically and irrespective of their relation to the acting self.

After Virtue and Virtue Ethics 17

praxis to *technē* or craft, which, unlike *praxis*, finds its aim or good in independent 'products' rather than in virtuous conduct *per se*. As Aristotle holds: 'some [ends] are activities, others are products … Where there are ends apart from the actions … the products … [are] better than the activities' (NE 1094a3–6; cf. 1105a26–33). Since, by hypothesis, virtuous action is not a craft (i.e. a productive activity), its good resides not in its results, but rather in itself. And second, to make virtue contingent on achievement would, for Aristotle, be to render it unstable and hence unworthy of the name *aretē*. As he maintains: 'the good we divine to be something of one's own and not easily taken from one' (NE 1095b25–6); '[t]o entrust to chance what is greatest and most noble would be a very defective arrangement' (NE 1099b24–5).[11]

What are we to make of this involuted conception of virtue? Where it seems to fall short is not in viewing virtue as having a constitutive aim – namely, virtuous action – but rather in occluding the constitutive teleology of virtuous action itself. For from the perspective of the virtuous agent, it is precisely one's goal (i.e. both one's motive and one's reason for action) to achieve certain independent *goods*, either primarily for others (as in justice) or primarily for oneself (as in temperance). Even the good of health, moreover, is also a social good, insofar as one's health impinges on others and their welfare. It follows that if one fails to achieve such goods, one has plausibly failed in action, and that – if the goods in question can nonetheless be achieved without one's agency – one will be satisfied (or at least consoled, in large part, for one's failure). For the *phronimos*, by contrast, things take on a different cast. Any failure to achieve goods pales in comparison with one's continued exercise in virtue, while others' provision of those goods appears – rather than satisfying or consoling – a derogation from one's own virtuous action.[12] This focus on the powers of the self may be appropriate from a third-personal standpoint, which is one of character appraisal or assessment rather than action. But from a first-personal or agential standpoint, it seems inappropriate. As Jozef Müller puts it, '[t]he generous person … is one who, say, donates money to charity … *because* it is beneficial to the

---

[11] Cf. 'virtuous activities … are thought to be more durable even than knowledge' (NE 1100b14–15). I would argue, further, that acting 'for the sake of the noble' – which characterises Aristotle's virtuous man or *phronimos* – is also an involuted end, referring not to any noble or fine results achieved through action, but rather to a particular mode of action and character, one embodied ideally in Aristotle's 'great-souled' man or *megalopsuchos*. (For argument along these lines, see Angier 2018b.)

[12] Unless, of course, it is virtuous to allow others to make such provision. But in that case, it seems inappropriate to welcome their provision of goods on the grounds that doing so is a mark of, or contributes to, one's own virtue. Rather, one should welcome their action owing to the independent goods it affords.

18   *Tom Angier*

right people not because she wants to donate for the sake of donating' (Müller 2018: §4, emphasis in original). Yet despite this diagnosis – that we should act for the sake of independent goods, not for that of being virtuous – we still find virtue ethicists like Hursthouse embracing involution. Justifying anti-racist education, she writes: 'we think it will make us better people, more charitable and just' (Hursthouse 1999: 117).

To put this critique in order, we can say that 'aiming at virtue' misses the mark in three fundamental respects. First, it gives a mistaken account of moral phenomenology, since the virtuous agent does not see their own virtue as their *telos*. Rather, they are focused on the goods to which virtuous action is intrinsically ordered and leave judgement of their own performance to others. At most, they will reflect on their performance in order better to devote themself to those goods. Second, virtue ethics *qua* aiming at virtue gives the wrong explanation for virtuous action. It explains it by invoking its contribution to virtuous character or by the good of virtuous action *per se*. But this is the wrong explanation: the right explanation is that one is seeking to achieve various goods, ones that lie beyond virtuous action as such and in the absence of which one's action remains radically inadequate and incomplete. Third, aiming at virtue is morally problematic because it provides the wrong motivation for virtuous action – viz. a condition of the self. The right motivation is, once again, the goods to which virtuous action is intrinsically directed, which need have nothing to do with the self.[13] As Hurka puts things, 'it is ... not virtuous ... to act primarily from concern for one's own virtue ... [this is to] be motivated ... in an unattractively self-indulgent way' (Hurka 2001: 246).[14] So on at least three grounds – moral phenomenological, explanatory and moral – 'aiming at virtue' misses the mark and renders virtue ethics self-effacing.[15]

1.3   Aiming at Happiness

Aiming at virtue and aiming at happiness have tended to go together for virtue ethicists, even though they are conceptually distinct. Aristotle and

---

[13] Though they may have, and very closely at that: take Aristotle's highest virtue, namely contemplation, which is an activity of the mind.

[14] It might be more accurate to say 'self-centred' than 'self-indulgent'. I shall come on to the appropriate terminology here when I discuss Robert Adams's work below.

[15] To escape the accusation of self-effacingness, some virtue ethicists try to separate moral motivations for acting virtuously from moral reasons for doing so. Hursthouse, for instance, declares that 'we are not insisting that [our ideal agent] have explicit thoughts about ... virtue, good action, or *to kalon* ... Such explicit thoughts are not a necessary condition for being morally motivated' (Hursthouse 1999: 140). I shall address this strategy of dissociating reason from motive in Section 1.3.

After Virtue and Virtue Ethics   19

Hursthouse, the paradigmatic virtue ethicists of antiquity and modernity respectively, affirm both. This raises the issue, inevitably, of how these aims are related. There are basically two options. One treats happiness as a substantive condition, both causally separate from and logically independent of virtue, to which virtue is a means. Since this conception of happiness reduces virtue to an instrument, whose value is wholly contingent on the realisation of happiness, I will relegate it to Section 1.5, where I investigate the consequentialist subordination of virtue ethics.[16] The far more common option is to understand happiness not as a product of virtue, but rather as constituted by it. Hurka calls this the 'formal', Copp and Sobel the 'moralised' conception of happiness,[17] and its most celebrated proponent remains Aristotle. Right at the start of the NE, Aristotle argues that *eudaimonia* – happiness, flourishing or fulfilment[18] – is the supreme or ultimate end of action, on pain of our *praxis* being 'empty and vain' (NE 1094a21).[19] But does virtuous action in fact have this constitutive aim? One might object that no such unifying and ultimate aim is necessary, since virtuous action can proceed piecemeal, as it were, aiming at an irreducible plurality of virtuous ends.[20] Alternatively, one could argue that virtuous action is a bad bet when it comes to happiness, or at least that virtue is insufficient for achieving it.[21] Finally, one might hold that happiness cannot be aimed at as such, so the whole idea of 'aiming at happiness' is philosophically too problematic to get off the ground.[22]

[16] Hurka notes that the 'substantive' conception of happiness entails the wholesale subordination of virtue, *à la* consequentialism (see Hurka 2001: 233). I take the notion of the 'subordination' of virtue from Solomon 1999.

[17] See Hurka 2001: 235 and Copp and Sobel 2004: 531 respectively.

[18] 'Fulfilment' seems the preferable translation, since Aristotle thinks one can be *eudaimōn* when facing severe adversity, or even after death. It is jarring to claim one can flourish or be happy under such circumstances.

[19] This applies to all action, whether virtuous or vicious or anything in between, since Aristotle believes that agency as such presses towards ultimate fulfilment.

[20] See, for example, Raz 2002 and Chappell 2014. If unity is needed, maybe it can be provided at the motivational – rather than eudaimonic – level. This is Slote's view: he holds that all virtuous action is unified by its origin in empathy or 'empathic caring' (see Slote 2010). But this seems a tall order: how can courage, justice, temperance, wisdom, etc., be realistically and informatively grounded in one master-motive? For similar criticism, see Hurka 2001: 244.

[21] The most notorious exponent of the first view is Friedrich Nietzsche, who frequently maintains that virtue is positively damaging to the well-being of the virtuous agent (for commentary, see Hursthouse 1999: 253–6 and Adams 2006: 60–62). For less extreme criticism, which is nonetheless sceptical of virtue as an (at least central) condition of happiness, see Conly 1988: 93–4, Hurka 2001: 240–43 and Copp and Sobel 2004: 527–8.

[22] See, for example, John Stuart Mill, who writes: 'Those only are happy ... who have their minds fixed on some object other than their own happiness; on the happiness of others,

20   *Tom Angier*

I want to put these three objections to one side. First, the virtue ethical tradition is saturated with the assumption that the happiness of the agent is a vital concern, even if it is not aimed at in every single action or context of deliberation. Hursthouse labels this the 'Platonic requirement', viz. that virtue be, in general, not only good, but also good for the agent (see Hursthouse 1999: 167). And this seems plausible: if virtue were of no benefit or of only very limited benefit to the agent, its first-personal appeal would be severely undermined.[23] Second, the claim that virtue is unnecessary for happiness is far less plausible than it may, at first, appear. If one's life were uniformly lacking in courage, temperance, justice and generosity, it is very unlikely – bar some very improbable circumstances – that one would, or could, benefit much from such an asocial and friction-filled existence.[24] True, it is also markedly implausible that virtue is sufficient for happiness. But Aristotle admits this, arguing that *eudaimonia* – even of the highest (contemplative) variety – requires a supply of 'external goods'.[25] So to frame the insufficiency of virtue for happiness as a decisive objection against eudaimonist virtue ethics is a very unpromising route to take. Third, the idea that happiness cannot, psychologically, be aimed at as such has some traction, insofar as Aristotle grants that virtue must be chosen *per se* (*di'auta*) in order to be eudaimonic (see NE 1105a30–32). But he holds also that it is chosen properly for the sake of *eudaimonia*, and he views these two *telē* as psychologically compossible. So to object that Aristotle, along with most of the virtue ethics tradition, is simply mistaken on this point is distinctly uncharitable. We should affirm this possibility, at least for the sake of argument.

In my view, the central problems with aiming at happiness lie elsewhere, and they closely parallel the problems with aiming at virtue. Indeed, if aiming at virtue is a self-effacing end, then aiming at happiness in and through virtue is so *a fortiori*. To begin with, the moral phenomenology of virtuous agency appears not only not to support but also to militate against such an end. For internal to that phenomenology,

---

on the improvement of mankind, even on some art or pursuit, followed not as a means, but as itself an ideal end. Aiming thus at something else, they find happiness by the way' (Mill 2018: 82). Cf. also Whiting 2002: 283, which examines Aristotle in particular.

[23] Hursthouse speaks of a 'pattern' of benefit, even if virtuous action is not beneficial in every case (see Hursthouse 1999: 172–4, 185).

[24] For an argument to this effect, see Angier 2020.

[25] See, for example, NE 1099a31–b8, 1100a8–9, b28–30, 1101a8–13. Cf. Adams 2006: 49 and Roberts 2015: 43. Unlike Aristotle or Aristotelian virtue ethicists, the Stoics do maintain that virtue is sufficient for *eudaimonia*. But they have not been the key shapers of the virtue ethics tradition. For an excellent introduction to Stoic ethics, see Klein 2012.

After Virtue and Virtue Ethics   21

as I've argued above, is a focus on independent goods, so to represent those goods as having a further and in fact supreme *telos* – namely, a condition of the agent themself – looks untoward. It amounts to a further involution of the ethical, and it appears warranted only or at best in what Bishop Butler calls a 'cool hour', once the main business of virtuous action is over. (Though even here there are real difficulties, as I will argue below.) Second, aiming at happiness gives the wrong explanation for virtuous action: as Hurka pithily puts it, 'that the action will make [one's] own life better or more flourishing … is not, intuitively, the right explanation. The right explanation is that the action will make the other's life better' (Hurka 2001: 248). Third, aiming at happiness is morally problematic, since it suggests that one is ultimately and properly motivated – across all contexts of virtuous action – by one's own well-being. And this seems inappropriately self-regarding, or, in Hurka's phrase, 'foundationally egoistic': 'A flourishing-based theory', he writes, '… says a person has reason to act rightly … ultimately because doing so will contribute to her own flourishing … But this egoistic motivation is inconsistent with genuine virtue, which is not focused primarily on the self' (Hurka 2001: 246).[26]

This tripartite critique of eudaimonist virtue ethics has met with formidable resistance. An initial objection is provided by Robert Adams. According to Adams, it is not self-regard *per se* that is the problem, or even 'self-love', but rather excessive or inappropriate versions of these (Adams 2006: 99). Such 'selfishness' usually shows up as insufficient regard for others, as, for example, in the vice of greed (Adams 2006: 100). Here, Adams avers, we are 'overly dominated by a desire for such objects as pleasure, convenience, wealth, or reputation' (Adams 2006: 101), so that we end up damaging others and depriving them of their proper goods. Such behaviours express what he calls 'vices of self-preference'. But there is also something he refers to as 'unselfish self-love' (Adams 2006: 101, §4). This is particularly visible in those recovering from 'disabling injury', who have to nurse themselves back to health, in the self-care incumbent on the old and in children, to whom we can justly say things like 'be a good boy and take your medicine; it's good for you' (Adams 2006: 106–107). The trouble with this defence, however, is that it bypasses the critique above. Those critical of eudaimonist virtue ethics can agree that one should not be greedy, but they will locate the ultimate ground for this not in the well-being accruing from

---

[26] Cf. Joseph Raz, who contends that, if one's happiness is made one's deliberate and intentional goal, this is 'unattractive' and 'narcissistic' and displays the 'wrong spirit' (see Raz 2002: 329–31).

22   *Tom Angier*

generosity, but rather in the harm done those unfairly deprived of goods. Like Adams, they will object too to improper self-preference or self-centredness, but not ultimately because it is self-loving to do so. Furthermore, they can accept the examples he cites, but they will also point out that the disabled, the old and children are *permitted* to give a more central role to their own well-being, precisely because they fall short of and are seeking to approximate normal adult functioning.[27]

Notwithstanding the force of these responses, they do not get to the heart of the issue between eudaimonist virtue ethics and its critics. For this, we must turn to Daniel Russell and Mark LeBar, who mount isomorphic defences of 'aiming at happiness'. Russell claims, boldly, that 'genuinely living one's life means being committed to giving oneself a good life, by living for things in which one will find fulfilment' (Russell 2012: 14). Even sacrifices can be brought under this rubric, since '[e]ven when our ends can cost us something, it can make sense to adopt those ends for the sake of eudaimonia' (Russell 2012: 31). Russell is careful to add that only 'immersion' in particular activities (e.g. golfing) is eudai-monic, since those activities themselves are *ways* of being happy (Russell 2012: 17).[28] But nonetheless, the ultimate explanation and justification for such activities is that they 'give ourselves the gift of a good life' (Russell 2012: 35). Russell is sensitive, here, to the charge that such aiming at happiness is inappropriate because, in Hurka's terms, it is 'foundationally egoistic'. He responds, however, by distinguishing 'two levels of reasons': 'reasons for acting in virtue of the ends one has' – which need have nothing to do with the self – and 'reasons to have those ends in the first place' (namely, because they contribute to one's happiness; Russell 2012: 26). These two levels of explanation correspond to 'two very different levels of justification' (Russell 2012: 33). At level (a), there are 'second-personal reasons' – viz. to act, generically, out of respect for others, for their sake rather than one's own – while at level (b), there are 'reasons for being someone who occupies the second-person standpoint' (Russell 2012: 33). The latter, (b)-level reasons 'are ultimately for the sake of the agent's eudaimonia' (Russell 2012: 33).

LeBar divides up the territory differently, but to similar effect. He recognises, at the outset, 'a worry that ["virtue eudaimonism", or VE] requires that agents be motivated by thoughts that are at best superfluous and at worst inappropriate' (LeBar 2013: 298). He counters this by

---

[27] They would be at fault, moreover – even though perhaps excusable fault – if they treated all action under the aspect of or as contributing to their own happiness.

[28] *Eudaimonia* is, as he puts it, 'an end that is largely indeterminate and malleable' (Russell 2012: 23).

After Virtue and Virtue Ethics 23

separating how virtuous agents deliberate from what justifies their actions (LeBar 2013: 299). When a virtuous agent deliberates how, for example, to save someone from drowning, they do not invoke the 'fineness and nobility' of such action, even less 'what will contribute to [their] living well' (LeBar 2013: 300). Such considerations are always, LeBar contends, 'in the background in deliberation' (LeBar 2013: 300). In the foreground are pertinent facts about the drowning person's urgent need. True, and as LeBar grants, these facts do not constitute 'the only line of inquiry we … might pursue *on other occasions* (occasions on which reflection, rather than action, is the order of the moment)' (LeBar 2013: 301, emphasis in original) – such reflection 'terminating', for VE, in the virtuous agent's own *eudaimonia* (LeBar 2013: 301). But this is simply irrelevant to the immediate context of deliberation and action. As LeBar puts things further on, 'ultimate justificatory question[s]' are 'global considerations' that should be sequestered from practical contexts, which he dubs 'smaller' or 'more localised' (LeBar 2013: 301–302). And he rounds things off with an analogy, borrowed from David Schmidtz.[29] Just as, when asked where the university is, it would be correct – but also useless and inappropriate – to respond 'North America', so it is correct, but also useless and inappropriate, to invoke *eudaimonia* as the ultimate aim of action *hic et nunc*. Such responses have their place – but they are far removed from that of actual practice.

These defences are intriguing and intelligent but ultimately unsuccessful. They both involve what could be called 'strategies of dissociation', which, although they are cast in terms of relevance or fittingness, are at root a function of embarrassment. In Russell's case, the dissociation is between levels of explanation and justification. When sacrificing my time for the local old age home, say, my ultimate explanation and justification is that this is a way of 'giving myself a good life'. But if so, don't I, as Hurka insisted above, have the wrong explanatory and justificatory priorities? Shouldn't my ultimate aim be the good of the elderly denizens *per se*? Russell can no doubt recur here to a different 'level' of motivation and reason-giving. But this looks less like a principled move than an *ad hoc* strategy deployed to avoid embarrassment. The dissociation between levels exists, that is, because of the discomfort felt at what are, after all, one's most basic commitments as a virtuous agent. In LeBar's case, the dissociation involved is temporal rather than abstract and theoretical,[30] and the focus is solely on justification. But the overall upshot is the same.

---

[29] See Schmidtz 2006: ch. 5.
[30] Cf. Glen Pettigrove's notion of a 'time-lag' between action and justification (see Pettigrove 2011: 192).

24   *Tom Angier*

My ultimate reason and motive for, say, saving the drowning person is my own happiness or 'living well'. But this ground is to be acknowledged only in contexts of reflection because, ostensibly, to invoke it here and now would be irrelevant. Yet one wants to ask: if it is correct, how is it not relevant? To have recourse to Schmidtz's analogy, moreover, won't help. For whereas the irrelevance of locating the university in North America is merely practical, the irrelevance of my own *eudaimonia* in contexts of rescue is moral. Better put, it is morally impertinent, and impugns VE from the ground up.

I have argued, then, that 'aiming at happiness' does not befit the virtuous agent. Even *qua* the formal or moralised aim that Aristotle, Hursthouse, Russell, LeBar and others take it to be, it is psychologically, explanatorily and morally self-effacing. At best, one can try to uphold some dissociation between reason and motive, so that what motivates me here and now is sequestered, somehow, from my architectonic reason for action (viz. happiness).[31] But this is a highly unattractive option given its systematic severance of theory from practice. As Allen Wood comments, 'moral theories should be first and foremost theories *for agents*. And there is no moral theorist who is not also a moral agent … [there is] no plausibility in a moral theory that takes as having independent and funda-mental value something that, by the theory's own lights, agents should not take [so]' (Wood 2011: 66, emphasis in original). In the end, Raz seems justified in holding that happiness (or, as he calls it, 'well-being') is not and should not be the kind of master-*telos* that eudaimonist virtue ethicists take it to be. As he maintains, '[g]oals and relationships they have or may want to have are what people have reason to care about, not their well-being as such' (Raz 2002: 319). 'Far from being able to assess the relative value of options for an agent by their possible contribution to his well-being, we cannot judge their contribution to this well-being except by reference to their value (i.e. their value independently of such contribution) … we can only choose what we believe to be of value, and … that value is independ-ent of our choice' (Raz 2002: 323–4). What falls out of this, once more, and as I have held consistently, is that the virtuous agent aims at substan-tive goods, not the involuted ends of virtue, or happiness, or both.

1.4   Aiming at Natural Ends

If aiming at virtue or happiness or both is, if not vicious, at least sub-virtuous, a third possibility raises itself: namely, that 'nature'

---

[31] Cf. Paul Guyer, who distinguishes (in the context of Kantian ethics) between the 'motive' and 'object' of morality (Guyer 2011: 211).

After Virtue and Virtue Ethics 25

supplies the requisite end or ends for the virtuous agent. This possibility is affirmed by Hursthouse (even though, as I've noted, she also affirms the two involuted ends above). What natural end or ends does she advocate? The ends she advocates are four-fold, and, as a set, explain (purportedly) why the virtues are the excellent and eudaimonic dispositions they are.[32] The first end is 'individual survival through the characteristic life span of [a species]'; the second is 'continuance of the species';[33] the third is 'characteristic freedom from pain and characteristic pleasure or enjoyment';[34] and the fourth is 'the good functioning of the social group'.[35]

The first question to ask concerning these ends is how 'natural' they are. Hursthouse presents them as 'objective', and hence as sponsored by naturalistic enquiry.[36] Indeed, as the above quotations make plain, she believes that insofar as *any* animal realises these ends, it is a good specimen of its kind and, moreover, flourishes. But is this the case? Several scholars have raised doubts on this score. Copp and Sobel, for instance, question whether '[any of] the items on Hursthouse's list ... is directly relevant to the good functioning of an animal. [Evolutionary biologists] are likely to say that the animal functions well ... not by preserving [itself] or by doing well at promoting the survival of the entire species but, rather, by caring for individuals that are especially closely related biologically to the animal' (Copp and Sobel 2004: 535). Copp and Sobel object further that 'it will have to be better explained why, even if we look for the normative in the natural, we should look especially to the evaluation of the individual as a member of the species ... rather than as the bearer of a specific genotype, as a member of the local herd or a local population, or as a member of a genus' (Copp and Sobel 2004: 536; cf. 542–3). Trenchant and sharp as these criticisms are, I propose we set them aside. For Hursthouse acknowledges that '[t]he long-term naturalistic project of validating the standard list of the virtues is Neurathian, and proceeds from within our ethical outlook' (Hursthouse 1999: 240). There is, she avers, no 'book of nature, as if human nature ... were [a] brute given' (Hursthouse 1999: 240). Hers is thus a highly qualified and non-scientific naturalism, so I suggest we accept her four 'natural' ends – at least for the sake of argument – and see what progress can be made on that basis.

A second question for Hursthouse is whether her four ends are mutually consistent. This question is particularly pertinent with regard to

---

[32] See Hursthouse 1999: 207–208, 235.   [33] Hursthouse 1999: 198.
[34] Hursthouse 1999: 199.   [35] Hursthouse 1999: 201.
[36] Hursthouse 1999: 202, ch. 11.

26   *Tom Angier*

'naturalism for rational animals',[37] since, as Hursthouse underlines, human 'characteristic ways of going on'[38] are far more complex than those of other animals. She acknowledges, on the one hand, that '[t]he ends in relation to which [living things] are evaluated can conflict, and when they do, the truth or falsity of the overall summing-up judgement is not always clearly determined'.[39] She asserts, on the other, that often enough such judgements are clearly determined. Citing the work of Philippa Foot, she refers, for instance, to an 'infertile cheetah', who, although she is free from certain pains and will survive herself, is not 'characteristic' of the species, because female cheetahs are due those pains and meant to reproduce. Similarly, a 'free-riding wolf' may enjoy his food and survive himself but does not experience 'characteristic enjoyment', because wolves are not meant to free ride – they are meant to contribute to the well-functioning of their group. What seems to be at work here is a holistic form of judgement, whereby – notwithstanding the ways in which Hursthouse's four ends can pull against or undermine each other – one can weigh their individual salience in context and arrive at well-founded, overall judgements. Still, given the difficulties of such weighing even in non-human contexts, it seems that aiming at natural ends may be more of a gestural idea than Hursthouse admits.[40] Indeed, rather than determining univocally the shape of virtue and happiness, those ends – depending on their individual saliences – may generate rival and incompatible conceptions of 'the good life'.

A third question for Hursthouse is whether her natural ends instrumentalise the virtues. For if those ends embody fixed points of goodness, it seems unclear why sub-virtuous or even vicious means should not (at least by Hursthouse's lights) be taken to them. If rape or ethnic cleansing, for instance, could promote individual or species survival, why not engage in them?[41] In response to this, Hursthouse contends that she is

---

[37] This is the title of Hursthouse 1999: ch. 10.   [38] Hursthouse 1999: 240.

[39] Hursthouse 1999: 204.

[40] Furthermore, it may depend, as Copp and Sobel argue, on conflating difference with deficiency. As they maintain, 'the point of [a snail's] shell is to be strong enough to resist predators. But suppose that one snail has a shell importantly stronger than the rest (and miraculously no heavier or cumbersome). Surely such a shell would be a wonderful snail shell. This example reveals that what is good in snail shells is not determined by what the textbooks tell us is characteristic but rather by the way in which the shell achieves the purpose of the snail's shell. Further, even if slowness in a snail is no defect, presumably a somewhat quicker snail that was able to outrun one of its predators would not thereby be defective. In short, deviation from the characteristic way that a species achieves survival and reproduction need not amount to a defect' (Copp and Sobel 2004: 538–9).

[41] Following Elijah Millgram, Micah Lott names this the 'Pollyanna Problem': why, that is, assume that 'natural' ends of the kind Hursthouse invokes are achieved best by virtuous means? See Lott 2012, esp. 410–18.

After Virtue and Virtue Ethics   27

mounting a merely 'hermeneutical' project, whose participants are 'not pretending to derive ethical evaluations of human beings from an ethically neutral human biology, but are already thinking about human beings in an ethically structured way'.[42] But if this 'ethically structured way' reduces to an antecedently accepted and independently justified (or perhaps just stipulated) set of virtues, it appears we have made little progress. At best, aiming at natural ends will deliver a highly indeterminate schema that has to be filled in using materials derived from elsewhere. As Scott Woodcock charges, 'the four ends specified ... set extremely broad limitations on the content of virtuous action. Yes, they will prohibit humans from extinguishing their own agency, extinguishing themselves as a species, and failing to promote pleasure, individual survival and group functioning in some way or another. But the range of ways in which these ends can be pursued is vast.'[43] At worst, aiming at natural ends turns out to be a pseudo-naturalistic schema designed to bolster virtues that it does little to subtend and much to undermine.

A fourth and final problem for Hursthouse's 'naturalistic' teleology centres on its role in deliberative agency. For even if we grant that her four ends are ultimate reasons for action, they do not constitute proper motivations. As Jennifer Frey puts things, those ends are 'too external to human practical self-consciousness' or to the 'first personal, practical point of view'.[44] And their externality consists in the fact that individual and species survival, pleasure and social functionality enter only rarely into the practical deliberations of the virtuous agent. Rather, and as I have elaborated above, virtuous agency is directed – intrinsically and by definition – at various goods, goods that do not prescind from people's everyday practical horizons. Natural ends in the *human* case consist in things like giving one's children a decent education, marrying one's chosen spouse and living in an affordable, at least minimally attractive house. By contrast, Hursthouse's four ends are extrinsic to this perspective. Clearly, she can appeal here to the distinction between reason and motive, maintaining, as she does, that '[t]he naturalistic conclusions are *not* intended to produce motivating reasons' (Hursthouse 1999: 194, emphasis in original; cf. 235). Motives are meant, in other words, to motivate *per se*, rather than devolve into a set of criteria for what makes a human life 'natural'. But as we saw in Section 1.3, this effects an unhelpful and unattractive bifurcation between theory and practice, dividing people between their theoretical and agential selves. The only difference is that, this time, the dissociation occurs not between virtuous motivation

---

[42] Hursthouse 2012: 174.   [43] Woodcock 2015: 31.   [44] Frey 2018: 57.

28   *Tom Angier*

and the involuted end of happiness, but between it and an essentially evoluted set of 'natural' ends.

1.5   Aiming at Utility or Duty

In sum, I have criticised Hursthouse's 'natural' ends on four grounds: they are not obviously natural, they tend to mutual inconsistency, they instrumentalise the virtues and they alienate reason-giving from moral motivation. Given the problems I've outlined with aiming at virtue, aiming at happiness and aiming at natural ends, it is time to look beyond virtue ethics *stricto sensu* and explore what David Solomon calls 'subordinating strategies' for the virtues.[45] On this type of view, the virtues are best understood as aiming at values traditionally assigned to and investigated by other ethical theories, such as utility (or good consequences) and duty (*qua* enjoined by deontic rules or principles). While adopting such strategies amounts, in a sense, to a defeat, since it concedes that virtue must be subsumed within a wider ethical framework, if this is the price for rescuing virtue as a central part of the theoretical landscape, then perhaps it is worth paying. Indeed, several philosophers have paid it (albeit not always with regret). The cohort of virtue-minded consequentialists plausibly includes David Hume, G. E. Moore and Julia Driver,[46] while among virtue-minded deontologists we can count Marcia Baron, Paul Guyer and Barbara Herman.[47] I will begin by considering virtue consequentialism (VC), the foundational commitment of which is that virtue aims at good (or perhaps the best) consequences, the latter being understood substantively (i.e. as causally separate and logically distinct from the virtues themselves). In this way, the substantive *telos* of VC is clearly demarcated from the formal *telos* of VE, which, as I detailed in Section 1.3, consists in the exercise of the virtues themselves.[48]

An initial, root-and-branch criticism of VC is that overall utility is a pseudo-aim, with no clear or fine-grained content. Judith Jarvis Thomson has articulated an argument to this effect,[49] and although I am sympathetic to it, it is too radical a criticism to repose weight on here. A more promising criticism, in this context, is that VC thoroughly

---

[45] See Solomon 1999.
[46] See (respectively) Hume 2007, Moore 1993 and Driver 2001.
[47] See (respectively) Baron 2011, Guyer 2011 and Herman 2011.
[48] There are several ways of unpacking the substantive aim of virtue consequentialism: as pleasure, preference-satisfaction, desire-satisfaction, etc. For present purposes, we can remain neutral on this issue.
[49] See Thomson 2008. Cf. Hurley 2009.

After Virtue and Virtue Ethics 29

instrumentalises virtue.[50] Not only does such instrumentalism directly contravene the virtue ethical project – which sees virtue as having intrinsic value – it also yields a destructive dilemma. For if utility consists in (say) overall pleasure or preference-satisfaction, then *either* virtue will be a very poor route to achieving this, *or* it will be reduced to what many antecedently consider to be vice. To illustrate this, imagine, on the one hand, how little pleasure or preference-satisfaction is generated by chastity,[51] and on the other, how much is generated by self-indulgence or untruthfulness. As Hurka puts matters, the first horn 'make[s] implausible claims about the place of virtue in … [consequentialist-type] flourishing' (Hurka 2001: 243), while the second invites agents either to positive vice or to the passive delights of Nozick's experience machine.[52] And there are further problems. Since VC casts virtue in a purely instrumental and 'hydraulic' role (i.e. virtue provides merely the motivational heft to realise independent and independently specified values), it effectively displaces virtue from any axiologically cognitive role, a role entrenched in virtue ethics.[53] Furthermore, whereas consequentialism is traditionally impartialist, virtue ethics has tended to foreground its partialism (i.e. the good of *not* giving equal weight to each individual's well-being).[54] On all these grounds, VC departs too egregiously from virtue ethics to be included within the fold.

As to virtue deontology (VD), similar objections are in order. VD also instrumentalises virtue: not for the sake of utility, but rather for that of duty (i.e. obeying certain rules or principles). Kant is quite explicit here: virtue is, he writes, 'moral strength of will', or 'the moral strength of a *human being*'s will in fulfilling his duty'.[55] As Allen Wood outlines Kant's view, virtue is reduced to 'moral strength of character, the strength of good maxims to secure compliance with duty in the face of recalcitrant inclinations' (Wood 2011: 59). Even Paul Guyer, who is more sympathetic to the virtue ethical project, acknowledges that, for Kant, 'the [deontic] moral ideal consists in the perfection of our will, choice, or autonomy', to which end '[t]he virtues are … instrumentally valuable' (Guyer 2011: 213). More generally, deontology obscures the goods to which virtue is intrinsically ordered, since it denominates the right as prior to the good and restricts all intrinsic value to acting on principle or for duty's sake. Indeed, in Kantian mode, deontology has no room for

---

[50] An exception here is Hurka, an avowed supporter of VC, who ascribes some intrinsic value to virtue. See Hurka 2001.

[51] Cf. Driver 1998: 125–6.

[52] Cf. Copp and Sobel 2004: 527–30 and Roberts 2015: 38–9 respectively.

[53] Cf. Solomon 1999: 96.   [54] Cf. Solomon 1999: 100.

[55] Kant 2017: 6: 405, emphasis in original.

30   *Tom Angier*

the goods towards which virtue is intrinsically aimed, since it views them as merely 'empirical' and hence not proper objects of the 'good will'. Finally, whereas deontology is preoccupied with duties, principles or rules of action, virtue ethics has tended to move away from these, insofar as its moral emphasis is particularistic and focused not on action, but character. On all these grounds, VD is a decidedly unpromising way of maintaining the centrality of virtue within ethical theory.

1.6   Conclusion

All in all, then, I have argued that, whether virtue ethics conceives of virtuous agents as aiming at virtue, aiming at happiness, aiming at natural ends or aiming at utility or duty – or any combination of these – it misses the mark. It does so because none of these aims is actually virtuous. They are either involuted (as are the first pair) or evoluted (as are the second) and thus too far within and too far beyond the virtuous agent respectively. The only proper aim for the virtuous agent consists in the various social and shared goods towards which the virtues are intrinsically ordered and without which they lack intelligibility: goods such as health and fitness (for temperance), saving the vulnerable from danger (for courage) and knowledge (for truthfulness). Crucially, these goods can be sought only in and through a host of practices, which are embedded, in turn, within various moral traditions. In my view, it is this triad of social goods, practices and moral traditions – rather than virtue *per se* or as such – that are at the heart of *After Virtue*'s argument and to which it rightly draws our attention. By contrast, virtue ethics has served to occlude the salience of this triad and has hence, on balance, done much to mislead ethical theory. On these grounds alone, we shall remain forever in *After Virtue*'s debt.

2   *After Virtue* and Happiness

Jennifer A. Herdt

It is an intriguing fact that the prevalence of the term 'utility' peaked in English-language books right around the time of the publication of *After Virtue*, followed by a steep decline. Meanwhile, use of the term 'happiness', having reached a summit in 1800, reversed a long subsequent decline at the same time.[1] And 'eudaimonia', while dwarfed in its usage by the others, witnessed an exponential rise starting in 1976, at a rate of increase that remains unabated up until the present.[2] *After Virtue*, in articulating a powerful Aristotelian challenge to utilitarianism, played an important role in these developments, absorbing energies from a nascent Aristotelian retrieval in philosophy, marrying it with Marxist impulses and mediating to a broad audience the sense that the ills of capitalist individualism were due to a loss of moral articulacy bound up with deep confusion about happiness.[3]

I will not in this chapter attempt to trace the influence of *After Virtue*'s reflections on happiness, since I take this to have been often subterranean and indirect.[4] I seek rather to unpack the substance of the corrective that

---

[1] Google Books N-gram Viewer, https://books.google.com/ngrams/graph?content=happiness%2C+utility&year_start=1700&year_end=2019&corpus=26&smoothing=3&direct_url=t1%3B%2Chappiness%3B%2Cc0%3B.t1%3B%2Cutility%3B%2Cc0, accessed 20 September 2021.

[2] Google Books N-gram Viewer, https://books.google.com/ngrams/graph?content=eudaimonia&year_start=1970&year_end=2019&corpus=26&smoothing=3&direct_url=t1%3B%2Ceudaimonia%3B%2Cc0, accessed 20 September 2021.

[3] On MacIntyre's lifelong connections with Marxism, including notably the British New Left, see Blackledge and Davidson 2008.

[4] It is surprisingly difficult to trace the influence of MacIntyre's reflection on happiness through the scholarly literature. The Philosopher's Index brings up no essays with both 'MacIntyre' and 'happiness' in the title, and only two with 'MacIntyre' and 'eudaimonia': Matthew Mendham, 'Eudaimonia and Agape in MacIntyre and Kierkegaard's 'Works of Love': Beginning Unpolemical Inquiry' (Mendham 2007) and Russell Hittinger, 'After MacIntyre: Natural Law Theory, Virtue Ethics, and Eudaimonia' (Hittinger 1989). The ATLA Religion Database brings up the same results. Similarly with edited volumes and monographs: *After MacIntyre: Critical Perspectives on the Work of Alasdair MacIntyre* (Horton and Mendus 1994) contains no index entries for happiness, eudaimonia or flourishing. The same is true of Peter McMylor's *Alasdair MacIntyre: Critic of Modernity*

MacIntyre sought to offer to dominant discourses about happiness, together with his constructive alternative, and to situate these in relation to several early works that indicate something of how MacIntyre's critique and corrective precipitated out of core concerns that have animated his career. A central thread is MacIntyre's critique of the intelligibility of pleasure as a reason for action and his pursuit of an objective conception of human flourishing to provide a standard for what is humanly worthy of desiring. The key challenge he faced along the way was to do justice to the socially and historically formed character of human flourishing. This led him to distance himself from Aristotle's 'metaphysical biology', and with it, from any ahistorical, falsely universal conception of human happiness or flourishing. This challenge was resolved in *After Virtue* through MacIntyre's embrace of social teleology and through the dialectical form of justification that MacIntyre went on to develop more fully in *Whose Justice? Which Rationality?*

MacIntyre's understanding of the relation between happiness and virtue is undoubtedly a form of eudaimonism. But which kind? Unpacking the distinction between a problematic welfare-prior eudaimonism and a defensible goodness-prior eudaimonism, I argue that MacIntyre's account straddles the two, failing to clarify whether a virtuous agent's ultimate reason for living well is because doing so enhances the agent's own well-being or simply because this is the fitting or appropriate way to live. MacIntyre's reflections on desire, pleasure, happiness and the well-lived life have nonetheless been vitally important to dispelling the deep-seated confusion on these matters that informs both philosophy and the culture at large.

2.1 MacIntyre's Early Critique of the Intelligibility of Pleasure as a Reason

In the mid-1960s, MacIntyre had already put his finger on a major weakness in contemporary philosophical discussions of happiness. In 'Pleasure as a Reason for Action', published in *The Monist* in 1965, MacIntyre pokes holes in the notion that 'pleasure', 'happiness' and/or 'enjoyment' are one thing, a single concept, of which Bentham, Aristotle

---

(McMylor 1993). In *Alasdair MacIntyre*, ed. Mark Murphy (Murphy 2003a), one finds only three glancing references to happiness and none to eudaimonia; flourishing is taken up briefly in essays by Jean Porter, J. L. A. Garcia and Terry Pinkard, but in none is it the focus. I have found the most sustained explorations of happiness and related concepts in MacIntyre's thought in Thomas D'Andrea, *Tradition, Rationality, and Virtue: The Thought of Alasdair MacIntyre* (D'Andrea 2006) and Christopher Stephen Lutz, *Reading Alasdair MacIntyre's* After Virtue (Lutz 2012).

After Virtue and Happiness

and others have different interpretations.[5] For hedonism pleasure is an end, whereas for Aristotelianism it 'supervenes upon activity successfully carried through' and hence cannot be an end of action. MacIntyre therefore sets out to disentangle the distinct concepts that have been muddled up together, with particular attention given to 'the role of the senses and of sensation in pleasure'.[6] He is particularly critical of reigning critiques of Benthamism, such as that of Ryle, which regard pleasure as enjoyment in activity, not noticing that this unitary account distorts as much as Bentham's and that one may fail to derive enjoyment from an activity either because of features of that activity or because of features of oneself. MacIntyre's overall thrust at this point is to lead us to attend to the contexts within which we learn to use concepts like pleasure, pain and enjoyment and thus to be able to distinguish primary from secondary uses, which are built on the former and from which puzzles arise when their secondary character is overlooked. Ethics cannot be done by distinguishing between 'different classes of judgment or kinds of statement', shorn of their context and hence of their intelligibility.[7] Along the way, MacIntyre argues in passing that 'a statement only provides someone with a reason for action if it is relevant to his wants and needs'.[8] Only if 'certain desires and aversions are standard for human beings' not in a statistical sense, but in the sense of being norms for what is humanly desire-worthy, embedded in our descriptive vocabulary, can descriptive statements furnish us with reasons for action. These would give us reasons apart from our subjective wants and needs. He does not here take any stand on whether such norms exist.

In this passing comment about 'standard' desires and aversions capable of constituting ethical norms for human beings, I take MacIntyre to be echoing Anscombe's 1958 comment that when it comes to defending the claim that a person can flourish only by being virtuous, 'philosophically there is a huge gap, at present unfillable as far as we are concerned, which needs to be filled by an account of human nature, human action, the type of characteristic a virtue is, and above all of human "flourishing"', where she admits that 'it is the last concept that appears the most doubtful', since 'it is a bit much to swallow that a man in pain and hunger and poor and friendless is "flourishing", as Aristotle himself admitted'.[9] MacIntyre contents himself at this stage with poking

---

[5] See MacIntyre 1965a: 217.   [6] MacIntyre 1965a: 218.

[7] MacIntyre 1965a: 228. This is also a core point made in another of MacIntyre's essays published in 1965, 'Imperatives, Reasons for Action, and Morals' (MacIntyre 1965b). Tellingly, this essay cites Anscombe's *Intention* (Anscombe 1957).

[8] MacIntyre 1965a: 229.   [9] Anscombe 1958: 1–19; here 18.

34   *Jennifer A. Herdt*

holes in the moral philosophy of the day; he offers no account of human nature or human flourishing that might offer norms for the humanly desire-worthy.

This same stance is also evident in *A Short History of Ethics*; the critique of happiness understood in terms of an individual's subjective states is clearly articulated, and MacIntyre is reaching for the possibility of a rational criticism of desire by reference to an objective conception of human flourishing, but the constructive proposal is a barest sketch. Virtue must have a telos, else it becomes pointless; meanwhile, happiness must 'constitute a satisfaction for a moralized human nature' or else 'it cannot be happiness for the kind of beings men are'.[10] The relation of virtue to happiness for Plato and Aristotle 'may constitute a problem', but the shape of the problem, and hence the shape of any potential solution, is clear. As Thomas D'Andrea notes, '*A Short History of Ethics* found Plato teaching us a permanent lesson about the rational criticism of desire – that a system of morality which is aimed at directing us towards our objective and progressively discoverable good must be a morality of desire-transformation, a morality of the virtues. In Aristotle's in some ways dated political ethics, MacIntyre has found a promising core of related theses showing us how virtue, moral rules, life in community, and happiness are internally connected.'[11] And yet – was it possible to fill in the 'huge gap', to offer a defensible objective account of human nature, action, virtue and flourishing? The possibility of resolving the relation between virtue and happiness, he suggests, lies in the form of community in which these concepts are embedded, not in any unpacking of the concepts as such. Where pursuing one's personal ideals is a matter of fulfilling social roles that help to constitute and sustain 'a well-integrated traditional form of society', personal ideals and social rules fit hand in glove. Not so where there is a tension between rules that sustain a well-functioning society and those ends or ideals (such as economic success) after which individuals strive and in which they find their personal satisfaction. Under the latter social conditions, 'the observance of rules will become either pointless or an end in itself', while 'it will be natural in this situation to conceive of the pursuit of pleasure and the pursuit of virtue as mutually exclusive alternatives'.[12] While MacIntyre here is discussing Cynics and Cyrenaics, Stoics and Epicureans, it is easy to discern the outline of his critiques of emotivism and of Kantian deontology.

[10] MacIntyre 1966: 66.   [11] D'Andrea 2006: 389; see also 50.
[12] MacIntyre 1966: 67.

2.2 *After Virtue*'s Critique of Reigning Conceptions of Happiness

By the time he writes *After Virtue*, MacIntyre has arrived at a distinctive response to the challenge of filling the 'huge gap' identified by Anscombe, one that joins his notoriously brusque rejection of Aristotle's 'metaphysical biology' with the affirmation of social teleology. The solution to the challenge of arriving at objective norms for what is humanly desire-worthy lies in running into the arms of historicism rather than seeking to circumvent it by way of any ahistoricist universalism. Happiness requires the transformation of our desires, the acquisition of the virtues that enable human flourishing in community, by way of participation in particular practices and traditions. Any general account of this must necessarily be highly formal, given the particularity of forms of life: 'the good life for man is the life spent in seeking for the good life for man'.[13]

Before considering what this proposal means for reflection on happiness as such, I want to take a step back to consider how MacIntyre in *After Virtue* frames the problem with reigning conceptions of happiness. In fact, MacIntyre's most sustained discussion of happiness in *After Virtue* takes place in the context of his chapter 6 discussion of the problems with modern moral theory understood through the lens of the failure of 'the Enlightenment project' (AV 62). Bentham's project is framed as that of providing a new teleology by which to vindicate the rules of morality, given a psychology in which the only motives for human action are pleasure and pain. On the basis of this psychology, Bentham argued that the telos of human action for the individual must be happiness understood as the maximisation of pleasure together within the minimisation of pain. This is capable of vindicating his 'moral thesis' requiring the choice of actions or policies that produce the greatest happiness of the greatest number, only if it is empirically the case that the 'enlightened' pursuit of one's own personal happiness, so construed, leads to the pursuit of the greatest happiness of the greatest number. Otherwise, it is psychologically impossible for the social reformer to set about making it the case that personal telos and social telos will coincide even for the unenlightened (AV 63). On MacIntyre's account, while John Stuart Mill set about putting utilitarianism on a stronger footing by revising Bentham's concept of happiness, 'what he had actually

---

[13] Alasdair MacIntyre, *After Virtue* [AV], 2nd edition (University of Notre Dame Press, 1984): 219.

36   *Jennifer A. Herdt*

succeeded in putting in question was the derivation of the morality from the psychology'. Bentham's project of developing a 'new naturalistic teleology' was bankrupt. 'Human happiness is *not* a unitary, simple notion and cannot provide us with a criterion for making our key choices' (AV 63, emphasis in original). There are many incommensurable pleasures and happinesses, and the activities by which these are achieved or constituted are not 'different means for providing the same end-state' (AV 64). Both pleasure and happiness are polymorphous and hence useless both as criteria for guiding the actions of individuals and for reforming societies.

2.3   Aristotelian Happiness in *After Virtue*

This does not mean, of course, that a particular understanding of happiness cannot provide an intelligible telos of human action. It does so within Aristotle's thought, as MacIntyre goes on to discuss when he returns to happiness in chapter 12. Happiness for Aristotle is eudaimonia, 'the state of being well and doing well in being well' (AV 148). Eudaimonia is achieved insofar as a human being realises their specific nature, which is made possible through the exercise of the virtues, which are not a means to happiness but partially constitutive of happiness, insofar as one can live well as a human being only through living virtuously: 'what constitutes the good for man is a complete human life lived at its best, and the exercise of the virtues is a necessary and central part of such a life' (AV 149). The virtues transform a person's emotions and desires such that they now can be made happy, in the sense of finding enjoyment or taking satisfaction, only in living virtuously. The content of eudaimonia is discovered only as and insofar as one becomes virtuous; only the good fully grasp the human good.

MacIntyre's core reservation about this Aristotelian construal of happiness, which he otherwise clearly endorses, is that it rests on Aristotle's 'metaphysical biology', the view that 'human beings, like the members of all other species, have a specific nature; and that nature is such that they have certain aims and goals, such that they move by nature towards a specific telos' (AV 148). Statements about the human good are thus a kind of factual statement. Now, MacIntyre's complaint here is not that the factual statement is erroneous, given that human beings can be shown not actually to aim at living virtuously. For what it means to say that human beings 'characteristically' aim at the good is not to be measured statistically, as a claim about what all or most human beings seek; it is, rather, a claim about what will realise or perfect members of this natural kind, as the telos of an acorn is to become an

After Virtue and Happiness   37

oak tree.[14] MacIntyre's complaint is not with this being a factual state-ment, which thus sidesteps the naturalistic fallacy insofar as it does not derive an 'ought' from an 'is' but discerns an ought teleologically built into the 'is'. However, the standard for human flourishing cannot be 'set by man qua animal, man prior to and without any particular culture' since 'man without culture is a myth' (AV 161). His specific concern is that Aristotle fails to see that his conception of flourishing human life is not universal but is rather a specifically Greek conception of what it means to flourish as a human being: 'Aristotle ... sets himself the task of giving an account of the good which is at once local and particular – located in and partially defined by the characteristics of the polis – and yet also cosmic and universal. The tension between these two poles is felt throughout the argument of the *Ethics*' (AV 148).

In what sense does Aristotle recognise the local and particular charac-ter of the good, on MacIntyre's account? Aristotle does recognise that the good life for human beings, as social animals, is possible only within the context of a community. This community, further, is of a particular kind, held together by its shared commitment to realisation of the human good and agreeing sufficiently on goods and virtues to be capable of sustaining civic friendship; that is, shared recognition of and pursuit of a good (AV 155). Aristotle rightly, on MacIntyre's account, assumes that the good life is realisable only within the context of such a community. But he wrongly maps this too closely onto the Greek polis of his day. He is guilty here both of idealising the Greek polis, failing to see the important respects in which it fails to provide a context for human flourishing, and of false universalisation, insofar as he takes precisely this sort of community to provide the only context for human flourishing. As MacIntyre notes, 'what is likely to affront us – and rightly – is Aristotle's writing off of non-Greeks, barbarians and slaves, as not merely not possessing political relationships, but as incapable of them' (AV 159). Aristotle's casual assumption that key virtues are available only to 'the affluent and those of high status', too, is objectionable. What MacIntyre does not say here, but which ought to be added, is that it follows from the ways in which the Greek polis provided a context only for the flourishing of Greek male elites, that it did not succeed in providing a context within which the good life, happiness, could be realised by *anyone*. The conception of the human telos was corrupted by false notions of justice, of what was due to other members of the

---

[14] 'Natural-historical' judgements of this kind play a central role in the Neo-Aristotelian theory of Michael Thompson, *Life and Action: Elementary Structures of Practice and Practical Thought* (Thompson 2008).

38 *Jennifer A. Herdt*

community and of friendship, insofar as certain members of the community were excluded from full participation in civic friendship.

What of the second failure, that of false universalisation? Here Aristotle is guilty of assuming that there is only one way in which to live humanly well. He does not grasp human beings as culture-creating creatures who construct myriad social practices within which diverse excellences can be achieved. He thus fails to take up the task of discerning amongst practices and communities which differences reflect injustice and other vices and which simply reflect alternative modes of flourishing: 'Aristotle writes as if barbarians and Greeks both had fixed natures and in so viewing them he brings home to us once again the ahistorical character of his understanding of human nature' (AV 159). Any would-be Aristotelian retrieval must come to terms with the existence of rival conceptions of human flourishing, unfolding historically, and the complex task of sorting through these in the effort to discern what it means to flourish, humanly speaking. No merely given conception of human flourishing may simply be taken as fully adequate. MacIntyre thus gestures towards the dialectical form of justification he will flesh out in *Whose Justice? Which Rationality?*[15]

2.4   MacIntyre's Socially Teleological Account of Happiness

MacIntyre's rejection of Aristotle's metaphysical biology is thus bound up with his understanding of human beings as essentially cultural and thus essentially historical creatures. We cannot make headway in arriving at a more adequate conception of human flourishing by cutting away culture and focusing solely on our species' nature. Conceptions of human flourishing are conceptions of what it is to flourish as a cultural and historical creature, and hence we must reckon with culturally and historically formed conceptions of human flourishing and their multiple and rival character.

MacIntyre thus arrives at his account of the good life, the life of genuine happiness or eudaimonia: 'the good life for man is the life spent in seeking for the good life for man' (AV 219). This is acknowledged to be 'a provisional conclusion about the good life', but it is not wholly empty. Realising one's specific nature as human requires engagement in the ongoing quest for the final good, 'the good which will enable us to order other goods'. It requires virtues that sustain this quest. And it

---

[15] I discuss MacIntyre's rationality of traditions more fully in 'Alasdair MacIntyre's "Rationality of Traditions" and Tradition-Transcendental Standards of Justification' (Herdt 1998).

After Virtue and Happiness   39

requires participation in communities that support civic friendship, and with it practices that sustain and deepen shared recognition of goods and shared cultivation of virtues.

As cultural and historical creatures, we must come to terms with the finite particularity of our grasp of the good. And yet, condemnation of false universals does not mean that we are reduced to relativism, to regarding the good that we seek as merely good 'for us', over against whatever might be good for those in other social contexts. That each of us must begin with whatever practices, whatever understandings of goods and virtues, into which we have been thrown does not mean that we must end there: 'without those moral particularities to begin from there would never be anywhere to begin; but it is in moving forward from such particularity that the search for the good, for the universal, consists' (AV 221). MacIntyre would of course go on to develop this more fully in his account of the rationality of traditions in *Whose Justice? Which Rationality?* and to recover a substantive account of human nature in *Dependent Rational Animals*, but it is worth underscoring that MacIntyre clearly rejects relativism in *After Virtue*, even as he underscores the danger of embracing false universals and foreclosing the quest for the final good.[16]

2.5   Competing Eudaimonisms: Welfare-Prior and Goodness-Prior

Thus far, I've retraced MacIntyre's path from the critique of happiness as understood from the Enlightenment onwards to his recovery of a usable notion of happiness from Aristotle and his revision of that Aristotelian notion through its historicisation. With that account in place, I want now to explore an instability in MacIntyre's moral psychology and, with it, in his account of the good. While MacIntyre does not describe his approach as a form of eudaimonism, it is standardly taken as such and certainly seems to qualify, insofar as it takes happiness or eudaimonia, understood as 'being well and doing well in being well', to require the virtues and to constitute the encompassing human good.[17] I want to suggest, however,

---

[16] *Dependent Rational Animals: Why Human Beings Need the Virtues* (MacIntyre 1999a): x. Defensible conceptions of human flourishing are diverse but not radically incommensurable, since they are constrained both by shared embodied vulnerabilities and capacities and by the virtues needed to sustain communal practical reasoning. By the time he gets to *Ethics in the Conflicts of Modernity*, MacIntyre is willing to go even further, enumerating eight basic goods 'whose contribution to a good life, whatever one's culture or social order, it would be difficult to deny', and about which there is 'in fact a surprising amount of agreement' (MacIntyre 2016: 222–3).

[17] Wood 2000: 261.

40   *Jennifer A. Herdt*

that MacIntyre's account wavers between a 'welfare-prior' and a 'goodness-prior' form of eudaimonism.[18] Despite his astute critique of Benthamite utilitarianism and its successor moral theories, MacIntyre's moral psychology remains too strongly shaped by the modern accounts he seeks to reject; while in the main he embraces a goodness-prior eudaimonism that is both more defensible and more aligned with ancient pagan and mediaeval Christian conceptions, his account remains entangled in problematic assumptions concerning justification and motivation.

By welfare-prior eudaimonism, I mean a view that regards the agent's own welfare as that which justifies and motivates the pursuit of the life of virtue. Welfare-prior eudaimonism recommends living well because this enhances the agent's own good. Goodness-prior eudaimonism, in contrast, recommends living well because this is the fitting or appropriate way to live; that is, because it is good. Goodness-prior eudaimonism does not dispute that it is indeed *good for* the agent to live well, but it regards the agent's well-being as supervening on pursuit of the *good as such*.[19] Neither welfare-prior nor goodness-prior eudaimonism takes the agent's desires and appetites as given. However, welfare-prior eudaimonism sees these desires and appetites as being transformed insofar as the agent arrives at a more adequate grasp of their own good and sees that it can be obtained only together with others in a life of virtue. Goodness-prior eudaimonism sees these desires and appetites being transformed insofar as the agent arrives at a fuller grasp of what is genuinely worthy of desire and devotion; that is, of what is independently good.

What is objectionable about welfare-prior eudaimonism is that it is a form of egoism: concern for others, and for the good as such, is conditional on the agent's pursuit of their own good. But this is the wrong kind of reason for concern for others and for the good.[20] Even if it is right to say that the right sort of concern for others and devotion to the good are constitutive of my own well-being as an agent, that I will find my true

---

[18] I more fully develop the contrast between these, defend goodness-prior eudaimonism and explore the rootedness of goodness-prior eudaimonism in both pagan and Christian thought in *Assuming Responsibility: Ecstatic Eudaimonism and the Call to Live Well* (Herdt 2022). The terminology draws on and modifies a distinction coined by Anne Baril, who contrasts 'excellence-prior' with 'welfare-prior' eudaimonism (Baril 2013: 512).

[19] Lott 2016: 366, discussing Toner 2010 and Baril 2013. That is, living well comes to be *specified* in terms of living virtuously; eudaimonia was not antecedently defined in terms of the agent's own good, but only in terms of living well, so even if (some) agents being formed in virtue must move from egoism to virtue, the theory itself does not need to overcome an in-built commitment to the agent's own good. See, e.g., Annas 2011: 218; Foot 2001: 97.

[20] See, e.g., Scheffler 1992: 116–17.

After Virtue and Happiness   41

happiness only in and through this sort of concern and devotion, this does not mean that they are rightly *contingent* on my own well-being.

What are the attractions of welfare-prior eudaimonism? Centrally, it appears to have a ready response to concerns about motivation. How can I bring myself to act well unless acting well is good for me? What reason would I have for acting virtuously if it were separated from my happiness? It is taken to be built into the very structure of practical rationality that it is orientated to the agent's own good, from which all reasons for action flow. This is seen as bound up with the natural and necessary character of living things as such, whose ultimate aim is taken to be that of enhancing their flourishing as the kind of things that they are. The welfare-prior eudaimonist can add that the modern ideal of altruism frames the relation between my good and the good of others in a falsely antagonistic way. There is no zero-sum game between these goods, since my good is only obtainable in community.

To this, the reply of the goodness-prior eudaimonist is that this is a misconstrual of the character of practical reason. It is simply not the case that the agency of all living things, or of practical reasoners, is intelligible only insofar as aimed at enhancing their own flourishing. Rather, living things perceive and respond to *particular* goods, things grasped as 'to be eaten', 'to be fled from', 'to be mated with'. It is when we as practical reasoners survey the shape of their activity that we may say that flourishing as the particular life form that they are is their final end. What it means to say this is to say that it is reference to this life form that makes sense of the shape of its activity and the range of goods to which it is sensitive. To be a practical reasoner, meanwhile, is to be a reason-giver, one capable of asking for and giving justifications. Practical rationality is orientated not merely to particular things grasped as good, as to be sought, but also to things *conceived of* as good. That is, of anything that we seek, value or devote ourselves to, it can always be asked of us whether it is appropriate to seek it, value it or devote ourselves to it, whether it is truly good. This becomes less, not more intelligible if we try to tack on here 'truly good *for me*'. The question is whether something is good *for me to value, and how*, not whether it is good for me in the sense of benefitting me. This certainly does not mean that the agent may not properly care about their own well-being, but that there are many other goods about which they properly care, and not only insofar as these contribute to their well-being. Goods are plural and appropriately valued in a host of ways; the point of speaking of 'the good as such' is not to deny this plurality, but simply to underscore that being a practical reasoner is bound up with the capacity to reflect on one's own pursuits and evaluations, to ask whether one's valuations are appropriate. There is nothing about this

42   *Jennifer A. Herdt*

reflexive evaluation of goods that limits it to reflection on *my* welfare, *my* own good. We can indeed say that we are perfected as practical reasoners insofar as we become more appropriately responsive to the full range of goods that we encounter. But its being good for me to be perfected in responsiveness flows from the independent goodness of that to which I respond. As Oliver O'Donovan notes, 'certainly, if an object is good, I, the subject, am involved with that object; it is good also for me, by virtue of the fact that I am part of the world in which and for which it exists as a good. But that "for me" is a mere implication of its goodness.'[21]

2.6 Welfare-Prior Eudaimonism in MacIntyre's Moral Psychology

There is strong evidence that MacIntyre was a welfare-prior eudaimonist early on in his career. As Thomas D'Andrea has noted, MacIntyre at that time argued that human actions can be understood only as they issue from an agent's desires, and that morality can be made intelligible only as 'instituted to serve long-term desire satisfaction': 'we affirm moral norms as indispensable guides to our actions – actions in which we seek to satisfy our desires in a reasonable and abiding and harmonious way, and in social contexts which are the necessary realm for human desire-satisfaction'.[22] MacIntyre is driven to embrace this position by his conviction that deontic considerations can be motivating for an agent only if they are taken to contribute to the agent's well-being. We saw this articulated in 'Pleasure as a Reason for Action', in which MacIntyre argued that 'a statement only provides someone with a reason for action if it is relevant to his wants and needs'.[23] On this view, as an agent acquires the virtues, their desires are transformed such that they come to desire what genuinely contributes to their well-being. They arrive at a transformed understanding of their wants and needs (according to which, importantly, their personal well-being harmonises rather than competes with the common good), but their reasons for action continue to flow from their understanding of what will contribute to (or help to constitute) their personal well-being.

Is it the case, though, that a statement provides someone with a reason for action only if it is taken to contribute to their well-being? MacIntyre in *After Virtue* suggests that this is built into the very structure of Aristotelian practical reasoning, itself 'a statement of necessary conditions for intelligible human action' (AV 161). Practical reasoning takes off from 'the wants and goals of the agent', adding 'the major premise, an assertion to

---

[21] O'Donovan 1994: 250. See also Hurka 1987: 71–3.   [22] D'Andrea 2006: 99.
[23] MacIntyre 1965a: 229.

After Virtue and Happiness

the effect that doing or having or seeking such-and-such is the type of thing that is good for or needed by a so-and-so' (AV 162). These, together with the minor premise that takes a particular this, here, to instantiate the type, leads to the conclusion. On this account, again, action is intelligible only if aimed at something taken precisely as good for or needed by the agent. What should be said in response to this account of practical reasoning? It is indeed the case that an agent can seek only something taken to be good. But this is analytic.[24] It is not the case that (as psychological egoism holds) an agent can seek only something under the aspect of its being good *for the agent*. For I may regard (and rightly regard) something other than my own good as more valuable and therefore more worthy of my devotion and pursuit than my own good. Further, as Joseph Butler astutely pointed out long ago, human beings value and pursue a host of goods for their own sake; these 'particular affections' may be for things that do not contribute to my long-term well-being, and need not be sought under that description: 'every particular affection, even the love of our neighbour, is as really our own affection, as self-love'.[25] So to say that I necessarily always seek something that I desire is not to say that what I desire is always sought as good for me.[26] Many things that we desire are not good for us, and in any case are not sought as good for me, but simply for their own sake. If I act well, doing so will in fact be good for me, in the sense that acting well serves to perfect my character. But I will not respond well to many of the goods I encounter if all my reasons flow from my well-being.

MacIntyre never disentangles welfare-prior from goodness-prior eudaimonism or repudiates the former. While he rightly argues that the pursuit of enjoyment or pleasure cannot guide action, even as these regularly supervene on living well, he never clearly states that the agent's personal good, too, *supervenes on* living well; that is, on appropriate responsiveness to a host of independent goods. However, much of what MacIntyre says in *After Virtue* is consistent with goodness-prior eudaimonism. For instance, he writes of the hypothetical character of moral judgements that they express 'a judgment as to what conduct would be teleologically appropriate for a human being' (AV 60). Here, the telos is

---

[24] Although this is admittedly contested, e.g., by Velleman 2000: 99–122.

[25] Butler 2017: 111.

[26] John Lemos develops a critique along similar lines in 'Virtue, Happiness, and Intelligibility' (Lemos 1997). However, Lemos concludes that 'there is no essential connection between being a good man (being virtuous) and achieving the good for men (happiness)' (Lemos 1997: 308). That is too strong. If happiness is 'being well and doing well in being well' (AV 148), then being virtuous is partly constitutive of doing well, and thus partly constitutive of happiness. There is, then, an essential connection between the two.

44 *Jennifer A. Herdt*

identified as acting well as a human being, not as the agent's well-being. He notes that the 'educated moral agent' 'does what is virtuous *because* it is virtuous', and that 'we cannot characterize the good for man adequately without already having made reference to the virtues' (AV 149, emphasis in original). That is, the virtues are good for the agent because they are good as such; they are 'what it is good for someone like him to do and to be' (AV 162). While the virtues tend to lead to the achievement of a certain class of goods, 'unless we practice [the virtues] irrespective of whether in any particular set of contingent circumstances they will produce those goods or not, we cannot possess them at all' (AV 198). Perhaps most importantly, he affirms that it is in our efforts to live well that we find ourselves embarked on a pursuit for the final good, '*the* good which will enable us to order other goods', starting with the contingent grasp of goods afforded by our particular embodied situations and 'moving forward from such particularity' (without leaving it behind) in 'the search for the good, for the universal' (AV 221, emphasis in original). There is here no insistence that I must take '*the* good' to be good *for me*, before I have a reason to respond to it as good.

2.7   After *After Virtue*

Has MacIntyre's stance become clearer since *After Virtue*? In *Ethics in the Conflicts of Modernity*, MacIntyre returns once again to the critique of the dominant conception of happiness as 'a state of only positive feelings'.[27] He notes that it makes sense to ask of such a state whether it is justified; that is, to ask whether, when we are feeling happy, we have a good reason for feeling or being happy. Among the conditions that he offers for its being the case that a person has a good reason for being happy is that 'that in which I take pleasure, that about which I am happy must be such that it contributes directly or indirectly to my good or the good of others for whom I have reason to care'.[28] He adds, further, that this must hold, rewritten, such that I have good reason for being unhappy when that about which I am unhappy contributes directly or indirectly to my 'harm or loss' or that of those for whom I have reason to care. Now, the disjunct here is intriguing; MacIntyre opens up the possibility that I may be happy not about my own good but about someone else's good, and unhappy

---

[27] MacIntyre 2016. I take this book to offer a significant rebuke to would-be 'traditionalist' appropriations of MacIntyre's thought and a clarification of the sense in which MacIntyre remains a Marxist; see my review essay in *Studies in Christian Ethics* (Herdt 2018) and also Tom Angier's review essay in *Religious Studies* (Angier 2017).

[28] MacIntyre 2016: 197.

After Virtue and Happiness | 45

not about my own harm or loss but about someone else's. But he does not say simply that I may be happy, and have good reason to be happy, simply because I am rightly responding to any number of goods that I rightly take to be good. My appropriate response might be one of admiration, or awe, or reverence; to be asking whether such goods contribute to my good is already to fail in appropriate response. Think, for instance, here of appropriate responsiveness to God, or to a frolicking pod of dolphins, or to a beautiful sunset.[29]

Presumably, if pushed, MacIntyre would say that the disjunct between my good and the good of someone else for whom I have reason to care disappears if we press on it. For he has long criticised the ideal of altruism that emerged when egoism came to be seen as the problem to be solved by morality. The problem of egoism, he argues, disappears when we recover an Aristotelian moral psychology: 'for what education in the virtues teaches me is that my good as a man is one and the same as the good of those others with whom I am bound up in human community' (AV 229). My pursuit of my good is thus not antagonistic to you pursuing your good. To this, the goodness-prior eudaimonist affirms, once again, that the agent's own good does indeed supervene on rightly responding to the various goods encountered by the agent, including as these affect other agents. There is indeed no zero-sum game between my living well as a human being and your living well as a human being. The disjunct here is merely apparent. Our ideal should not be altruism, but appropriate responsiveness to the good. But it is also unhelpful to insist that I have good reason to be happy only in response to something that is contributing to some person's good, whether mine or someone else's. For this is to occlude the fact that there are objects in themselves good that therefore elicit our positive valuation. To rightly value goods we encounter, including but not limited to the good of the persons we encounter, is certainly good for me. But, to echo O'Donovan once again, 'that "for me" is a mere implication of its goodness'.[30]

2.8   Conclusion

MacIntyre's clear-eyed critiques of common conceptions of happiness as they are operative in moral philosophy, in positive psychology and in the culture at large are threaded throughout his career, and they assumed in

---

[29] Iris Murdoch, drawing on Simone Weil, influentially developed the concept of 'attention' along these lines in 'The Idea of Perfection'. See *The Sovereignty of Good* (Murdoch 2014 [1970]: 17–19).

[30] O'Donovan 1994: 250.

After Virtue a mature and deservedly influential form. Since happiness continues to be understood as a state of positive feeling, and taken as a proper individual and social goal, with increasing attention from the social sciences in particular, MacIntyre's astute deconstruction of this dominant conception remains invaluable.[31] As he wisely notes, given the state of the world, and of we ourselves, we often have good reason to be dissatisfied, even outraged: 'the good life, the fulfilled life, may be and often is unhappy by the standards of happiness studies'.[32] Yet he never quite distinguishes between welfare-prior and goodness-prior eudaimonism. His position straddles the two in ways that leave his eudaimonism open to critique as inappropriately self-regarding. The core issue here is an overly narrow notion of reasons for action that took root early in MacIntyre's intellectual development and that has remained operative throughout.

While more work therefore needs to be done in order to recover and defend a viable eudaimonism, that enterprise is unimaginable in the absence of MacIntyre's contributions as philosopher and social critic. He has succeeded in driving home in extraordinarily compelling ways the point that each of us as a practical reasoner faces a task, that of acting in a way that is appropriate to our character as practical reasoners. As finite embodied practical reasoners, we are situated in and formed by our various social and historical locations and responsible for sorting through these to the best of our ability. In so doing, we move ourselves and our social practices towards greater care and greater justice. To have helped his readers see the goodness of this calling, and therefore to ignite in them the desire to seek it, has been a contribution not merely to moral philosophy but to ethical formation itself. MacIntyre, like Aristotle before him, rightly thinks that the two cannot be separated.

---

[31] Since the focus of this chapter is on *After Virtue*, I do not delve here into MacIntyre's astute critique of positive psychology in *Ethics in the Conflicts of Modernity* (MacIntyre 2016: 194–6).

[32] MacIntyre 2016: 202.

3 *After Virtue*
Nietzsche or *Aristotle, Institutions* and *Practices*

Kelvin Knight

Alasdair MacIntyre has often said, in symposia and conversation, that if he had not become an Aristotelian he would be a Nietzschean. *After Virtue*'s structural bifurcation and conclusion with chapters juxtaposing Aristotle with Friedrich Nietzsche, '*the* moral philosopher of the present age' (MacIntyre 2007: 114; MacIntyre's emphasis), are therefore more than merely the greatest of its dramatic devices. In arguing that the Enlightenment project of justifying morality failed, it concurs with Nietzsche. No less than Nietzsche, it considers this failure to be of profound importance for all us moderns. The German described modernity as nihilistic, as having negated all previous values; *After Virtue*, borrowing from the vocabulary of an 'English-speaking philosophical world' still, in 1981, unfamiliar with Nietzsche, described it, less dramatically, as 'emotivist' (MacIntyre 2007: 21). For Nietzsche, the only hope for overcoming this wretched condition was for individuals who have the will to create their own values to impose them on others; for *After Virtue*, Nietzsche's self-assertive creation, 'the *Übermensch*', belongs 'in the pages of a philosophical bestiary rather than in serious discussion' (MacIntyre 2007: 22).

After Virtue commends Nietzsche for anticipating the fate of modern moral philosophy. Beyond that, it concedes only that 'the attractiveness of Nietzsche's position lay in its apparent honesty' (MacIntyre 2007: 258). Had its author become a Nietzschean, he would have done so because of the 'importance of being ... finally undeceived, being, as Nietzsche put it, truthful at last' (MacIntyre 2007: 129). The book's objection to Nietzsche's standpoint is therefore already in that pre-Enlightenment tradition at which he aimed his most powerful, genealogical critique and which would never have been defended by Aristotle, from whom Nietzsche 'borrow[ed] the name and notion of "the great-souled man"' (MacIntyre 2007: 117; cf. Kaufmann 1974: 382–4) who was no less enamoured of noble magnificence and who 'would certainly not have admired Jesus Christ and ... would have been horrified by St Paul' (MacIntyre 2007: 184). This allegiance was missed by many of

48 *Kelvin Knight*

the book's early reviewers. They might not have missed it had they attended to its case against Nietzsche. 'Nietzschean man, the *Übermensch* ... "wants no 'sympathetic' heart, but servants, tools; in his intercourse with men he is always intent on making something out of them"', a 'characterization of "the great man"' that MacIntyre considers both incredible and repellent (MacIntyre 2007: 257–8, quoting Nietzsche's *The Will to Power*). No less than Kant, it is the traditional, Christian virtues that MacIntyre most wants to justify in terms of a specifically *practical* reason. What adds most drama to his defence, beyond the failure of that Enlightenment project that culminated in Kant, is Nietzsche's sustained attack upon those virtues as slavish self-deceits.

3.1 Institutions

When *After Virtue* first poses the question 'Nietzsche or Aristotle?', in chapter 9, it does so by referring neither to Nietzsche nor to Aristotle but to Max Weber's predictive superiority over Karl Marx. 'The contemporary vision of the world' is so 'Weberian' that when 'Marxists organize and move toward power they always do and have become Weberians in substance', and this for the Weberian reason that 'all power tends to coopt and absolute power coopts absolutely' (MacIntyre 2007: 109). This reasoning might be thought to differ from that of both Nietzsche and Marx. It differs from that of Nietzsche in being sociological, by explaining individuals' actions in terms of shared beliefs and reasons more than in terms of their inner, purely voluntary, *psycho*logical drives, passions or emotions. It differs from Marx's reasoning in refusing to reduce historically effective shared beliefs to those of conflicting, amoral, material, class interests.

When still a Marxist, MacIntyre was persuaded of the historical complicity of a vocational 'work ethic' in motivating capital's accumulation. So persuaded, he abandoned historical materialism for what was often described as a historically causal idealism, commending the 'enormous achievement' of Weber's *The Protestant Ethic and the Spirit of Capitalism* in attributing to Protestantism a practical 'rationality' and economically causal role, even whilst criticising Weber's interpretation of evidence for attributing Calvinists' behaviour more to psychological anxiety than to shared reasoning in resolving a contradiction in their beliefs about how one ought to act (MacIntyre 1962: 48–9, 54–5). In fitting the later Weber into a history of modern German thought, he proposed that 'all subsequent sociologists were to be ... pupils' of Weber's sophisticated way of interpreting actions' meanings for actors. The 'technical, fact-finding rationality' that informed early entrepreneurial action extended into

Nietzsche *or* Aristotle, Institutions *and* Practices   49

'a disenchanted world' of bureaucratic rationalisation of endless means, in which 'bureaucratic values must not be allowed to be ultimate'. Unfortunately, the sophistication of a sociology that 'introduces the notion of status' alongside that of 'class' seemed to allow 'no general answer' to the question of how to resist bureaucratisation (MacIntyre 1972: 435–9).

As yet, MacIntyre himself had no such answer. *A Short History of Ethics*, which surveyed the historical ground on which he would build *After Virtue*'s argument, concluded by proposing that one should simply 'choose' between moral beliefs (MacIntyre 1966: 216, 268), without, as yet, taking either his belief in the capacities of shared reasoning or his critique of Weber, which that belief informed, so far as to propose that such reasoning might afford one criteria by which to judge between the relative truthfulness of, say, Nietzscheanism and Aristotelianism. The book's history of ethics had begun by following Nietzsche, both back to 'prephilosophical' Greece and in describing the original, Homeric meaning and use of ἀγαθός or 'good' (MacIntyre 1966: 5–13, 223), before crediting him as 'the most perceptive of German moralists' (MacIntyre 1966: 225–6). A couple years later, reviewing Walter Kaufman's edition of *The Will to Power*, MacIntyre acknowledged that Nietzsche's critique of 'the false objectivism of liberalism' offered 'a rival scheme of *the* virtues', albeit 'as only aristocratic virtues, as class virtues' (MacIntyre 1969a: 81; MacIntyre's emphasis). Later still, MacIntyre began a very short history of 'modern German thought' not with Luther, Kant or Hegel but with Nietzsche, because it was he who stepped out of his country's 'established order' to assert 'all the excellences of which the personality is capable'. Before moving on to Weber, he posed the *Übermensch* as Nietzsche's response to modernity's 'bureaucratisation of life' (MacIntyre 1972: 428–30). This response is repudiated in *After Virtue* as an intentionally irrational proposition to 'make ourselves into autonomous moral subjects by some gigantic and heroic act of the will' (MacIntyre 2007: 114). Assimilating Nietzschean genealogy to a tradition of distinctively modern moral philosophy, it presents the *Übermensch* as successor to Kant's autonomous actor once all possible grounds for categorical imperatives appear to have been annihilated. What Nietzsche portrayed as archaic individuals' 'self-assertion', *After Virtue* describes as a form 'of assertion proper to and required by a certain role … a social creation, not an individual one' (MacIntyre 2007: 129). His apparent honesty about the vital, impersonal universality of a will to power it adjudges to be the self-deceit of an 'inventive literary construction' animated by 'his own nineteenth-century individualism'. Nonetheless, *After Virtue* argues that Nietzsche's

50   *Kelvin Knight*

construct *does* represent *something* fundamental; not in life as such but within the individualised inhabitants of post-Enlightenment, 'emotivist culture'. What characterizes this 'emotivist self', in its various guises, is the amoral manipulativeness of its social relations, in contrast to the genuine virtues exemplified by Homer's heroes or Weber's ascetic, Calvinist entrepreneurs. Whereas such pre-modern roles exemplified moral excellences recognised by entire societies, the emotivist self demonstrates modernity's loss of moral unity and belief.

After Virtue exceeds Nietzsche's concern with heroism in characterising entire past societies, if not an entire stage of human development, by the term 'heroic', supplementing, like him, Homeric poetry with Norse saga to illustrate such societies' domination by heroic warriors (MacIntyre 2007: 121–31). In describing mediaeval society's 'transition out of ... heroic society' (MacIntyre 2007: 166), the book ignores the moralities both of Nietzsche's resentful slave and of the saint, Christianity's moral hero. The leading roles that emerged in post-'heroic', mediaeval society, such as the conflictual ones performed by Thomas Becket and Henry II or Thomas More and Henry VIII, were already institutionally defined (MacIntyre 2007: 166–73). MacIntyre is as aware as Weber that transition to 'the modern mass ... *bureaucratic* army' made any such social role as that of the 'Homeric hero' redundant (Weber 1994: 146; Weber's emphasis), with *After Virtue*'s conclusion seeming to echo Weber's proposition that 'the communist warrior' of Trotsky's Red Army was the 'perfect counterpart to the monk' living the ascetic, 'garrisoned and communistic life' that St Benedict had once instituted (Weber 1978: 153). Its distinction between social 'roles' and modern, socially symbolic 'characters' reflects that between moral language's meaning and emotive use, thereby exceeding Nietzsche and Weber's favoured, non-deductive mode of arguing through presentation of culturally characteristic moral 'types'.

MacIntyre's employment of such 'characters' accommodates Weber, as a typical 'Wilhelmine ... Professor' (MacIntyre 2007: 27–30), even if not Nietzsche, who, having 'rejected Wilhelmine Germany' and its professoriate, he cast as the altogether more idiosyncratic, taboo-busting 'Kamehameha II of the European tradition' (MacIntyre 2007: 113, 129). The character that is of greatest importance, not least because it displaces Marx's capitalist whilst simultaneously constituting the state, is that of 'the bureaucratic manager – the essential instrument for organising modern work' (MacIntyre 2007: 228), complemented by the character of 'the rich aesthete' as unproductive consumer of the work of others (MacIntyre 2007: 24–5). Such managers are the agents of 'the continuously reestablished dominance of markets, factories and finally

Nietzsche *or* Aristotle, Institutions *and* Practices

bureaucracies over individuals' (MacIntyre 2007: 228), their unheroic quest for power and position exemplifying the 'suppressed Nietzschean premises' of 'the Weberian managerial forms of our culture'. He presents Weber's critical account of modernity as modernity's own self-image. 'Weber and Nietzsche together provide us with the key theoretical articulations of the contemporary social order' (MacIntyre 2007: 114–15). Assimilating the perspectives of both Germans to that of a kind of philosophising about morality of which he had long been critical, he calls them 'emotivists' (thereby identifying them as the strongest link between the Enlightenment project and what *After Virtue* portrays as its eventual philosophical and cultural fate). The proposition that one must 'simply choose' between moral beliefs in a way about which 'reason is silent' he now disowns, instead attributing it to Weber as a mark of the sociologist's characteristically emotivist inability to draw any 'genuine distinction between manipulative and non-manipulative social relations' (MacIntyre 2007: 21–3, 26; cf. MacIntyre 1962: 67–8).

In America, where MacIntyre wrote *After Virtue*, Weber's reputation was well established. He was known as the great theorist of 'The Modern Western Institutional System', 'of the sociological and institutional foundations of the modern economic and social order' and, indeed, of 'the institutional structure of the modern world as a whole' and as 'a total institutional order', who had invented 'a quite new institutional kind of analysis' and a 'comparative institutional sociology' (Parsons 1947: 78, 4, 52, 79, 54, 78). Even those 'radical critics' (MacIntyre 2007: 75) who contested Weber's view of capitalist 'institutions … as the very embodiment of rationality' appealed to his understanding 'of capitalism as a unit[ary] … configuration of institutions, which by the logic of their own requirements increasingly narrow the range of effective choices open to men', whom they reduce to 'actor[s] of social roles', capitalism having co-opted 'other institutions into its own image' of 'bureaucratic management' (Gerth and Mills 1946: 49, 65, 73, 66, 49–50). Weber was understood as the sociological institutionalist complementing America's indigenous, constitutionalist politics, post-war 'pluralist' political science and older, 'institutionalist' school of economics.

MacIntyre had long been developing his critique of Weber's account of bureaucratic domination. Weber he considered as social science's pre-eminent methodologist, and he understood 'social science methodology as the ideology of bureaucratic authority' (MacIntyre 1998a), arguing in *After Virtue* that it is a gross error to presume that social scientists' methodological expertise enables them and the managers they inform to reason in a way unavailable and superior to that of those whose behaviour they claim to explain and control (MacIntyre 2007: 75–108).

52   *Kelvin Knight*

'Civil servants and managers alike justify themselves and their claims to authority, power and money' in a way that is consistent with Weber's 'insistence that the rationality of adjusting means to ends in the most economical and efficient way is the central task of the bureaucrat', applying 'a set of universal law-like generalizations'. On MacIntyre's account, it was by such insistence that 'Weber provided the key to much of the modern age', insisting himself 'that how we ought to answer the question of the moral and political legitimacy of the characteristically dominant institutions of modernity turns on how we decide an issue in the philosophy of the social sciences' (MacIntyre 2007: 86–7). His way beyond both Marx and Weber was to argue that 'the fetishism of commodities has been supplemented by ... that of bureaucratic skills', 'that a metaphysical belief in managerial expertise has been institutionalised in our corporations' (MacIntyre 2007: 107–108), and that state and corporate institutions would be delegitimised, and their managers' 'claim to status and reward ... fatally undermined', when it is acknowledged that this fetishistic metaphysics endows them with no real expertise (MacIntyre 2007: 106). Methodology apart, MacIntyre charges that Weber reserves 'rational criteria' for 'that type of bureaucratic authority which appeals precisely to its own effectiveness', so 'that bureaucratic authority is nothing other than successful power' (MacIntyre 2007: 26).[1] Refusing this appeal, he finds the idea of 'managerial and bureaucratic expertise' and 'effectiveness' to be a 'moral fiction' (MacIntyre 2007: 74–7).

After Virtue's scepticism about bureaucracy belies its origin in MacIntyre's thinking through of the moral limitations of Marxist theory and practice. The book's concluding praise of Trotsky's predictive acumen, condemnation of 'the barbarous despotism of the collective Tsardom which reigns in Moscow' (MacIntyre 2007: 74–7) and prediction that Stalinism's bureaucratic collectivism was 'doomed' because 'the totalitarian project will always produce ... rigidity and inefficiency' all reflect its author's political past (MacIntyre 2007: 106). Marxism, he had concluded, shared with 'liberal individualism' 'the *ethos* of the distinctively modern and modernising world'. If he was to establish 'a rationally and morally defensible standpoint from which to judge and to act' (MacIntyre 2007: xvii–xviii), he had to understand what was mistaken in the rationality of a theory capable of concluding that, if the state appropriated all capital, it would wither away rather than increase its

---

[1] Although MacIntyre has scarcely been influenced by Leo Strauss, it is conceivable that by 1981 his view of Weber owed something to that other, *anti*-historicist German's critique of Talcott Parson's American Weber.

Nietzsche *or* Aristotle, Institutions *and* Practices 53

social dominance. Weber's reasoning here succeeded where that of Marx failed. The 'pessimism' MacIntyre shared with Weber was that of practical, political reason's inability to see any 'tolerable alternative set of political and economic structures ... to replace the structures of advanced capitalism' (MacIntyre 2007: 262). Stalinism's moral rejection required a critique of states and of capitalist corporations as, alike, bureaucratic and managerial 'institutions'.

In adding the non-Marxist category of power as domination (e.g. MacIntyre 2007: 140) to Marxism's critique of capital, besides using 'status' to signify the kind of social hierarchy exemplified by bureaucracy, *After Virtue*'s conceptual scheme exceeds those of both Nietzsche and Marx in its Weberian reach; the ends to which means are adjusted and matched by bureaucratic rationality are the accumulation of both power and capital. The way in which the book moves beyond both Marxist and Weberian sociologies to confront Nietzsche with Aristotle is intended to raise fundamental issues of moral agency. As it rightly says, 'even Kant, who sometimes seems to restrict moral agency to the inner realm of the noumenal, implies otherwise in his writings on law, history and politics' (MacIntyre 2007: 23). That said, MacIntyre's ethical sociology and 'historicism' (MacIntyre 2007: 266–72) go far beyond anything expressed in Kant's 'moral anthropology'. They are no less radical than Hegel's historicism, whilst refusing his identification of ethical rationality with corporately and politically institutionalised actuality. By invoking Aristotle, MacIntyre clearly distinguishes his own rejection of Hegel from that of Marx, of Nietzsche and of Weber. More substantively, he provides a general answer to the question of how moral agency might counter modernity's threat of bureaucratic and managerial domination in what *After Virtue* says of practices.

3.2   Practices

The MacIntyre of *After Virtue* might have surprised his earlier self more by becoming an Aristotelian than he would have done had he become a Nietzschean. That his formal education well equipped him for his new role cannot be doubted; what might have surprised the communist classics student was his revival of the ethics of that philosopher who took as 'the paradigm of human excellence ... the Athenian gentleman' (MacIntyre 2007: 182; cf. MacIntyre 1966: 28, 67, 78; Kaufmann 1967: 208–209). However, what MacIntyre took himself to be reviving in *After Virtue* was no culturally particular paradigm of human excellence but, rather, 'a long tradition' to which 'Aristotle's account of the virtues' is 'central' (MacIntyre 2007: 146). As he took care in elaborating, this tradition may be 'corrected and transcended in a way that leaves the present open to being in turn corrected and transcended by some yet more adequate future point of view' (MacIntyre 2007: 146).

Aristotelianism might well now be thought to have been corrected by the more adequate point of view elaborated in *After Virtue*. It transcends the patriarchal views typical of Athenian slave-owners by analysing the argument of Aristotle's *Nicomachean Ethics* as 'a threefold scheme in which human-nature-as-it-happens-to-be (human nature in its untutored state) is initially discrepant and discordant with the precepts of ethics and needs to be transformed by the instruction of practical reason and experience into human-nature-as-it-could-be-if-it-realized-its-*telos*' (MacIntyre 2007: 53), going on to argue (in chapters 10–13) that this tripartite conceptual scheme has been successfully adapted to different conceptions of the human end and used to justify different moral precepts. The Enlightenment project failed because it rejected this scheme. Therefore, the tradition of the virtues pioneered by Aristotle has *not* been defeated and survives to contest Nietzsche's claims.

After Virtue's objections to Aristotle go far deeper than his aristocratic prejudices and precepts. Aristotle's own application of the three-fold scheme is now unsustainable, it contends, because it is premised on an erroneous, ahistorical conception of human nature. Its first edition denied 'any teleology in nature' (MacIntyre 1981: 183; cf. MacIntyre 2007: 196). 'We must', subsequent editions have continued to insist, reject Aristotle's 'metaphysical biology' (MacIntyre 2007: 162). When it describes belief in managerial expertise as 'metaphysical', it means that what is believed is a rationalist fiction. In contesting what it takes to be 'conventional *philosophy* of social science', it claims alignment with 'the practice and ... findings of *empirical* social science' (MacIntyre 2007: 106; emphases added). Relatedly, in bearing the subtitle 'a study in moral theory', it already implies that its task is largely critical. On MacIntyre's view, the practicality of moral reasoning is incompatible with any isolation of a metaphysics of morals from its anthropology, such that pure practical reason might determine how individuals 'ought' to act irrespective of social rules, relations or roles. His antipathy to metaphysics was not born of ignorance. After his education in classics, English Dominicans had published his first philosophical paper on the eminently Thomist and Aristotelian subject of 'analogy in metaphysics' (MacIntyre 1951a), whilst the third and most modern source of his understanding of Aristotle was from that Oxonian interpretative tradition, which, notwithstanding its concern with an ethics of social roles (MacIntyre 1994c; Knight 2011a), he criticised as combining Aristotle with Hegel 'to perform social analysis in a highly metaphysical style' (MacIntyre 1966: 245).

Nietzsche *or* Aristotle, Institutions *and* Practices 55

MacIntyre's historicism informs *After Virtue*'s critique of Nietzsche as well as its critique of Aristotle. He criticises both for being too metaphysical. Notwithstanding Nietzsche's own critique of 'historians of morality' for being '*by nature* unhistorical' (Nietzsche 1967a: 25; Nietzsche's emphasis), he regarded Nietzsche as having worked in the shadow of Kant's realm of the noumenal, where individual psychology transcended social time and place by wilful exercise of resolution, courage and maturity in questing for a single, universalisable paradigm of autonomous excellence and self-mastery. Against Nietzsche's intellectual creation of an impersonal 'will to power' as life's vital, inescapable force, MacIntyre reverts to the Marxist thought that, 'if moral utterance is put to uses at the service of arbitrary will, it is someone's arbitrary will; and the question of *whose* will it is is obviously of both moral and political importance' (MacIntyre 2007: 110; MacIntyre's emphasis). This was a question that MacIntyre resolved to answer after *After Virtue*, the task of which was to elaborate a practical rationality capable of contesting modernity's notionally impersonal, bureaucratic rationality of institutionalised domination.

Not until chapter 14 does MacIntyre spell out what he calls his 'core concept of the virtues'. He specifies 'three stages in the logical development of the concept which have to be identified in order' because 'each later stage presupposes the earlier, but not *vice versa*', and because each stage 'has its own conceptual background' (MacIntyre 2007: 186–7). The first stage is that of 'a "practice"', which he defines as 'any coherent and complex form of socially established cooperative human activity through which goods internal to that form of activity are realised in the course of trying to achieve those standards of excellence which are appropriate to, and partially definitive of, that form of activity, with the result that human powers to achieve excellence, and human conceptions of the ends and goods involved, are systematically extended'. As examples he cites football, chess, architecture, farming, painting, music, 'politics in the Aristotelian sense, the making and sustaining of family life' and 'the enquiries of physics, chemistry and biology' and of history. Each of these forms of activity has two kinds of goods internal to it: first, 'the excellence of the products' or performances that the particular activity involves, giving it 'point and purpose in a progress towards and beyond a variety of types and modes of excellence'; and second, 'the good of a certain kind of life'. If one commits to the 'living out of a great … part of' one's life as, for example, a painter, then one *might* say – although *After Virtue* does *not* – that one has painting as *a vocation*. Had MacIntyre used the same term as translators of Weber's two most famous late lectures – on *Science*, which covered Weber's own vocation, and on *Politics*, which is the other vocation that Weber (had he lived

56   *Kelvin Knight*

longer) might have had – then MacIntyre's account of the ethics of social practices might have complicated his critique of Weberian social science. What is clearly consistent with that critique is his insistence that both kinds of good internal to a practice 'can only be identified and recognised by the experience of participating in the practice in question', so that 'those who lack the relevant experience are incompetent thereby as judges of internal goods' (MacIntyre 2007: 187–90).

MacIntyre contrasts internal goods to those goods of money, power and status, which are 'objects of competition' and which 'when achieved … are always some individual's property and possession', so that normally 'the more someone has of them, the less there is for other people'. Such goods are only 'externally and contingently attached to' practices. Here the reach of MacIntyre's conceptual scheme exceeds that of Weber, author of the most famous sociological use of the expression 'external goods' when, in concluding *The Protestant Ethic*, he proposed that the past rationale of their accumulation for the sake of one's salvation had led to modernity's entrapment by their pathological pursuit (Weber 2016: 487), leading him to his subsequent theorisation of bureaucratic rationality. For Weber, as for Aristotle and Aquinas, goods are either internal or external to individual persons.[2] For MacIntyre, goods may *also* be understood as either internal or external to practices in which individuals participate. It was recognition of this similarity of his own, ethical sociology to Aristotle's practical philosophy that occasioned MacIntyre's sudden identification with an Aristotelian tradition in *After Virtue*. That no such sociological distinction between kinds of good was drawn by Weber, and that it would have been denied by Nietzsche, explains MacIntyre's criticism of both as emotivists. Having drawn an ethical and newly sociological distinction between 'internal' and 'external' goods, he uses it to motivate and delineate a distinction between practices and institutions:

Practices must not be confused with institutions. Chess, physics and medicine are practices; chess clubs, laboratories, universities and hospitals are institutions. Institutions are characteristically and necessarily concerned with what I have called external goods. They are involved in acquiring money and other material goods; they are structured in terms of power and status, and they distribute money, power and status as rewards. (MacIntyre 2007: 194)

This conceptual distinction of 'practices' from 'institutions' was no less innovative than *After Virtue*'s redeployment of Aristotelianism. Both

---

[2] Scholarly exegesis relates Weber's *äußeren Güter* back, beyond Baxter and Luther, to Aquinas's *bona exteriora*; Weber 2016: 245. I trace the idea of internal goods forward from Aristotle in Knight 2007.

of the juxtaposed terms were commonplace in post-war sociology and philosophy, especially in works by followers of Weber and of Ludwig Wittgenstein. Usage by one of the latter, John Rawls, was typical in all respects except that of its analytical clarity. Elaborating 'the practice conception of rules' with which he criticised the logic of utilitarian justice, Rawls 'use[d] the word "practice" throughout as a sort of technical term meaning any form of activity specified by a system of rules which defines offices, roles, moves, penalties, defenses, and so on, and which gives the activity its structure' (Rawls 1955: 3). In *A Short History* MacIntyre repeated Rawls' 'distinction between two logically distinct types of rule' after specifying examples of 'a rational, because rule-governed, discipline' with impersonal standards of performance and 'criteria of success or failure' as 'an established and recognised practice' (MacIntyre 1966: 241, 88–9). Only later would he be called a communitarian critic of Rawls. By then Rawls, having previously described 'justice ... as a virtue of social *institutions*, or what I shall call *practices*' (Rawls 1958: 164; emphases added), had reversed that usage in his finished theory of distributive justice as 'the first virtue *of institutions*' (Rawls 1971: 3; emphasis added). A decade later, *After Virtue* began by similarly using the two terms as virtual synonyms. MacIntyre's conceptual, sociological and ethical innovation is introduced only with chapter 14's famous, stipulative definition of 'a practice' and distinction of them from institutions.

The principal point of *After Virtue*'s critique of emotivism is to contest the legitimation of modern corporate and state institutions. Its corresponding implication regarding 'the will to power' is to be found not in the incredible figure of Nietzsche's *Übermensch* but in managers' institutionalised pursuit of money, authority and manipulation of others, thereby demoralising both those others and themselves. On MacIntyre's view, the Weberian account of modernity accurately describes how claims to expertise, authority and power really are effective, if not in controlling reality at least in legitimating managers' domination of their subordinates. On his own Aristotelian analysis, social activity is ordered not only by the coercive imposition of institutional rules but, still more, by the pursuit of commonly conceived goods. His contemporary, sociological Aristotelianism identifies, besides Aristotle's *polis* and economic community of the *oikos*, innumerable other communities of shared reasoning and practice, each of which is unified by pursuit of common goods to which participants devote their efforts, and all of which he contrasts to those modern state and corporate institutions the ethical legitimacy of which he contests.

Since capital accumulation, 'institutionalized acquisitiveness' or '*pleonexia*, a vice in the Aristotelian scheme, is now the driving force of

58   *Kelvin Knight*

modern productive work', 'on a production line, for example', practices have 'been removed to the margins of social and cultural life' (MacIntyre 2007: 227). What remain amidst the moral wilderness are institutions inhabited by emotivist selves. This is why he argues 'that the tradition of the virtues is at variance with central features of the modern economic order'. No less does his Aristotelianism reject 'the modern political order ... for modern politics itself expresses in its institutional forms a systematic rejection of that tradition' (MacIntyre 2007: 254–5). Whilst 'private corporations' justify their activities in ways he calls Weberian, 'government itself becomes a hierarchy of bureaucratic managers' (MacIntyre 2007: 85). The problem is that practices require organisation. Even if practices and practitioners were to be organised in ways that are less bureaucratic, managerial and manipulative than is now normal, it would remain true that no practices can survive for any length of time unsustained by institutions. Indeed, so intimate is the relationship of practices to institutions – and consequently of the goods external to the goods internal to the practices in question – that institutions and practices characteristically form a single causal order in which the ideals and the creativity of the practice are always vulnerable to the acquisitiveness of the institution, in which the cooperative care for common goods of the practice is always vulnerable to the competitiveness of the institution. In this context the essential function of the virtues is clear. Without them, without justice, courage and truthfulness, practices could not resist the corrupting power of institutions (MacIntyre 2007: 194).

Pursuit of goods internal to practices is necessarily susceptible to institutionalised pursuit of money, power and status, and to morally fictitious, manipulative disguises of managerial self-assertion; conversely, insofar as those whom an institution subjects to arbitrary domination do still share in some common practice, managerial power may be resisted by a rival conception of goods and its rival rationality. Since these two kinds of rationality are incommensurable, conflict between them is inevitable. Were it possible for institutional rationality to remove its rival even from modernity's margins, then we really would inhabit the nihilistic world in which the only realistic ethic would be that postulated by Nietzsche.

For MacIntyre, practices are the schools of the virtues. Participation in pursuit of their internal goods requires us 'to learn to recognise what is due to whom; ... to be prepared to take whatever self-endangering risks are demanded along the way; and ... to listen carefully to what we are told about our own inadequacies and to reply with the same carefulness for the facts'. In 'any practice with internal goods and standards of excellence' we are obliged to learn 'the virtues of justice, courage and

Nietzsche *or* Aristotle, Institutions *and* Practices 59

honesty'. To cheat, to be dishonest, renders one's participation in the 'practice pointless except as a device for achieving external goods' (MacIntyre 2007: 191). One might respect Nietzsche's honesty in reporting the untutored condition of his own desires and will whilst nonetheless supposing that, to achieve true excellence, one must be prepared to *learn* from working and acting with others. To acknowledge this is to accept that there really are goods greater than oneself and greater than one's own desire for domination.

Whilst what MacIntyre says of practices owes nothing to Nietzsche, the subsequent, second stage of his core concept of the virtues may owe something, at least by way of critical engagement. He quotes Nietzsche's injunction '"*to become those we are*"', observing that 'the core of a Nietzschean moral philosophy' is the task of wilfully making 'ourselves into autonomous moral subjects' (MacIntyre 2007: 114, quoting Nietzsche's *The Gay Science*; Nietzsche's emphasis). In *Ecce Homo* the egoistic anti-nihilist narrated how he became 'so wise', 'so clever' and 'dynamite' (Nietzsche 1967b: 222, 236, 326). To be perceived as such by others was enough for Nietzsche. For MacIntyre, in contrast, to be an independent practical reasoner one must first narrate one's reasons to others, not simply to oneself, and one must do so to learn from them, not for them to admire one's self-mastery, self-assertion and dynamism. His injunction is to become what we might best be and to discover what that is by acting and reasoning *with* one another. This is why what he writes of self-narration presupposes what he has just written of shared practices and goods, to which he adds that everyone must quest for a way of reconciling and ordering otherwise compartmentalised and conflicting goods within a coherent conception of the good life.

The third and final stage of MacIntyre's historical sociology of the virtues is that of 'tradition'. As yet, this remained his tradition of the virtues, with its idea of a human good the actualisation of which gives purpose to humans' cultivation of excellences of character. When, a couple of years earlier, he had 'introduced' the concept 'of a social tradition', it was to restrain the tragic, 'Heraclitean view of social life in which conflict, rivalry and strife are the fundamental features', happily acknowledging that Weber had 'originally introduced the concept of bureaucratic authority precisely in order to contrast it with that of traditional authority. But his account of tradition was so inadequate that the point of the contrast was partly lost' (MacIntyre 1966: 67). Having clarified that contrast's point, MacIntyre contrasts his own concept of tradition with that of 'conservative political theorists' by stipulating that 'a living tradition ... is an historically extended, socially embodied argument, and an argument precisely in part about the goods which

60   *Kelvin Knight*

constitute that tradition', such that when, as it should ideally be, 'an institution – a university, say, or a farm, or a hospital – is the bearer of a tradition of practice or practices', it would sustain 'continuous argument' about what medicine, farming or 'a university is and ought to be' (MacIntyre 2007: 221–2). In this ideal case, an institution would be legitimated in terms of a traditional authority and ethical, practical rationality rather than that bureaucratic authority derived from successfully distributing money, power and status as rewards for obedience. What this pointed to differs from those aspects of tradition that would preoccupy him for the next decade, when defending the concept against charges of relativism thrown at him by philosophical critics and, in so doing, defining it against the 'Nietzschean perspectivism' that, in *After Virtue* (MacIntyre 2007: 129) and thereafter, he considers a more serious philosophical challenger. In defending his own tradition he defined its rivals as themselves traditions, restraining the historicism of this by exploring the theoretical rationality of Aristotelianism's epistemological realism. What now got at least partly lost, amidst such theoretical conflict with rival traditions, was his own original, ethical point in starting from the cooperative care for common goods of shared reasoning and practice.

3.3   Ethics and Politics

After Virtue may be accorded two kinds of importance. *Historically*, it is important because it marked the irruption of Aristotelianism, understood as a distinctive philosophical and ethical standpoint, into contemporary thought. One aspect of this was the advent of 'virtue ethics' within academic moral philosophy as a theoretical rival to deontology and utilitarianism, a development from which its author has increasingly distanced himself. Whilst it also stimulated interest in Nietzsche in the Anglophone world, its use ensured that Nietzsche would be marginal to academic virtue ethics and Aristotle central. Within the subsequent proliferation of Aristotelianisms, MacIntyre soon added his weight to the identification of the origin of a contemporary Aristotelianism in the tradition of Thomas Aquinas's successful 'synthesis' of Aristotle's arguments with those of Augustine, and especially with Augustine's analysis of the will (MacIntyre 1988: 152–207).

Since traditions, like practices, need to be sustained by institutions, MacIntyre joined both the Roman Catholic Church and America's leading Catholic research university. The former had twice been responsible for reviving Thomism in response to theoretical challenge, most incisively at the time that Nietzsche was announcing the death of God and exploring its implications. A century after Nietzsche's breakdown and the Church's adoption of Thomism as its official philosophy, MacIntyre brought the two into confrontation within his *Three Rival Versions of Moral Enquiry*. Although this book acknowledges the Church's role as the source of Thomism's second great revival, although it includes much about universities as sites 'of institutionalised conflict' between such rivals (MacIntyre 1990: 222) and although MacIntyre has written much of Catholic universities elsewhere (especially in MacIntyre 2009a), he still says little of the Church as an institution and has written nothing of it with reference to *After Virtue*'s moral critique of institutions. As an institution sustaining the practice of worship, he has prescinded from critical discussion of it. In this, he differs from his friend Stanley Hauerwas, from Weber (and still more from Weber's friend Ernst Troeltsch), from Kant and from many fellow Catholics; he does *not* differ from how he normally acted as a loyal (albeit theoretically heterodox) member of Marxist parties, even when they resembled the charismatically led sects of which Weber wrote. Such conformity to the rules of those few institutions whose aims he has shared undoubtedly constrains generalised criticism of institutions and of their devotion to goods external to any practice. He acted under no such constraint when writing *After Virtue*.

That book's radical historicism, defended and refined in MacIntyre's next two books as Thomistic Aristotelianism's exemplary 'rationality of tradition' (MacIntyre 1988: 349–69; 1990: 127–48), has been opposed even by many fellow Thomists. Some have embraced it, taking his calls for others to join him in progressing that rationality so seriously as to help establish an International Society for MacIntyrean Enquiry, many of the most fruitful enquiries of which have concentrated upon interrogating and extending *After Virtue*'s elemental account of practices and institutions. A very different way in which MacIntyre's historicism might be thought to have strengthened Thomistic Aristotelianism is in provoking Terence Irwin to write an *anti*-historicist history of ethics much longer than any by MacIntyre, postulating Aristotle's first, metaphysically biological principles as those with which to correct and transcend the future ethics even of Kant, proposing Aquinas as that standpoint's central protagonist and differing from MacIntyre by making much of Thomism's first revival (especially in Francisco Suárez's work), but nothing expressly of that ongoing, second revival in which it participates alongside all of MacIntyre's work since *After Virtue* (Irwin 1989; 2007–2009).

Whether *After Virtue* still has a second, *philosophical* kind of importance might be thought to be at issue between the first group and critics such as Irwin. From the latter perspective, *After Virtue*'s positing of a core concept of the virtues independent of Aristotelian and Thomistic metaphysics is likely to appear as an overly audacious, if not arrogant, rejection of traditional reasoning from which its author has prudently, if perhaps still insufficiently, since retreated. From the former (now institutionally 'MacIntyrean') standpoint, that core concept will seem more like an invaluable supplement to such metaphysical naturalism (with which the idea of practices is reconciled in MacIntyre 1999a; cf. Pozo 2022), which could not have occurred without MacIntyre's engagement with Marx and Nietzsche, Weber and Wittgenstein, and which now enables the tradition to contest its rivals' claims in ways for which the convert has sometimes been too modest to argue against his co-traditionalists.

After Virtue's elemental, ethical distinction of practices from modern institutions might indeed be understood to identify a sociological – or, as it contends 'Aristotle would have said, political' (MacIntyre 2007: 148) – starting point for a general answer to the challenge of what it terms 'the bureaucratic culture of the age' of 'bureaucratically managed modern societies' (MacIntyre 2007: 114), of 'bureaucratic individualism' (MacIntyre 2007: 35, 71, 225) and of 'institutional arrangements for imposing a bureaucratized unity on a society which lacks genuine moral consensus' (MacIntyre 2007: 254). Nietzsche's answer to this nihilistic challenge was not for humanity in general but only for those few with the courage to assert their own will to power. Likewise, Weber's more modest answer was that those few who have the will to lead ought to exercise it responsibly by regarding 'politics as a vocation' (Weber 2004: 53–94).

Although MacIntyre has never publicly engaged with Weber's famous lecture, we may suppose it to be a cause of much of his antipathy towards Weber and, perhaps, even of his antipathy towards modern states. In it, Weber argues that 'the modern state can be defined sociologically only by the specific *means* that are peculiar to it' – namely, its '*monopoly of legitimate physical violence* within a particular territory' (Weber 2004: 33; translation adapted, Weber's emphases) – and not of any determinate end. The state can therefore be defined sociologically neither as Lenin's instrument for the suppression of one class by another nor as Aristotle's, Aquinas's or Oxonian idealists' pursuer of 'the common good'. Whilst, in this, MacIntyre concurs with Weber's politically realist interpretation of our modern, institutional condition, he nonetheless demands some other, more general and more fundamental, political response.

The principal political point of *After Virtue*'s critique of 'moral fictions' is to deny that either 'rights' or 'utility' (MacIntyre 2007: 64, 68–71; or, as the US Constitution has it, 'the general welfare') can really endow modern states with any moral justification of their power. Its condemnation of managerial effectiveness as another moral fiction is also politically important, not least in denying even Weber's realist attempt to legitimate his ideal-typical modern state. This fits with *After Virtue*'s conclusion about the 'exhaustion' of 'every … political tradition within our culture'. What it does not do is offer any prospect of an Aristotelian politics of the common good. Although MacIntyre denies 'that the moral tradition which I am defending lacks any contemporary politics of relevance', his notorious equation of the moral barbarism of endless managerial domination with those 'Dark Ages' that Homeric poems and Icelandic sagas recalled does not overplay the virtue of hope (MacIntyre 2007: 262–3). As he has recently said, '[t]here's nothing to be done about the state … It's there', offering both 'resources and … obstacles but it isn't itself an instrument of the common good' (MacIntyre 2021, post-presentation answer).

MacIntyre's greatest attempt to do for politics what *After Virtue* had done for ethics was undertaken as a research project on 'Common Goods and Political Reasoning' at the secular London Metropolitan University's Centre for Contemporary Aristotelian Studies in Ethics and Politics (CASEP). Here he aimed at writing 'a book, provisionally entitled "The Politics of the Common Good In and Against the Politics of the Modern State"'. The project's original aim was to discover 'whether and in what ways' a Thomistically Aristotelian conception of the common good 'might find application in the politics of modern societies'. Its anticipated conclusions were 'that the institutional prerequisites for effective political reasoning aimed at achieving the common good of political societies are not just different from, but incompatible with [,] the institutional structures of the modern state and of the advanced economies with which the activities of the modern state are increasingly integrated' (MacIntyre 2009b: 1–2). Although he wrote that 'for me … questions about truth and power need to be put in terms of the relations between institutions and practices' (MacIntyre 2010a: 2), few of the papers he presented as a part of the project (or of associated projects; MacIntyre 2011a; 2020) made much of those two concepts.[3] Whilst debate failed to falsify his anticipated conclusions, it also failed to get far in identifying institutional prerequisites for contemporary political community. In retrospect, this was due to a failure to rework the first stage of *After Virtue*'s 'core concept' in which other members of CASEP shared.

Whilst MacIntyre's completed project has no parallel in the work of Nietzsche, whose projected, apolitical *Will to Power* had, like Weber's

---

[3] That which made most – MacIntyre 2012 – anticipated much of what would be published on their relation in *Ethics in the Conflicts of Modernity* (MacIntyre 2016).

64   *Kelvin Knight*

Economy and Society, to be compiled by others, it *does* have a parallel in Kant's vocational narrative. As *After Virtue* noted, whereas 'Nietzsche and Aristotle agree' 'that we need to attend to virtues in the first place in order to understand the function and authority of rules', 'on the modern view the justification of the virtues depends upon some prior justification of rules and principles' (MacIntyre 2007: 119). Therefore, Kant first separated moral autonomy from natural causality and, in *The Groundwork of the Metaphysics of Morals*, justified moral rules as categorical imperatives before allowing himself to speculate about virtue's reward in his second *Critique*. Only then, before his time ran out, did he write the long-anticipated *Metaphysics of Morals*, dividing his rationalist metaphysics between his political 'Doctrine of Right' and, only thereafter and inferentially, a 'Doctrine of Virtue'. That what Kant had long projected as the culmination of his Critical Philosophy did not achieve the coherence of politics with ethics that he desired does not detract from the seriousness that infused his philosophical practice, revealing the final end of his critique of practical reasoning: a legitimation of states' sovereignty and of the supposedly impersonal rationality of the rule of their law as the condition of individuals' 'external freedom' and rights against one another. MacIntyre's political project demonstrates a similarly resolute seriousness and sustained exemplification of the moral and intellectual virtues. The pity is that his completed project issued in no book dedicated to political reasoning. Fortunately, what it did contribute to was *Ethics in the Conflicts of Modernity*.

This sequel to *After Virtue* differs from the original in obvious ways. It differs in its lack of historical, narrative structure, the philosophical substance of its first four chapters being as purely analytic as are the works of those renamed 'expressivists', whose arguments it contests. It differs also in eschewing all such dramatic devices as the earlier book's confrontation of Aristotle with Nietzsche. Having originally criticised irrational manipulation, MacIntyre's subsequent intention to keep his means of literary persuasion within the bounds of reason alone is nowhere more obvious than in the careful argument of *Ethics*. He therefore never expected this last book to have the immediate impact secured by *After Virtue*, often saying that he expects it to be a slow burner. In renouncing rhetorical manipulation he has abandoned confrontation with Nietzsche in Nietzsche's dramatic terms, mindful that resort to such means would signify a greater desire for victory than for truth.

In many respects *Ethics* refines, updates and illustrates the reasoning of *After Virtue*, including much of that about narrative and conflict. If *After Virtue* shared Nietzsche's concern with 'the Homeric insight that tragic conflict is the essential human condition' (MacIntyre 2007: 157) in a way

Nietzsche *or* Aristotle, Institutions *and* Practices 65

that MacIntyre has since renounced, *Ethics* retains 'a Sophoclean insight' in MacIntyre's continuing argument 'that it is through conflict and sometimes only through conflict that we learn what our ends and purposes are' (MacIntyre 2007: 164). The earlier book criticised Aristotle for failing to learn from either insight, blaming this failure on the metaphysical theology that he took from Plato and placing Sophocles in 'confrontation' both with Aristotle (MacIntyre 2007: 157) and with Aquinas (over whom the otherwise unlikely Alan of Lille is therefore favoured; MacIntyre 2007: 171, 179), siding against both with the tragedian. It sided with Sophocles also against Weber, for the rather different reason that, whereas the Greek believed in the objectivity of both moral order and moral dilemmas arising in the dramas of human life, 'the Weberian individualist life of itself has ... no form, save that which we choose to project on to it in our aesthetic imaginings' (MacIntyre 2007: 144). The later book gives a far more refined account, especially in its fourth, concluding chapter's four narratives of lives educated by conflictual conditions and conflicting desires to quest both for a rational ordering of those desires and for a common good enactable within and against the politics of modern states. These narratives do not enliven any political philosophy. Rather, they illustrate MacIntyre's 'NeoAristotelian' case against the expressivism for which he continues to regard Nietzsche as having provided the, 'even now' in 2016 (MacIntyre 2016: 59), inadequately acknowledged inspiration, an inspiration he takes Nietzsche to have instead intended as an imperative for wilful 'philosophers ... to become commanders and law-givers', mindful that 'their "knowing" is *creating*, their creating is a law-giving, their will to truth is – *will to power*' (MacIntyre 2016: 43, quoting Nietzsche's *Beyond Good and Evil*, Nietzsche's emphases).

What the later book omits is the crucial place that the earlier accorded to practices, to their internal goods and to those external goods that are the currency of institutions and of their structurally manipulative management. The terms remain but the guiding argument does not. *Ethics* still refers to 'ends' and 'goods internal to practices' (MacIntyre 2016: 49, 52; cf. 38), still juxtaposes practices to 'institutions' (MacIntyre 2016: 110, 166–7), still protests at standards being 'imposed by external managerial control' and still questions 'the legitimacy of established hierarchies of power' distributing 'financial and other rewards' (MacIntyre 2016: 171, 211). What it no longer does is articulate any sociological or political opposition of practices' internal goods to either institutions or external goods. MacIntyre still encourages others to pursue systematic enquiry into such socially systemic conflict, but, for better or worse, he has now entrusted such enquiry entirely to us, *After Virtue*'s readers.

66   *Kelvin Knight*

Does it follow from the continuing lack of a distinctively NeoAristotelian political philosophy that the moral tradition that MacIntyre defends lacks any contemporary politics of relevance? Not at all, he maintains (MacIntyre 2016: 176–83), if we think of politics in terms of those 'local forms of community within which ... moral life can be sustained' for which *After Virtue* first called (MacIntyre 2007: 263). *Perhaps* not, either, if we think of his politics as a 'revolutionary Aristotelianism' addressing society's structural conflict between practices and institutions (MacIntyre 1998b; 2011b; 2015; Knight 2007: 102–225; 2008; 2011b; 2013; Blackledge 2009; Callinicos 2011; Gregson 2019; Nicholas 2021). He has maintained for over forty years that the managerial rationality of institutions conflicts with the rationality of those practices that would always have money, status and power subserve their more particular, common goods, himself sharing the belief of many practitioners that such common goods participate in a still more social and potentially political, architectonic common good, whilst aware that conflicts with arbitrary managerial power continue amongst those 'mundane transactions of everyday life' that 'define the working tasks of so many of our contemporaries' (MacIntyre 2007: 115, 25) and, further, that such conflicts are sometimes motivated by such belief and, still now, often by a desire to defend goods internal to shared practices. This is an ethics that may inform the actions of any of us as 'plain persons' (MacIntyre 1998c), and especially of anyone who thinks of their work both as a personal vocation and as the performance of a social role. Perhaps, however, truthfulness demands admission that exercising justice and courage in defence of practices against the corrupting power of institutions falls far short of any Thomistically Aristotelian politics of *the* common good. Perhaps no such politics is now possible, at least beyond local confines. *If so*, NeoAristotelians should abandon the quest for a way of imitating Aristotle's *politics* in terms of a modern sociology, even whilst hoping that practices will continue to imbue social life with common goods. It is a NeoAristotelian – or, more specifically, MacIntyrean (cf. MacIntyre 2020) – *ethics* of goods and virtues that demands justice, courage and truthfulness in defending practices from a managerial will to power that is now so widely and deeply institutionalised.

Part II

After Virtue and Political Theory

4 *After Virtue*'s Critique of Liberalism

David Rondel

> My ... critique of liberalism derives from a judgment that the best type of human life ... is lived by those engaged in constructing and sustaining forms of community directed towards the shared achievement of those common goods without which the ultimate human good cannot be achieved. Liberal political societies are characteristically committed to denying any place for a determinate conception of the human good in their public discourse ... On the dominant liberal view, government is to be neutral as between rival conceptions of the human good, yet in fact what liberalism promotes is a kind of institutional order that is inimical to the construction and sustaining of the types of communal relationship required for the best kind of human life.
>
> Alasdair MacIntyre, *After Virtue*

After Virtue is most centrally a book about the loss of our moral culture, about how, in its author's words, 'morality is not what it once was' (MacIntyre 1981: 22). Morality is in a bad way because what we have access to now are only 'fragments of a conceptual scheme, parts which now lack those contexts from which their significance derived'. We have no trouble deploying moral concepts or using moral language. Yet morality today is in a state of 'grave disorder' because these practices have been severed from the sources that originally gave them meaning. What we possess nowadays are only shards of past moral traditions, fragments of past frameworks. But we lack any comprehensive, let alone coherent, moral picture (MacIntyre 1981: 2, 256). And the result is that our whole moral sense – our capacity to reflect on the nature of the good, to wisely resolve moral conflict, to evaluate the 'rival and heterogeneous moral schemes which compete for our allegiance' – has been badly diminished (MacIntyre 1981: xviii).

I am grateful to Galen Gorelangton, my former student, whose superb 2019 MA thesis on MacIntyre's critique of liberalism – 'MacIntyre in the Wasteland' – I had the great pleasure to supervise at the University of Nevada, Reno. Thanks are also due to the students who participated in a 2019 graduate seminar I taught on 'Liberalism and Its Critics' in which MacIntyre's work figured prominently. I'm also grateful for various discussions with James Bondarchuck, Simone Gubler, Carlos Mariscal and Chris Williams.

70   *David Rondel*

After Virtue tells the story of a fall from grace, a story of deterioration and impoverishment. Stephen Holmes colourfully (albeit with a tinge of sarcasm) summarises the narrative and tone of MacIntyre's book:

> Past societies were orderly and healthy, while ours is dishevelled and sick ... Things used to be good; now they are bad. Once whole, the vase of culture now lies shattered ... People who were once firmly implanted in harmonious communities are now rootless. Vital social relations have been desiccated by arid individualism. A warm, solidary, and emotionally satisfying communal order has yielded to a chilly, egoistical, and morally hollow one. The social faculties of prelapsarian souls have been grievously damaged by Western rationalism. Generosity, friendship, and joy have nearly vanished. Niggardliness and misery are all-pervasive. Idyllic normative consensus has been supplanted by sickeningly endless disagreement. Thick preindustrial forms of social identity have been displaced by thinner and more universal ones. As a result, mankind is clueless about how to live, what to do. (Holmes 1993: 89–90)

How did things get so bad? And what is fundamentally to blame for this steep moral-cultural decline? The main culprit, MacIntyre tells us, is something called 'modernity' or 'individualism' or 'liberalism' (or sometimes co-extensive groupings of these like 'liberal individualism' or 'modern liberal individualism'). Even though the word 'liberalism' itself appears somewhat infrequently in *After Virtue*, the rise of a certain liberal individualist picture is at the very root of what MacIntyre is lamenting in that book. The main business of this chapter is to try to piece that argument together.

Section 4.1 provides a broad-stroked overview of MacIntyre's critique of liberal individualism. Special attention is given to liberalism's obsession with procedure over moral substance, its notorious claim to neutrality, and to the conception of the human self on which, according to MacIntyre's diagnosis, the intelligibility of the liberal tradition depends. I also try to show how these different elements of the liberal worldview hang together in a mutually reinforcing whole. In Section 4.2, I consider the ideal of liberal neutrality in more detail. The repudiation of neutrality is the piece of MacIntyre's critique of liberalism that has probably received the most scholarly attention, from defenders and critics alike. That is not accidental in my view. For if I am right, neutrality is the decisive ground on which MacIntyre's case against liberalism ultimately succeeds or fails. If liberalism *can* justifiably claim some sort of neutrality, then this gives liberal government a special prerogative to legitimate authority. It suggests that, given the intractable fact of pluralism in modern societies, liberal government has a unique right to rule. But if liberalism's claim to neutrality is untenable – if, its own protestations to the contrary notwithstanding, liberalism really is its own unique

After Virtue's Critique of Liberalism 71

comprehensive tradition – then, in the words of John Rawls, 'liberalism becomes but another sectarian doctrine' in a sea of sectarian doctrines (Rawls 1999: 409). Without neutrality, in short, liberalism is on a par with all the other traditions and doctrines that compete for our allegiance. And liberal government as a result cannot claim any special right to rule. Finally, in Section 4.3, I offer some scattered thoughts about how MacIntyre's critique of liberalism connects with other anti-liberal arguments (both older and more contemporary; both from the left and the right), and I assess how well the arguments in *After Virtue* hold up, as it were, forty years after the publication of MacIntyre's remarkable book.

4.1 MacIntyre's Critique of Liberalism Summarised

Four interrelated theses together represent the core of MacIntyre's critique of liberalism in *After Virtue* and subsequent writings.

(1) Liberalism relies on a deflationary, preference-based conception of the human self. This diagnosis of the liberal self comes out early in *After Virtue*, as part of MacIntyre's observation that 'people now think, talk and act *as if* emotivism were true, no matter what their avowed theoretical stand-point may be' (MacIntyre 1981: 22, emphasis in original). The emotivist or modern self is thought to have the ability and the right to do and choose as it pleases. Nothing is off-limits. Opportunities for self-creation are boundless. Moral judgement is 'criterionless'. There is nothing external to the emotivist self that can be appealed to for moral guidance, unless of course the emotivist self *itself* happens to prefer some such appeal (Bernstein 1984). As MacIntyre writes:

The specifically modern self, the self that I have called emotivist, finds no limits set to that on which it may pass judgment for such limits could only derive from rational criteria for evaluation and, as we have seen, the emotivist self lacks any such criteria. Everything may be criticized from whatever standpoint the self has adopted, including the self's choice of standpoint to adopt. (MacIntyre 1981: 31)

In a world where everyone behaves as if emotivism were true, moral agency becomes thoroughly democratised. 'Anyone and everyone can ... be a moral agent since it is in the self and not in social roles or practices that moral agency has to be located' (MacIntyre 1981: 32). To be a moral agent on this kind of view, MacIntyre has it, is 'precisely to be able to stand back from any and every situation in which one is involved, from any and every characteristic that one may possess, and to pass judgment on it from a purely universal and abstract point of view that is totally detached from all social particularity'. This specifically modern self has the ability and the right 'to evade any necessary identification

72   *David Rondel*

with any particular contingent state of affairs'. Such a self 'can … be anything, can assume any role or take any point of view, because it *is* in and for itself nothing' (MacIntyre 1981: 31–2, emphasis in original).

This modern conception of self is at the very centre of the liberal individualist picture that *After Virtue* sets itself against. The self that MacIntyre opposes is depicted as little more than the owner of contingent desires and preferences, as having 'no history', as lacking all the thick 'particularity' that real human beings in the real world cannot function without (MacIntyre 1981: 221). The ability to make choices is the liberal self's defining feature, and, as such, this self owes fidelity to no relationship or association that it did not voluntarily select for itself. From the standpoint of the liberal self, then,

> I am what I myself choose to be. I can always, if I wish to, put in question what are taken to be the merely contingent social features of my existence. I may biologically be my father's son; but I cannot be held responsible for what he did unless I choose implicitly or explicitly to assume such responsibility. I may legally be a citizen of a certain country; but I cannot be held responsible for what my country does or has done unless I choose implicitly or explicitly to assume such responsibility. Such individualism is expressed by those modern Americans who deny responsibility for the effects of slavery upon black Americans, saying 'I never owned any slaves'. (MacIntyre 1981: 220)

In *Why Liberalism Failed*, a book whose indebtedness to MacIntyre's thought is obvious, Patrick Deneen claims that liberalism's master idea involves the imperative to ground politics in the idea of 'voluntarism' – the idea that only those features of a person's situation that have been voluntarily opted for are morally binding and legitimate. Deneen writes, 'Liberalism begins a project by which the legitimacy of all human relationships – beginning with, but not limited to, political bonds – becomes increasingly dependent on whether those relationships have been chosen, and chosen on the basis of their service to rational self-interest' (Deneen 2018a: 31–2). If we are all emotivists now – if we all behave *as if* emotivism were true – what legitimates our various relationships and associations is merely the fact that they were voluntarily opted into. And the inverted version of the same argument is that any unchosen relationship or association is, on that same basis, illegitimate.[1]

---

[1] Similarly, the animating principle in liberal or 'luck' egalitarianism is that, as I once described it, 'justice requires compensating people for the inequalities that derive from the arbitrariness of the natural lottery, whereas inequalities that can be traced back to the choices that people have made (about how best to live their lives, or about what sorts of endeavors to pursue or avoid) need not be corrected by justice. The only permissible inequalities, from the point of view of justice, are those that originate from the choices that individuals have voluntarily made' (Rondel 2007: 117).

After Virtue's Critique of Liberalism 73

In *After Virtue* and elsewhere MacIntyre famously argues against the attractiveness and coherence of this liberal conception of the self. For MacIntyre, healthy human selfhood requires that one be in possession of a story – a narrative – about who one is, where one comes from, what one cares about. Human beings are invariably born and grow up somewhere. They are formed by the people, language, culture and traditions around them, and these facts constitute the 'given' or 'moral starting point' against which any attempt at self-creation must take place. As MacIntyre explains, in a beautiful passage from *After Virtue*:

> I am someone's son or daughter, someone else's cousin or uncle. I am a citizen of this or that city, a member of this or that guild or profession. I belong to this clan, that tribe, this nation. Hence what is good for me has to be good for one who inhabits these roles. As such, I inherit from the past of my family, my city, my tribe, my nation, a variety of debts, inheritances, rightful expectations and obligations. These constitute the given of my life, my moral starting point. This is in part what gives my life its own moral particularity. (MacIntyre 1981: 220)[2]

What healthy human selfhood requires, then, liberalism deems out of bounds. Instead of understanding human beings as essentially social creatures who derive direction and meaning from their membership in enduring communities, from the social roles they inhabit, liberalism insists that the human self is, at bottom, an 'unencumbered' chooser of ends, a mere satisfier of preferences.[3] From the point of view of modern liberal individualism, 'a community is simply an arena in which individuals each pursue their own self-chosen conception of the good life, and political institutions exist to provide that degree of order which makes such self-determined activity possible' (MacIntyre 1981: 195). Incorrect and unattractive though it may be, MacIntyre is confident that this modern, liberal conception of the self has become culturally and politically the dominant one.

(2) The ascendency of a liberal conception of self goes hand in hand with a commitment to neutrality. If human beings are understood as essentially the bearers of preferences and desires, and if there is no objective or non-arbitrary way to parse or rank these various preferences and desires, it follows, as MacIntyre puts it, that '[e]very individual is to

---

[2] A similar view about the nature of the self can be found in Taylor 1989: 3–38.

[3] The complaint that the liberal self is erroneously celebrated as 'unencumbered' is at the centre of the 'communitarian' critique of liberalism. See most notably Sandel 1982. MacIntyre is frequently lumped in among the so-called communitarian critics of liberalism, although he has consistently rejected that characterisation. As he makes plain in *After Virtue*'s prologue: 'a communitarian … [is] … something that I have never been' (MacIntyre 1981: xiv). See Murphy 2003b for an illuminating discussion of MacIntyre's rejection of the communitarian label.

74   *David Rondel*

be equally free to propose and live by whatever conception of the good he or she may adhere to, unless that conception ... involves reshaping the life of the rest of the community in accordance with it' (MacIntyre 1988: 336). Liberals (*qua* liberals) are expected to refrain from endorsing or disparaging the content of anyone's desires and preferences. The existence of desires and preferences is supposed to be taken as brutely given from a moral or evaluative point of view. From the point of view of modern liberal individualism, MacIntyre explains, 'there are no facts about what is valuable. "Fact" becomes value-free, "is" becomes a stranger to "ought" and explanation, as well as evaluation, changes its character as a result of this divorce between "is" and "ought"' (MacIntyre 1981: 84).

It cannot be the task of government on this kind of view to promote one specific conception of the good life at the expense of others. It is up to individual men and women, one by one, to determine for themselves the kinds of lives that are most worth living. 'Government and law are, or ought to be, neutral between rival conceptions of the good life for man, and hence, although it is the task of government to promote law-abidingness, it is on the liberal view no part of the legitimate function of government to inculcate any one moral outlook' (MacIntyre 1981: 195).

This is ultimately what makes markets so beloved on the liberal way of thinking. Markets are thought to be *neutrality preserving* insofar as they simply report *that* certain preferences exist, while simultaneously abstaining from judgement about the goodness or badness of their content. For MacIntyre, then, liberalism envisions a social world in which preference satisfaction is the *summum bonum*, a world in which customer service is more important than virtue. And the upshot, as can be observed all around us, is a politics that shrinks away from discussion of the human good, a politics that relies on anonymous polling and focus group-tested talking points rather than moral argument. Another consequence is that political life begins to look increasingly like a kind of etiquette or manners – individualistic to the core, everything boiling down to the actions and decisions of discrete individual actors. This is a politics whose parameters are defined by what Marx dubbed 'bourgeois morality'.

Provided no one else is being directly harmed by an individual's desires and preferences – provided no formal rights are being violated – liberalism abstains from judgements about the merits or demerits of different conceptions of the good life. It stays quiet, as it were, about questions concerning what is conducive to human flourishing and what is not so conducive. As Loren Lomasky writes, in approval of this liberal picture:

Liberalism ... holds out no comprehensive catalog of the virtues, refrains from endorsing any specific conception of the good life, supplies no depiction of the

After Virtue's Critique of Liberalism 75

delights of intimate association or communal solidarity. Its range of prescriptions can be summarized as: Respect the rights of others. Beyond that, liberalism does not tell people what to do. (Lomasky 2002: 50)

The injunction to 'not tell people what to do' will sometimes be celebrated by its defenders as evidence of liberalism's commitment to tolerance and healthy open-mindedness. Critics will read it as an expression of liberalism's relativism or nihilism, proof positive of Robert Frost's quip that 'a liberal is a man too broadminded to take his own side in a quarrel'. For his part, MacIntyre thinks that liberalism *really does* tell people what to do. However, since liberalism never advertises (or even concedes) its own prescriptivity and coerciveness, this tends to happen in more covert ways. On MacIntyre's analysis, as we will see, liberalism is a comprehensive tradition that has trouble speaking its own name. Despite its avowed commitment to neutrality, liberalism 'does indeed have its own broad conception of the good', MacIntyre writes, 'which it is engaged in imposing politically, legally, socially and culturally wherever it has the power to do so, but also in so doing its toleration of rival conceptions of the good in the public arena is severely limited' (MacIntyre 1988: 336). Liberalism's conception of the good turns out to be nothing other than liberalism itself – 'the continued sustenance of the liberal social and political order' (MacIntyre 1988: 345). The implication is that, in the best of all possible worlds, a liberal social and political order would remain permanently, enduringly in place.

(3) A major consequence of its avowed commitment to neutrality is that liberalism places much more emphasis on rules and procedures than it does on questions of moral substance. Liberals are enamoured of the Rawlsian slogan according to which the 'right is prior to the good'. They generally believe that procedures for determining how debate should proceed enjoy a certain theoretical priority over debate about the substantive ends to be pursued. As MacIntyre claims, for the liberal, 'rules become the primary concept of the moral life', so that to accept some moral stance is at least to some strong degree to accept the rules or procedures that permit it, the rules or procedures from which the stance is a consequence (MacIntyre 1981: 119). Liberalism shuns first-order discussion about the good in favour of second-order procedural negotiation about the right. As MacIntyre writes, in a stunning sentence from *Whose Justice? Which Rationality?*, 'The lawyers, not the philosophers, are the clergy of liberalism' (MacIntyre 1988: 344).

In his 1950 volume *The Liberal Imagination*, Lionel Trilling famously complained about liberal literature's lack of romance. 'The sense of largeness, of cogency, of the transcendence which largeness and cogency

76   *David Rondel*

can give, the sense of being reached in our secret and primitive minds –
this we virtually never get from the writers of the liberal democratic
tradition at the present time' (Trilling 1978: 301). Trilling's complaint
makes a lot of sense in the light of liberalism's lawyerly prioritisation of
rules and its flight from moral substance. After all, a well-functioning
bureaucracy does not reach us in our 'secret and primitive minds'. There
is no poetry in proceduralism. *Robert's Rules of Order* rarely makes the
human heart leap up.

(4)   Liberal individualism gives rise to a series of new 'characters'.
Most central here are the aesthete, the therapist and the bureaucratic
manager. The bureaucratic manager in particular is the 'central character
of the modern social drama', and their prominence is intimately associated with the rise of the liberal individualist picture (MacIntyre
1981: 76–7).

The bureaucratic manager is the chief representative of a new ruling
elite that flourishes under liberalism. If we all behave as if emotivism were
true – if there are only people's various *yays* and *boos* but no objective
moral truths, no facts about what a human life well lived consists in – this
carves out space for a new kind of 'morally neutral' expertise that bureaucratic managers are thought to be in possession of. Managers claim
justified authority in virtue of their expertise in 'systematic effectiveness',
and there are two central elements to this claim (MacIntyre 1981: 74).
'One concerns the existence of a domain of morally neutral fact about
which the manager is to be expert. The other concerns the law-like
generalizations about their applications to particular cases derived from
the study of this domain' (MacIntyre 1981: 77). In this sense, the
manager's expertise is alleged to 'mirror' claims made by the natural
sciences. Like scientific knowledge, the manager's expertise is supposed
to be morally neutral, disinterested, impersonal, merely descriptive. So,
to take one kind of example, economic 'experts' will debate about
whether some policy or initiative will be 'good for the economy'. And
such experts will claim to know what will happen if taxes are raised to
such and such a degree, or if interest rates are lowered by such and such a
percentage, and so on. But there is no public debate about what an
economy is ultimately for – about the moral ends in the service of which
it should be regulated, about the human habits, institutions and virtues it
should seek to cultivate and strengthen. On the contrary, the bureaucratic manager arises as a prominent figure at the very moment that these
deeper questions of value begin to appear quaint or unanswerable. Once
everyone becomes convinced that there are no final, non-question-beg-
ging answers to these sorts of questions (as the emotivist centrally
insists), then turning things over to bureaucratic managers who have

After Virtue's Critique of Liberalism 77

expertise in morally neutral 'efficiency' and 'effectiveness' seems like the logical next step. Bluntly put, if there are no objective moral truths around which to structure our lives and institutions, why not let the normatively neutral technocrats be in charge? Why not trust the only real 'experts' left? Much more insidiously, however, it is very much in the interest of the elite bureaucratic managerial class that ordinary people do not spend too much time pondering fundamental questions about the human good. As we have just seen, the manager's claim to authority rests precisely on the assumption that there are no answers to these sorts of fundamental questions.[4]

It is easy to see how the four large theses outlined above hang together in a mutually reinforcing web. If we human beings are really just bundles of desires and preferences, and if it is not possible to rank or order these various desires and preferences in any non-controversially final way, it follows that the state cannot advocate for the superiority of some ways of life over others. The state should be neutral among competing conceptions of the good life. As a direct result of its stated commitment to neutrality, liberalism shuns first-order debate about the nature of the good and retreats to a bland bureaucratic proceduralism. So, for instance, instead of reflecting on whether legalised prostitution or recreational drugs, say, are detrimental to the flourishing of its citizens, a liberal government will obsess about the rules and procedures by which restriction and permission can or may function. Such rules and procedures constitute the vocabulary in which the liberal bureaucratic manager is fluent. And such fluency is thought to justify the manager's influence and power, in turn.

So much for the package of views that, more or less, constitute MacIntyre's critique of liberal individualism in *After Virtue*. As always, there is much more to be said and many details to consider. Some of that will occur in Section 4.3. Before that, in Section 4.2, I want to consider the debate about the ideal of liberal neutrality in more detail. I suggested earlier that liberalism's claim to justified authority rests on a more abstract claim that a liberal regime is (uniquely among the available alternatives) able to achieve neutrality among competing conceptions of the good life. If that more abstract claim is untenable, as MacIntyre argues, the consequences for liberalism would be momentous to say the least.

---

[4] As MacIntyre writes, in a later essay, '[L]iberalism is the politics of a set of elites, whose members through their control of party machines and the media, predetermine for the most part the range of political choices open to the vast mass of ordinary voters. Of those voters, apart from the making of electoral choices, passivity is required. Politics and its cultural ambiance have become areas of professional life, and among the most important of the relevant professionals are the professional manipulators of mass opinion' (MacIntyre 1995b: 153).

78   *David Rondel*

4.2   Liberal Neutrality and Its Discontents

The ideal of a neutral state looms large in liberal theory. Such an ideal is and can be defended in various ways, but most often the argument that a state has an obligation to be neutral is understood to be the direct consequence of what Rawls (1993) has famously dubbed 'the fact of pluralism' – the fact that modern, democratic societies have within them many rival comprehensive conceptions of the good life. As Charles Larmore summarises this common line of argument:

> In modern times we have come to recognize a multiplicity of ways in which a fulfilled life can be lived, without any perceptible hierarchy among them. And we have also been forced to acknowledge that even where we do believe that we have discerned the superiority of some ways of life to others, reasonable people may not share our view. Pluralism and reasonable disagreement have become for modern thought ineliminable features of the idea of the good life. Political liberalism has been the doctrine that consequently the state should be neutral. (Larmore 1987: 43)

But how could a state possibly be neutral? Every law it upholds or fails to uphold, every policy it enacts or refrains from enacting, every incentive or disincentive it confers or withholds represents an affirmative stance of some kind. Every action or omission on the part of the state furthers some kind of agenda. Try though it might, there is simply no way for a state to avoid having a point of view. As Cheryl Misak writes:

> A state has no choice but to make choices and it thus promotes a particular culture in countless ways. The law often takes a controversial position on what is good. In our regime it recognises monogamous marriages and punishes bigamous ones ... prohibits digging up corpses, defecating in public, and so on. Statutory holiday schedules, national anthems, oaths, and the like also reflect certain values. In my society these are Christian values, despite the fact that not all citizens are Christian. My state advertises on television and on the subway against the drug culture; encourages 'high' culture by subsidising the arts, but not tag-team wrestling; offers tax credits for contributions to 'recognized charities', but doesn't recognize white supremacist groups who want to set up a charitable foundation for 'victims' of affirmative action; regulates against pornography and against using the F-word, as my seven-year-old says, during prime time television, and so on. Neutrality, that is, is a myth. (Misak 2000: 113)

There is no way for a state to avoid taking sides, no way to avoid advancing some conception of the good. The question cannot be about *whether* to permit the state to have an effect on individuals and culture. Rather, since the individuality- and culture-shaping power of the state is inescapable, the question becomes how such shaping should be undertaken. In light of what? To what ends and to what extent? With what

After Virtue's Critique of Liberalism

kinds of ideals in mind? MacIntyre might have also emphasised that doing nothing is a form of social engineering too. A politics of *laissez-faire* will shape people and culture no less assuredly than any other way of making decisions. It can no more claim 'neutrality' than any other manner of proceeding. 'Even the purest libertarianism is just one more brand of technocracy' (Rondel 2018: 99–100).

Does it follow then that the ideal of an ethically neutral state is a chimera? Liberals have usually responded to these kinds of arguments by distinguishing between various sorts and degrees of neutrality. So, for instance, Larmore clarifies that, on his preferred conception, 'The state should not seek to promote any particular conception of the good life because of its presumed *intrinsic* superiority – that is, because it is supposedly a *truer* conception' (emphasis in original). (A liberal state may naturally restrict certain ideals for *extrinsic* reasons because, for example, they threaten the lives of others. See Larmore 1987: 43.) A natural rejoinder to Larmore's clarification is to insist that the intrinsic/extrinsic distinction he draws rarely makes a difference in the real world. No one ever says: 'Well, at first I was angry that the state was non-neutrally taking sides against my values and way of life. But now I see that my anger was misplaced. Now I understand that the state never affirmed the *intrinsic* inferiority of my values. It merely set itself against my values for *extrinsic* reasons.'

Be that as it may, Larmore's clarification represents an example of a frequently invoked distinction within the literature on liberal neutrality. Instead of endorsing *neutrality of effect* or *neutrality of outcome*, liberal theorists now more commonly claim that the kind of neutrality that matters is a *neutrality of justification*, the kind of view, as Richard Arneson glosses it, 'which requires that any policies pursued by the state should be justified independently of any appeal to the supposed superiority of any way of lie or conception of the good over others' (Arneson 2003: 193). *Neutrality of justification* is a thesis about the kinds of reasons a liberal society can properly appeal to in the justification of political decisions.

It is easy to see how the turn from *neutrality of outcome* towards *neutrality of justification* demonstrates, yet again, liberalism's proclivity for rules and procedure over moral substance. Instead of promoting neutrality as a first-order moral position in its own right, increasingly neutrality becomes a second-order package of considerations about the rules that should govern political justification and discourse. But there is another point here that brings into focus one of the central elements of MacIntyre's critique of liberalism in *After Virtue* and elsewhere. On MacIntyre's view, the introduction and proliferation of just the sorts of

80   *David Rondel*

distinctions of which the turn to *neutrality of justification* is a prime example are precisely what make liberalism an authentic tradition in its own right. This expansion of the discursive terrain is the quintessentially liberal move. The interminability of the dispute about what justice requires in a world where there are many different conceptions of the good *is itself* the conception of the good that liberalism seeks to promote. This is one of MacIntyre's most important insights. In *Whose Justice? Which Rationality?* he puts it this way:

> [L]iberalism, which began as an appeal to alleged principles of shared rationality against what was felt to be the tyranny of tradition, has itself been transformed into a tradition whose continuities are partly defined by the interminability of the debate over such principles. An interminability which was from the standpoint of an earlier liberalism a grave defect to be remedied as soon as possible has become ... a kind of virtue.

And again, several pages later:

> [L]iberalism requires for its social embodiment continuous philosophical and quasi-philosophical debate about the principles of justice, debate which ... is perpetually inconclusive but nonetheless socially effective in suggesting that if the relevant set of principles has not yet been discovered, nonetheless their discovery remains a central goal of the social order ... What has become clear ... is that gradually less and less importance has been attached to arriving at substantive conclusions and more and more to continuing the debate for its own sake. For the nature of the debate itself and not its outcome provides underpinnings ... of the rules and procedures of the formal legal system. (MacIntyre 1988: 335, 343–4)

Because liberalism's conception of the good requires open-ended yet inconclusive deliberation about how to justly mitigate disagreement about the good, we end up getting endless debate, the perpetual refinement of principles, the proliferation of ever-more subtle distinctions, ever-more granular formulations of 'public reason', and so on.[5] Again, the point of these exercises is not the discovery of the morally correct answers. The goal is to keep the conversation going for its own sake.

---

[5] On the liberal proclivity to proliferate ever more distinctions and refinements, consider Gerald Gaus's rundown of some of the different ways that the ideal of liberal neutrality has been understood: '(1) *Justificatory neutrality* (that is, neutrality as a constraint on the kinds of reasons and arguments that may be advanced to justify coercive state action). (2) *Consequential neutrality*: the effects of state action must somehow be neutral. (3) A doctrine about the aims of or the intent of legislators. (4) A doctrine about the proper functions of the state. (5) A prohibition on the state "weighing in" or "taking a stand" on some controversial moral issue. (6) The prohibition of the state in enforcing moral character; it being forbidden to engage in the "care of souls". (7) That the state simply be "impartial" (as Brian Barry famously argued). (8) Or, neutrality may be a requirement of a theory of justice, not a theory of state action' (Gaus 2003: 138).

After Virtue's Critique of Liberalism 81

As Christopher Stephen Lutz nicely puts the point, liberalism 'ends up locked in controversy over the definition of the universal rational principles whose existence it dogmatically asserts' (Lutz 2004: 54).

The whole project of justificatory liberalism – the retreat from *neutrality of outcome* to *neutrality of justification* – is one more piece of evidence for liberalism living out its very own conception of the good. Indeed, this is what fundamentally transforms liberalism into a tradition of its own, on MacIntyre's analysis:

> The starting points of liberal theorizing are never neutral as between conceptions of the human good; they are always liberal starting points. And the inconclusiveness of the debates within liberalism as to the fundamental principles of liberal justice ... reinforces the view that liberal theory is best understood, not at all as an attempt to find a rationality independent of tradition, but as itself the articulation of an historically developed and developing set of social institutions and forms of activity, that is, as the voice of a tradition. (MacIntyre 1988: 345)

The ultimate conclusion is that liberalism can no more achieve neutrality among competing conceptions of the good than any other tradition can. The contemporary state 'is not and cannot be evaluatively neutral' (MacIntyre 1999b: 213).

Despite the obvious power of MacIntyre's critique, there is an ideal of neutrality (or, if not neutrality *per se*, an ideal in the same conceptual neighbourhood) that seems to many of us something very much worth preserving. Richard Rorty gives a sketch of the sort of ideal I have in mind when he writes:

> We do not really want doctors to differentiate between the values of the lives they are saving, any more than we want defense lawyers to worry too much about the innocence of their clients, or teachers to worry about which students will make the best use of the education they are offering. A society built around procedural justice needs agents who do not look too closely at such matters. (Rorty 1991: 205)

What Rorty is describing here is something like the virtue of fairness or even-handedness, something like a personal virtue of neutrality that should prevail in a liberal 'society built around procedural justice'. This virtue emphasises the importance that people – agents of the state in many instances – discharge their duties in a spirit of consistency and fair-mindedness, without prejudice or unjustified partiality. All of us should recognise the value in this ideal, even if we agree that the state is not and cannot be neutral. MacIntyre himself comes extremely close to agreeing with Rorty on this issue. A neutral state may be a fiction, but 'it is very much to be desired', he writes in a later essay, that the 'agencies of the state'

82   *David Rondel*

... should provide for the equal protection of the state's subjects from a wide variety of harms, and that this protection should be characterized so that it preserves an ostensible neutrality on the part of the state. Even although that neutrality is never real, it is an important fiction, and those of us who recognize its importance as well as its fictional character will agree with liberals in upholding a certain range of civil liberties. (MacIntyre 1999b: 214)

4.3   *After Virtue* in the Tradition of Anti-liberalism

One of the most striking things about MacIntyre's critique of liberalism in *After Virtue* is how it cuts across arguments from both left and right. Unsurprisingly, MacIntyre's book frequently has an unapologetically Catholic feel, drawing from Aristotelian and Thomistic arguments about the human *telos*, about 'the hierarchy of goods which provide the ends of human action', about the richness of the ancient and mediaeval virtue traditions (MacIntyre 1981: 84). At other times, one gets the sense that MacIntyre is channelling a young Karl Marx. (It has been plausibly suggested, incidentally, that MacIntyre's real genius consists in having shown that Marx was fundamentally a 'revolutionary' Aristotelian, someone who conceives of human life in properly teleological terms and shows how capitalism damages and inhibits the human *telos* – what Marx would sometimes call our 'species being').[6] Still, the greatness of *After Virtue* is captured in large part by the fact that it cannot plausibly be pigeonholed.

But even after conceding its great originality and power, it sometimes remains unclear what, precisely, the target of MacIntyre's critique really is and what register the critique is supposed to be operating in. Is the 'liberal individualism' that MacIntyre rejects a philosophical or political doctrine at bottom? Is it an ideology or a theory? A kind of *Weltanschauung*? Or does it more centrally involve something like an ethos or a sensibility – what Wendy Brown (2015), in her illuminating discussion of neoliberalism, calls a 'governing rationality'? It is not easy to say. Sometimes MacIntyre writes as though he is contributing to a standard political-philosophical debate, as if engaging directly with the ideas of John Rawls, Ronald Dworkin or Robert Nozick. At other times, MacIntyre's critique feels more nebulously cultural. And indeed, this distinctively cultural register has a long and important history in the tradition of anti-liberalism.[7] Critics of liberalism – from de Maistre to

---

[6] See the essays collected in Blackledge and Knight 2011a.

[7] Harvard law professor Adrian Vermeule, himself a fierce critic of liberalism, provides a good example of the sort of thing I have in mind. In an essay about what he claims to be the essentially 'sacramental' character of liberalism, Vermeule is clear that he does not mean to criticise liberalism as a political theory, 'let alone the recondite academic versions

After Virtue's Critique of Liberalism 83

Strauss, from Schmitt to MacIntyre himself – virtually always engage in *Kulturkritik*. Their criticisms of modern culture follow a fairly standardised format according to which the repudiation of liberalism goes hand in hand with a more general lamentation over the 'moral and spiritual degeneration of modern society' (Holmes 1993: 5). For better or for worse, this is the genre to which *After Virtue*'s critique of liberalism undeniably belongs.

Yet it is sometimes unclear just how much of the moral and spiritual degeneration of the present age it is appropriate to lay at the feet of liberalism as such. No one can really gaze out on the world and pinpoint exactly where the contributions of something called 'liberalism' are located – as distinct from myriad other ideas, forces and contingent historical events. Can anyone ever really show that certain forms of degeneration in contemporary societies are the direct upshot of a few key philosophical ideas from the seventeenth and eighteenth centuries? As if there was a straight line from John Locke's *Two Treatises* to the prevalence of Tinder. As if the moment we agree with J. S. Mill that the only 'freedom which deserves the name, is that of pursuing our own good in our own way', we are inexorably on the road to a culture in which there is no self-control, no cultivation of the virtues, a culture in which pornography and selfishness and gluttony rule the day (Mill 1989: 16). We can trace the lines of those connections if we squint. And it can be exhilarating to argue in this way. But it is also difficult to seriously substantiate causal claims at this level of abstraction, over such long periods of time. In the real world, the story about how we got here is almost certainly much more complex, circuitous and contingent than liberalism's critics, MacIntyre among them, sometimes make it out to be. It seems right to say that, in a good number of instances, *After Virtue*'s critique of liberalism is most convincing when it is most broad-brushed and impressionistic. As soon as more definitional and causal precision is

---

of that theory, worked out to the nth decimal, with distinctions among perfectionist and anti-perfectionist liberalism and so forth. The latter is definitely not my topic and I will be impatient with complaints that I have not spoken to the latest minor paper on Rawlsianism or the latest argument for transhumanism.' Rather, Vermeule means to criticise liberalism 'in a sociological vein' and to conceive of it 'as a lived and very concrete type of political-theological order' (Vermeule 2019). All the great contributions to the tradition of anti-liberalism – from the French revolution to the present day – make use of a distinction in this general vicinity, between conceiving of liberalism as a political theory, on the one hand, and as a lived order of some kind, on the other. I think it is correct to say that critics of liberalism are not always as careful as they should be in keeping these different registers of analysis separate. As Holmes claims, 'the unwillingness to examine liberal theories and liberal societies separately is a trademark of antiliberal thought' (Holmes 1993: xiv).

84 *David Rondel*

demanded, some of its critical and rhetorical sting is diminished. Or so I would contend.

Asking about whether something as big and amorphous as liberalism might be right or wrong, virtuous or vicious, conducive to human flourishing or wholly non-conducive is not particularly helpful in my view. Liberalism is too variegated for anyone to be sensibly 'for' or 'against' it. Too many things can plausibly be counted as 'liberal'.

And yet, the story MacIntyre tells in *After Virtue* about how we have lost our way rings true. Loudly so. And the ringing is even louder, it seems to me, when one makes liberal *society* rather than liberal *theory* the main character in that story. Amazingly, the ringing is also louder today than it was four decades ago, in 1981, when *After Virtue* was first published. For to the extent that liberalism these days is in deep trouble all over the world (and nobody can deny that liberalism is in deep trouble), this is because we have watched a number of MacIntyre's key claims (about the increasingly powerful role that elite bureaucratic managers play in our lives, about liberalism's compulsive proceduralism and its flight from moral substance, about how liberal individualism weakens close-knit communities) play out in real time, as it were. Forty years on, *After Virtue* remains a vital touchstone in moral and political philosophy. Anyone curious about both the rise of liberal individualism and its future prospects cannot afford to ignore it.

5 *After Virtue* and the Rise of Postliberalism

Nathan Pinkoski

As its subtitle indicates, *After Virtue* is primarily a study in moral theory. Nevertheless, in the decades following the book's publication, its political implications have set off heated debates. Central to this controversy is Alasdair MacIntyre's critique of liberalism. Most of MacIntyre's critics were themselves friends of liberalism, as well as friends of the Enlightenment project that MacIntyre argues is complicit in the advance of liberalism. This dynamic obliged him to clarify his ultimate assessment of liberalism and the Enlightenment, but in ways that were sometimes ambiguous.

In the last decade, however, a different dynamic has emerged. A political postliberal movement has taken off that is unabashedly hostile to liberalism. For these postliberals, the liberal political tradition has failed and must be replaced. Because *After Virtue* concludes that liberalism is an exhausted tradition, MacIntyre has been an inspiration for postliberal thinkers, although postliberals depart from him in key ways. I shall argue that this new dynamic discloses persistent ambiguities in MacIntyre's own treatment of liberalism, just as the old dynamic did.

In Section 5.1, I explain the core features and nuances of *After Virtue*'s critique of liberalism. In Section 5.2, I describe MacIntyre's politics and evaluate three misinterpretations of his positions – the conservative, communitarian and reactionary – which emerged following *After Virtue*. MacIntyre's responses to these misinterpretations, I contend, evince some tensions in his own assessment of liberalism. In Section 5.3, I describe the MacIntyrean features of the postliberal project. While there are important similarities, postliberals break from MacIntyre in several respects. However, these ruptures between contemporary postliberalism and MacIntyrean postliberalism reinforce the same ambiguous tensions in MacIntyre's own treatment of liberalism disclosed in his response to the political misreadings of his work. In Section 5.4, outlining MacIntyre's analysis of proto-liberal moments in the history of philosophy, I explain

86 *Nathan Pinkoski*

why for MacIntyre these suggest that liberalism cannot be replaced now or in any discernible future, constraining postliberal ambitions.

5.1 *After Virtue*'s Critique of Liberalism

From *After Virtue* onwards, MacIntyre has made two major arguments.[1] His critical argument explains the failure of liberalism to provide an adequate moral theory, or a theory of practical reasoning. The constructive argument explains why the Aristotelian tradition is the best theory of practical reasoning so far to correct liberalism's failure; it alone helps human beings become independent practical reasoners (MacIntyre 1994a: 258, 263; 1999a: 81–98; 2011b: 329; Lutz 2012: 30–32).

Understanding liberalism as modern liberal individualism, MacIntyre criticises the theoretical basis of modern liberal individualism and the social culture it produces through a historical, genealogical critique that seeks to identify the roots of liberal theory and practice. In this sense, it is a radical critique of liberalism.

Because this critique brings MacIntyre to scrutinise the ambitions of modernity and the Enlightenment project, it appears that he targets the Enlightenment, regarding it as a catastrophe (see, e.g., Beiner 2014: 169 n., 186–8). Zealous to defend modernity and Enlightenment, MacIntyre's critics have primarily attacked him on normative theoretical grounds, accusing him of refusing to acknowledge the Enlightenment's

---

[1] MacIntyre describes himself as being 'engaged in a single project' since 1977, when, after years of self-reflection, he finally developed an account of why the theory to which he was attached in his youth, Marxism, had failed (1991: 267–9). In MacIntyre's 'single project' from 1977 onwards, *After Virtue, Whose Justice? Which Rationality?*, *Three Rival Versions of Moral Enquiry* and *Ethics in the Conflicts of Modernity* are the central works, defining and updating the core theses of his research project (Lutz 2004: 7, 10–32). The initial formulation of his project in *After Virtue* – as for any research project – could not be comprehensively formulated but must be open to refinement and development. Consequently, MacIntyre acknowledges that he has refined and developed his views, and that some remain open-ended (2007: ix; D'Andrea 2006: 397–402; Knight 2007: 224–5). Critics incorrectly interpret *After Virtue* and his other books as almost independent treatises, with occasional *errata* directed at prior positions. Cf. Nussbaum: '[In *Whose Justice? Which Rationality?*] MacIntyre quietly drops *After Virtue*'s interesting account of the importance of story-telling in giving moral terms their meaning ... Nothing of comparable power has replaced it' (Nussbaum 1989). Nussbaum does not consider how he could be complementing his original argument. Cf. Blakely 2017: 2–3. Blakely acknowledges that MacIntyre makes corrections to *After Virtue*. But he still thinks it qualifies as an immanent critique of MacIntyre to quarrel almost exclusively with the MacIntyre of *After Virtue*, because it is 'by far the most influential MacIntyre – the culturally pessimistic, antiliberal Aristotelian we meet in the pages of *After Virtue*'. See also Pinkoski 2019: 557.

After Virtue and the Rise of Postliberalism 87

benefits.[2] This attack has tainted MacIntyre with the charge of promulgating conservative or even reactionary ideas.[3]

Yet MacIntyre's more positive assessment of the Enlightenment was already implicit in the text of *After Virtue*. As a close reading of the 'disquieting suggestion' at the start of *After Virtue* suggests, his genealogical critique of liberalism does not target the Enlightenment (2007: 1).[4] The original 'catastrophe' in moral philosophy that the opening passage invites us to look for lies not with the figures of Enlightenment or Protestantism. Rather, it is their 'late mediaeval predecessors' who 'embody a new conception of reason' (MacIntyre 2007: 53; 1990: 155; Lutz 2012: 44–6). The catastrophe is the construction of metaphysical voluntarism. Late mediaeval metaphysics, not Enlightenment's politics nor the Reformation's theology, structures the fundamental choice of late modernity. The choice between Nietzsche or Aristotle is for voluntarism and against teleology on the one hand, or for teleology and against voluntarism on the other (MacIntyre 2007: 109–20; D'Andrea 2006: 249). Enlightenment does not bear the responsibility for producing this catastrophic theoretical mistake. Its responsibility is diminished because it inherited that catastrophe. MacIntyre's position is therefore closer to Louis Dupré, who sees the origins of modernity in late mediaeval theology, than those who posit a sharp break from antiquity originating in either the Renaissance, Reformation or Enlightenment.[5]

---

[2] Some critics also attacked on historical grounds, accusing him of misunderstanding the Enlightenment's multi-faceted character. In reply, MacIntyre demonstrates his awareness of the various historical and philosophical strands of the Enlightenment. He wanted to emphasise common features between these strands, and the transformative social and political *projects* that the thinkers of the Enlightenment endorsed. See 1995a: esp. 172; as well as Perreau-Saussine 2005: 57.

[3] 'Reactionaries are not conservatives. This is the first thing to understand about them' (Lilla 2016: xii). While conservatives might be characterised as inclined to preserve what exists, reactionaries are hostile to modernity, juxtaposing it to a political, nostalgic longing for a lost pre-modernity. As part of their political nostalgia, they imagine pre-modernity as a 'happy, well-ordered state' and blame modernity *tout court* for destroying it. In modernity, humanity has entered a new dark age. Unlike conservatives, reactionaries are radicals and often revolutionaries, hoping to overturn modernity for the sake of pre-modernity (Nussbaum 1989; Lilla 2016: xii, xiv; Blakely 2017: 1). Blakely places himself in a tradition of similar works that accused MacIntyre of being a reactionary, including Mark Lilla as well as Holmes 1993.

[4] In the new preface to *After Virtue*, MacIntyre realises that his argument was misunderstood because few of his critics grasped that *A Canticle for Leibowitz* was the reference (2007: xv–vi).

[5] Cf. Dupré 1995 with Maritain 1970, who places the rupture with René Descartes and Martin Luther. Early in his career, Leo Strauss argued that the modern rupture began in the Enlightenment period proper, in the seventeenth century with Thomas Hobbes; see Strauss 1953. Later, however, Strauss argued that the modern rupture began with Machiavelli in the sixteenth century; see Strauss 1958. In both cases, however, Strauss

88   *Nathan Pinkoski*

Yet the Enlightenment project intensified the problem concealed in the theory of voluntarism. It sought to free the will from any kind of thinking as directed by another. From this position, ostensibly free from any reliance on one's society or culture, it aimed to provide a single set of universal moral rules that did not mention social roles (MacIntyre 1995a: 174–5; 2007: 54). Translating this moral theory into practice, moral rules could be accepted by all, spreading the ideals of liberty and equality in modern society. MacIntyre agrees that several of the specific values Enlightenment thinkers promoted, such as negative liberty and tolerance, challenged unjust and illegitimate institutions. By promoting these values, which became values associated with liberalism, the Enlightenment brings positive outcomes (MacIntyre 1995a: 180; 2011b: 325–7; 2016: 123–4).

Yet the promised translation from moral theory to practice never happened because of the Enlightenment's flawed moral theory, its flawed theory of practical reasoning. The Enlightenment's most sophisticated moral theorists ended up endorsing the view that the self is essentially constituted by its autonomy and chooses its own good. Drawing on Elizabeth Anscombe's condensed critique of Kantianism, MacIntyre argues that this concept of morality is groundless; liberalism, which depends on this conception of morality, is likewise groundless (Anscombe 1958: 2; D'Andrea 2006: 346; MacIntyre 2007: 86; 1990: 39–40). The arbitrariness of modern morality lies in its voluntarist roots. For Anscombe, the voluntarist project was only rational and intelligible when it presumed the theological framework of divine command theory. When modern thinkers removed the theological framework, the obligation to obey one's own will became arbitrary. MacIntyre makes a parallel argument. By inheriting the late mediaeval metaphysical error, the Enlightenment could not avoid the same collapse into arbitrariness. Whether in its Kantian or utilitarian form, the liberal moral agent has no criterion to justify their choice for the moral law other than their own autonomous choice. But the basis for this choice lacks any rational criteria (MacIntyre 2007: 44–6; Lutz 2012: 86–7).

MacIntyre describes at length the social and political consequences of this theoretical deficiency. Bad theory produced bad practice. In their first iteration, in the seventeenth and eighteenth centuries, Enlightenment values brought positive results. They delegitimised the unjust institutions of the *ancien régime*. However, they could not cope with what Karl Polanyi termed 'The Great Transformation': the

---

emphasises a topic MacIntyre does not address: a radical transformation in the conception of science and the attitude towards technological development.

After Virtue and the Rise of Postliberalism 89

emergence of new political, economic and social structures that dislodged the embedded relationships hitherto assumed in human communities (MacIntyre 2007, 239; 1988: 211). In this new social context, the theoretical weakness of Enlightenment values became more and more acute. Because Enlightenment theory repudiated the contention that values require an articulated social context to give them meaning, Enlightenment's values remained ambiguous. Efforts to define these values produced irresolvable disputes over their ultimate meaning and justification. This resulted in the proliferation of rival moral theories that could not justify themselves effectively over and against one another. For these reasons, the ideals associated with Enlightenment could not in practice be realised. It is in this way that the Enlightenment project's hopes must remain unfulfilled (MacIntyre 2011b: 326).

MacIntyre's social critique also includes an ideological critique. Arbitrariness in moral theory transforms modern social practices. For MacIntyre, emotivism is the social theory that best describes how modern human beings think and act in this changed situation. Modern human beings regard judgements about what is good to be mere expressions of preferences and feelings. When liberal emotivist selves take over practice-based communities, they upset the capacities of these practice-based communities to discover and realise the common good, as well as the human good of the rational agents therein. As the emotivist culture spreads, it becomes hard to acknowledge the substantive interconnections across different realms of human activity. Social life becomes more and more compartmentalised (MacIntyre 2007: 18–35, 51–78; McMylor 2011: 228–40; Lutz 2012: 123).

Coupling Marxian insights with Weberian ones, MacIntyre extends his ideological critique to attack liberalism's chief political form: the bureaucratic managerialism of the modern nation-state. This state, or more precisely the managers who rule it, boasts that it has the legitimate authority to govern a pluralistic society and that it has brought political conflicts to an end (MacIntyre 2007: 26–7). MacIntyre attacks this political form on two fronts. He contends that the state derives its pretentions to legitimate authority from managerial expertise. But managerial expertise is a fraud. It is premissed on a false conception of reality and of human practical reasoning. Presuming that law-like generalisations can predict the behaviour of rational agents, managerial bureaucrats assert exclusive competency to make the laws that would engineer positive social reform (MacIntyre 2007: 85–7). But no agents, managerial experts or otherwise, can make such laws because such predictions are impossible to make. Hence managers cannot justify their authority. MacIntyre contends that the political form of the managerial state is

90   *Nathan Pinkoski*

itself illegitimate. Rather than benefitting human society, managerialism is a cover for manipulation and domination. Social conflict has not come to an end. The belief that politics reduces to management suppresses alternative political and ethical visions (Breen 2012: 160–65).

The second front on which MacIntyre attacks the liberal state is its flawed conception of justice. He argues that it rests on an incoherent conception of justice, which hides behind the neutrality paradigm. This paradigm purports to resolve conflict and adjudicate fairly between the subjective goods of citizens. But to do so, the state must endorse a particular set of goods and command obedience from citizens because of its claim to satisfy that set of goods. This conception of politics, MacIntyre argues, privatises the good, turning it into subjective preference. It is at the service of emotivist culture. The liberal state, then, privileges a particular theory of justice and does not allow it to be challenged (MacIntyre 1988: 392; 1990: 235). While at some level of debate liberals acknowledge this, MacIntyre holds that their position is without philosophical foundation, rooted as it is in the flawed ethical theory of the Enlightenment. What masquerades as sophisticated philosophical theory is in fact muddled compromise that favours established interests.[6]

As MacIntyre argues, those with power, status and money are particularly adept at playing the managerial system and 'neutral' justice of the liberal nation-state to their advantage. They hijack the vocabulary of liberalism (particularly the vocabulary of the Scottish Enlightenment: utility, contract and individual rights) and the new social circumstances created by the Great Transformation to advance their preferences.[7] These forces rearrange the economic and state institutions in order to further their own interests. Their success makes it difficult to schematise alternative political and ethical visions. This cements managerial rule and confirms the grip that the ideology of liberalism holds over the rest of society. This near-universal trend makes it almost impossible for the surviving practice-based communities to achieve the common good, and it stymies the capacities of rational agents to realise human flourishing.

5.2   The Politics of *After Virtue*

The ending of *After Virtue*, where MacIntyre announces the 'exhaustion' of Marxism and 'every other political tradition' and laments the new

---

[6] See MacIntyre 1988: 342–5.
[7] Note that the failure of the Scottish Enlightenment to provide an intelligible ethics and its susceptibility to capture by capitalist ideology is unintended by its architects. See MacIntyre 2007: 229–33. C.f. Polanyi 2001: 71–80, 141–70.

After Virtue and the Rise of Postliberalism

'dark ages' that have beset us, indicates the extent of his pessimism about reconstructing communities that achieve the good (2007: 263–4). But what is *nearly* impossible is not impossible; MacIntyre does not think we are consigned to a 'generalised social pessimism' devoid of any 'politics of relevance' (2007: 263; Blackledge and Knight 2011a: 1). *After Virtue* left an intriguing opening for a political programme. The basis for this political programme is MacIntyre's theory of practices. Working together in communities, human agents cultivate the qualities of mind and character – the virtues – necessary to achieve the good (MacIntyre 2007: 187, 191, 219, 223). MacIntyre's political exhortation to pursue 'the reconstruction of new forms of community within which the moral life could be sustained' (2007: 264) was, however, misunderstood in turn as conservative, communitarian or reactionary.

In one sense, it is correct to describe MacIntyre as 'conservative', because he holds that all human activity, including thinking, is historically rooted and conditioned. Human agents reason by reference to the specific historical communities and traditions that shape them (Lutz 2004). For some critics, the political implications of this tradition-constituted rationality seemed to be that MacIntyre takes communities and traditions as they are, subjecting the exercise of power therein to neither justification nor critical scrutiny (Frazer and Lacey 1994: 267, 270–75).

However, this was not an accurate interpretation of MacIntyre's account of rationality, for MacIntyre stressed the fallibility of the standards of reasoning communities and traditions provide (2007: 221–2). This criticism also misunderstood the political implications of his theory of practices. Far from taking communities as they were, MacIntyre's theory subjects the exercise of power within communities to critical scrutiny by contrasting practices with institutions. Practices are the sites where human beings discover the goods internal to those practices. Institutions are the sites where goods external to practices, such as money, status and power, are pursued and realised. Institutions are not inherently bad; they are needed to sustain practices across time. The external goods they pursue are certainly useful and important. But the danger is that they can be confused with the overall human good and become obstacles to achieving it (D'Andrea 2006: 277; MacIntyre 2007: 194; Knight 2011b: 25–6).

The task of rational agents is not just to interpret the world but also to change it, deploying Aristotelian practices to change society (MacIntyre 1995b: 156; Knight 2011b: 20–34). Applying the theory of practices to their own actions, rational agents can initiate a political programme that scrutinises and challenges institutions that do not assist in the discovery

92   *Nathan Pinkoski*

of the human good. For that reason, MacIntyre's neo-Aristotelian theory of practices provides a way to resist and subvert the justifications contemporary institutions use to deploy their power. This 'revolutionary' account of MacIntyre's politics remains important as a refutation of the charge of conservatism. MacIntyre himself endorsed it and wrote a new prologue for the twenty-fifth anniversary edition of *After Virtue* in order to criticise conservatism (MacIntyre 2007: xv–vi; cf. 222).[8]

MacIntyre argues that the apparent disagreement between contemporary liberal-leftists and conservatives masks a deeper agreement on the fundamental tenets of modern liberal individualism. For example, conservatives absolutise individual property rights against one's community, religion or government. Liberal-leftists absolutise individual privacy rights against one's community, religion or government. Both essentially agree on the importance of individual autonomy; both therefore use individual autonomy to attack and destroy social structures, exacerbating the compartmentalisation of modernity and the triumph of the emotivist self (MacIntyre 2007: 18–35, 51–78, 222; 1994a: 258; 2016: 115, 118).[9]

During the twenty-five years following the publication of *After Virtue*, MacIntyre was also labelled a 'communitarian'. While communitarians soften the edges of their critique of liberalism, they seek to counter liberalism with a community-centred alternative that would reorientate the state in directions less friendly to global capitalism and more friendly to local cultures, minorities and communities (Mulhall and Swift 1996). Nevertheless, describing MacIntyre as a communitarian misunderstands his relationship to the modern state. As an intransigent critic of both the modern state and modern economic power, MacIntyre disavows the 'communitarian' label, because he does not think state power can be used to rein in the excesses of economic power (1998b: 243–6). Such a project would only maintain or strengthen the unjust institutions that prevail in many local communities. It is seldom appreciated that in the liberal-communitarian debate, MacIntyre ratifies the liberal critique of communitarianism (Beiner 2013: 171).

---

[8] 'For an accurate and perceptive discussion of my political views see Kelvin Knight, "Revolutionary Aristotelianism"' (MacIntyre 1998b: 235).

[9] For the purposes of this chapter, I understand the left–right (or left–conservative) political divide in a classical sense, since a key part of MacIntyre's argument is that the modern, contemporary left and right share a liberal philosophical and political outlook. I use 'left' or 'left-wing' to refer to those who embrace a political project that seeks the open-ended emancipation of individuals and societies and 'right' or 'right-wing' to refer to those who embrace a political project that seeks to preserve or reconstruct the authority of communities, institutions and societies.

After Virtue and the Rise of Postliberalism

Ultimately, the 'conservative' and 'communitarian' epithets fail to apprehend how MacIntyre continues to endorse, as he did in his youth, a Trotskyist, Marxist critique of society. This targets the modern bureaucratic state and particularly the modern capitalist economy, which for MacIntyre 'provides systematic incentives to develop a type of character that has a propensity to injustice' (1995b: 149).

Those who charge MacIntyre with advocating a reactionary political programme at least grasp that, on the basis of the Trotskyist conclusion to *After Virtue*, MacIntyre demands the 'radical negation of present society' (Blakely 2017: 11–12). They believe MacIntyre advocates restoration of pre-modern, traditional communities on an Aristotelian basis, and so is a reactionary (Holmes 1993: 89; Sayers 2011: 83; Blakely 2017: 12). Yet the text of *After Virtue* punctures this argument. The 'exhaustion' of 'every other political tradition' extends to the pre-modern tradition MacIntyre is allegedly out to restore, namely Aristotelianism. MacIntyre acknowledges that Aristotle's political programme advocates the *polis* as the ideal form of political community. But because the historical circumstances that led to it were unique to the ancient world, attempts to reconstruct Aristotelianism in present circumstances must face the challenge that replicating the *polis* is now impossible (MacIntyre 2007: 163). Moreover, MacIntyre stresses the normative failures of pre-modern Aristotelianism. The *polis* is a community that lacks the virtue of justice. To become a just community, the *polis* would have to admit artisans, women, slaves and non-Greeks to citizenship, allowing them to participate fully in the life of the *polis*. But Aristotle would not accept this proposition (MacIntyre 1988: 105; D'Andrea 2006: 421–6; Lutz 2012: 179–80). MacIntyre believes that efforts at reformulating Aristotle's politics for modern circumstances credit the theory with more coherence than it possessed. A *polis* that included everyone would contradict Aristotle's own understanding of the human end (MacIntyre 2016: 86). In taking this position, MacIntyre accepts much of the content of Aristotle's more hostile modern critics (Callinicos 2011: 64–5). As MacIntyre's application of the liberal critique of communitarianism indicates, he holds communities to a high normative standard that aligns more with modern egalitarian demands than with ancient ones. For MacIntyre, most communities, especially pre-modern communities, are wanting in theory and practice.

The decades in which MacIntyre fended off criticisms of his project as conservative and communitarian disclosed common features of his interlocutors. The conservative or communitarian thinkers who appropriated MacIntyrean insights tended to be friendly critics of liberalism. Similarly, the critics who delivered the more aggressive polemics accusing

MacIntyre of conservative or reactionary thinking tended to be attached to a particular set of liberal values. Generally, MacIntyre was facing down critics who tended to be inspired by the Marxian left and those who held strong liberal and egalitarian sympathies.

MacIntyre's responses, however, have moved in divergent directions. Faced with conservative or communitarian appropriations of his work, MacIntyre contended that conservatism or communitarianism affirmed essential tenets of liberalism. He emphasised how he rejected those tenets, demonstrating his distance from liberalism and thereby demonstrating his distance from conservatives and communitarians. But faced with spirited attacks by the defenders of liberal values, MacIntyre points out that he shares many of those values. He thereby confirmed that in several respects he was more sympathetic to the norms associated with liberalism than his critics believed.

The tension in MacIntyre's stance stems less from his endorsement of these norms; as he argues, some of them admit of non-liberal and Aristotelian manners of justification. It stems more from MacIntyre's belief that a revitalised, reinvigorated Aristotelian political tradition is presently unavailable to be put into wide-scale practice. We are still waiting for such a political theory to come into existence. The project to replace liberalism and bring us into a genuinely postliberal era is therefore incomplete. Because it is incomplete, we must rely on aspects of liberalism (and sometimes ally with the liberal state) to defend practice-based communities from even worse forms of domination and control (MacIntyre 1998b: 252). This concession to liberal politics as the lesser evil could go very far – even to the point of legitimising the modern state and liberalism itself (cf. Michéa 2007; Duff 2021).

5.3 MacIntyrean Resonances and Dissonances within Postliberalism

Whatever his compromises in the present, MacIntyre maintains clarity about his hope for a new, postliberal political order. He points towards the sources to help us construct the Aristotelian theory that would bring an end to this period of concession and replace liberalism. Openness to both Christian and Marxist sources – neither of which, he contends, are antagonistic to each other – would remedy the defects of Aristotelianism (MacIntyre 1995b: 145–6). This political theory would be based on the insights of Aristotle's ethics without being dependent on the particularities of his politics, and it would be capable of critiquing advanced capitalism (Hibbs 2004: 377). In the years following *After Virtue*, MacIntyre concluded that Thomistic natural law reasoning, with some

After Virtue and the Rise of Postliberalism 95

revisions and developments, would provide such a theory (MacIntyre 2007: x–xi; 1988: 164; 1990: 124–5; 1995c: 62–3).[10]

In the third decade following the publication of *After Virtue*, a new kind of postliberal movement has taken off on the Anglo-American right that appears to fulfil MacIntyre's demands. It desires precisely the Aristotelian, Thomistic political theory that is critical of advanced capitalism which MacIntyre advocates. The postliberalism now ascendent in political theory gathers dissidents from the Anglo-American right who contend that the liberal political tradition has failed and must be replaced. These discussions generate much ongoing commentary in print and online publications, so it is impossible to describe, let alone evaluate, the entire movement and its chief advocates here.[11]

My modest aim is to compare Anglo-American political postliberalism with MacIntyrean political postliberalism. To that end I shall focus my analysis on two academic texts, which contain both critiques of liberalism as well as constructive arguments as to what should replace liberalism, and which aim to be canonical works for the ongoing political postliberal project.[12] These texts are John Milbank's and Adrian Pabst's *The Politics of Virtue* and Adrian Vermeule's *Common Good Constitutionalism*.[13]

---

[10] MacIntyre admits he was wrong on three major points in the first edition of *After Virtue*. He had claimed Aristotle was reliant on flawed metaphysical biology and that he neglected tragic moral dilemmas, and that Aquinas was wrong on the unity of the virtues (2007: 157–8, 179–80; cf. xi; MacIntyre 2006a: viii–ix; 1988: x). Correcting these mistakes prepares the way for MacIntyre's acceptance of Thomism.

[11] Versions of postliberalism have developed for decades in a variety of fields, notably in theology (e.g. Milbank 2006: xi–xv). I do not have space to treat versions of postliberalism beyond political theory here, even though MacIntyre has inspired some of the discussions in theological postliberalism (e.g. Rowland 2003). MacIntyre's approach is secular philosophical, not theological (1994a: 266), and so it is too speculative to conjecture what his response would be to theological appropriations of his thought.

[12] Patrick Deneen is an influential postliberal thinker whose critique of liberalism is rhetorically and substantially indebted to MacIntyre (see esp. Deneen 2016: 196; 2018a: 42). There are three reasons why I do not consider him here. First, at the time of writing, Deneen has only published one critical book-length argument against liberalism and no constructive book-length argument outlining the features of the postliberal politics that will replace it. His conclusion in fact affirms aspects of liberal politics (Deneen 2018a: 180–82, 196–7). Second, Deneen conceives of a much sharper rupture between modernity and pre-modernity than MacIntyre does, and he is more hostile to modernity and favourable to pre-modernity than MacIntyre is (Pinkoski 2019: 531–63). Third, because Deneen has endorsed Vermeule's common good constitutionalist project and Vermeule (2018) endorsed Deneen's critical argument, we can regard the two as sharing a common postliberal vision and focus on the text that outlines the constructive argument – the juridical-political project – in more detail.

[13] They have conservative or rightist sympathies in that they seek to defend authoritative practices and traditions – the source of their breach with the left (Vermeule 2022: 7, 37, 67). Milbank and Pabst are more of an outlier as they would not identify with this

These postliberals are different from earlier postliberals in that, like MacIntyre, they regard the present political and social order as the culmination of liberalism and hope for a better, postliberal future.[14] The structure of their argument has three important MacIntyrean cadences. First, they take up MacIntyre's diagnosis of the prevalent political parties' sharing a basic agreement. They argue that a seemingly conflictual relationship between the contemporary left and right conceals a relationship of mutual support in promoting individual autonomy. For Milbank and Pabst, the socio-cultural liberalism of the left has been in a 'tacit, secret alliance' with the economic liberalism of the right; they show how these two have advanced a similar political and social project based on unencumbered individual freedom (2016: 1). Focusing on constitutional jurisprudence, Vermeule's strategy is to demonstrate that originalism (the right's jurisprudence) and living constitutionalism (the left's jurisprudence) work in tandem with rather than in opposition to one another, advancing social progressivism in the name of the liberation of the will (2022: 16–17, 97–108, 164).

Second, as their description of the contemporary political landscape shows, they conceive of liberalism as modern liberal individualism. Liberalism represents a single, *unified* theory (see esp. Milbank and Pabst 2016: 28–46; Vermeule 2022: 169, 180–81).[15] Milbank and Pabst contend that the primacy of individual autonomy stems from late mediaeval metaphysics, including voluntarism (2016: 33). Likewise, Vermeule condemns both originalism and progressive constitutionalism for representing 'the ultimate valorisation of will at the expense of natural reason' (2022: 133). He sees this shift beginning in the early modern period; the American Founding era is a moment that 'was already in

political labelling (2016: 69). Nevertheless, their defence of Toryism and Edmund Burke – attacked by MacIntyre – shows that they share certain sympathies with the right (2016: 41–5).

[14] Cf. Gottfried 1999. Although he sympathises with MacIntyre's critique of emotivist culture (95), he departs from MacIntyre by denying that there is a unified liberal tradition (37). If liberalism once meant anything, it meant a form of bourgeois representative government that was defeated in the twentieth century by the mass democratic welfare state. The new managerial state that emerged is not ultraliberal but postliberal. So unlike in MacIntyre's thinking, we should not look forward to a distant but better postliberal future but instead acknowledge the presently existing disorder as postliberal. Postliberalism is a troubling rather than a hopeful concept.

[15] There are some variations from MacIntyre on what constitutes the unified theory of liberalism. Milbank and Pabst draw attention to the theological errors of the Reformation, which culminate in Jansenism and Deism (Milbank and Pabst 2016: 43). Vermeule's focus on jurisprudence means he singles out the rise of legal positivism and the demise of a classical and Thomistic natural law tradition, a breach that happened very recently, sometime after the Second World War (Vermeule 2022: 24, 176). But both see voluntarism as essentially constituting liberalism.

After Virtue and the Rise of Postliberalism   97

transition from a classical conception of law and rights to a modern liberal conception' (Vermeule 2022: 202–203, n. 133).

Third, their constructive argument for what shall replace liberalism contends that the political and legal order should affirm the primacy of the common good and be ordered towards achieving it. To overcome liberalism's neglect and mischaracterisation of social life, coupled with its false neutrality paradigm for justice, they focus on reconstructing the common good of society as a whole, without resort to aggregate interests or utility maximisation (Milbank and Pabst 2016: 53, 70; Vermeule 2022: 26–8).[16] While a full treatment of their account of the common good is not possible here, the point to emphasise is that their account of the common good departs from the conservatism MacIntyre criticised in *After Virtue*. For Vermeule, the libertarian absolutisation of 'property rights and economic rights will have to go' (2022: 42). Postliberals come not to praise advanced capitalism, but to bury it (see esp. Milbank and Pabst 2016: 72–88, 93–171).

Yet MacIntyre is a revolutionary. He sees the reconstruction of the common good as serving one particularly subversive project. The reconstruction of the common good recovers the exceptionless precepts of the natural law that all rational agents 'recognise as indispensable … for the achievement of our goods and of our final good, because they direct us toward and partially define our common good' (MacIntyre 1995c: 49). This link between affirming exceptionless precepts, defining the common good and scrutinising the law for whether it conforms to the common good was already present in *After Virtue* (MacIntyre 2007: 150). Clarifying this link in later writings and giving it a Thomistic basis, MacIntyre argues that the commitment to exceptionless precepts of justice helps challenge liberal institutions by constantly scrutinising those who rule, calling into question the legitimacy of their actions. Since any breach of an exceptionless precept threatens the common good, and since every rational agent in a community (not simply the ruler) can assess whether a law breaches a precept, rational agents 'can never lose their capacity for judging when they ought and when they ought not to

---

[16] Although some polemics tend in this direction, postliberals do not set up a false dichotomy between an account that affirms the common good on one hand and one that rejects it on the other. Just as MacIntyre does, they raise the Thomistic question of which common good to affirm. All law, insofar as it is law, necessarily connects to a common good, even the law promulgated by a tyrant (*Summa Theologiae*, question 92, article 1). Likewise, liberals also have an understanding of the common good, even if it is a truncated one. Postliberals see themselves as rejecting an implausible liberal account of the common good on the one hand for a more adequate account of the common good on the other (e.g. Milbank and Pabst 2016: 71–2; Vermeule 2022: 170; cf. MacIntyre 1998b: 239–43).

98   *Nathan Pinkoski*

obey the human laws enacted by their rulers' (MacIntyre 1995c: 49). According to MacIntyre, the task of Thomistic political theory since its inception has been to subvert the excessive power and authority of 'the institutions of the nascent nation-state' (1995c: 42).

That subversive project is not shared by postliberals. Vermeule wants to reject jurisprudence informed by accounts of the common good that are 'highly restrictive of governmental authority' and that 'sharply restrict the ruling power of the state' (2022: 67). Vermeule sides with the expansive power of federal government articulated since Roosevelt's New Deal, including a *de facto* general federal police power (2022: 33–4, 40–41, 61–2). And while Milbank and Pabst, like MacIntyre, are sympathetic to the traditions of British socialism that defend local communities and are suspicious of the centralised state (2016: 78–80), they do not share his revolutionary critique of state institutions.

Affirming Gladstone's liberal constitutionalism and vision of parliamentary representative government, Milbank and Pabst defend the post-war British welfare state as a natural culmination of long-term associative trends, especially in its most prized institution, the National Health Service (Milbank and Pabst 2016: 79, 81). They see a decisive shift away from these achievements in the 1970s, writing that the prior landscape looks 'Aristotelian' when 'compared with what we now experience' (Milbank and Pabst 2016: 51). By contrast, the young MacIntyre attacked post-war triumphalism concerning the welfare state and the purported accomplishments of parliamentarism; this informs the older MacIntyre's critique of managerialism (Perreau-Saussine 2005: 19–32). Milbank and Pabst aspire to recover personalised government directing the bureaucracy and a greater role for the head of state. In contrast to MacIntyre's hostility towards the assertive monarchy of Louis IX, they argue that monarchy can defend the many against the few. It is a healthy populist antidote to oligarchy (Milbank and Pabst 2016: 207–209, 218–19). They also reject regional separatist movements in the United Kingdom and elsewhere in Europe, whereas MacIntyre tends to support them (Milbank and Pabst 2016: 365–6; Perreau-Saussine 2005: 40–41, 48–51). And rather than regarding international state alliances as a temporary necessity to ward off worse evils – MacIntyre's concession to international politics (1998b: 252) – they regard the task of building a commonwealth of nations with similar social and cultural ties as a persistent one of politics, suggesting permanent alliance structures that solidify nation-state stability (Milbank and Pabst 2016: 351). Finally, they endorse 'ever-closer union' in Europe to handle security concerns and a larger civil service bureaucracy in the European Union (Milbank and Pabst 2016: 363–4, 370). MacIntyre supports the European Union

After Virtue and the Rise of Postliberalism

project for instrumental reasons: to disrupt Westminster's power over the United Kingdom (Perreau-Saussine 2005: 50).

The splits between these postliberals and MacIntyre on these matters run deeper than policy disagreements. Postliberals see the task of political theory as affirming a substantive common good that must at times make use of the resources of the nation-state and sometimes strengthen them. MacIntyre, however, sees subverting and weakening the managerial and centralised bureaucratic state as an important task of political theory. Thomism demonstrates 'a set of legal, political, and moral possibilities for structuring communal life' that is superior to the 'emerging nation state and its later bureaucratic heirs' (MacIntyre 1995c: 42–3). Postliberals see a compatibility between the modern bureaucratic state and flourishing communal life. Their problem is that, in the 1960s or 1970s, this welfare or administrative state brusquely turned away from policies conducive to the common good. MacIntyre sees this claim of compatibility as the endorsement of an illegitimate political form that has been extending its power for centuries at the expense of communal life. Endorsing this political form would be to endorse liberalism.

But MacIntyre is content to concede other elements of political life to a liberal framework. He endorses the separation of church and state because the modern state, including the nascent modern state of the Middle Ages, 'cannot generally be trusted to promote any worthwhile set of values' (1999b: 214). Equally, there is no subordination of the temporal power to the spiritual power of the church. Even when the state is governed by a 'morally sophisticated' man like Louis IX, MacIntyre criticises him and his state for setting up a temporal order governed by spiritual concerns: this gave his edicts a 'quasi-infallibility' they should not have had (1995c: 45–6). In this context, arguing that human laws stem not from Christian theology but natural reason 'has radical implications' (MacIntyre 1995c: 47). Appealing to natural reason subverts the state ordered by specifically Christian premises.

MacIntyre's position rests partly on the need to put all political authority – including the claims of theological authority, but especially the claims made by the nascent modern state – to the question philosophically. This severely curtails the temporal power's deference to the spiritual power (MacIntyre 1996: 247; 1995c: 48, 54, 62–3; 1999b: 208, 214). Moreover, MacIntyre accepts state neutrality as 'an important fiction' for protecting rational enquiry and the goods discerned through conflict between competing perspectives (1999b: 214). This suggests that the contemporary law-giver should not fix on promoting any more substantive good than tolerating a plurality of rational enquiries that different human beings might take. Since MacIntyre first wrote *After Virtue*, he has

100   *Nathan Pinkoski*

been more forthright about the substantive descriptions of the highest good or final end of the human being. Nevertheless, his emphasis remains, as in the text of *After Virtue*, on the human being's 'quest' for the highest good, rather than on the content of the highest good itself (MacIntyre 2007: 218–20; cf. 2016: 52–4).

As a result, MacIntyre's account of the common good is much thinner than the substantive account that postliberals defend. According to his Thomistic political theory,

Aquinas thus disagrees with both later puritans and later liberals. Like those puritans and unlike those liberals he understands law as an instrument for our moral education. But, like those liberals and unlike those puritans, he is against making law by itself an attempt to repress all vice. (MacIntyre 1995c: 47)

MacIntyre's Thomistic political theory holds that coercion through law is ineffective for educating an agent into the virtues. And for MacIntyre, the common good is first and foremost about rational agents learning to become independent practical reasoners who understand what the good is. To that end, he understands the common good as a community of political learning and participation in rational enquiry (MacIntyre 1998b: 246). Defining and achieving the common good requires 'an active and enquiring attitude toward radically dissenting views' (MacIntyre 1998: 251). When agents debate, agree and achieve a shared understanding of the good in their particular society, it is legitimate to develop coercive laws to confirm it and to call upon a higher society to enforce them (e.g. MacIntyre 1995c: 60–61). Yet such a high standard to legitimise legislation favours small societies. It is almost impossible to achieve for large ones (MacIntyre 1998: 249). So at the larger scale, where that shared understanding is absent, the use of power to impose one account of the good on others is unjust because the legitimacy obtained through agreement is not available in the first place. One must fall back on the virtue of toleration (MacIntyre 1998: 251).

In short, MacIntyre's account of the common good is more friendly to liberal norms than it might otherwise appear. His opposition to the state's promulgating authoritative values is more Lockean than John Locke (Pinkoski 2019: 561–2). His stress on agreement as a precondition of legitimacy favours a pure democracy that postliberals reject for the sake of a mixed regime (Milbank and Pabst 2016: 205–12; Vermeule 2022: 47–8). His advocacy of church–state separation stands in sharp contrast to postliberals, some of whom defend an established church (Milbank and Pabst 2016: 230–39). In this respect, MacIntyre's account of the common good diverges from postliberals who, drawing on St Thomas Aquinas (*Summa Theologiae*, question 92, article 2), hold that the

After Virtue and the Rise of Postliberalism 101

law-giver should be fixed on the true good (cf. Milbank and Pabst 2016: 235, 240; Vermeule 2022: 29). They are open to the view that the true common good is the good of the most complete society, the city of God, and that it is therefore the task of the temporal power to guide persons towards that universal and complete common good. MacIntyre agrees with the former but not the latter (cf. 1999b: 207–208).

Comparing MacIntyre's positions to those held by prominent postliberals demonstrates how his thinking reinforces the results of the same dialectic he faced earlier. It exhibits his ambiguous account of liberalism. Contemporary postliberals attempt to decouple neutrality from the centralised state, asserting that the state, equipped with a better account of justice, can become an instrument to achieve the common good. MacIntyre, by contrast, regards the state as bound up with assumptions about the merits of centralisation and managerial expertise that cannot command legitimacy. Without the delegitimisation of managerial authority, the liberal political project persists. Just as with MacIntyre's rejoinders to his conservative and communitarian critics, so MacIntyrean rejoinders to postliberals show that their attitude toward the state affirms rather than negates an essential tenet of liberalism.

MacIntyre's account of what good should be pursued in common in the present situation, however, displays a different side of his thinking. To preserve rational enquiry and the goods obtained through rational debate, he affirms that tolerance and the preservation of pluralism are legitimate ends of government. Postliberals, by contrast, call these ends into question so that the law may be fixed towards a more complete account of the common good. Just as MacIntyre's most spirited critics on behalf of liberalism discovered, postliberals inspired by MacIntyre find he is more sympathetic to the norms associated with liberalism than he initially appears.

5.4 Overcoming Liberalism, Ancient and Modern

MacIntyre is cautious about breaking from norms associated with liberalism because, unlike postliberals, he does not think that, at the present time, liberalism can be replaced with something better. MacIntyre's provocative suggestions about how prior ages responded to proto-liberal dominance helps clarify what postliberalism would have to accomplish today, and why, on MacIntyre's terms, we should not expect to see a successful postliberalism emerge in the present.

MacIntyre portrays two historic encounters with versions of proto-liberalism. The first occurs in classical Athens, during the fifth and fourth centuries BCE. Following the lead of classicist Eric Havelock, MacIntyre

102   *Nathan Pinkoski*

holds that the teachings of the sophists and their effects resemble those of modern liberals (MacIntyre 1998b: 87, 392).[17] The sophists, sceptical of defining the good in terms of fulfilment of one's social role, emphasised, against traditional practices, the goods of individual effectiveness. They promised that these goods could achieve new forms of individual and communal success, but, lacking rational justification, their conception of human goods endorsed the pursuit of power, status and money. The goods of the sophists failed to unify Greece's fragmenting communities, intensifying division and conflict. Despite their failings and inconsistencies, however, most Greeks preferred to remain with the inconsistencies of the sophists; though some radicalised their theses to embrace wholeheartedly the pursuit of individual power, as Callicles, the proto-Nietzschean, does in Plato's *Gorgias* (MacIntyre 2007: 140). Despite the emergence of figures such as Socrates, Plato and Aristotle, who honed arguments to refute sophistic positions, the sophists continued to dominate Greek culture. The influence of Isocrates was greater than the influence of Socrates (MacIntyre 1988: 86–7). Only gradually did the competing tradition of the goods of excellence displace the sophists and inaugurate a post-sophistic age. MacIntyre grants that the superiority of the arguments that Socrates, Plato and especially Aristotle presented exposed the weaknesses of sophistry. Yet it is in retrospect that we see how the critical conversation bore fruit; only in the long run did their achievement lead to the downfall of sophistry.

This analogy is instructive for telling us what we cannot expect in the present. Today, no such tradition could displace the modern equivalent of sophistry, namely liberalism, because the liberal tradition and its opponents have grown too far apart. The traditions of the goods of excellence and the goods of effectiveness could engage with and criticise each other, as they shared a common source in the Homeric tradition. They both sought to answer the question, 'what kind of person shall I become?'; they both refused to separate the good from human desires; and they both presupposed teleology (MacIntyre 2007: 118).

But modern liberalism, informed by Kantian ethics, does not understand the task of ethical practice in that way (cf. MacIntyre 2007: 140). This is the significance of late mediaeval metaphysics, rejecting teleology to embrace voluntarism. That shift dismembers ethical practice from the common assumption that once informed debates about practical

---

[17] See Havelock 1957. Adkins 1960 also plays a role (MacIntyre 2007: 138–9). For Havelock, the liberal sophists are good and the illiberal Plato and Aristotle are bad. MacIntyre simply reverses Havelock. See also Perreau-Saussine 2005: 117. Cf. Strauss 1995: 26–64.

After Virtue and the Rise of Postliberalism   103

reasoning. The liberal tradition shares no common source with a tradition that could displace it, preventing rational debate. The only other extant tradition that shares the common source of metaphysical voluntarism, Nietzschean genealogy, intensifies and embraces the voluntaristic weaknesses of the liberal tradition. Unlike in classical Athens, the gap between liberalism and its alternatives is too great for the critical conversation to take place that would lead to the collapse of liberal tradition.

The second proto-liberal moment concerns the social, institutional situation of the late Middle Ages. At that time, it would seem that a tradition – Thomism – had emerged that synthesised the best insights of the two most important traditions of the period: Augustinianism and Aristotelianism. If, according to MacIntyre, Thomism is the best theory of practical reasoning to have emerged thus far, should we not expect this good theory to translate into good practice – as MacIntyre believes good theory does (1994b: 233–4; 1995b: 156; 1996: 235)? However, he believes this translation did not happen. Despite Aquinas's providing the theoretical resources to resolve the conflicts between Aristotelianism and Augustinianism and to integrate them, his theory was not embodied in the mainstream social practice of rational enquiry.

According to MacIntyre's account of the mediaeval period, Aquinas was a marginal and 'highly deviant' figure (2007: 178). His intellectual project was primarily thwarted by the institutional transformation of the mediaeval university. The late mediaeval curriculum abandoned the unified intellectual enquiry that had made the achievement of Aquinas possible. Instead, it opted for a new liberal arts programme that separated study into subjects studied without reference to each other, such as logic, ethics and metaphysics (MacIntyre 1990: 151; 2009a: 97–8; 2016: 93; D'Andrea 2006: 363). The university thus institutionalised a study of unified intellectual traditions, namely Aristotelianism and Augustinianism, which nonetheless broke these traditions apart according to the artificial divisions of the curriculum. Distinct and often incompatible approaches developed in each subject, with less and less conversation between these approaches taking place. The mediaeval university failed to reckon 'with insights and arguments of thinkers of widely different points of view' – a critical MacIntyrean benchmark for a good university (2013b: 213–14). This institutional failure encouraged fracture, conflict and the promulgation of rival forms of Augustinianism and Aristotelianism. Augustinians and Aristotelians retreated into compartmentalised discussions and stopped debating with their opponents. In short, the mediaeval university developed a form of compartmentalisation 'that foreshadows the compartmentalisation of later enquiry' (MacIntyre 1988: 206). This proto-liberal social and institutional order

104   *Nathan Pinkoski*

then gained advocates to justify it. The Augustinianism of Duns Scotus shut out possible Aristotelian developments of Augustinian theses (MacIntyre 1990: 152–4, 162). William of Ockham denied outright that theoretical enquiry has a unified goal or subject. For Ockham, rational enquiry is irreducibly heterogeneous (MacIntyre 1990: 158, 161–2; 2009a: 101–102; D'Andrea, 2006: 364). Ockham's stance mimics the intellectual justification for the modern situation. It entails that we cannot secure rational moral agreement – unity – and that we are resigned to widespread disagreement and heterogeneity (cf. MacIntyre 2007: 6; 2009a: 97–112).

MacIntyre's history teaches that even when a viable theory exists that could resolve the philosophical problems of other traditions and displace the defective ones, institutions have kept this theory marginal. MacIntyre's history of philosophy stresses Thomism's limited influence, even in the Catholic context. Interest in Thomism only revived in the late nineteenth century, with the 1879 publication of *Aeterni Patris* by Pope Leo XIII. But this marked a victory at the level of papal politics rather than a widespread intellectual and social transformation. Partly because of the limitations of a centralised papal project to promulgate Thomism and partly because of an undue focus by Thomists themselves on epistemological questions, the intellectual triumph of Thomistic theory did not take place (MacIntyre 1990: 72–8; 2009a: 151–64, 173–80). And because it did not triumph intellectually, its political influence remained marginal. Aquinas's subversion of Louis IX's political project, for example, did not stop the latter being a 'remarkably successful attempt' to expand royal control and extend centralised bureaucracy, which obscured Aquinas's legal and political theory (MacIntyre 1995c: 50).

So on MacIntyre's account, the one theory that has the capacity to replace liberalism has existed for centuries but has never managed to displace liberalism. On the contrary, it is liberalism that has displaced its rivals (Knight 1998b: 21). There has been no gradual reversal or change in this situation. For the immediate future, then, there is no reason to expect a rapid transformation of these institutions so that Thomism suddenly becomes politically mainstream. The preponderance of historical evidence indicates the persistence of liberal orders.

5.5   Conclusion: All Postliberalisms Must (for Now) Fail

The political project of *After Virtue*, to subvert and overcome liberalism's destructive social and political culture, is a postliberal project. Yet its appeal has been limited. Most of MacIntyre's critics – even the conservatives who admired MacIntyre – at heart disagreed with MacIntyre's

After Virtue and the Rise of Postliberalism 105

analysis that liberalism was an exhausted political tradition. The same is true of the ostensibly postliberal left. They hold hard to the Enlightenment's promise of universal emancipation. This, they concede, must involve the destruction of practices and traditions that claim authority. By contrast, MacIntyre defends the authority of practices and traditions, albeit with significant qualifications (Callinicos 2011: 75–8). As MacIntyre argues in *After Virtue*, the problem with Marxian leftism remains its theoretical failure to develop its own moral theory. Because Marxist humanism owes so much to Kantianism, it cannot shake itself free from liberal moral theory (Kolakowski 1978; MacIntyre 1998e: 34). Marxian-leftist postliberalism becomes an argument for ultra-liberalism, for greater fidelity to the autonomy principle. This failure makes leftists, just like liberals, subservient to the rule of wealth, status and power (MacIntyre 1998e: 36, 49; 2007: 262; 2016: 280).

What MacIntyre did not anticipate in *After Virtue* is that the effort to reconstruct the insights of Aristotle's ethics independent of the particularities of his politics, which would be capable of critiquing advanced capitalism, would eventually be taken up by those who completely rejected the left. Defending authoritative practices and traditions, rejecting Kantian and utilitarian ethics and denouncing the liberal tradition as a complete failure, these postliberals repudiate leftism as ultra-liberalism but also regard Anglo-American conservatism as a collaborator in the same liberal project. To replace liberalism, they offer a political agenda orientated towards achieving the common good. Does their project align with MacIntyrean postliberalism?

There are three important ways in which it does not. First, postliberals are much more favourable towards the modern political form – the centralised administrative state – than MacIntyre. Even postliberals critical of the modern state eschew MacIntyre's radical commitment to subverting it; they often defend the institutions of the mid-twentieth-century state. On this terrain, they are more liberal than MacIntyre, as he connects the institutions of the modern state more completely to modern liberalism. They stress a post-war rupture (which takes off sometime in the 1960s or 1970s) with a prior, better welfare and administrative state. MacIntyre does not. In the immediate triumphalism of the post-war scene, when the welfare state appeared both successful and benign, MacIntyre was already a revolutionary critic of it. His support for the Thomistic natural law tradition does not alter that.

The second divergence lies in the nature of the common good. Faced with critics who wanted to accuse him of promoting reactionary ideas, MacIntyre emphasised that he shared several liberal values, including toleration. For MacIntyre, law can teach what is good, but only in a

106   *Nathan Pinkoski*

qualified sense, when agreement as to what the good is has been secured. Because that agreement is not possible to achieve on a large scale, at the level of mass politics, he therefore affirms the separation of church and state, as well as state neutrality regarding which values to promote. This account of the common good clears MacIntyre of the charge of promoting reactionary politics, but apparently by affirming liberal politics. These efforts to clarify the political positions suggested in *After Virtue* are sometimes baffling and make his position less clear (Hibbs 2004: 367–72). Nevertheless, MacIntyre's motivation for endorsing these positions is that he posits an account of a more limited common good defined as a community of learning. But to maintain this high intellectualist goal – a goal that is possibly fantastical and impossible to achieve – requires a low but solid normative standard, which respects the freedom of the individual at the price of achieving more substantive projects. To learn, we must prevent the evil of domination and maintain openness to radically dissenting views. Despite MacIntyre's postliberal language, he has affirmed in substance an account of the common good that certain liberals also endorse (Perreau-Saussine 2005: 7–18).

The third divergence pertains to what lesson MacIntyre draws from the history of philosophy. MacIntyre's history emphasises conflict over the nature of the good. Conflict presents a problem to be solved: debate, followed by accord and agreement as well as the rejection of false accounts of what is good, precedes political decision and legislation. In this way, the ancient world eventually overcame and replaced the flawed proto-liberal tradition of the sophists. But the proto-liberalism of the late Middle Ages – not for MacIntyre a period of homogenisation but one of conflict and division (1995c: 41; 2007: 165) – could not be defeated. That period introduced the institutions that compartmentalised rational enquiry, thwarting robust debate between conflicting accounts and making accord and agreement impossible. Despite its superiority, Thomism could not gain a proper hearing in that setting. It had no control over the institutions. That is the same problem that faces any theoretical and practical challenge to liberalism today. *After Virtue* concludes that liberalism is likely to continue to be dominant for the foreseeable future. Even if postliberals could demonstrate that their political project is more feasible than the ultra-liberal pseudo-alternatives promoted by the left and right, there is no reason to believe that the situation established in past centuries will rapidly change. History does not predestine liberalism to permanent dominance, but it does suggest a very long-term dominance. Like the Thomas Aquinas of *After Virtue*, it appears that (for now, at least) postliberals must remain marginal and highly deviant.

6   *After Virtue* and Conservatism

David McPherson

Is *After Virtue* a conservative book? MacIntyre is sometimes *charged* with being a conservative (as if that were obviously a bad thing), or even with being a reactionary.[1] For his part, MacIntyre has been concerned to disclaim affiliation with conservatism. Nevertheless, despite his protestations, one can find strong conservative elements in his work, though these exist alongside unconservative, even radical elements. In this chapter I will identify and assess both the conservative and unconservative elements of *After Virtue*. In Section 6.1, I will offer an account of conservatism as I think it is best understood. In Section 6.2, I will use this account to identify conservative elements of *After Virtue*, focusing on MacIntyre's critique of what he calls 'the Enlightenment project'. In Section 6.3, I will discuss MacIntyre's anti-conservatism. While in some cases I will argue that he is more conservative than he allows, nevertheless there is one way in which he is especially unconservative: namely, in the predominant emphasis he gives to a repudiation of the present state of things. I will argue that this is in fact the most problematic aspect of his thought.

6.1   What Is Conservatism?

Conservatism is typically understood as a political philosophy or outlook. However, it can also be understood in broader terms as a *life-orientation*; that is, as a way one orientates and lives out one's life in relation to the world. Indeed, I think we cannot properly understand a conservative political outlook without understanding this broader life-orientation.

Conservatism, as a life-orientation, can be characterised as a disposition to conserve what is seen as good in the given world, and connected with this, it involves a cautiousness or hesitancy regarding change and, in

---

I thank Tom Angier and Ian James Kidd for helpful comments on earlier drafts of this chapter.

[1] See, e.g., Nussbaum 1989; Freytag 1994; Lilla 2016: 74–5; Blakely 2017.

108   *David McPherson*

some cases, a resistance to change, especially radical change. This does not mean that the conservative is opposed to change as such, or merely affirms the status quo. Indeed, the work of conservation will often require some change or reform; as Edmund Burke says about the political realm: 'A State without the means of some change is without the means of its conservation' (Burke 1999 [1790]: 108). But the conservative typically prefers gradual, piecemeal change when change is needed. When we talk about change here, it should be noted, we are concerned not with trivial change (such as a change of clothes), but rather with change in matters important to human well-being.

We can gain a better understanding of conservatism as a life-orientation by exploring the reasons why conservatives are cautious or hesitant regarding change, and in some cases resistant to change. I will discuss three main reasons.

6.1.1   *Recognising Human Limits*

Perhaps the most common reason that conservatives cite for being cautious or hesitant regarding change, particularly in complex human affairs, has to do with a recognition of epistemic and character limitations in human life. Otherwise put, conservatives often embrace a scepticism about the reach of human reason and a pessimism about the perfectibility of human nature (see Tosi and Warmke 2022: 580–81).

Human life involves good and bad things. In light of this, people are motivated to seek change because they hope to improve their condition; that is, they hope to enhance the good things and reduce the bad things. Conservatives will often take up this endeavour, but they do so cautiously, especially when the endeavour concerns complex human affairs (such as is the case with politics, economics and culture). The worry motivating this cautiousness is that in our efforts to improve our condition we may in fact make things worse: we may unnecessarily lose important good things in the effort to reduce what is bad. The conservative life-orientation thus expresses a certain risk aversion.[2] The conservative acknowledges that the best-laid schemes of human beings regarding complex human affairs often go awry because of our limited knowledge about the workings of these complex affairs and how they should be arranged. They also often go awry because of the character limitations inherent in human life, which are related to the fact that human beings

---

[2] When people speak colloquially about taking a 'conservative' approach, they often mean taking a less risky approach compared to some more risky alternative.

After Virtue and Conservatism

are a mixed bag, with good and bad tendencies.[3] This means we should not expect human beings to become perfect in virtue.

What are the implications of recognising epistemic and character limitations? To begin with, conservatives will embrace a *politics of imperfection* rather than a politics of perfection (see Quinton 1978).[4] While a politics of perfection puts forward a utopian ideal that exists nowhere except in the imagination ('utopia' literally means 'no place'), a politics of imperfection acknowledges that perfection in politics is not feasible, and it embraces somewhere in particular with all its imperfections: it seeks improvement where needed, but it recognises that we also need to find a way to be at home in the world amidst imperfection. A politics of imperfection therefore seeks a *good enough* condition and is especially concerned to avoid the worst evils. As an example of this politics of imperfection, consider Alexander Hamilton's defence of the US Constitution in *The Federalist* (Hamilton, Jay and Madison 2001 [1787–1788]). In *Federalist* No. 6 he says that we should reject those 'Utopian speculations' and 'idle theories' that promise us 'an exemption from the imperfections, the weaknesses, and the evils incident to society in every shape', and instead we should 'adopt as a practical maxim for the direction of our political conduct, that we, as well as the other inhabitants of the globe, are yet remote from the happy empire of perfect wisdom and perfect virtue'. In *Federalist* No. 9 Hamilton identifies the 'regular distribution of power into distinct departments; the introduction of legislative balances and checks; the institution of courts composed of judges, holding their offices during good behaviour; the representation of the people in the legislature, by deputies of their own election', as the 'means, and powerful means, by which the excellencies of republican government may be retained, and its imperfections lessened or avoided'.

Another implication of the conservative recognition of human limits, particularly epistemic limits, is an opposition to rationalistic or abstract theoretical approaches to human affairs and an affirmation of a *prudent traditionalism*. Speaking about the conservatism of the English (in contrast with the revolutionaries in France), Burke writes:

We are afraid to put men to live and trade each on his own private stock of reason; because we suspect that this stock in each man is small, and that the individuals would do better to avail themselves of the general bank and capital of nations, and of ages. Many of our men of speculation, instead of exploding general prejudices, employ their sagacity to discover the latent wisdom which prevails in them. If they

---

[3] As David Hume puts it, while we may have a 'particle of the dove' within us, this exists alongside 'elements of the wolf and serpent' (Hume 1975 [1751]: 271).

[4] In this paragraph I draw from McPherson 2022: 109–10, 121–2.

110   *David McPherson*

find what they seek, (and they seldom fail) they think it more wise to continue the prejudice, with the reason involved. (Burke 1999 [1790]: 182)[5]

Burke's appeal to 'prejudice' here is an appeal to inherited wisdom about how best to live that has been built up and handed down over the generations. Such inherited wisdom proves itself in the way that it has been shown to be reliable over the ages for navigating complex human affairs; in other words, it has shown itself to be 'tried-and-true'. As John Kekes puts it, conservatism 'values and aims to protect the tried and true; both together, because the tried alone may have little in its favor and much against it and because the true needs to be tried, and tried again, to be shown to be true' (Kekes 1998: 5). The appeal to inherited wisdom (the tried-and-true) shows a commitment to traditionalism. A *prudent* traditionalism is needed because it takes prudence to know how to apply inherited wisdom to present circumstance.[6]

In the realm of ethics, conservatives embrace 'traditional morality', which places emphasis on the importance of (1) character (i.e. the virtues) and responsibility, (2) associative duties (i.e. duties of loyalty to family, friends and fellow citizens, and duties of neighbourliness, including to strangers we come upon, as in the Parable of the Good Samaritan) and (3) absolute prohibitions rooted in a recognition of the sanctity of human life.[7] Traditional morality is often taken as the contrast case to supposedly 'enlightened' forms of morality that are said to have superseded it, such as utilitarianism and liberal Kantianism (i.e. autonomy-centred ethics).[8] In the terms of contemporary moral philosophy, traditional morality can be understood as an expression of an *anti-theory* approach to ethics, which builds up ethical understanding from concrete ethical experience rather than simply applying abstract principles.[9] Traditional morality seeks to attend to the common human fund of moral experience and conserve whatever is good in this experience, in line with Aristotle's method of beginning with common beliefs (*endoxa*) and seeking to preserve what is true in them (see Nussbaum 2001 [1986]: ch. 8). Philosophy has a role to play, but its role consists primarily in

---

[5] Similarly, Quinton writes: 'political wisdom ... is not to be found in the theoretical speculations of isolated thinkers but in the historically accumulated social experience of the community as a whole. It is embodied, above all, in ... traditional customs and institutions [and in people with] extensive practical experience of politics' (Quinton 1978: 16–17). See also Michael Oakeshott, 'Rationalism in Politics', in Oakeshott 1991 (1962).

[6] For more on the role of prudence in conservative political thought, see Hörcher 2020.

[7] See McPherson 2017, which I have drawn from in this discussion of traditional morality.

[8] See, e.g., Dworkin 1994; Singer 1995.

[9] On anti-theory in ethics, see Williams 1985: esp. chs 1, 5, 6, 10; Clarke and Simpson 1989.

After Virtue and Conservatism

overcoming inconsistencies, clarifying and articulating our inchoate sense of things and offering justification. The sort of 'theory' that traditional morality is against is that which seeks to offer a decision procedure (the principle of utility, the universalisation requirement, etc.) that prescinds from concrete moral experience and any particular tradition-informed moral community.[10]

A particularly problematic feature of such moral theories is their reductionism: they reduce the complexity of our ordinary moral experience, especially regarding substantive moral judgements about the various good and bad things that help to define for us the good life. They do so by offering a basic principle or decision procedure that is supposed to take precedence in the moral life. However, they do not prescind entirely from substantive moral judgements, since accepting the precedence of their basic principle or decision procedure requires a substantive moral judgement about, for example, the goodness of universal benevolence (in the case of utilitarianism) or the importance of autonomy (in the case of liberal Kantianism).

Granting these are good things, why think they are the only good things or that they should take precedence? According to traditional morality, benevolence (or compassion) is a virtue, but not the only one. There are other virtues such as loyalty and justice with which it must be made consistent. Likewise, in certain respects autonomy is indeed a good, though it should be constrained by other goods, such as virtue and the sanctity of human life, and the value of autonomy is itself derivative from the goodness of freely choosing for the good. Thus defenders of traditional morality see supposedly more enlightened forms of morality as mere 'fragments' torn from the larger whole of traditional morality. As C. S. Lewis puts it in his defence of traditional morality (or the Tao, as he calls it):

What purport to be new systems [of value] ... all consist of fragments from the Tao itself, arbitrarily wrenched from their context in the whole and then swollen to madness in their isolation, yet still owing to the Tao and to it alone such validity as they possess. ... The rebellion of new ideologies against the Tao is a rebellion of the branches against the tree: if the rebels could succeed they would find that they have destroyed themselves. (Lewis 1944: 43–4)[11]

I will return to this 'fragments thesis' when discussing *After Virtue*.

---

[10] This leaves room for saying that traditional morality can count as a 'theory' in a non-offending sense; indeed, it is often developed as such in what is known as 'natural law theory' (see Angier 2021).

[11] Cf. Burke: 'We know that *we* have made no discoveries, and we think that no discoveries are to be made, in morality' (Burke 1999 [1790]: 181, emphasis in original).

112   *David McPherson*

For now, having briefly discussed conservative approaches to politics and ethics, I want to mention a point that is relevant to conservative economics, which is also connected with the conservative recognition of epistemic limits: namely, there is a general preference for decentralised, self-correcting spontaneous (i.e. organic) order over centralised, planned order in complex human affairs (such as in economics, politics and culture), and this means that conservatives have a general preference for free-market economies over command economies (see Scruton 2006). Indeed, free-market economies have proven themselves to be tried-and-true in their ability to create prosperity and reduce poverty, while the same cannot be said for command economies, which lack the efficiency provided by the price signals of free-market economies.

At the same time, conservatives will often feel ambivalence about free-market economies because their 'creative destruction' (Schumpeter 2008 [1942]) can undermine traditional ways of life and forms of belonging when left unconstrained by considerations of the human good (not to mention that large corporations overall have hardly proven themselves to be friendly to traditional values; see Deneen 2018b). Indeed, conservatives will sympathise with Marx's essentially conservative lament about the effects of capitalism: 'All fixed, fast-frozen relations, with their train of ancient and venerable prejudices and opinions, are swept away, all new-formed ones become antiquated before they can ossify. All that is solid melts into air, all that is holy is profaned' (Marx and Engels 2000 [1848]: 248). Surely 'all' is too strong here, but the basic sentiment is readily appreciated by conservatives (see Kolozi 2017). Free-market economies encourage us to be what Wendell Berry calls 'boomers' rather than 'stickers': 'boomers' are 'those who pillage and run', who want 'to make a killing and end up on Easy Street', and they are 'motivated by greed, the desire for money, property, and therefore power'; by contrast, 'stickers' are 'those who settle, and love the life they have made and the place they have made it in', and they are 'motivated by affection, by such love for a place and its life that they want to preserve and remain in it' (Berry 2012: 10–11). 'Conservative' is another name for a 'sticker'. Conservatives will therefore endorse constrained forms of free-market economies with the aim of promoting the common good and their way of life within a particular place.

This discussion of being a 'sticker' brings us to the second reason conservatives can be hesitant and, in some cases, resistant with regard to change.

6.1.2   *Love and Attachment*

The conservative is often hesitant and, in some cases, resistant with regard to change for reasons of love and attachment: we want to hold

After Virtue and Conservatism

on to that which we love (or value) and to which we are attached. As Roger Scruton puts it: 'Conservatism is the philosophy of attachment. We are attached to the things we love, and wish to protect them against decay' (Scruton 2014: 29). And we should add: we wish to protect them from destruction. Also consider Michael Oakeshott:

> The general characteristics of [the conservative] disposition ... centre upon a propensity to use and to enjoy what is available rather than to wish for or to look for something else; to delight in what is present rather than what was or what may be. Reflection may bring to light an appropriate gratefulness to what is available, and consequently the acknowledgement of a gift or an inheritance from the past; but there is no mere idolizing what is past and gone. What is esteemed is the present ... on account of its familiarity: ... [Here one is disposed to say:] *Stay with me because I am attached to you.* ... In short, it is a disposition appropriate to a man who is acutely aware of having something to lose which he has learned to care for. (Oakeshott 1991 [1962]: 408, emphasis in original)

John Kekes makes a similar point when he notes that in seeking to be understood conservatives can make appeal to a natural conservatism that all human beings share: 'If there were beings who did not enjoy having what they valued and were not afraid of losing it, they would not be recognizably human. The [conservative] attitude then is basic to human psychology, but it need not be conscious or articulate.' However, it is when we become aware of a threat to the good things to which we are attached that such natural conservatism 'must be transformed into a reflective one that can meet it' (Kekes 1998: 5–6).

But the question arises: why prefer a present good thing to which we are attached if it could be replaced with some other good thing that might be better in certain ways? Consider G. A. Cohen's defence of the conservative attitude that is concerned with conserving 'existing value'. This attitude, he says, 'exhibits a bias in favor of retaining what is of value, even in the face of replacing it by something of greater value' (Cohen 2013: 149).[12] He distinguishes between three aspects of this conservative attitude: (1) valuing and seeking to preserve that which is intrinsically valuable (i.e. 'particular valuing'); (2) valuing and seeking to preserve that which is personally valued (i.e. 'personal valuing'); and (3) 'accepting the given'. I focus on (1) and (2) here, though I will discuss (3) in my own terms in the Section 6.1.3.

In the case of 'particular valuing', Cohen says: 'a person values something as the particular valuable thing that it is, and not merely for the value that resides in it' (148). The key point is that 'we devalue the valuable things we have if we keep them only so long as nothing even

---

[12] In the following paragraph, when page numbers alone are provided in-text, they are for Cohen 2013.

114   *David McPherson*

slightly more valuable comes along': 'Valuable things command a certain loyalty' (153). Although Cohen speaks of valuing *something* here (which can include valuing *somewhere*; that is, 'a place and its life', as Berry puts it), his point applies just as much to valuing *someone*. Furthermore, once we experience such loyalty we are then in the realm of 'personal valuing', where 'a person values something [or someone] because of the special relation ... to that person' (148); namely, because of their attachment. Cohen goes on to say: 'We are attached to particular things [or persons] because we need to belong to something [or someone], and we therefore need some things [or persons] to belong to us' (168). Indeed, a conservative will acknowledge identity-constituting forms of belonging and attachment, which we cannot forgo without ceasing to be ourselves. In other words, conservatives embrace what Michael Sandel calls an 'encumbered' conception of the self (see Sandel 1984).

The human need for belonging also takes an existential form as a need to be at home in the world, and this brings us to the third reason for the conservative attitude towards change.

6.1.3   *Becoming at Home in the World*

The first two reasons for being hesitant or cautious regarding change – and in some cases resistant to it – are commonly voiced by conservative thinkers though not always brought together. However, the third reason for the conservative attitude towards change has often not been properly recognised, but I believe it is the most important and fundamental. It concerns our orientation towards the given, which we can call an 'existential stance'. The given here is of two general kinds: the cultural-political given and the natural given. The cultural-political given is that which human beings have built up and handed on over the generations, and it includes political institutions and moral precepts along with achievements of art, literature, philosophy and religion as well as the forms of belonging (families, neighbourhoods, nations, etc.) we find ourselves in. The natural given includes the wider natural world as well as our human nature and our own natural talents and abilities.

As I have argued elsewhere,[13] a conservative life-orientation should seek to discover, appreciate, affirm and conserve what is good in the world *as it is* or *as given*, and one should do so in order to be *at home* in the given world as far as possible. The aim here is to overcome the alienation or not-at-home-ness that is fundamental to the human

---

[13] See McPherson 2019, which I draw on in this section.

After Virtue and Conservatism

condition due to its connection with the emergence of rational self-consciousness. Unlike non-rational animals who cannot be alienated from their environment, we are tasked with finding our place in the world and thereby overcoming alienation. This means discovering a meaningful life-orientation. A key issue that must be addressed here is the problem of cosmodicy, which is the problem of justifying life in the world as meaningful and worthwhile in the face of evil and suffering.

Given this concern with overcoming alienation, the conservative will therefore be resistant to efforts to change things that arise out of existential stances that emphasise repudiation of the given world and so exacerbate the experience of alienation or not-at-home-ness. One such stance is that of the radical progressive who repudiates the given world in light of some imagined ideal future world. Another such stance is that of the person who repudiates the given world in light of some supposed 'golden age' of the past. By contrast, for the conservative there is an emphasis on affirming and inhabiting the present. We saw this in Oakeshott's description of the conservative disposition as centring on 'a propensity to use and to enjoy what is available rather than to wish for or to look for something else; to delight in what is present rather than what was or what may be', though he acknowledges that reflection 'may bring to light an appropriate gratefulness to what is available, and consequently the acknowledgement of a gift or an inheritance from the past; but there is no mere idolizing what is past and gone'.

The radical progressive and the golden ageist agree in finding the given world to be a disappointment, which raises the problem of cosmodicy. For the radical progressive this can be answered positively only insofar as we see ourselves as moving towards realising some ideal future. Likewise, for the golden ageist we must see ourselves as recovering some ideal past. But the danger in both cases is that we will despair over attaining or even approximating the ideal given that the world as it is will often fall drastically short of the ideal. The conservative, by contrast, aims to address the problem of cosmodicy not by attempting to realise some ideal future or to recover some ideal past, but rather by seeking to discover, appreciate, affirm and conserve what is good in the given world, which enables one to find one's way to an affirmation that life in the world is good and worthwhile and to feel at home within it.

The conservative can and should acknowledge that there is a great deal of evil in the world that should not be affirmed and indeed should be fought against precisely because of the good that is affirmed. For instance, affirming that human life is a 'gift' to be cherished, promoted and protected means that one must stand opposed to what threatens it.

116 *David McPherson*

Thus the conservative will undertake actions aimed at removing such threats, which are done precisely in order to conserve what is good. However, the conservative also believes that evil will never be fully eradicated from our finite, earthly condition and yet the given world is worth affirming.

The crucial point is about our orientation towards the given world. We can state what is at issue here in terms of the following question: is our basic outlook on the world-as-it-is centred on affirmation or repudiation, yes-saying or no-saying? These are not mutually exclusive options, but the question concerns the emphasis of a particular outlook. The conservative, in contrast to the radical progressive and the golden ageist, is fundamentally affirmative: there is an emphasis that the world, as it is and in spite of its evils and imperfections, is meaningful and worth affirming; that is, the given world as a whole is good and is a source of joy and fulfilment, even if not everything about it is good and even if there are ways, whether minor or major, that it should be made better. Radical progressivism and golden ageism are of course not without affirmation, but the focus of affirmation is on an ideal future or an ideal past by which one critiques and seeks a thoroughgoing change of the present. Their attitude towards the given world emphasises repudiation and a sense of indignation. The conservative, by contrast, first seeks to count his or her blessings, to take stock of what is good about the given world, before figuring out how to make it better. There is an emphasis on gratitude or appreciation, which enables one to become at home in the world.

In the foregoing I have identified three reasons for why conservatives are cautious and sometimes resistant with regard to change, which have to do with (1) recognising human limits, (2) love and attachment and (3) becoming at home in the world. It is possible that one could affirm any one of these three reasons and be considered a conservative, but conservatism in the fullest sense, in my view, affirms all three. I will now turn to discuss the conservative elements of MacIntyre's *After Virtue*, and then after that I will discuss the unconservative elements.

6.2 MacIntyre's Conservatism

MacIntyre begins *After Virtue* with the 'disquieting suggestion' that the language of morality in the modern world is in a state of 'grave disorder' such that what we possess 'are the fragments of a conceptual scheme, parts which now lack those contexts from which their significance derived', and so 'we have – very largely, if not entirely – lost our comprehension, both theoretical and practical, [of] morality' (MacIntyre 2007

After Virtue and Conservatism 117

[1981/1984]: 2; see also 54–5, 59–60).[14] Here MacIntyre endorses a 'fragments thesis' about our contemporary moral predicament that is akin to what C. S. Lewis endorses when he says (as cited earlier): 'What purport to be new systems [of value] ... all consist of fragments from the Tao itself, arbitrarily wrenched from their context in the whole and then swollen to madness in their isolation.' MacIntyre does not acknowledge the influence of Lewis here, though perhaps it is second-hand, since he does acknowledge the influence of Elizabeth Anscombe (53), who puts forward a similar fragments thesis, describing modern secular conceptions of obligation as 'survivals' from an earlier theistic conception of ethics.[15] She too does not acknowledge the influence of Lewis, but it is plausible to think there might have been an influence, since both were at Oxford at the same time, and they also partook in a famous debate (see Lipscomb 2022: 145–8).

Like Lewis, MacIntyre is also concerned with defending a form of traditional morality, which he calls 'the tradition of the virtues', against supposedly enlightened forms of morality that are said to supersede it. Indeed, central to MacIntyre's overarching argument in *After Virtue* is a critique of 'the Enlightenment project', which sought to provide a rational vindication for morality apart from any teleological conception of the human good and any divine authority, and which brought us moral theories such as the various versions of utilitarianism and Kantianism that seek to offer a decision procedure that prescinds from concrete moral experience and any particular tradition-informed moral community. The Enlightenment project is precisely the sort of rationalistic or abstract theoretical approach to human affairs that we have seen that conservatives oppose. MacIntyre argues convincingly that it failed because of its inability to secure rational agreement (evidenced by the interminable debate between a great variety of conflicting moral viewpoints). The result of this failure, he contends, is the rise of an 'emotivist' culture where the appearance of rational argument masks what are in fact attempts to manipulate others in service of one's arbitrary preferences. This emotivist culture is what MacIntyre had in mind when he spoke of the grave disorder of modern moral discourse.

The emotivist culture encourages a certain understanding of the self, which MacIntyre calls 'the emotivist self'. This is what Sandel calls 'the

---

[14] In what follows when page numbers alone are provided in-text they are for MacIntyre 2007 (1981/1984).

[15] See G. E. M. Anscombe, 'Modern Moral Philosophy' (1958), in Anscombe 1981: 26, 30–31, 33.

118   *David McPherson*

unencumbered self', which prizes individual autonomy such that what matters most is not the ends we choose but the capacity for choice itself, and where the self is understood as independent of any binding loves and loyalties, rather than as constituted by them, as with 'the encumbered self', which I said the conservative affirms. MacIntyre writes of the emotivist (unencumbered) self that it 'cannot be simply or unconditionally identified with *any* particular moral attitude or point of view ... just because of the fact that its judgments are in the end criterionless' (31, emphasis in original). To be a moral agent on this view, MacIntyre says, is 'to be able to stand back from any and every situation in which one is involved, from any and every characteristic one may possess, and to pass judgment on it from a purely universal and abstract point of view that is totally detached from all social particularity' (31–2). The self, so understood, 'has no necessary social content and no necessary social identity', and so it can 'be anything, can assume any role or take any point of view, because it *is* in and for itself nothing' (32, emphasis in original). MacIntyre later writes: 'the price paid for liberation from what appeared to be the external authority of traditional morality was the loss of any authoritative content from the would-be moral utterances of the newly autonomous agent. Each moral agent now spoke unconstrained by the externalities of divine law, natural teleology, or hierarchical authority; but why should anyone else now listen to him?' (68).

So MacIntyre identifies the symptom of a problem, namely the grave disorder of modern moral discourse (the emotivist culture), and he also diagnoses the problem as resulting from the failure of the Enlightenment project. What remedy then does he propose? The answer is: a recovery of the tradition of the virtues. MacIntyre offers a 'socially teleological account' of the virtues where they are understood in terms of their role in practices, traditions and the narrative order of a human life. According to this account, the virtues are first of all needed in order to achieve goods internal to practices (e.g. productive crafts, artistic activity, intellectual activity, games and the making and sustaining of family life and political life) through which our 'human powers to achieve excellence, and human conceptions of the ends and goods involved, are systematically extended' (187). Secondly, the virtues are also needed to sustain our 'narrative quests' in which we seek, along with those others with whom we share in community, an answer to the question: what is the good for our lives as a whole? Thirdly, because the starting points for our enquiry are always provided by our communities and their particular histories, which constitute the larger narratives wherein we live out our individual narratives, the virtues are needed to sustain a tradition; that is, 'an historically

After Virtue and Conservatism 119

extended, socially embodied argument' about the nature of the good life for human beings (219–23).[16]

Here we see MacIntyre adopt an 'anti-theory' approach to ethics, which I said conservatives adopt and which builds up ethical understanding from concrete ethical experience rather than simply applying abstract principles. We see this in MacIntyre's emphasis on the importance of cultivating the virtues within the context of practices for understanding and realising goods internal to practices. We also see here that MacIntyre accepts a prudent traditionalism, which relies on the 'tried-and-true'. He writes:

A practice involves standards of excellence and obedience to rules as well as the achievement of goods. To enter a practice is to accept the authority of those standards and the inadequacy of my own performance as judged by them. It is to subject my own attitudes, choices, preferences and tastes to the standards which currently and partially define the practice. Practices ... have a history ... Thus the standards are not themselves immune from criticism, but nonetheless we cannot be initiated into a practice without accepting the authority of the best standards realized so far. (190)

In other words, practices are situated within traditions, which, MacIntyre notes, 'never exist in isolation [from] larger social traditions' (221). An important point here is that against the Enlightenment project MacIntyre affirms the necessary situatedness of ethical enquiry, and against the unencumbered conception of the self he affirms a narrative conception of the self that is constituted by social and historical situatedness. He writes:

I am never able to seek the good or exercise the virtues only *qua* individual ... [we] all approach our own circumstances as bearers of a particular social identity. I am someone's son or daughter, ... I belong to this clan, that tribe, this nation. Hence what is good for me has to be the good for one who inhabits these roles. As such, I inherit from the past of my family, my city, my tribe, my nation, a variety of debts, inheritances, rightful expectations and obligations. These constitute the given of my life, my moral starting point. This is in part what gives my life its own moral particularity. (220)

MacIntyre notes that this sort of perspective is likely to appear alien to someone who inhabits the standpoint of modern individualism (exemplified in the emotivist, unencumbered self): 'From the standpoint of [that] individualism I am what I myself choose to be. I can always, if I wish to, put in question what are taken to be the merely contingent social features

---

[16] See McPherson 2020: 14–17 for further discussion of MacIntyre's 'socially teleological account' of the virtues.

120 *David McPherson*

of my existence' (220). By contrast, from the standpoint of the narrative (encumbered) self, MacIntyre says: '[The] story of my life is always embedded in the story of those communities from which I derive my identity. I am born with a past; and to try to cut myself off from that past, in the individualist mode, is to deform my present relationships' (221). Indeed, it is also to deform oneself.

All of this sounds very much in line with my account of conservatism in Section 6.1. So why not regard MacIntyre as a conservative full stop? To understand why not, we need to consider MacIntyre's own professed anti-conservatism.

6.3   MacIntyre's Anti-conservatism

We see MacIntyre's concern to disclaim affiliation with conservatism (lest he be charged with it) in the way in which he contrasts his appeal to tradition with what he regards as a 'Burkean' conception of tradition. He writes:

We are apt to be misled here by the ideological uses to which the concept of a tradition has been put by conservative political theorists. Characteristically such theorists have followed Burke in contrasting tradition with reason and the stability of tradition with conflict. Both contrasts obfuscate. For all reasoning takes places within the context of some traditional mode of thought, transcending through criticism and invention the limitations of what had hitherto been reasoned in that tradition ... Moreover when a tradition is in good order it is always partially constituted by an argument about the goods the pursuit of which gives to that tradition its particular point and purpose. ... Traditions, when vital, embody continuities of conflict. Indeed when a tradition become Burkean, it is always dying or dead. (221–2)

Since MacIntyre does not cite any specific conservative political theorists besides Burke, one might suspect that what we are dealing with here is a caricature of conservatism. I think this is indeed the case. MacIntyre gives us a picture of Burkean conservatism as being anti-reason, homogeneous (not allowing conflict) and simply seeking to preserve the status quo. However, none of these characterisations are true with respect to Burke. He does not oppose tradition to reason, though, as we saw earlier, he thinks our 'private stock of reason' is small, and so rather than depend on this private stock alone, we do better to avail ourselves of 'the general bank and capital of nations, and of ages'; that is, we should avail ourselves of the wisdom of tradition, which is found in what Burke calls 'prejudice'. When we come to understand this wisdom, Burke says, we should 'continue the prejudice, with the reason involved'. Burke also endorses a role for conflict and debate in determining how best to live;

After Virtue and Conservatism 121

for instance, he was in fact one of the early defenders of contending political parties (see Burke 1999 [1770]). Furthermore, Burke does not simply seek to preserve the status quo and so promote a static social order; as we saw earlier, he says: 'A State without the means of some change is without the means of its conservation.' Indeed, on my account of conservatism, conservatives will often seek improvement, promoting the good and avoiding the bad as best as one can. However, they will do so *cautiously*, especially when the endeavour concerns complex human affairs such as politics, economics and culture, since without this cautiousness we may in fact make things worse.

When MacIntyre speaks of conservatism he seems to have in mind the sort of 'conservatism' that was in fashion in the 1980s; namely, what might be called Reagan–Thatcher 'conservatism', which is really a kind of liberalism that endorses unfettered capitalism, though with a few nods to traditional values. We can see this when MacIntyre writes: 'modern conservatives are for the most part engaged in conserving only older rather than later versions of liberal individualism. Their own core doctrine is as liberal and as individualist as that of self-avowed liberals' (222). We also see this view of conservatism expressed in MacIntyre's primary political conclusion in *After Virtue*, which is that we should reject the modern liberal order due to its individualism and acquisitiveness, along with its inability to secure agreement on the nature of justice and the common good. MacIntyre writes:

This does not mean that there are not many tasks only to be performed in and through government which still require performing: the rule of law, so far as it is possible in a modern state, has to be vindicated, injustice and unwarranted suffering have to be dealt with, generosity has to be exercised, and liberty has to be defended, in ways that are sometimes only possible through the use of governmental institutions. But each particular task, each particular responsibility has to be evaluated on its own merits. Modern systematic politics, whether liberal, conservative, radical or socialist, simply has to be rejected from a standpoint that owes genuine allegiance to the tradition of the virtues; for modern politics itself expresses in its institutional forms a systematic rejection of that tradition. (255)

What MacIntyre encourages then is a politics of local community that is also a politics of resistance to the corrosive influences of the liberal order. 'What matters at this stage', he writes, 'is the construction of local forms of community within which civility and the intellectual and moral life can be sustained through the new dark ages which are already upon us ... We are waiting not for a Godot, but for another – doubtless very different – St. Benedict' (263).

Now, the endeavour to construct and sustain communities of virtue in the face of threats to such a way of life is a quintessentially conservative endeavour, and it is certainly much more recognisably conservative than the Reagan–Thatcher 'conservatism' that MacIntyre identifies as being in fact a form of 'liberal individualism', albeit with a few nods to traditional values. But this suggests that MacIntyre recognises that this is not really conservatism properly understood. As I have said, conservatives will often feel ambivalence about free-market economies. On the one hand, they will certainly prefer free-market economies to command economies because of their general preference for decentralised, self-correcting spontaneous order over centralised, planned order and given that free-market economies have been proven to create prosperity and reduce poverty. On the other hand, conservatives will also worry about the way in which free-market economies can undermine traditional ways of life and forms of belonging, and so will want constraints on the free market. Notably, this conservative form of modern politics does not express a systematic rejection of the tradition of the virtues.

If conservatism is understood in this way, as it should be, then MacIntyre is much closer to being a full-blown conservative. He is in fact in good company as a Marxist who ended up moving in a conservative direction; other instances include G. A. Cohen (cited earlier), Christopher Lasch, Eugene Genovese, Leszek Kołakowski, James Burnham and George Orwell. Sometimes this is explained in terms of being 'mugged by reality', given feasibility problems for Marxism, and given the atrocities of the Soviet Union. Furthermore, while there are important differences between Marxism and conservatism, there are also affinities between them, such as opposition to liberal individualism and an ambivalence about the changes unleashed by modernity. Thus it is not altogether surprising to see such movements towards conservatism, especially when one becomes disillusioned with Marxism as a concrete political programme.[17]

So MacIntyre is much closer to being a full-blown conservative than he allows. However, there is an important way in which he is decidedly unconservative: namely, in his golden ageism, which is expressed in the title *After Virtue*, suggesting that there was a golden age of virtue, but which is now behind us. A conservative will find this posture just as problematic as utopianism, since, as stated earlier, both emphasise repudiation rather than affirmation of the present state of things and so exacerbate the experience of alienation or not-at-home-ness.

---

[17] I am indebted to discussions on social media for helping me to clarify my thoughts on this matter. For a helpful discussion of MacIntyre's disillusionment with Marxism, see Knight 2019: esp. 82, 94.

After Virtue and Conservatism

One of the main criticisms of MacIntyre's *After Virtue* is in fact that it expresses a problematic nostalgia for a bygone age that never existed, since there has always been moral disagreement, virtue and vice and inarticulacy about the ethical life (see, e.g., Nussbaum 1989). MacIntyre responds to this nostalgia charge in the prologue to the third edition of *After Virtue*:

> Because I understand the tradition of the virtues to have arisen within and to have been first adequately articulated in the Greek, especially the Athenian *polis*, and because I have stressed the ways in which that tradition flourished in the European middle ages, I have been accused of nostalgia and of idealizing the past. But there is, I think, not a trace of this in the text. What there is is an insistence on our need to learn from some aspects of the past, by understanding our contemporary selves and our contemporary moral relationships in the light afforded by a tradition that enables us to overcome the constraints on such self-knowledge that modernity, especially advanced modernity, imposes. We are all of us inescapably inhabitants of advanced modernity, bearing its social and cultural marks. (xi)

It is surely incorrect to say that there is 'not a trace' of nostalgia in the text. However, it is true that MacIntyre is not suggesting that we simply seek a return to some golden age that is thought to have existed in the past, which he rightly sees as impossible. Nonetheless, the impossibility of return can in fact be part of the appeal of golden ageism, just as the unrealisability of utopia can be part of the appeal of utopianism, since both provide a vantage point (even if only in the imagination) from which to critique and repudiate the present state of things (including our political, economic and cultural conditions).[18] This appeals to those who would like to see themselves as prophets of their age and want to pronounce critical judgement upon it by, for instance, starkly declaring it to be a 'new dark age' that can be resisted only through constructing and sustaining small neo-Benedictine communities of virtue.

As I have said, the endeavour to construct and sustain communities of virtue in the face of threats to such a way of life is a quintessentially conservative endeavour, and I think this should be endorsed. However, what is problematic from a conservative viewpoint is the background framing in terms of a declinist narrative where we have moved from a golden age of virtue to a dark age of moral confusion and vice. To begin with, all those who affirm what C. S. Lewis calls 'the Tao' – which he also calls traditional morality or the natural moral law – should agree with Charles Taylor in his response to MacIntyre when he says that we should

---

[18] A point along these lines about the unrealisability of utopia is made in Scruton 2010: 69–70.

124   *David McPherson*

not take modern rejections of the tradition of the virtues at face value and regard our age as being 'after virtue'; rather, we should recognise that these rejectors 'will always be in truth more "Aristotelian" than they believe, surreptitiously relying on notions like "virtue" and "the good life", even while they repudiate them on the level of theory' (Taylor 1994: 22). What we need, then, is to bring out these rival visions of the good life and make a case for which is best.

The conservative will be sceptical of both declinist and progressivist narratives that offer us a Manichaean contrast between an age of darkness and an age of light, which seem to have the ideological function of reinforcing political power and/or a self-serving function in puffing up one's self-image as being on the side of light against the darkness. The conservative will instead see every age, like human nature itself, as a mixed bag, containing both good and bad. We can see much good that has come about in the modern world, but which often also comes with problematic aspects: for instance, modern democracy allows for people to have a voice in their government, but it also allows for greater disagreement; modern freedom counters oppressive government action, but it can also encourage a problematic ideal of autonomy that is opposed to the life of virtue; and modern capitalism has reduced poverty around the globe, while at the same time it has increased economic inequality and created environmental problems. For the conservative, the task in this age, as in every age, is to discover, appreciate, affirm, conserve and promote the good in the given world and to reduce the bad as best as we can, while acknowledging that there is no utopia to be realised or golden age to which we can return. What matters most is the orientation we bring to this task: to recall what I said earlier, the conservative first seeks to count his or her blessings, to take stock of what is good about the given world, before figuring out how to make it better, and it is this emphasis on gratitude or appreciation that enables one to become at home in the world amidst its imperfections.

7 *After Virtue* as a Real Utopia

Jason Blakely

Forty years since its first publication, Alasdair MacIntyre's *After Virtue* still does not lack for brilliantly energised, philosophically dazzled readers. At present it belongs to a small group of the most dynamic philosophical treatises of the last half-century. Not only did *After Virtue* spectacularly revive virtue ethics with a creativity and scope missing from nearly all other such contemporary defences, but simultaneously it offered a teleological basis for resisting the hegemony of positivism and naturalism in the human sciences (Blakely 2016). As if these accomplishments in ethics and philosophy of social science were not enough, in political theory *After Virtue* fuelled the critique of proceduralist liberalism, thereby inspiring prominent thinkers from highly heterogeneous ideological perspectives (D'Andrea 2006; Knight 2007; Blackledge and Davidson 2008; Deneen 2016; 2018a; Dreher 2017; Lilla 2018). If – as the ancient Greeks believed – theory is a form of sight, then *After Virtue* undoubtedly enhanced our vision and illuminated spaces that otherwise would have remained murky.

In the present chapter I do not pretend to shave off more than a sliver of the insight offered by MacIntyre's brilliant book. My limited aim is two-fold: first, to cast doubt on the reduction of *After Virtue* to a reactionary, illiberal tract; and second, to suggest it might alternatively be read as offering resources for the utopian humanist and ethical socialist tradition, albeit in ways that go beyond it (Holmes 1993; Lilla 2016: xii, 74–5). Indeed, my view is not that *After Virtue* is simply a left-wing tract. To the contrary, it offers sharply critical alternatives to contemporary left-wing socialism's tendency to slide into structuralism, technocracy, abstract utopian ideals and a neglect of the central role of virtue and tradition in politics.

In Section 7.1, I critically reconstruct reactionary readings of *After Virtue*, which stress themes like the inexorable moral decline of liberalism and the call for traditionalists to isolate themselves in small communities of virtue. As part of this, I highlight dilemmas facing reactionary readings of MacIntyre's political thought. In Section 7.2, I interpret *After Virtue* as

126   Jason Blakely

instead echoing the young MacIntyre's search for a humanistic socialism that rejected Marxism as well as any abstract idealism. This section presents MacIntyre's *After Virtue* as resolving certain dilemmas that face orthodox Marxism and continue to vex the modern socialist tradition.

To be clear, I do not offer an argument about MacIntyre's own self-understanding (a task for the historian of thought and something upon which MacIntyre himself can opine with far greater authority). Rather, I hope to illuminate the sheer philosophical and hermeneutic richness of *After Virtue* by making plausible an alternative reading to the reactionary, illiberal one that is prominent among a number of both MacIntyre's critics and admirers. As part of this, I also hope to make clear to readers on the left that they have not taken sufficient note of *After Virtue* as both a resource and a corrective to their politics.

None of this is to say that *After Virtue* is straightforwardly a treatise fitting the left–right spectrum. On the contrary, part of the brilliance of MacIntyre's book is that it uncovers genuinely original philosophical ground that remains in some senses beyond our constrained ideological map of the contemporary world. My intention is not to replace one error (equating *After Virtue* with right-wing politics) with another (equating it with left-wing politics). Instead, I wish to see a greater appreciation of the plural political possibilities stemming from thoughtfully reading *After Virtue* – a testament to its enduring genius. And who more than MacIntyre has shown us that all great ethical-political texts eventually inspire rival readings?

7.1   Reactionary Readings of *After Virtue*

A number of high-profile critics of MacIntyre have assumed his political thought is reactionary. For example, Stephen Holmes (1993: 88) dubbed *After Virtue* an 'antiliberal catechism' that is 'hostile to Enlightenment universalism', while Mark Lilla (2016: xii) identified MacIntyre as a source for the rise of a radically nostalgic politics that rejects modernity in favour of a purportedly earlier, 'happy, well-ordered state'. Where conservatives advocate gradualism and cautious reform of the status quo, Lilla argues that reactionaries instead seek revolutionary change in order to restore a past order of moral harmony and lost greatness.

But reactionary readings have also been suggested by admirers of MacIntyre. For example, Rod Dreher (2017) writes that his much-discussed book, *The Benedict Option*, is derived from what he sees as *After Virtue*'s call for traditionalists to withdraw from liberal modernity into homogeneous, religious enclaves. Dreher draws heavily on one stirring passage at the end of *After Virtue*, in which MacIntyre

After Virtue as a Real Utopia

(2007: 263) refers to liberal society as a 'new dark ages' and calls for the formation of 'local forms of community within which ... moral life can be sustained'. Another right-wing admirer of MacIntyre – the political theorist Patrick Deneen – has argued that liberalism is destined to decline morally and collapse. For Deneen (2018a: 3), liberalism's failure is a sociological inevitability due to an 'inner logic' that 'generate[s] patholo-gies'. Chief among these is liberalism's purported tendency to atomise individuals, who then slip into 'wholly relativist belief and practice, untethered from anything universal or enduring' (2018a: 71) .

Both critics and admirers read *After Virtue* as associated with the thesis that liberalism is inescapably tied to moral decay and decline. To under-stand why such a reading of *After Virtue* is not uncommon – if also misguided – we must reconstruct part of MacIntyre's defence of virtue and critique of emotivism. MacIntyre's ethics begins from Aristotle's (2011: 33) definition of virtues as embodied dispositions that render an individual excellent in acting in ways that make human flourishing pos-sible. According to Aristotle, vices thwart goal-directed agency. For example, individuals who lack the virtue of courage will be unable to face the slightest risk and may even stop leaving the house altogether. Or someone lacking in the virtue of moderation, who is too gluttonous or abstemious, might either eat or deprive themselves to the point of sickness. Thus Aristotle (1984a: 197) holds that humans always require some share of a number of complex virtues – including 'courage, moderation, justice, or prudence' – simply to flourish as agents navigating the world.

One of *After Virtue*'s many innovations is to elaborate on this familiar Aristotelian line of thought by introducing the concept of 'practices'. Practices, MacIntyre (2007: 187) writes, are 'any ... socially established cooperative human activity through which goods internal to a form of activity are realised' and are 'systematically extended'. Some examples of practices are chess, water polo, farming, portrait painting and studying maths. Essential to practices is that there be some internal good that 'cannot be had in any way' but by participating in it (MacIntyre 2007: 188). This does not mean practices are unrelated to other external goods – such as honour, money or power – but external goods are defined by the fact that they can be accomplished in any number of ways and are not necessarily attached to a particular practice. For this reason, MacIntyre distinguishes practices from institutions, the latter being organisations concerned with securing the external goods needed to sustain a practice.

What is crucial to see for my purposes is that practices – which MacIntyre takes as forming at the grassroots level in human societies – follow the Aristotelian line of argument in requiring virtues to achieve a

128   *Jason Blakely*

telos or goal and not fall into self-defeating actions. To become an excellent maths student, painter and so on, MacIntyre (2007: 191) argues that one needs to 'recognise what is due to whom' (i.e. the justice to recognise rational authority), 'take … risks' (i.e. the courage to fail) and 'listen carefully to what we are told about our own inadequacies' (i.e. the humility to be teachable). Properly formed practices are thus schools of virtue in which participants instruct and model the character traits necessary to flourish in attaining goods internal to a practice.

These same practices are corrupted when external goods override virtues and distort internal goods. This happens at the communal level when an institution's desire for money, power and prestige corrupts the very practices it is supposed to protect. But it also happens at the level of single individuals. MacIntyre (2007: 188) gives the example of a young chess player who never learns intrinsically to love the game of chess but instrumentalises it as a vehicle for external goods like money and celebrity. Such a player has 'no reason not to cheat'. Rather than excellence at a practice, this player might cheat if victory requires violating the integrity of the practice.

Thus there is a political dimension to virtues as sustainers of practices. As MacIntyre (2007: 193) puts it, practices 'might flourish in societies with very different codes; what they could not do is flourish in societies in which the virtues were not valued, although institutions and technical skills serving unified purposes might well continue to flourish'. This brings us to a key feature of the reactionary reading of *After Virtue* – namely, the critique of liberal societies as unable to sustain virtue, and even actively corrupting it by subverting goods internal to practices. On this reading, liberal societies *necessarily* remain neutral on what constitutes a good life while handing over power to a technocratic managerial ideology that manipulates society as a means, treating practices as a route to external goods such as economic prosperity or political security (cf. MacIntyre 1998a). Liberal states and markets are composed of institutions that corrupt practices in favour of profit and order.

The result of this corruption of practices as small-scale schools of virtue is the proliferation of individuals who struggle to form a unified sense of self. This is one way to interpret MacIntyre's (2007: 18–35) account of the 'emotivist self'. The emotivist self sees all the goods of their life as subjective expressions of a kind of market preference. Because there is no shared political conception of the good, each individual has autonomy as a goal. Relative to this autonomous individual all goods, practices and traditions are subordinated to subjective-preference satisfaction. Everything comes to appear instrumentalised in reference to an exaggeratedly autonomous subject who relativistically decides what is

After Virtue as a Real Utopia 129

good or bad. Such individuals lack awareness of the objectivity of goods internal to practices and traditions.

On the reactionary reading, the problem with liberalism is that it must decline into an emotivism incapable of virtue. This line of thought brings me to the first problem with the reactionary interpretation of *After Virtue*: namely, what exactly is the nature of the link between liberalism and emotivism? One possibility is that the bond between liberalism and emotivism might be construed as having to do with the kinds of people that tend to occupy key institutional positions in a liberal order. So key institutional figures – managers, political representatives, bureaucrats and therapists – are emotivists. The reactionary reader might point to later passages where MacIntyre (2016: 129) writes that 'individuals can only function as modernity requires them to function, if their desires are expressed, contained, and ordered in certain ways'. That is, the only way modern states and markets function is if the individuals running them act as if they were emotivists. To participate in the institutions of modernity is necessarily to become some kind of emotivist or quasi-emotivist.

However, this is a highly problematic reading of MacIntyre. This is partly because the idea that occupying key institutional positions necessitates certain beliefs is philosophically incompatible with MacIntyre's critique of naturalist forms of causation in chapter 8 of *After Virtue*. In that chapter, MacIntyre persuasively argues that the human creative capacity to contingently modify beliefs makes it impossible to formulate necessary law-like generalisations determining human beliefs and actions (akin to those found in the natural sciences). To argue that whenever agent X occupies institutional space Y their beliefs will be Z is to formulate just such a naturalistic prediction.

By contrast, MacIntyre's argument against a predictive science of human behaviour entails that a particular institutional setting does not exclude the possibility that an agent might creatively adopt new beliefs or modify existing ones. This line of argument draws on a much longer and highly important engagement by MacIntyre with the social sciences, in which he claims that the necessary, mechanistic causal bonds of the natural sciences are inappropriate to explaining human behaviour (Blakely 2016). Therefore, an individual who participates in institutions might transform them by drawing on practices and traditions to which they also belong (say, local sports leagues, musical communities and parish life) in such a way that displays virtue. Indeed, such an individual might become a sign and source of virtue within an institution by displaying unusual honesty, courage or other such character traits. This would imply that it is sociologically possible that liberals and leading liberal figures can be virtuous and not emotivistic within modern institutions.

130   *Jason Blakely*

But might not a reactionary reading posit instead that the link between emotivism and liberalism is not about mechanistic, predictive causality but is a philosophical or conceptual claim? After all, emotivism is a philosophical doctrine – 'the doctrine that all evaluative judgments and more specifically all moral judgments are nothing but expressions of preference, expressions of attitude or feeling' (MacIntyre 2007: 11–12). A number of passages in *After Virtue* do seem to imply that although some people still think of themselves as natural rights theorists, utilitarians and so forth, the failure of these projects entails emotivism. In other words, those who have not adopted Aristotle *ought* to be Nietzscheans even if they have not realised it yet. For this reason, MacIntyre (2007: 117) suggests that the *philosophical* choice is Aristotle versus Nietzsche:

it was because [the Enlightenment] project failed, because the views advanced by its most intellectually powerful protagonists ... could not be sustained in the face of rational criticism that Nietzsche and all his existentialist and emotivist successors were able to mount their apparently successful critique of all previous morality.

Yet here another problem arises for those who read *After Virtue* as positing a thesis of inexorable decline. For one could accept MacIntyre's critique of the Enlightenment and adoption of Aristotle and still maintain that liberalism is able to foster virtue. One way of briefly illustrating this philosophical possibility is by drawing on Alexis de Tocqueville's *Democracy in America* and presenting it as a form of virtue liberalism (or a synthesis of liberal practices and virtue theory's emphasis on character traits).

For Tocqueville, the strength of nineteenth-century American democracy was precisely the way in which deliberating and debating within a certain kind of liberal tradition encouraged practices of self-government and awareness of a wider public good. Famously, Tocqueville (2004: 84) believed that 'Americans combat the effects of individualism by free institutions'. This was possible because the 'legislators of America' tried to 'multiply to an infinite extent opportunities of acting in concert for all members of the community', which allowed citizens to 'constantly feel their mutual dependence on each other' (2004: 85). Tocqueville believed that federalist liberal institutions, with their open opportunities for participation at the local level, helped engender the civic virtues associated with self-rule and deliberation. So he wrote that 'when the members of a community are forced to attend to public affairs, they are necessarily drawn from the circle of their own interests'; then the individual citizen 'begins to perceive that he is not so independent of his fellow-men ... that in order to obtain their support, he must often lend them his cooperation' (2004: 84).

After Virtue as a Real Utopia

In other words, the institutions of liberal democracy might (at least in principle) house practices – the practices of democratic self-rule and deliberation. These practices in turn can feed and sustain higher levels of representative, liberal government. As Tocqueville (2004: 86) put it: 'the free institutions which the inhabitants of the United States possess, the political rights of which they make so much use, remind every citizen, and in a thousand ways, that he lives in society'. Thus, according to Tocqueville, the virtues in American society are not just the result of extra-liberal influences or features of civil society, but can (at least in principle) be helped and supported by the liberal order itself. The point is not to advocate Tocqueville's admittedly heterodox virtue-liberalism, which has inspired both the American left and right (Bellah et al. 1996: xxx; Mansfield 2010: 23). Rather, it is to note that, philosophically speaking, liberalism can at least *philosophically* be linked to virtue. Of course, MacIntyre's criticism of liberalism would still be withering, but it would only hold for certain traditions of liberalism – perhaps neoliberal ideological variants that actively encourage a kind of society entirely constructed around self-interest and the instrumentalisation of social life (Blakely 2020a: 3–43).

If this line of thought is cogent, then it also casts doubt on a further major theme of reactionary readings of *After Virtue* – namely, the claim that traditionalists must abandon contemporary society and enter isolated enclaves of virtue. Such a reading of *After Virtue* is evident in Dreher's (2017: 17) writings, where he claims MacIntyre as the inspiration for 'leaving society and starting a new community' free from the elite 'barbarians' of liberal society who are 'at work demolishing the faith, the family, gender, even what it means to be human'.

Dreher's reading of *After Virtue* is particularly muddled, as MacIntyre has consistently maintained that the reconstitution of a tradition of virtue ethics must occur in a society with a diversity of ethical schools of thought witnessing and dialoguing with one another. This is because, according to MacIntyre (1998d: 202), ethical and political traditions gain objective status only through a practical as well as theoretical exchange with rival positions (see also: MacIntyre 2006c; Blakely 2013: 451–6). To self-isolate will condemn one to a diminished form of ethical reasoning, as one is unable to compare rival answers to what makes for a good human life. Dreher's Benedict Option will lead (at best) to ethically and rationally immature individuals.

How is this comparative form of objectivity accomplished? MacIntyre argues that comparative objectivity can be established in terms of internal dilemmas, fruitfulness and the ability to account for a rival's position better than that rival can. One way to decide which of two rival theories is superior is to inhabit one of the theories in order to discern any dilemmas, problems, anomalies or contradictions that are internal to it. Doing so requires the 'exercise of philosophical and moral imagination', learning 'to think, feel, and act from the standpoint of some alternative or rival standpoint' (MacIntyre 1998d: 219). Such imaginative action can occur hermeneutically only when there is serious engagement dialogically with defenders of that way of life. Only when this is done is it possible 'to put in question the conceptual framework of [a] particular standpoint from within the framework itself' (1998d: 219). If a theory or tradition is better able to resolve or overcome anomalies that remain insuperable for its rivals, this counts in its favour (1998d: 218).

In his published work since *After Virtue*, MacIntyre has affirmed that a continual exchange among a diversity of rival, incompatible views – Marxist, Nietzschean, Thomist, Confucian, etc. – is necessary in order to rationally establish the philosophical superiority even of Aristotelianism itself. So MacIntyre (1990: 235) has written that 'systematic debate' between these rival traditions should be a 'central preoccupation of our shared cultural and social life'. In addition, he has written generously about neo-Nietzscheans such as Raymond Geuss and made appeals to discursive inclusiveness such as: 'a dialogue about issues in moral philosophy in which Marxists were not participating would be a defective and inadequate conversation', as would one 'from which contemporary Thomists were absent' (MacIntyre 2013a: 475). In recent years, he has also argued for engaging non-Western sources of philosophy such as Confucianism, writing: 'American philosophy can only flourish as a conversation of diverse voices from conflicting standpoints, among which a range of Chinese voices have an important place' (MacIntyre 2004: 203).

This poses a massive (perhaps even insuperable) dilemma for 'Benedict Option' readings of MacIntyre's philosophy. If epistemological progress requires comparative work between sociologically embodied and extended traditions, it follows that some kind of pluralism would be normatively desirable for epistemic and ethical reasons within society. Indeed, MacIntyre (2004: 203) has even written that 'we now inhabit a world in which ethical inquiry without a comparative dimension is obviously defective'. And yet reactionary readers like Dreher (2017: 9) insist that MacIntyre is his inspiration for declaring that 'the public square has been lost' and that traditionalists should hastily retreat into isolated monocultures away from the 'hostile secular nihilism' that has supposedly 'won the day'. Postliberals like Sohrab Ahmari, Patrick Deneen, C. C. Pecknold and others have similarly assumed that the goal of a well-ordered polity is the hegemony of a single ethical or perhaps even national, religious tradition (Ahmari et al. 2019).

After Virtue as a Real Utopia   133

None of this requires that MacIntyre's philosophy somehow be committed to liberalism. After all, it is in principle possible that traditionalism might be made compatible with pluralism. But certainly, the reactionary impulse to suppress deep diversity and disagreement appears an untenable reading of MacIntyre's political thought. On the contrary, *After Virtue* points to a situation in which rival traditions respectfully dialogue over 'radically dissenting views on fundamental issues' (MacIntyre 1998b: 251). Pluralism and deep ethical disagreement are positive features of a just and humane society.

7.2   A Utopian Reading of *After Virtue*

Reactionary appropriations of *After Virtue* face a cluster of dilemmas – involving both the social scientific dimensions of claims to inexorable decline as well as the normative programme of establishing the hegemony of a single tradition within society. By contrast, reading *After Virtue* in reference to the socialist tradition resolves problems and opens new avenues of development and exploration. Such an epistemic move is, of course, partly how MacIntyre taught us to think about objective progress in ethical and political inquiry. It also resonates with MacIntyre's (2010b: 393–4) continual insistence that socialism should be seriously engaged and learned from against what he called the 'mindless mouths of the American Right for whom "Socialism" has been reduced to a term of abuse'. In what follows, I only begin to sketch a few ways in which *After Virtue* might inspire an ethical socialism that resists the influence of Marxism, abstract idealised utopianism and the tendency to veer into structuralism and manipulative technocracy.

One way to frame such a discussion is in terms of the young MacIntyre's participation in the British New Left's heterodox socialism, which was highly critical of Marxism on precisely such humanistic, ethical grounds (Blakley 2016: 24–37). In 1958's 'Notes from the Moral Wilderness', MacIntyre (1998e: 32) observed that the socialist tradition had come to be dominated by a mechanistic theory (not unlike the one we observed in those like Deneen above) in which liberal capitalism was predicted to collapse due to certain 'objective laws' of economics. This was tightly associated with a technocratic conception of politics in which 'human agency is essentially ineffective' and an 'enormous faith' was placed in 'the levers of social engineering' (1998e: 36).

Orthodox Marxism posits that the transition to post-capitalism will be brought about by economic structures triggering the radicalisation and mobilisation of the working class and other revolutionary agents. A classical expression of this view is found in Marx and Engel's

134   *Jason Blakely*

(1978: 483) *Manifesto of the Communist Party*, which claims that capitalism will produce 'above all, … its own grave-diggers' by immiserating the poor and being 'incompetent to assure an existence to its slave within his slavery' (cf. MacIntyre 2008b). The wider socialist tradition has continued to struggle with what Erik Olin Wright (2010: 273) has called 'the fundamental problem of a theory of transformation' from 'within [the] economic structures of capitalist societies'.

Part of the problem is that these mechanistic theories of transition continue to be frustrated by the actual course of political events, in which, far from mass-scale radicalisation, significant portions of the working class align with conservative and even reactionary sentiments. As MacIntyre (2008b: 259) observed, the underlying problem is a 'mechanistic error' in Marxism that assumes there is a predictive science of human behaviour. But a properly Aristotelian, teleological anthropology makes clear that there is no fixed, developmental logic to political culture, because individual agents are able creatively to interpret and modify their own beliefs and goals. As MacIntyre (2007: 89) argued in detail in chapter 8 of *After Virtue*: 'the social sciences are predictively weak' and 'do not discover law-like generalisations'.

But without a predictive sociology for the transition to post-capitalism, the socialist tradition appears caught between ineffectual 'utopian' dreaming (in the sense of idealised fantasies with no connection to the actual social world) and dark visions of voluntaristic state takeover. Indeed, perhaps the dominant form of socialism has come to pursue post-capitalism via a sheer act of the political will embodied by a statist executive, or perhaps a vanguard administrative elite (MacIntyre 2008b: 255). Today such a voluntaristic tendency is evident in major thinkers on the socialist left like Fredric Jameson (2016: 19), who argued in 'An American Utopia' that the best way to transition to post-capitalism would be for a holder of the executive office to declare 'emergency powers' and conscript the entire populace into the military, thereby extending healthcare and education benefits to all. Clearly this involves an authoritarian willing of socialism via top-down bureaucratic action. Jameson believes this kind of technocratic implementation of a 'new social structure' will usher in a 'transformation of subjectivities' (2016: 20, 35).

And yet MacIntyre's critique of the social sciences in *After Virtue* makes clear that Jameson's vision of political transformation is a form of magical thinking. Specifically, it assumes a mechanistic vision of social engineering that neglects the role of human agency and existing traditions in the creation of political culture. The notion that a new kind of socialistic self can simply be imposed from the top down misses the self-interpreting features of human agency that are embedded in existing

After Virtue as a Real Utopia

135

traditions. Here socialist thinkers like Jameson would benefit from a serious engagement with *After Virtue* – not only with its critique of positivistic and structuralist thinking, but also as offering an alternative theory of transition that is neither top-down nor voluntaristic. Ironically, the Marxists converged on a similar fusion of positivistic error and executive hierarchical politics to that of the reactionary postliberals.

By contrast, MacIntyre's conception of practices as schools of virtue provides a kind of real, existing utopian or post-capitalist form of association. To be clear, these kinds of real communities of practice here and now are utopian in the sense of post-capitalist but not in the sense of idealised abstractions. To the contrary, Aristotelian practices are organised to immediately transform an untutored self (one perhaps indoctrinated in vicious habits of materialistic, neoliberal self-interest) into virtuous habits that are orientated to the value of goods internal to a community of practices. Such bottom-up associations of practice and virtue generate a 'political community' that is aware of the need to 'exercise the virtues for its own sustenance' (MacIntyre 2007: 195). In such communities, individuals are offered an 'education in the virtues' that 'teaches me ... that my good as a man is one and the same as the good of those with whom I am bound up in human community' (2007: 229). Associations of virtue thus organise around goods internal to practices and offer an education that defies the atomistic, self-interested notion of agency of the neoliberal tradition. Post-capitalist society needs a different culture of self and community – this might be a different way to think of 'the construction of new forms of community' that MacIntyre calls for in the closing pages of *After Virtue* (2007: 263).

By contrast, at present the socialist left has no robust account of how individuals substantively transform and shift away from atomistic – at times even emotivistic – sources of self towards new forms. Instead, the contemporary left either opts for authoritarian voluntarism or wishful, abstract utopian thinking of some future community with no connection to the present. Communities of practice, however, engender a solidarity or form of social friendship around the telos of a shared good. Individual sacrifice in material terms – both security and profit – becomes reasonable within a community whose good is a shared practice. A solidaristic courage with the community of practices goes beyond individualistic atomism and generates a 'concern for individuals, communities, and causes' outside self-interested, Hobbesian visions of polity (MacIntyre 2007: 192). This neo-Aristotelian notion of community is subsumable neither into the neoclassical vision of *Homo economicus* as maximising a preference schedule nor within the liberal theory of individuals entering a social contract contingent on a desire to preserve mere material existence.

MacIntyre's notion of practices might suggest, therefore, a form of bottom-up transformation of the political world. Transition, on this view, will not come via mechanistic structural change, voluntaristic, statist imposition or abstract ideals. If post-capitalism is to come about at all, it will require the difficult work of individuals entering into new kinds of associational life that transform capitalism from hyper-individualistic cultures into something truly different. This is an alternative conception of communities of virtue – not Dreher-like isolation, but active transformation of the political culture from within.

This line of thought is closely related to a second dilemma that the young MacIntyre diagnosed within the dominant form of Marxist socialism: namely, its inability to form a consistent ethic to guide practice. Neglecting Aristotle and virtue, socialists under the influence of Marxism not only lacked a distinctive moral theory, but in fact inherited individualistic systems of thought that had been developed to help buttress capitalist economic organisation. Ironically, socialists vacillated incoherently between Kantian claims about the absolute dignity of individuals and Benthamite cost–benefit analyses in which an action is justified if and only if it maximises overall social utility. As MacIntyre (2007: 261) put it: 'Marxists have always fallen back into relatively straightforward versions of Kantianism or utilitarianism'.

The absence of a coherent socialist ethic was also related to the problem of the transition to post-capitalism, as there was no clear sense of what motivated the revolutionary shift. Was a socialist agent supposed to be motivated by the absolute dignity of individuals and never treat them as means to an end? Or were they instead to follow a utilitarian calculus, in which revolutionary, even violent confrontation with political adversaries was justified by the end-state of post-capitalist society? MacIntyre diagnosed very early on a problem that continues to bedevil the socialist tradition – are opponents to be respected as agents of moral worth, or are they to be manipulated and coerced in the name of mass-scale social consequences?

Perhaps an unintended consequence of this philosophical failure is that socialists in political life often cede virtue ethics to conservatives and religious traditionalists. At the same time, much of the socialist tradition has opted for an ultra-autonomous libertarianism – for example, moralities of avant-gardism that view themselves as pitted openly against traditions of virtue. Great confusion reigns in the contemporary socialist tradition over what kind of character traits are necessary to sustain a new kind of politics. The turn to increasingly libertarian moralities of rational self-control and technological domination unwittingly reproduces neoliberal visions of human life as composed of atomistic autonomy.

After Virtue as a Real Utopia

Yet the socialist tradition might instead learn from MacIntytre's *After Virtue* that his Aristotelianism provides the basis for the formation of selves that resist the vicious impulses of mass consumerism and individual isolation. Virtue communities focus not only on the tutoring of human desire, but also on the formation of collectivities that reject the tendency in neoliberal culture to atomise the individual into a purely economic agent who prizes preference maximisation in private life. In this vein, MacIntyre's analysis of practices being corrupted by the external goods of institutions might be viewed as a resource for a revived ethical socialism – one that shuns the technocratic, anti-humanist tendencies of the mainstream left and also does not remain at the level of simply abstract dreaming. Where neoliberalised persons continually instrumentalise relationships and practices for the sake of utility schedules and profit, those shaped by the virtues will instead be ethically capable of social friendship and solidarity. As MacIntyre (2007: 254) puts it: 'the tradition of virtues is at variance with central features of the modern economic order and more especially its individualism, its acquisitiveness, and its elevation of the values of the market to a central social place'.

Virtuous individuals in a community of practice will not calculate foremost in terms of economistic outcomes or attachments to wealth and celebrity. Instead of, say, learning music for the sake of profit and fame, such individuals will see their chief good as constituted by belonging to a tradition of musicians bound by the integrity of a craft. To resist the siren call of institutional bribes requires certain virtuous character traits such as 'truthfulness, justice, and courage' in the form of genuine 'excellences' (MacIntyre 2007: 192). On the socialistic reading of *After Virtue*, we have something that both overlaps and contrasts with the humanistic, ethical utopian socialism of William Morris that focused on the importance of local crafts and a society that prized beauty over efficiency in economic life (Bevir 2011: 85–105). MacIntyre, on this reading, might share with the utopian socialists a focus on bottom-up ethical transformation within small communities that resist capitalist logics. However, unlike the utopian tradition, MacIntyre (2010b: 394) rejects motivation by a mere 'abstract ideal' because it does not offer individuals a way to 'relate such ideals to the ends for which' they 'recurrently struggle' in their 'everyday lives'. Instead of utopia as idealised abstraction, MacIntyre advocates real communities of practice – here and now – that, like G. K. Chesterton's 'distributists', understand that 'the only viable politics of the exploited ... is one that enables them to defend what they rightly value in the present against the threats of capitalism and the modern state' (2010b: 394).

MacIntyre was also prophetic in his perception that a socialistic left, lacking any coherent ethic, would be tempted to turn to a dark anti-humanism – a Nietzschean will to power in which politics bottoms out into a play of might. This is an alternative way to understand MacIntyre's provocative dilemma near the conclusion of *After Virtue*: namely, whether one is to select Nietzsche or Aristotle. The point is not whether there are other logical possibilities (of course there are) but whether, politically, one will be tempted to resolve the ailments of society via an outburst of violent domination or through patient communities of virtue and social friendship.

Unlike the incoherent and unstable ethics surrounding current socialist accounts of the transition to post-capitalism, MacIntyre provides a theory in dialogue with traditions of wisdom – such as faith traditions. This is another way in which one might opt for Nietzsche's actively hostile atheism, or instead an Aristotelianism that sees ethical truth in the world's great religions (such as Christianity, Judaism, Islam, Buddhism, Confucianism and so on). Any politics that wishes to mount a genuine resistance to capitalism and the allure of materialism will need deep sources for moral conversion. MacIntyre reconciles religious traditions and radical resistance to capitalism via Aristotelianism. By contrast, the contemporary left continues to blunder insofar as it neglects, belittles or denigrates the world's great religious traditions as sources of virtue. As long as left-wing politics persists in having little to say about virtue and vice – ceding thick moral languages and religious traditions to conservatives, nationalists and reactionaries – it will have vastly impoverished and perhaps even rendered impossible its own ability to generate a different politics (Albertson and Blakely 2021).

This brings us to a final problem internal to the socialist tradition which *After Virtue* might resolve: namely, the dilemma of an unrealistic idealism about post-capitalism. Once there is no ethical or social scientific theory of transition, socialism is reduced to an idealised fantasy about the future. Paradoxically, the Marxist tradition in particular is vulnerable to takeover by figures like Joseph Stalin or other authoritarian 'realists' who wrap themselves in the moral authority of socialist idealism, all the while enacting a politics of extreme hierarchy. Indeed, near the end of *After Virtue*, MacIntyre (2007: 262) warns that while 'Marxism had recommended itself precisely as a guide to practice', it was unable to 'illuminate the future', and its proposed 'path to human liberation had in fact led to darkness'. In the same passage, he notes that the problem was that Marxism lacked any notion of where the new, post-socialist community would be concretely located inside the 'moral impoverishment of advanced capitalism' (2007: 262).

After Virtue as a Real Utopia

By contrast, *After Virtue*'s communities of practice and traditions of virtue might be interpreted not as nostalgic, ethnically homogeneous enclaves (Dreher) but as already accomplished cells of post-capitalist society. They would be what socialist theorist Erik Olin Wright dubbed 'real utopias', or actual communities that organise in the present according to principles that defy the economic logic of neoliberalism. This is a form of socialism that rejects state-centred approaches in favour of a cumulative, bottom-up shift towards new kinds of life. Sounding somewhat reminiscent of MacIntyre, Wright (2010: 332) observed that the socialist tradition, in the 'absence' of some actual community of 'social empowerment', would 'unleash strong centralizing and authoritarian tendencies' that in turn would 'lead to a consolidation of an oppressive form of statism'. The concept of a real utopia within recent ethical socialist philosophy is not abstract idealisation but one of actual, existing communities that do not conform to market organisation. MacIntyre (2016: 106–10) goes far beyond any present theorist in the socialist tradition by thinking through ethical sources for the formation of these new communities that can in turn draw from the wisdom of ancient religion. The reconstruction of existing practices and traditions within society itself is the basic locus for the creation of new, post-capitalist forms of community and self.

Rather than the ambiguous and historically discredited ambitions of the dictatorship of the proletariat, MacIntyre's communities of virtue already exist in germ form wherever humans are attempting to pursue practices excellently. They are *utopian* in the sense of a new kind of community beyond the reach of capitalism that also serves as an icon for a much broader-scale future society. But they are *real* in the sense that they are not idealisations but the intensification of already-existing social realities. MacIntyre (2007: 255) provocatively notes in *After Virtue* that 'modern systematic politics, whether liberal, conservative, radical or socialist, simply has to be rejected from a standpoint that owes genuine allegiance to the tradition of the virtues'. The problem with the modern iterations of these ideologies is precisely that they are abstract mobilisations whose goal is state takeover, without attending to the deeper problems of self and culture (something to which ancient Greek philosophy was far more profoundly attuned). But the real utopias of a humanistic, ethical socialism are precisely not programmes for systemic power over the state for the sake of the central imposition of policy. Instead, they are attempts to revolutionise and overcome the culture of contemporary capitalism by replacing it from within through the formation of new kinds of social organisation sustained by new kinds of selfhood. As in ancient political philosophy, politics and ethics are intimately fused.

In short, MacIntyre's *After Virtue* is – while remaining a text that lies beyond the reductions of any contemporary ideological tradition – also capable of inspiring complex dialogical interventions in the current political situation. It holds within it resources for a constructive project, as well as complex criticisms of both left-wing socialist and right-wing reactionary thought. While not beholden or reducible to any one tradition, it has conceptual resources that put pressure on all political forms. It is therefore not surprising that, although *After Virtue* now lies forty years in the past, it will continue to beckon us to new and unexpected political futures.

Part III

After Virtue and Narrative

8   Form, Style and Voice in *After Virtue*

Stephen Mulhall

8.1

It's clear from the opening pages of *After Virtue* that its readers are not entering a conventionally composed philosophical work.[1] The first chapter, entitled 'A Disquieting Suggestion', invites us to imagine a post-apocalyptic world of a kind that 'is very like one that some science fiction writers have constructed' (AV 2), one in which the natural sciences suffer radical disruption inflicted by populist riots and political movements that hold scientists responsible for environmental disasters. So when enlightened people attempt to reconstruct these enterprises long after the catastrophe, they must do so from isolated assertions, partly comprehended tools and charred pages torn from textbooks – surviving fragments from the antediluvian world, but now lacking the broader contexts (of beliefs, instruments and practices) that gave them their sense and significance.

This is not a thought experiment of the kind familiar to readers of contemporary analytical philosophy: it is not a direct and radically simplified recasting of reality intended to isolate certain of its features and thereby clarify and refine our judgements about their importance. It offers a concise speculative-fictional narrative about the natural sciences as an analogue to an extended non-fictional narrative about the history of Western European moral thought and practice – quite as if the reality it portrays will come fully into focus only by means of a dialectical encounter between two modes of storytelling. Instead of using fiction to strip the flesh from reality's bones, MacIntyre offers one story as an anticipatory X-ray of the basic structure of another story, the tale that it will take the rest of the book to tell; his speculative fiction displays the bare narrative bones of that ensuing philosophical history, in which reality appears as always already clad in the rich, multi-layered complexity of our (physical and cultural) embodiment over time.

---

[1] MacIntyre 1981 – hereafter 'AV'.

144   *Stephen Mulhall*

For the thought experimenter, flesh and blood only get in the way of clearly grasping reality's fundamental articulations; the simplest of fictions can directly disclose that hidden essence. For MacIntyre, reality's bones are inherently enfleshed: they serve their body and are disclosed by its actions and expressions. But he proposes to enhance their accessibility to us by exploiting our willingness to suspend disbelief about fictional tales – particularly those we think of as extrapolating aspects of our present or imminent reality – in order to soften us up for a non-fictional narrative that he knows will beggar belief. For if we find that we can imaginatively inhabit such dystopian tales of the future, why should we not be willing to re-imagine the present as having already attained that dystopian condition?

By inviting us to see an analogy between a fictional future condition of natural science and the supposedly factual present state of moral understanding, MacIntyre's tactic already encourages his readers to accept a fateful assumption, one that governs the whole of his ensuing account, for better and for worse, without ever being fully confronted – that claims to objectivity and authority in the moral field are essentially identical in nature to those advanced in chemistry or physics. But for my purposes in this chapter, what matters more is that his opening exercise in speculative fiction enacts a methodological perception that is equally pervasive in the rest of the book, for which it explicitly argues, and to which its form is responsive in various ways – that there is an internal relation between the fictional and the historical, and that this has a constitutive role in establishing, maintaining and transforming our shared reality.

8.2

To accept the opening analogy that MacIntyre offers is, however, to acknowledge that the one offering it confronts a very particular kind of difficulty. To begin with, MacIntyre claims that the post-apocalyptic condition of what passes for natural science would go entirely unnoticed by philosophers – in particular, by both analytical and phenomenological philosophers, both of whom restrict their focus to careful descriptions of the way things manifest themselves to us in experience, thought and speech, and so would concern themselves with investigating the structure and presuppositions of the prevailing, internally coherent simulacra of genuinely scientific discourse that people have managed to construct from its ruins. The same would therefore be true of philosophy if our real moral life were as MacIntyre's speculative fiction suggests; and MacIntyre further suggests that the resources of historical enquiry, being now pervasively shaped by post-apocalyptic assumptions, would be

Form, Style and Voice in *After Virtue*

equally incapable of detecting the nature of the problem. Indeed, insofar as the contemporary academic curriculum as a whole – its conception of the differences between certain disciplines and so their modes of legitimate interaction – has been shaped by the catastrophe, its reality and significance will be invisible to any of those disciplines. And since ordinary people unreflectively assume that the current dispositions of moral discourse are in order as they stand, they will be no better placed than academics to recognise their post-apocalyptic disorder.

But this means that no one will be in a position to hear MacIntyre's claims as anything other than the expression of mental instability – even a kind of insanity. Every available mode of discourse in terms of which to articulate his sense of pervasive disorder lurking beneath the illusion of order belongs to that illusion and so will apprehend his perspective as itself disordered – a mere simulacrum of insight. The fact that this predicament is exactly what the truth of his claim entails does not mitigate that predicament – it intensifies it. For it shows not only that MacIntyre confronts a dilemma: either everyone else's mind has lost its moorings, or else that fate belongs to him alone. It also suggests that insisting on the truth of such apparently unintelligible claims might result in one's becoming mad.

This is the structure of what MacIntyre (in an essay originally published before *After Virtue*) calls an epistemological crisis, in which alternative and rival schemata yield mutually incompatible accounts of what is going on and mutually incompatible accounts of the evidence available on which to base that choice. And since he believes that not a single substantial account of this phenomenon is to be found in the academic philosophical literature, he characterises it further by offering a reading of *Hamlet*.[2] According to MacIntyre, Hamlet has a multitude of ways of interpreting events at Elsinore and thereby of rewriting the dramatic narrative of his family and his kingdom in the light of responses to his probing of its present condition. That probing is informed by two ideals, truth and intelligibility, and MacIntyre points out that the pursuit of both is sometimes not easily reconciled:

The discovery of a hitherto unsuspected truth is just what may disrupt a hitherto intelligible account ... To be unable to render oneself intelligible is to risk being taken to be mad, is, if carried far enough, to be mad. (EC 5)

In effect, then, the author of *After Virtue* invites his readers to think of him as an avatar of Hamlet. And to acknowledge that this is a

---

[2] In 'Epistemological Crises, Dramatic Narrative and the Philosophy of Science' (MacIntyre 2006c) – hereafter 'EC'.

146   *Stephen Mulhall*

melodramatic gesture (the likely fate of any invocation of apocalypse, however calmly it is conjured) does not necessarily constitute grounds for its dismissal; it might rather help to specify its mode of significance.

For instance, readers of Stanley Cavell might thereby consider MacIntyre as a brother of the unknown women who populate a genre of cinematic melodrama that Cavell has intensively studied. For those women – such as Ingrid Bergman's Paula in *Gaslight* or Bette Davis's Charlotte in *Now, Voyager* – find that the terms for self-understanding and self-expression provided by their social world (often epitomised in an offer of marriage from a man who stands for that world) offer them no way of making sense of themselves and their present, persistent sense of bewilderment or disorientation. It renders them mute, depriving them of a voice in their own history, and it incites them to judge that world as a whole as uninhabitable until it undergoes complete transformation (rather than piecemeal improvement), a project for which they take a stand by withdrawing their consent, hoping thereby to prompt questions and conversation about what in that world might be so radically awry as to prompt such withdrawal. This is a vision of melodrama not as a distinctively feminine emotional responsiveness disproportionate to its cause or occasion, but as the manifestation of a specific kind of radical socio-political critique rooted in a sense of inarticulable suffering.[3]

What intensifies the suffering in MacIntyre's case is the extent to which he had previously been at home in, and nursed high hopes for, the discursive systems from which he is now alienated. As he makes clear in the preface to the first edition of *After Virtue*, 'This book emerged from extended reflection upon the inadequacies of my own earlier work in moral philosophy, and from a growing dissatisfaction with the conception of "moral philosophy" as an independent and isolable area of enquiry' (AV vii). Such disappointment indicates something of the initial aspirations MacIntyre had for moral philosophy and his own work in it; and its bitterness finds indirect expression in another prefatory remark, in which he declares:

The dedication of this book expresses an indebtedness of a more fundamental order; if I had only recognized its fundamental character earlier, my progress towards the conclusions of this book could have been a good deal less tortuous. But I would not perhaps ever have been able to recognize it in a way that could help me towards these conclusions had it not been for what I owe to my wife, Lynn Sumida Joy – in this as in so much else *sine qua non*. (AV ix)

That dedication, which precedes the preface and so begins the whole text, is to 'the memory of my father and his sisters and brothers'. So his

---

[3] Cf. Stanley Cavell, *Contesting Tears* (Cavell 1996).

Form, Style and Voice in *After Virtue*   147

prefatory citation of it tells us that MacIntyre's philosophical disorientation was rooted in a deep alienation from those who brought him into the world and brought him up, those without whom he would not be (the author of this book), and so in a deep alienation from himself – someone whose commemoration of those elders in his dedication naturally culminates with a Gaelic rendering of a passage from the Song of Solomon (*Gus am bris an la*: 'until the day breaks'). And it further declares that a new marriage, and its creation of a new shared world, was a condition for the possibility of his beginning to understand himself as so alienated. It could hardly be clearer that the crisis of which MacIntyre speaks in the first chapter is not simply that of his broader culture, with he alone untouched by its subjection to illusion. The dramatic historical narrative that the rest of the book goes on to supply is as fully in the service of his own transformation as it is that of his interlocutors and thereby of the transformation of a world that they both inhabit.

8.3

Like Cavell's unknown women, then, MacIntyre withdraws his consent from the standing modes of discourse available to him – in moral philosophy, in philosophy more generally and even in the current modes of non-philosophical discourse. I do not mean by this that he altogether refuses to engage with them: on the contrary he confronts an unusually broad range of individual thinkers whose claims to intellectual authority are uncontroversial. But he does so in a tone of voice distinctly lacking in decorum or civility: he rejects complex bodies of thought in breathtakingly brief stretches of argument, offers sweeping dismissals of whole approaches to certain kinds of problem and repeatedly deploys terms of criticism that go beyond expressions of intellectual disagreement to tap registers of disdain and condescension. Thus Moore is charged with 'naïve and complacent apocalypticism', and his disciples with 'great silliness' (AV 15); we are told that Nietzsche's overman and Sartre's existentialist hero 'belong in the pages of a philosophical bestiary rather than in serious discussion' (AV 21); and that all those who theorise on the basis of utility or rights are deploying concepts that have the same sheerly fictional status as those of unicorns and witches (AV 67). That a certain enjoyable vein of dry wit runs through these harsh denunciations – as when MacIntyre claims that in the UN's Universal Declaration of Human Rights 'what has since become the normal UN practice of not giving good reasons for *any* assertions whatsoever is followed with great rigour' (AV 67, emphasis in original) – doesn't make them any less harsh.

148 *Stephen Mulhall*

There is, however, a philosophical justification for this rhetorical brutality: for it is required by the otherwise overwhelming authority exercised over us all by what MacIntyre takes to be the consensual hallucination we inhabit. The text's denunciatory tone helps constitute an authorial subject-position for whom the hollowness of the phenomena it is confronting is so self-evident, their inadequacies so immediately apprehensible, that it empowers the reader seriously to consider the otherwise instantly dismissible possibility that what they have hitherto taken to be not only genuinely substantial but compulsory resources for understanding their world might in fact amount to structures of air. By constructing a persona for whom the official interpretative schema for social reality is so blatantly lacking in conviction, the text makes space for the disorientating realisation that the way things have hitherto seemed might not be the way things are. The tone of rebuke is equally apposite, insofar as it seeks to make us ashamed of our having previously identified reality with this threadbare interpretative schema. As Emerson knew, having learnt it from the prophets of ancient Israel as well as Jesus, cultivating a properly impersonal shame (impersonal because it links us with such intellectual luminaries as Kierkegaard, Kant and Mill rather than distinguishing us from them, and so it does not indicate a merely personal inadequacy) is an exceptionally effective way of motivating reflection and reconsideration on the part of those whom we know to be capable of doing better, of thinking and living otherwise.

A related authorial strategy also makes more sense when considered against this background. For another striking aspect of MacIntyre's intellectual style is that he can often be found making use of the concepts and methods of those he subjects to particularly ferocious criticism. One small example is his willingness to abuse Moore for his apocalypticism mere pages after having deployed his own version of that rhetorical register; at the very least, this shows a real confidence on MacIntyre's part that he can tell naïve and complacent forms of such discourse from their mature and self-aware counterparts. But there are larger examples of the same strategy. For instance, as part of his attempt to relegate rights to the status of unicorns and witches, MacIntyre tries to bring out a conceptual connection between the rise of rights talk, the salience of protest and the prevalence of strategies of unmasking. The link turns on the thought that invoking rights allows us an effective way of protesting against being manipulated by others and thereby legitimates not only increasing levels of indignation but also the attempt to unmask the other's interference with my autonomy as a mere exercise in manipulation. In short, we utilise one fictional tool to indignantly protest against others' attempts to do likewise. And yet, what is the basic purpose

Form, Style and Voice in *After Virtue*

of *After Virtue* if not to protest indignantly about the inherently manipulative world we currently inhabit and to unmask the many and varied ways in which this takes place?

There's an analogous structure implicit in MacIntyre's critique of Nietzsche – *the* modern thinker who he claims offers a cogent alternative to rehabilitating Aristotle, and to whom he accordingly devotes particularly ferocious critical attention. And yet, Macintyre reiterates crucial elements of various aspects of Nietzsche's work in his own. As what he calls an act of 'poetic justice' to Nietzsche (AV 113), he begins his reconstruction of the history of Aristotelian moral culture from the Homeric texts with which Nietzsche begins his own critique of slave morality; indeed, he even offers us a two-paragraph etymological genealogy of the term 'morality' from its Greek through its Latin and English translations, as if deliberately mimicking Nietzsche's own decision to motivate his genealogy of morality by utilising etymological clues (AV 37). The book's Gaelic dedication to a hoped-for daybreak itself invokes the title and pivotal figure of a Nietzschean text; and of course, MacIntyre's attempts to disclose a new future for our moral lives by revising the narrative we tell ourselves about our development from the Greeks to liberal democracy, showing the unpredictable interactions of cultural contingency and conceptual structure that drove those processes, is strongly reminiscent of Nietzsche's genealogical method.[4]

This may look like sheer inconsistency; but it is better thought of as turning the enemy's weapons against them. More precisely: if the world of simulacra is the only available source of words with which to articulate one's critique of it, then that critique can be articulated only by turning those words against themselves – by taking them up and turning them to a different use, one which transfigures them from emptiness to genuine substantiality, from a pattern of employment that occludes reality to one that brings it properly into focus. This amounts to treating each of them – in a very Nietzschean vein – as a site of interpretative conflict, as incorporating layers of meaning accrued over time that might be made to pull against one another and thereby reshape each word's future usefulness. And if these words achieve their current obfuscatory function only as part of a total discursive field, then they can be troped or turned individually only if they are all so turned. For MacIntyre, the essential medium for this operation is historical narrative of a very particular kind.

---

[4] I offer a more extended account of Nietzsche's method in the 'Introduction' to my *The Ascetic Ideal: Genealogies of Life-Denial in Religion, Morality, Art, Science and Philosophy* (Mulhall 2021).

150   *Stephen Mulhall*

8.4

A central reason for MacIntyre's turn to the historical emerges in his rational reconstruction of an Aristotelian approach to human flourishing. For that account incorporates a conception of human actions as comprehensible only as episodes in larger stories, from which it follows that the rationality of our choices as agents, the unity of our lives and the coherence of the practices and traditions within which we live them out are all inherently narratival in their nature and so are most perspicuously presented as unfolding in time and history. For MacIntyre, then, historical narrative simply elicits and elucidates the story-shaped form of human life.

But the specific kind of historical narrative he constructs in *After Virtue* has distinctive features that cannot be explained simply by reference to this (highly controversial) conceptual claim. To understand that specificity, we need to take seriously the fact that his narrative is responsive to an epistemological crisis; for on MacIntyre's account, epistemological crises can and must be resolved by 'the construction of a new narrative which enables the agent to understand *both* how he or she could intelligibly have held his or her original beliefs *and* how he or she could have been so drastically misled by them' (EC 5, emphasis in original). Readers of MacIntyre's subsequent work will recognise this as a version of the account of conflict resolution between rival traditions contained in the final chapters of the sequel to *After Virtue* – *Whose Justice? Which Rationality?*[5] It's as if *After Virtue* shows what the earlier essay and sequel say. One might even say that the provision of that narrative is the first step in making possible genuine interlocution with others not currently in the grip of this crisis, since it aims to render the way things currently are questionable – that is, to disclose them as involving the taking of a particular evaluative stance and so to conjure at least the possibility of taking another stance, thereby inviting us to consider whether we wish to continue taking responsibility for maintaining the cultural world in its current dispensation.

This is a central reason why MacIntyre's historical narrative is not presented to us in what might otherwise seem the obvious way – as a chronologically ordered story, beginning with the Homeric mythological origins of our Western European moral culture, incorporating its catastrophic caesura at the Enlightenment and then tracing its increasing entropy or disorder in the post-Enlightenment period until it terminates

---

[5] MacIntyre 1988.

Form, Style and Voice in *After Virtue* 151

with the present. Instead, MacIntyre begins with the present and gradually works backward from it, excavating each preceding cultural dispensation until he reaches the Enlightenment and its project of justifying morality. (It's not so much that he needs to retell that history otherwise – although he does; it's more that he needs to recover for us the very idea of the present as having a history, as opposed to exemplifying timeless necessities of thought, speech and action.) Having outlined the reasons why the Enlightenment project was bound to fail (the loss of the concept of a human telos), he then returns to the present (via an account of its relation to the nineteenth century) in order to pose the pivotal question: Nietzsche or Aristotle? Only then does he return to our Homeric origins and tell a chronologically continuous tale linking Homer to mediaeval modes of virtue-centred moral culture – that is, to the brink of the catastrophe, the caesura as viewed from its other side. This gives him enough material to provide an extended rational reconstruction of an Aristotelian account of morality, which he then uses to track that tradition's slow degeneration after the Enlightenment (shifting between distortions of its central insights and belated reformulations of them, up to the time of Austen and Cobbett) and to work out the only ways in which we might recover or revive that tradition in the future – by accepting Trotsky's critique of the state as a locus of genuine moral and political justice and taking guidance from St Benedict's example by turning towards more local sites at which moral practices, institutions and traditions continue to inform genuinely valuable forms of human flourishing.

In short, in ways that have bewildered many readers, the order of the historical narrative and the order of its narrating come apart: the latter takes the form of an anti-chronological archaeology of modernity whose telos is essentially diagnostic, followed by a chronology of pre-modernity that is orientated by the need to attract our investment in an Aristotelianism of the future. This is what will make intelligible our cleaving to beliefs that have drastically misled us, alienating us from ourselves and from others. And it is a genuinely philosophical history, in the sense MacIntyre associates with Hegel and Collingwood (AV 3): its narrative is shaped by an evaluative goal, and its episodes are (re-) ordered so as to provide the necessary resources for the phases of more purely philosophical work of conceptual analysis and argumentation that punctuate it – most obviously, the critique of emotivism as a theory of meaning in chapter 2, the argument in chapter 5 designed to convince us that the Enlightenment project had to fail and the rational reconstruction of an Aristotelian perspective on morality in chapters 14 and 15.

This is one central way in which MacIntyre writes against the conception of moral philosophy as an independent and isolable area of enquiry

152   *Stephen Mulhall*

(and against the strictly chronological structure of his own earlier work, *A Short History of Ethics*).[6] But the structure of his historical narrative also manifests other aspects of that resistance: in particular, it treats a wide of range of philosophical issues usually assigned to distinct sub-branches of the discipline, and certainly segregated from the branch devoted to ethics; and it treats the task of understanding philosophical concepts, claims and practices as requiring the resources of a broad range of other intellectual disciplines usually segregated from philosophy. The philosophical issues that MacIntyre deems pertinent to his enquiry include the nature and methods of the natural sciences, the feasibility of theoretical knowledge of social phenomena, the nature of action and intention, the possibility of radical conceptual innovation, game theory, contractualism in political philosophy, and so on. Moreover, in treating any of them, he is as willing to draw on authors belonging to what is still called 'Continental' philosophy as on those usually assigned to the Anglo-American analytical traditions: for MacIntyre, that distinction is just one more isolating and baleful illusion, another strategy for depriving us of a voice. The disciplines other than philosophy that he draws upon in his quest to grasp the reality beneath our ethical simulacra include sociology, psychoanalysis, anthropology, biography and life-writing, the practice and theory of literature and art more generally, not to mention history. And of course, each holistic register or dimension interacts crucially with the other: it could hardly be otherwise, since MacIntyre's willingness to deploy the results of anthropological or sociological enquiry presupposes a defence of their status as genuinely knowledge-generating enterprises, just as his philosophical analyses of intention, action and interpretation will inevitably reframe the claims of non-philosophical modes of enquiry to social and intellectual authority.

In articulating and elaborating his account in this way, MacIntyre is echoing Nietzsche's rejection of the ways in which Enlightenment culture attempted to facilitate the autonomy of the various dimensions of human cultural life – assigning distinct logics to aesthetics, politics, religion, morality, science and philosophy – and thereby dismembered the inter-related unity of that life in pre-Enlightenment eras, especially that of the ancient Greeks. For Nietzsche, this merely reflects the emphasis on individual autonomy so central to the ethics and politics of modernity, and that forms an essential part of its claim to have liberated us from external constraints on the pursuit of both individual and collective freedom; but this appearance of emancipation is simply a further

---

[6] MacIntyre 1966.

Form, Style and Voice in *After Virtue* 153

manifestation of the ascetic ideal that is rooted in the slave moral value system that overturned the ancient Greek world, and so in truth enhances the power of a fundamentally unified evaluative world view that achieves Judaeo-Christian goals by other means – including that of disavowing any relation to Judaeo-Christianity.

In one way, MacIntyre's account inverts Nietzsche's, since he wishes to demonstrate that the appearance of a coherent, integrated modern moral culture masks an essentially fragmented and gravely disordered reality. But his response to the situation in which he finds himself mirrors that of Nietzsche: for both aspire to embody resistance to the catastrophe they have diagnosed by refusing to accept their culture's assumption that properly rigorous thinking requires respecting fundamental differences between the domains of religion, ethics, politics, aesthetics, science and philosophy. Just as Nietzsche's early riposte to the Socratic annihilation of the tragic world view is to construct and deploy a conception of philosophy as always already informed by ethical, political, aesthetic and scientific modes of engagement with reality (the conception embodied in the tragic dramatic narrative of *The Birth of Tragedy*),[7] so MacIntyre aims to construct a vision of meaningful postlapsarian human life by drawing simultaneously on every means by which human beings have gained a reliable grip on the reality they inhabit. This is one reason why *After Virtue* is importantly mischaracterised when it is viewed as a contribution to the revival of virtue theory in its competition with deontological and consequentialist rivals. For the book aims not only to recover but to embody a vision of human flourishing that precisely rejects any conception of ethics as limitable to one self-contained sector of our lives and of moral philosophy as the single, self-contained branch of philosophy that is appropriately devoted to its study.

8.5

The register of this holistic mode of enquiry upon which I want to focus for the remainder of this chapter is the one that tends to be neglected in comparison with the others I just listed: the aesthetic. In a sense, of course, everything I have said so far is also focused on that aesthetic dimension of MacIntyre's book – for what are analyses of its narrative structure or plot, its critical evaluations of fictional concepts, its deployment of fictional tales to illuminate non-fictional ones, its strategy of

---

[7] *The Birth of Tragedy and Other Writings* (Nietzsche 1994).

154 *Stephen Mulhall*

turning or troping key concepts and images against themselves and the carefully calibrated tones of its authorial voice (rebuking, self-excoriating, rueful, enraged and enraging) if not exercises in a kind of criticism that is as much literary as it is philosophical? In another sense, however, I have so far passed over some of the more obvious ways in which art – and literature in particular – plays a significant role in MacIntyre's marshalling of his philosophical forces.

One is his tendency to focus his analyses of the history of philosophy on authors whose writings incorporate distinctively aesthetic strategies for attracting and convincing their readers. In chapter 4, for example, MacIntyre's route back into the Enlightenment begins with Kierkegaard's *Either-Or* and then contextualises Kant by invoking Diderot's *Rameau's Nephew* rather more extensively than Hume's *Treatise*. More generally, the shadow of Hegel's highly dramatised and rhetorically complex approach to philosophical history-writing (epitomised in his *Phenomenology of Spirit*) informs the broad shape of MacIntyre's project at least as much as does Nietzsche's willingness to deploy unprecedentedly heterogeneous tonal registers across the body of texts that constitute his attempt to revalue modern values. From MacIntyre's perspective, each may exemplify more or less egregious errors in the philosophical conclusions at which they arrive. But each, in their different ways, also realise a conception of philosophy with which he is in deep sympathy – one which regards it as crucially dependent for its own flourishing upon its willingness to deploy aesthetic strategies of the kind that led Socrates to expel the poets from the just republic and the well-ordered human soul.

Another role played by art in MacIntyre's project is to be seen in the ways he draws upon practitioners of literary fiction as part of his strategies of persuasion. His engagements with Jane Austen and Henry James are perhaps the two most salient examples of this. Austen appears as a late, revitalising representative of the classical Aristotelian approach to morality, who identified the primary enclave within which the practice of the virtues still remained viable as a particular kind of marriage, and the kind of household that placed such marriages at their centre. The centrality of marriage reflects broader cultural and economic changes: in particular, the outsourcing of productive forms of activity from the domestic sphere left many single women with no way of contributing to their own upkeep or that of their household and so made the act of refusing marriage (and the financial security it could promise) an act of great moral courage. In Austen's novels (particularly *Emma* and *Persuasion*, which in this respect function as distal sources for the film genre Cavell calls 'Comedies of Remarriage', from which the melodramas we cited earlier are generated

Form, Style and Voice in *After Virtue*

by negation),[8] an acceptable marriage was one that could facilitate both spouses' happiness or flourishing, where that was understood in terms of a broadly familiar synthesis of Christian and Aristotelian conceptual resources – but one into which Austen introduced some additional elements.

First, unsurprisingly given the degenerate state of the broader moral culture, Austen places unprecedented emphasis on the ability to detect counterfeits of the virtues, and in particular individuals whose ability to imitate virtuous behaviour masked their subjection to passions uncultivated by appropriate upbringing and self-discipline. Mirroring this is a high regard for self-knowledge and a deep appreciation of the costs involved in acquiring it – the price of overcoming self-deception. And since the narrative unity of the self presupposed by Aristotelian accounts of human flourishing could no longer simply be taken for granted, Austen focuses persistently on the importance of the relatively new virtue of constancy. MacIntyre concludes his analysis as follows:

Jane Austen's moral point of view and the form of her novels coincide. The form of her novels is that of ironic comedy. Jane Austen writes comedy for the same reason that Dante did; she is a Christian, and she sees the *telos* of human life implicit in its everyday form. Her irony resides in the way that she makes her characters and her readers see and say more and other than they intended to, so that they and we correct ourselves. The virtues and the harms and evils which the virtues alone will overcome provide the structure both of the life of which the *telos* can be achieved and of a narrative in which the story of such a life can be unfolded. (AV 226)

It is Austen's sense that the life of the virtues was being afforded very little social and cultural space that leads MacIntyre to endorse a claim advanced by one of Kipling's characters – that she was the mother (perhaps better the grandmother) of Henry James (AV 226). For James's novels narrate versions of a world in which that space is becoming all but impossible to find, and in which accordingly the substance of morality is rendered increasingly elusive. But note the care with which MacIntyre associates Austen's choice of ironic comedic form with her Christianity. Given that MacIntyre presents himself in this book as a secular thinker, the pervasively ironic form of his own text (with its unceasing vigilance over counterfeits of morality, its incessant disclosure of gaps between what people say and what they mean, its recurrence to gestures of unmasking and its search for the means for self-reliant constancy) cannot serve comedic purposes. Its postdiluvian perspective

---

[8] *Pursuits of Happiness* (Cavell 1981).

156   *Stephen Mulhall*

instead finds expression in a genre one might baptise 'ironic tragic drama'.

The example of Henry James should also remind us of another literary strategy that plays an early, and determining, role in MacIntyre's diagnosis of our emotivist condition – his use of the notion of 'characters', a term MacIntyre chooses because of the way it links the dramatic and the moral.

> There is a type of dramatic tradition – Japanese Noh plays and medieval morality plays are examples – which possesses a set of stock characters immediately recognizable to the audience. Such characters partially define the possibilities of plot and action. To understand them is to be provided with a means of interpreting the behaviour of the actors who play them, just because a similar understanding informs the intentions of the actors themselves; and other actors may define their parts with special reference to these central characters. So it is also with certain kinds of social role specific to certain particular cultures. (AV 26)

Characters in this sense pick out a very particular kind of social role, one that places a certain kind of moral constraint on the personality of those who would inhabit them. In such cases, role, personality and morality fuse. Characters are the moral representatives of their culture because of the way in which moral and metaphysical ideas and theories assume through them an embodied existence in the social world; they are the incarnation of moral philosophies. Whereas most social roles tolerate varying degrees of distance between the values they embody and those occupying them (the faithless priest, the politically cynical trade unionist), because a character is an object of others' regard – because he or she furnishes them with a cultural and moral ideal – those who occupy such roles confront the demand that role and personality be fused, that social and psychological type coincide. (In this respect, characters have a more proximate artistic source, in Hollywood movies of the Golden Age, which are stocked by roles Cavell has called types or individualities – the Sergeant, the Fallen Woman, the Gangster).[9]

Just as the Victorian Headmaster in England and the Professor in Germany provided the moral focus for a whole cluster of attitudes and activities in those nations in the nineteenth century, so on MacIntyre's view modern emotivist culture is embodied in the Rich Aesthete, the Therapist and the Manager. For as he argues in chapter 3, each in their own way represents the obliteration of the distinction between manipulative and non-manipulative social relations that MacIntyre sees as the

---

[9] Cf. ch. 5 of *The World Viewed* (Cavell 1971).

Form, Style and Voice in *After Virtue*

fundamental characteristic of emotivist world views. The Aesthete, as described in James's novels, staves off boredom by inducing others to behave in ways that satisfy their jaded appetites; the Therapist aims to transform neurotic individuals into ones well-adjusted for the existing social and economic roles their culture imposes; and the Manager directs both the human and non-human resources of their organisation so as to achieve goals determined by others (CEOs and shareholders) as effectively as possible. And their centrality to modern culture is evinced no less decisively by opposition to their claims to authority than it is by their acceptance; for insofar as rebellion organises itself around such characters, it confirms their defining significance, both individually and collectively.

That said, MacIntyre sees significant differences between these three emotivist characters, ones which turn on their relation to the conceptual fictions (such as rights and utility) that he takes to be central to modern moral culture's self-deceptions. According to MacIntyre, the Aesthete is least likely to be their victim, because Aesthetes specialise in the hermeneutics of suspicion in order to free themselves of unwanted demands; whereas the Therapist is most likely to fall prey to them, and indeed is the most likely to be seen to be deceived, since devastating critiques of the intellectual bases of Therapists' claims to authority are so freely available that it seems miraculous that they continue to function as characters at all. Of all three, however, such fictions belong to the very definition of the role only in the case of the Manager: for their claim to effectiveness depends upon their having genuine knowledge concerning how to predict and alter human behaviour, and MacIntyre devotes two full chapters to showing that the very idea of such knowledge – the very idea of law-like generalisations governing human behaviour and thereby rendering it predictable and controllable – is chimerical. He does so because he believes that demonstrating this gap or absence at the heart of a character so central to our culture's self-understanding will have a particularly disturbing impact on our theatre of illusions.

However that may be, the idea of characters as a dramatically derived lens through which perspicuously to survey a culture's self-image, as individuated crystallisations or exemplars of their evaluative universe, gives MacIntyre a way of making manageable the critical task on which he has embarked – that of criticising his culture as a whole, of putting his world as such (with all of its complex, inter-related discursive fields) under judgement. And their salience in that context gives us a way of understanding why MacIntyre's narrative of the processes whereby our present world was constructed from its predecessors systematically invokes exemplary individuals. Aristotle and Aquinas, Diderot and

Kierkegaard, Austen and James are, in effect, characters in this dimension of MacIntyre's diagnostic dramatic narrative – individualities whose role in the drama fuses personality and morality, rather than proving that MacIntyre believes in a 'Great Men and Women of Ideas' theory of history. (There is a further point of connection here with Nietzsche's tragic dramatic narrative of the birth, death and rebirth of the spirit of tragedy, which recounts Dionysus' and Apollo's repeated rebirth in different cultural types and forms, until their contemporary re-marriage in Wagner's remaking of opera as a total work of art.)[10]

If we put together this vision of *After Virtue* as a richly populated character drama with my earlier claim that MacIntyre aspires to articulate his envisaged transformation of the present world by turning its key concepts and figures to his own purposes, then we arrive at the thought that we might use the Aesthete, the Therapist and the Manager – suitably reinterpreted – as a way of grasping MacIntyre's place in his own philosophical narrative. We have already seen how that narrative has therapeutic designs on its readers – diagnosing them as disorientated, as inhabiting fantasies whose overcoming is a requirement for them to flourish. We have just seen that a central part of that therapeutic process involves organising a large cast of characters and characterisations so that they contribute as effectively and perspicuously as possible to the enterprise's overall goal of self-overcoming, but doing so by deploying a narratival model of making sense of human agency rather than one invoking wholly fictional law-like generalisations. And we can now see that this chapter as a whole confirms the indispensability of aesthetic resources and techniques to this book's work, but in a way that does not amount to the immoral consumption of others but rather to their ethical production – to their creation as genuine others, as potential sites of genuine interlocution, and so to the creation of the agent of this process as genuinely other to his others, and so to himself. In this sense, the three distinct characters of emotivist modernity function as dismembered fragments from which the author of *After Virtue* constructs a unified image of himself as the *sine qua non* of his own and his readers' achievement of true emancipation.

---

[10] I develop this interpretation of Nietzsche at more length in 'Orchestral Metaphysics', in *The Self and Its Shadows: A Book of Essays on Individuality as Negation in Philosophy and the Arts* (Mulhall 2013).

9 *After Virtue*, Narrative and the Human Good

Micah Lott

> I dreamed a realistic chronicle. I began gazing into his life – not his life as a god or a demigod in whose triumphs one could exult as a boy but his life as another assailable man.
>
> Philip Roth, *American Pastoral*

In this chapter, I explore some ways an Aristotelian approach to moral philosophy might be enriched by attending to narrative, as well as some limits to what Aristotelians should expect from narrative. Can we better understand action and character by reflecting on the nature of stories? Can we gain insight into the human *telos* by considering how our lives might themselves have a narrative structure? I will pursue these questions by examining the work of Alasdair MacIntyre, paying special attention to his account of the narrative self and narrative unity in *After Virtue* and his notion of complete lives in *Ethics in the Conflicts of Modernity*.

9.1   Agents, Ends and Complete Lives

On an Aristotelian account of human agency, we each act for the sake of a final end, or *telos*.[1] Your final end is something you value for its own sake. It is also something for the sake of which you act even when you are pursuing other ends, including those ends you value for their own sakes. How this can be true is explained by the fact that our final end is understood in a highly general way: the end of *living well*. So the basic idea is that in everything you do, *qua* rational agent, you aim at living well (as you understand it), which is something you value for its own sake, and other particular things you do for their own sakes (e.g. celebrating a friend's birthday, studying French history) you also choose to do *as ways* of living well. And, importantly, our aim is not to act well merely in this or that respect, or *qua* this or that role (e.g. mother, physician). Rather, *qua* rational agents, we aim to act and live well *haplōs* (overall, in an

---

[1] In this chapter, I will use the term 'Aristotelian' to refer to a family of views with common features, including views that might be labelled 'Neo-Aristotelian'.

160   *Micah Lott*

unqualified way). Living well can be appropriately characterised as living *virtuously*. However, at this stage and level of generality this is not yet a claim about what, in substance, the human virtues are. It is simply a way of making clear that 'living well' is a matter of doing well with respect to thought, feeling and choice insofar as they are governed by reason – and the virtues, whatever those turn out to be, are those states of character and intellect that enable us to think, feel and choose *well*.

Aristotelians add that living well should be understood as human flourishing, or realising *the human good*. The phrase 'the human good' might suggest that there is only one narrowly defined way for humans to flourish. But Aristotelians need not be committed to this. They can acknowledge that human flourishing takes many forms and varies across time and place, even as there is a common core to living well for human beings.[2] In addition, we can distinguish between generalisations about *the* human good and any individual's distinctive way of realising that good – *your* particular way of living well, as manifested in the details of your life.

Of course, there are many things we do that can accurately be described as part of living well but that are not all equally valuable as ends in themselves. For instance, cleaning the family bathroom might be part of your living well. Suppose you clean virtuously, and cleaning is a necessary task in a life that is, overall, a life of human flourishing. Still it is unlikely that bathroom cleaning is the focus of your living well, or that you take bathroom cleaning to be just as finally valuable as, say, lively conversation with your friends or joyful play with your children. So within living well, we need to recognise the particular ends that are a person's focus – the orientating activities, projects and relationships that give rational shape to how someone lives. And just as we distinguished between the human good and your way of realising that good, here we can distinguish between human final ends described in general terms – friendship, knowledge, play, art, etc. – and your specific way of pursuing such ends and giving them a place in your life.

In addition to characterising our final end as living well, Aristotelians sometimes describe it as *the good life*.[3] At first glance, 'living well' and 'living a good life' might seem like two ways of talking about the same thing. But consider what we might say about a person who dies in an accident at the age of twenty-five: 'her life was cut short'. This expression implies some sense of the proper, or adequate, *duration* of a human life. And it is not, at least in the first instance, an evaluation of *how* the person

---

[2] A point that MacIntyre emphasises in both MacIntyre 1984 and MacIntyre 2016.
[3] See, e.g., MacIntyre 1984 and Russell 2013.

After Virtue, Narrative and the Human Good

was living in the time before she died. We might say 'her life was cut short' about someone who was living either virtuously or viciously before she died. The evaluation applies to the *life* rather than to how the person is *living*. One plausible suggestion here is that in thinking about your life as 'cut short' (or not), we are thinking about a life as a kind of temporal whole, with a beginning, middle and end. And we operate with some sense of the stages that properly belong to a human life as it unfolds over time.

One thing an Aristotelian might say at this point is that there is a distinct kind of living well that belongs to each stage of life (e.g. a special place for obedience while a person is young or for dispensing acquired wisdom in old age). On this view, our final end is living well in the distinctive ways that are appropriate to each stage of a human life. Aristotle himself does not go quite that far. But he does acknowledge a temporal dimension to our final end. As he says: 'the human good turns out to be activity of the soul in accord with virtue and, if there are more virtues than one, then in accord with the best and most complete. Furthermore, in a complete life (ἐν βίῳ τελείῳ), for one swallow does not make a spring, nor does one day.'[4] The completeness or perfection that Aristotle has in mind here is evidently not the same as the completeness or perfection of *how* the person is living. For the whole point of talking about a complete *life* is to add a further element to our understanding of the human good, beyond the notion of living well or virtuously. Aristotle has already made the point that the actions and activities of living are completed, or perfected, when performed virtuously – 'each is completed well (ἀποτελεῖται) when it is done in accord with the virtue that properly belongs to it'. That is a point about *how* you are living. The idea of a complete life adds, over and above this, a thought about the temporal duration of a life in which such completed activities take place.

9.2 *After Virtue*: Practices, Virtues and Narrative Selves

There is much more to explore here. But let this stand as a rough sketch of the basic Aristotelian framework for moral philosophy. In *After Virtue* (*AV*), MacIntyre argued for a return to Aristotelianism, and he developed his own Aristotelian account of action, character and the human good. One of the most creative and distinctive aspects of MacIntyre's account is the central place it gives to *narrative*. Human actions, MacIntyre says, are 'enacted narratives', and the unity of

---

[4] *Nicomachean Ethics* 1198a16–20. For further discussion, see Emilsson 2015 and Lear 2015. See also *Eudemian Ethics* II.1.

162   Micah Lott

a person's life is 'the unity of a narrative embodied in a single human life'.[5]

MacIntyre presents his view in several stages. In the first stage, he introduces the idea of a practice, and he distinguishes between internal and external goods. This makes possible an initial, tentative definition of human virtue: '*A virtue is an acquired human quality the possession and exercise of which tends to enable us to achieve those goods which are internal to practices and the lack of which effectively prevents us from achieving any such goods.*'[6]

In the next stage, MacIntyre highlights an important limitation of this definition: it does not yet address the place of the virtues in a life viewed *as a whole*, since it makes reference only to practices (plural) and not a final end towards which all practices are ordered. At the end of chapter 14 of *AV*, MacIntyre spells out three problems that follow from this limitation. First, if we have a practice-only approach to the virtues, without a notion of the human good, then individuals have no rational way to navigate the potentially incompatible claims made by different practices and the goods internal to each of them, in which case 'it may seem that the goods internal to practices do after all derive their authority from individual choices, for when different goods summon in different and incompatible directions, "I" have to choose between their rival claims'.[7] This means that 'unless there is a *telos* which transcends the limited goods of practices by constituting the good of a whole human life, the good of a human life conceived as a unity ... a certain subversive arbitrariness will invade the moral life'.[8]

The second problem with the practice-only approach concerns the characterisation of any particular virtue: 'without an overriding conception of the *telos* of a whole human life, conceived as a unity, our conception of certain individual virtues has to remain partial and incomplete'.[9] The basic idea, I take it, is an Aristotelian point about virtue: genuine ethical virtues (as opposed to mere natural virtues) are governed by practical wisdom, which includes an understanding of what matters in life overall and the ability to apply this understanding in particular situations, leading one to act well overall, not just in this or that respect. In order to act wisely, and hence virtuously, we need a conception of how to order various goods and how to integrate various practices within a single life.

The third problem that MacIntyre points out concerns a specific virtue: integrity or constancy. Such a virtue, MacIntyre suggests, makes

---

[5] MacIntyre 1984: 211, 218.   [6] MacIntyre 1984: 191, emphasis in original.
[7] MacIntyre 1984: 201–202.   [8] MacIntyre 1984: 203.   [9] MacIntyre 1984: 202.

After Virtue, Narrative and the Human Good   163

sense only if we recognise a human life as a unified whole, not merely the site for a grab-bag collection of practices and goods: "'Purity of heart", said Kierkegaard, "is to will one thing." This notion of singleness of purpose in a whole life can have no application unless that of a whole life does'.[10]

The limitations of the practice-only approach all point towards the need for a final *telos* – an end that belongs to a different order from any particular good and for the sake of which we act when pursuing other goods. MacIntyre understands the final *telos* as a certain kind of life: the good life for a human being.[11] This notion in turn requires that we are justified in thinking of a human life as a unified whole. And thus MacIntyre asks: '[I]s it rationally justifiable to conceive of each human life as a unity, so that we may try to specify each such life as having its good and so that we may understand the virtues as having their function in enabling an individual to make of his or her life one kind of unity rather than another?'[12] This sets up the next stage in MacIntyre's presentation of his account – the idea of the narrative self, and the claim that narrative unity provides the way to understand the unity of a human life.

In chapter 15 of *AV*, MacIntyre lays out a 'concept of a self whose unity resides in the unity of a narrative which links birth to life to death as narrative beginning to middle to end'.[13] MacIntyre begins by arguing that actions are (fully) intelligible only when we view them in wider contexts that go beyond discreet 'behaviours' narrowly construed. One sort of wider context is the social setting in which an action occurs and which partly defines its meaning. Another sort of wider context is provided by the longer-term intentions towards which shorter-term intentions are directed. MacIntyre stresses that both these sorts of wider contexts require thinking in *narrative* terms. Social settings of any kind have a history that can be given in narrative form, and it matters for the meaning of an individual action when in that history the action takes place. And in relating shorter-term to longer-term intentions, we are 'involved in writing a narrative history'.[14] Thus narrative is essential for understanding human action: 'Narrative history of a certain kind turns out to be the basic and essential genre for the characterization of human actions.'[15]

---

[10] MacIntyre 1984: 203.   [11] MacIntyre 1984: 148, 175, 184.
[12] MacIntyre 1984: 203.   [13] MacIntyre 1984: 205.   [14] MacIntyre 1984: 208.
[15] MacIntyre 1984: 208. Some of MacIntyre's comments in *AV* suggest the view that all action explanation is narrative explanation, or at least that narrative explanation is always the most important way of explaining human action. But I do not think that MacIntyre needs to be committed to such strong claims about narrative explanation, and it seems that in his later works MacIntyre moves away from such strong claims.

164   *Micah Lott*

To these claims about intelligibility MacIntyre adds a closely related point about *accountability*. Human beings, characteristically, can be held accountable for their actions. Justifying ourselves requires that we make clear what is valuable or worthwhile in our action. And this requires providing a narrative context for what we are doing, since 'action itself has a basically historical character'.[16]

For MacIntyre, accountability for our actions is connected to a certain conception of the *self*. This is the self as 'the subject of a narrative that runs from one's birth to one's death' and that is 'accountable for the actions and experiences which compose a narratable life'.[17] This notion of the self provides a distinctive account of personal identity: 'personal identity is just that identity presupposed by the unity of the character which the unity of a narrative requires'.[18] And thus we have a circle of concepts that come together as a package, each presupposing and helping to explain the others: 'The concepts of narrative, intelligibility and accountability presuppose the applicability of the concept of personal identity, just as it presupposes their applicability and just as indeed each of these three presupposes the applicability of the two others.'[19]

With this circle of concepts in view, MacIntyre returns to the issue left outstanding at the end of chapter 14. Are we justified in supposing that an individual human life is a unified whole, such that we can make claims about *its* good, not simply this or that particular good? MacIntyre's answer centres on narrative:

In what does the unity of an individual life consist? The answer is that its unity is the unity of a narrative embodied in a single life. To ask, 'What is the good for

For an insightful discussion of the importance of non-narrative explanations of actions and practices, see Moran 2015. Taking up MacIntyre's example of the practice of gardening, Moran writes: '[G]iving an historical narrative of the development of the social practice of gardening, for example, will depend on a prior understanding of the synchronic structure of the practice itself: such things as the difference between planting flowers and growing food, the different forms of dependence on time (time of day versus growing season), and the relationship between ownership of land, the act of labor, and the ownership of what is grown. This natural and cultural background constitutes the intelligibility of a practice like gardening, and will be presupposed in any temporally ordered narrative of the development of gardening, but this context does not itself have anything like a narrative structure. Rather, the structure consists in such facts as the relation between the specific practice and general human needs, the relations of dependence between different components of the practice, the social relations between producer, product, and owner, and the rules and techniques that define mastery of the practice' (Moran 2015: 25–6). One of the forms of intelligibility that Moran mentions here – relating specific practices to general human needs – is especially important for the kind of ethical naturalism that MacIntyre develops in *Dependent Rational Animals*.

[16] MacIntyre 1984: 212   [17] MacIntyre 1984: 217.   [18] MacIntyre 1984: 218.
[19] MacIntyre 1984: 218. For discussion of how this set of ideas comes together as a package, see Rudd 2012.

After Virtue, Narrative and the Human Good 165

me?' is to ask how best I might live out that unity and bring it to completion. To ask 'What is the good for man?' is to ask what all answers to the former question have in common ... The unity of a human life is the unity of a narrative quest. Quests sometimes fail, are frustrated, abandoned, or dissipated into distractions; and human lives may in all these ways also fail. But the only criteria of success or failure in a human life as a whole are the criteria for success or failure in a narrated or to-be-narrated quest.[20]

9.3   Your Life as a Whole

Having sketched MacIntyre's account in *AV*, let's now consider how this appeal to narrative might enrich the Aristotelian framework outlined in Section 9.1. An initial answer is clear: the narrative self provides a way to conceive of each human life *as a whole*, and hence as the sort of unified thing that might have *its good* (i.e. a final end). This might not seem like very much. After all, there is something slightly odd about the question that motivates MacIntyre's turn to narrative, whether it is 'rationally justifiable to conceive of each human life as a unity'. What exactly is the worry supposed to be? Isn't it fairly obvious that a human life is a unity of *some* kind (i.e. one thing, with different aspects and phases)? And is this worry specific to human lives, or is there a corresponding question about whether the life of each, say, wildebeest is a unity?

We need to distinguish two issues here. The first is our *need* as agents to think of our lives as wholes. In *AV*, this need is set out in the discussion of the inadequacy of the practice-only approach to the virtues in chapter 14. The second issue concerns *challenges* to thinking of our lives as wholes. In *AV*, this point shows up at the beginning of chapter 15, where MacIntyre highlights 'two different kinds of obstacle, one social and one political' that tend to prevent us from envisioning our lives as unified wholes. The social obstacles come from the way that 'modernity partitions each life into a variety of segments, each with its own norms and behaviours'.[21] The philosophical obstacles come from two different tendencies: the tendency to think atomistically about human action (typical of analytic philosophy) and the tendency to make a sharp distinction between individuals and the roles they play (typical of sociology and existentialism).

---

[20] MacIntyre 1984: 219. Even this account, however, is not quite complete. For MacIntyre holds that human practical thinking, when it is well-ordered, operates within a 'living tradition'. I set aside here MacIntyre's claims about tradition because they are beyond the scope of this chapter.

[21] MacIntyre 1984: 204.

166   *Micah Lott*

It is these social and philosophical obstacles that narrative is meant to overcome by providing an interpretation of the relevant notion of *your life as a whole* (or, equivalently, *your whole life*). To appreciate this point better, let's compare the account in *AV* with another broadly Aristotelian discussion of our final end. In *Intelligent Virtue*, Julia Annas also highlights the connections between rational agency, a final end and the conception of one's life as a whole. She does not, however, connect these ideas to narrative. Consider the following passage:

> Reflection thus both triggers and then furthers thinking about how to achieve the goals I have in light of the constraints I have (time, money, energy) and their mutual achievability. This thinking is unifying about the goals because they are *my* goals, and I need to have an integrated and unifying way of achieving them because I have only one life, the life I am living ... This is a *global* way of thinking about my life: I come to see that I have various goals that I aim at, and that in the one life I have, and which I am already living, these goals need to be structured in a *unifying* way in order for me to achieve them ... the result is that I am faced with a *task*, namely the task of organizing the goals I am working towards and shaping my life as a whole. It is this – the idea of what my life as a whole is aimed at – which in ancient ethical theories is called the *telos* or overall good of life.[22]

Although Annas does not make this explicit, her explanation of a life's *telos* implies two different ways of thinking about 'life as a whole'. On the one hand, there is a kind of wholeness that is an *achievement*. At any given time, various practical concerns make a claim upon my time, energy and other resources.[23] As a rational agent, however, I aim to act well overall, and thus I need to avoid acting well in one role at the cost of acting badly in another role, or betraying one of my values by how I pursue another of my values, or forwarding one of my projects while undermining another of my projects. What I need, then, is *practical integration*. This is, essentially, a matter of giving each of my practical concerns their due as parts of something larger – my life as a whole. Making your life whole or integrated is the aim of a *task* that rational agents must face. Wholeness in this sense is a kind of success.

At the same time, the very task of achieving wholeness in this sense depends upon another sense of life as a whole in which wholeness is regarded not as an achievement but as a *given*. The reason I must strive for integration among my various goals is that I am *already* living a life that possesses some sort of unity – 'I have only *one* life'; 'the *one* life

---

[22] Annas 2011: 122–3, all emphases in original. For a similar line of argument, see Rudd 2012: 187–8. Drawing on MacIntyre and others, Rudd connects the notion of 'a whole life' to narrative in a way that Annas does not.

[23] Annas emphasises the need to organise your *goals*. I have opted for the more general phrase 'practical concerns'.

After Virtue, Narrative and the Human Good 167

I have'. Indeed, unless there is already a single life whose different aspects and phases are parts of a whole, it is hard to see how there could be a need for practical integration and a task of achieving it.

What can narrative add to this picture? First, the narrative self explains the sense of your life as a whole that Annas takes as a given and refers to as 'the life I am living'. We might be tempted to think of 'life' here as *animal* life, or the life of an organism. In that case, the corresponding sense of life as a whole would apply equally to wildebeests. And indeed it may be that an organism is a special sort of unity, and that we can speak about a wildebeest's 'life as a whole'. But to leave it there would be misleading. For it doesn't capture the distinctly human way of living and the distinctive sort of unity that applies to a human life. Narrative selfhood is an attempt to characterise the special way of living that belongs to human beings as creatures who are rational, linguistic, accountable and always positioned in a particular historical context. Life as a narrative quest points to a sense of your life as a whole that applies to distinctly *human* lives.[24]

Related to this, narrative selfhood suggests that the practical integration we need to achieve, *qua* rational agents, has both synchronic and diachronic dimensions. The practical integration that Annas emphasises is synchronic, insofar as it is something we can bring into view by taking a 'snapshot' of a person's activity at a given time and considering how their practical concerns are (dis)organised at that moment. However, viewing action as enacted narrative implies that what any such snapshot depicts will be fully intelligible only in narrative, and hence diachronic, terms. And it suggests our need to achieve practical integration across the temporal phases of our life (however exactly we characterise those phases). We might call success in the synchronic dimension of practical integration *living with integrity* and success in the diachronic dimension *living with constancy*. Both of these contrast with living in ways that are

---

[24] Compare Charles Taylor's claims about identity, selfhood and narrative in *Sources of the Self*: 'We are not selves in the way that we are organisms, or we don't have selves in the way we have hearts and livers. We are living beings with these organs quite independently of our self-understandings or -interpretations, or the meanings things have for us. But we are only selves insofar as we move in a certain space of questions, as we seek and find an orientation to the good.' And later: 'I have been arguing that in order to make minimal sense of our lives, in order to have an identity, we need an orientation to the good, which means some sense of qualitative discrimination, of the incomparably higher. Now we see that this sense of the good has to be woven into my understanding of my life as an unfolding story. But this is to state another basic condition of making sense of ourselves, that we grasp our lives in a *narrative*' (Taylor 1989: 34, 47, emphasis in original).

168   *Micah Lott*

fragmented, random, self-contradictory or self-undermining, either at a given moment or across time.

9.4   Narrative Unity, Good Lives and Practical Deliberation

The discussion so far suggests some important ways that narrative ideas might enrich the basic Aristotelian framework. Our final end is the good of a whole human life, and thus to make claims about our final end we need to be justified in thinking of our lives as wholes. We also need an adequate characterisation of the notions of *living* and *life* as they figure in claims about living well or the good life. Narrative selfhood, and the conception of life as a narrative quest, can help by providing a way of spelling out the abstract idea of *your life as a whole*.[25]

On its own, however, this tells us little about the content of our final end. A conception of your life as a whole might be necessary for evaluating how you are living overall and for saying whether and how your life has realised its good. And narrative notions might provide the best way of thinking about your life as a whole. But can narrative notions tell us anything more substantive about what the human good *is*, about the activities, purposes and values that are central to living well or are essential for a good life?

Suppose we grant that a human life should be conceived as a narrative quest. By itself this tells us little about the proper aims of a human quest, or how such a quest should be conducted, or what counts as success or failure in such a quest. Suppose we grant, too, that practical integration, in both its synchronic and diachronic dimensions, is a task for all rational agents and a necessary condition for achieving the human good. This still gives us little insight into our final end. After all, you might live with integrity and constancy in service to false values or shallow goals. That would not be living well. Can narrative notions take us any further in providing a substantive characterisation of our final end? Can thinking of your life as a story, an enacted narrative, provide any guidance when it comes to thinking about how to act and live? I doubt it. In this section,

---

[25] In saying this, I am only pointing towards the potential contribution that narrative notions can make to Aristotelian ethics. To make good on this potential, these narrative ideas would need to be developed in much more detail and various objections addressed. For an attempt to do this that draws on Kierkegaard, see Rudd 2012. For a position in personality psychology that finds a major role for narrative in the constitution of the self, see McAdams 2013. For some worries related to thinking about a whole life in narrative terms, see the discussion of 'fictionalizing tendencies' and their possible pitfalls in Goldie 2012: 161–73. In my view, Goldie raises genuine concerns about how narrative thinking can go awry, but these are not decisive objections to the notions of a narrative self or life as a narrative quest.

After Virtue, Narrative and the Human Good 169

I develop several reasons for thinking that narrative notions, on their own, cannot provide much help here. This is not the role we should expect narrative to play.

Let's start with the idea of narrative unity. Is the narrative unity of a human life a kind of success, something that helps to spell out what good human lives look like? The short answer is: no. Setting aside extreme or limit cases, every human life will have the unity of an enacted narrative, whether or not it is a good, well-lived life. The various forms of success or failure that a life might possess are not a matter of achieving or failing to achieve narrative unity per se. Rather, they are a matter of what can figure into the content of a true narrative about a life. So in trying to grasp what the good life amounts to, either for an individual or for human beings in general, we don't gain much insight from narrative unity. A human life might be a 'narrative quest', but the success or failure of such a quest depends on its content (i.e. on what *kind* of quest it was, how it was conducted, towards what ends, with what results, etc.). Narrative unity per se tells us little about what counts as a successful or failed quest. It provides little with regard to the content of the *telos* of a life as a whole.[26]

Still, we might wonder: if someone fails utterly in achieving practical integration, won't it be difficult, even impossible, to tell a unified narrative of the person's life? Imagine someone drifting through life with little direction, oscillating between various goals and commitments. Won't it be hard to tell a coherent story about such a life, to say what it all adds up to? Very roughly speaking, a unified narrative requires an appropriate beginning, middle and end and appropriate connections among events: a story with nothing essential left out.[27] But here we need to distinguish between: (1) unity as a feature of a narrative itself – of how the story is told; and (2) unity as a feature of the subject matter of a narrative – the thing that the story is about. As Bernard Williams points out, a narrative of failure is not the same thing as a failed narrative.[28] Likewise, a life that lacks unity in the sense of practical integration could nevertheless be described in a unified narrative. On the other hand, a perfectly unified life could be described in a narrative that was fragmented, disjointed and

---

[26] My claim here is about the ideas themselves, not the interpretation of *AV*. But I also believe this is MacIntyre's own view as presented in *AV*. So as a matter of interpreting *AV*, I disagree with Bernard Williams when he says: 'When MacIntyre writes "the unity of a human life is the unity of a narrative quest", I take it that the large ambiguity of his statement is to be resolved in favour of his meaning the quest for a narrative, rather than the narrative of a quest' (Williams 2009: 305–306).

[27] For a lucid and insightful discussion of narrative and narrative thinking, including the process of 'emplotment', see Goldie 2012: 1–25.

[28] Williams 2009: 309–10.

170   *Micah Lott*

incomplete. Someone who merely drifts through life might thereby be open to criticism. But that criticism applies to how they are living, not to how their living is narrated. And it isn't clear why even a life that was highly deficient in integrity and constancy couldn't be described in a unified narrative.[29]

What, then, about the role of narrative in practical deliberation? MacIntyre claims, 'I can only answer the question, "What must I do?" if I can answer the prior question, "Of what story or stories do I find myself a part?"'.[30] Understood as a point about the conditions required for practical deliberation to get off the ground, this claim is highly plausible. By the time we are able to deliberate, we are already embedded in relationships, practices and institutions. These provide our 'moral starting point'.[31] And stories are a crucial way of grasping the relationships, practices and institutions in which we find ourselves, and of making intelligible our goals, commitments and values. So our moral starting point must be given largely in narrative terms. In this way, narrative is necessary for practical deliberation to begin.

That said, we cannot simply 'read off' the correct way to act and live from the stories we find ourselves in. For depending on the stories in which you find yourself, and your part in those stories, acting well might require different responses (loyalty, resistance, aspiration, indifference, etc.). Your practical thinking needs to focus on the genuine goods, values and norms that are at stake in whatever narrative contexts you are a part of. So the stories you find yourself in are of limited significance for your practical deliberation.

Suppose I am considering a radical change in life. Up to the age of forty my life has been focused largely on making money. I come to suspect that I've been living by distorted values, and I consider changing my life's focus. Consulting the story of my life so far cannot tell me, in any direct way, how to proceed. For the right way to understand that story – the story of a wealthy person with a successful career in finance – is in large measure what I am trying to discern. Have I been achieving great things or wasting my time? Making the world a better place or functioning as a parasite on the work of others? Likewise, the goal of living out a unified life narrative is not much help. For whatever I decide to do with my life, the result can be narrated in a unified way. If I change course, then my life's story will have a different shape than it would

---

[29] Limit case: if the person were to lack integrity and constancy altogether, we could not see them as having any genuine commitments or values. We would then lose our grip on them *as* a rational agent.
[30] MacIntyre 1984: 216.   [31] MacIntyre 1984: 216.

After Virtue, Narrative and the Human Good 171

otherwise, and perhaps it will belong in the genre of conversion story. But such a story can be perfectly unified as a narrative. On the other hand, if I continue with my current way of living, it is a poor justification for this to say, 'Well, I've lived like this so far, so I should remain consistent!' Acting well cannot be assumed to be equivalent to acting consistently with prior behaviour.

To approach this issue from a slightly different angle, consider a person who aspires to 'live out' an imagined life story (e.g. the story of being an excellent and influential journalist). Understood one way, such an aspiration is a familiar, perhaps necessary, part of practical thinking. When we consider a long-term goal, it makes sense to consider what it might look like to pursue that goal successfully over time. And the typical, perhaps essential, form of such thinking is a narrative. This suggests that narrative thinking matters for practical thinking not only as a way of understanding the stories of which we are a part, but also for imagining possible future stories (i.e. possible courses of action and ways of living to which we might aspire).[32]

At the same time, there is a way of aspiring to live out a story that amounts to regrettable alienation from one's own activity. Suppose I tell you that I aspire to be a great journalist – 'I want *that* story to be the story of my life'. But suppose, too, that I have no love for the craft of journalism, no appreciation for the virtues of truthfulness and tenacity that are required of good journalists, no sense of journalism's role in a well-functioning society and no desire to investigate matters of public importance. Upon inspection, my position is scarcely intelligible. What is missing is my appreciation of the goodness or value of a possible career in journalism. Such an appreciation is precisely what you need to bring into view if you are to understand *why* I aspire to live out the story of a great journalist. And it is what I need to bring into view for myself, if my own aspiration is not to confront me as a strange and inexplicable urge that I must deal with.

By contrast, when we are not alienated from our own desires and aspirations, we are drawn to potential courses of action because we perceive some goodness in that way of acting. I might want to live out the story of a being a great journalist because I have been impressed by the insight and boldness that journalism requires, or I have been moved by journalism's capacity to expose injustice, etc. In the language of *AV*: I am drawn to the practice of journalism by some initial awareness of the internal goods of the practice of journalism. If I pursue a career in

---

[32] For discussion of this point in relation to our powers of memory and imagination, see Murphy 2020: 145–76.

172   *Micah Lott*

journalism, and if all goes well, then my understanding of those goods will deepen, together with my capacity to realise those goods in my own activity *qua* journalist. In this case, narrative modes of thinking might be essential for my understanding of both the practice of journalism and its possible place in my life as a whole. Even so, my motivation to 'live out the story' of a great journalist is a matter of direct, first-personal appreciation of the goods that define the practice of journalism. Indeed, unless I remain alive to those goods, then I cannot *be* living out the story of a great journalist, since a great journalist is motivated by an appreciation of those goods.

9.5   *Ethics in the Conflicts of Modernity*: A Complete Life?

So far I have examined MacIntyre's appeal to narrative notions in *AV*, and I've identified some ways that narrative ideas can, and cannot, contribute to an Aristotelian approach to moral philosophy. I now turn to the place of narrative in some of MacIntyre's later work.

Eighteen years after *AV*, MacIntyre published *Dependent Rational Animals* (MacIntyre 1999a; *DRA*). Central to *DRA* is the claim that our final end should be construed as *human flourishing*, and that human flourishing should be understood within a broader, naturalistic account of flourishing that also applies to non-human animals. In *AV* MacIntyre describes his view as a 'socially teleological account' in contrast to Aristotle's 'biologically teleological account'. But in the preface to *DRA*, MacIntyre explicitly repudiates his earlier strategy of separating ethics from biology. *DRA* develops a version of Aristotelian ethical naturalism.[33] And in striking contrast to *AV*, *DRA* contains no discussion of narrative.

However, MacIntyre did not simply jettison narrative for a return to nature. *Ethics in the Conflicts of Modernity* (MacIntyre 2016; *ECM*) appeared seventeen years after *DRA*, and *ECM* offers a view that integrates the naturalistic framework of *DRA* with *AV*'s account of social practices and their internal goods. And in *ECM* MacIntyre argues that in order to understand human flourishing we must draw on the resources of narrative thinking.[34] In returning to narrative, MacIntyre reiterates a number of points from *AV*, including the claim that the unity of a human

---

[33] For a discussion of MacIntyre as an Aristotelian naturalist, see Beier 2020. For MacIntyre's own brief remarks on his view as a kind of ethical naturalism, see MacIntyre 1999a: 78–9.

[34] Many of the claims about narrative in *ECM* also appear in MacIntyre's 2014 essay 'Ends and Endings'.

After Virtue, Narrative and the Human Good   173

life is 'the unity of a narrative'.[35] In addition, *ECM* contains four narratives of individuals who lived and died in the twentieth century. MacIntyre cites two reasons for including these narratives. First, in order to understand ethical concepts, we must see how they apply to real-life cases. And second, ethical theory needs to be informed by the consideration of particular cases, and vice versa.[36]

With regard to the connection between narrative and our final end, I take one of MacIntyre's central points in *ECM* to be this: we have no way to understand, in any significant or satisfying way, whether and how someone has lived *a good life* – whether or not, and in what ways, someone has attained or failed to attain their final end – apart from the narrative(s) of the person's life. And our most important stories about human lives presuppose some conception of a human *telos* that shapes how we tell the stories of individual lives, especially with regard to the various kinds of success and failure that figure in those stories.

I accept this central point. However, I wish to raise some doubts about MacIntyre's specific understanding of how we should conceive of our final end, and by extension how we should tell the stories of human lives. In particular, I want to focus on MacIntyre's understanding of the claim that our final end 'completes and perfects the life of the agent who achieves it'.[37] Consider the following passage:

Of any life which has come to an ending or is about to come to an ending, whether our own or that of an another we can ask, 'What, if anything, makes this life, qua the life of a human being, significantly imperfect and incomplete? What is or was lacking in it which would have brought it to completion?' To answer these questions is to have found application for the concept of a final end for human beings and to have posed the problems about the relationship between our ends and our endings, about how we should tell the stories of lives that go well and lives that go badly.

What is the sense of 'complete' that we should have in mind here? At the most abstract level, the notion of a complete life refers to an *ideal* life. In this sense, a complete life lacks nothing we can appropriately wish for, a life that is no way defective or marred: our final end. As we saw in Section 9.1, the Aristotelian notion of our final end also identifies two more specific senses of complete as aspects of an ideal life: (1) complete as a matter of how you are living – your activity is not defective or lacking, you are doing excellently; and (2) complete as a matter of the duration of your life – your life is not cut short (or extended too long, perhaps). Evidently, MacIntyre is here referring to a complete life in an

---

[35] MacIntyre 2016: 231.   [36] MacIntyre 2016: 243, 311.   [37] MacIntyre 2016: 53.

174   *Micah Lott*

encompassing sense that includes *both* of these aspects of completeness. For if we were only interested in how you are living, there would be no need to wait until your life has 'come to an ending or is about to come to an ending' to ask about that. And if we were only interested in the temporal duration of your life, that would not be sufficient to tell us the extent to which you had realised your final end. After all, you might live to a ripe old age, passing through all the stages of life, and yet live viciously and miserably at each stage.

However, in the final paragraph of *ECM*, MacIntyre considers those who die before attaining the particular final ends that give focus and orientation to their lives, and he insists that it would be a mistake to suppose that such persons must have fallen short of completing their lives, or to think that they might have done so if only they had lived longer. Why is this a mistake? Here is MacIntyre's explanation:

> To live well is to act so as to move toward achieving the best goods of which one is capable and so as to become the kind of agent capable of achieving those goods. But there is no particular finite good the achievement of which perfects and completes one's life. There is always something else and something more to be attained, whatever one's attainments. The perfection and completion of a life consists in an agent's having persisted in moving toward and beyond the best goods of which she or he knows.[38]

There are several different claims here. One claim is that whatever your attainments, there is always something more to attain. Is this true? Of course, human finitude means that there is more to discover, create, nurture, etc., than anyone can do in a single lifetime. But is there always more for *you* to attain, in the sense of something that is the appropriate object of your striving? Consider someone who says, 'I've lived a full life and done all that I was put here to do'. Must such a person be mistaken about the human *telos*? A lot seems to depend on the sort of goods we have in mind. Suppose the good is a project like founding a hospital and working to make it effective and sustainable. It does not seem unreasonable if, after working for decades on a hospital, someone concludes that *their* task with the hospital is finished – they have attained all there is for them to attain with respect to this good – and it is time to pass on the work to others. Is MacIntyre's claim, then, that no matter your attainments of such goods, there is always more of this sort of thing that you should work towards? More hospitals to found, more paintings to paint, more books to read, etc. Personally I find this an appealing suggestion. But I do not see why someone must accept this vision of living well. You

[38] MacIntyre 2016: 315.

After Virtue, Narrative and the Human Good 175

need not think there is some *particular* finite good the achievement of which perfects your life. But you might think that a certain configuration of finite goods, or a range of achievements, can be sufficient for a complete life (i.e. a life lacking nothing that a human can reasonably hope for, a life that reaches its *telos*). This would not, presumably, be a perfect life in every sense, but still a fine example of the good life, and not incomplete because it left hospitals unbuilt, paintings unpainted, books unread, etc.

On the other hand, consider goods of a different sort. It does not make sense to say that you have attained, once and for all, the good of being a good friend or good neighbour. Nor is the task of being a good friend or good neighbour ever fully finished.[39] More generally, as long as you are living as a rational agent, you face the task of living virtuously. And there is always room to expand and deepen your understanding of what it means to live justly, kindly, truthfully, etc. So we might say that the task of living well is *never finished*. This, however, is a rather different way of interpreting the idea that there is always something more to be attained, since it appeals to different sorts of goods from hospitals, paintings, books, etc., and since the task of living well is not one project or goal among others, alongside building, painting, reading, etc.[40]

Another claim in the passage above is that the perfection and completion of a life 'consists in an agent's having persisted in moving toward and beyond the best goods of which she or he knows'. On the one hand, this is a welcome invitation to think of living well as something dynamic rather than static. On the other hand, this formulation sets the bar for our final end too low. Imagine someone who grows up committed to false values, after being educated into a distorted and hateful ideology. Such a person might persist in moving towards and beyond the best

---

[39] Perhaps someone might object at this point: 'But being a good friend is no longer *mine to do*; my time for taking up that task is over.' Or perhaps: 'The way that I am to be a good friend requires me to do something that will end my life, so I can only live up to the task of being a good friend by doing that which will bring my pursuit of that task to a stop, an ending.'

[40] This last point is a version of the point we encountered earlier, as part of MacIntyre's discussion of the limits of the practice-only approach to the virtues. It is a point that MacIntyre has made in multiple places in slightly different ways. For example, in 'Ends and Endings', he writes: 'Types of activities are as various as mountain climbing, chimney cleaning, coal mining, playing the cello, and trimming one's toenails. But the project of developing and exercising the power of being moved by good reasons to achieve the genuinely desirable is not one more such type of activity, something undertaken in the time left over from mountain climbing, chimney cleaning, coal mining, playing the cello, and trimming one's toenails. It is a project less or more successfully implemented in all those types of different activity, indeed in every type of activity' (MacIntyre 2014: 816).

176   *Micah Lott*

goods *of which he knows*, but still not progress very far towards a true appreciation of genuine human goods. There might be something to respect about this movement in the right direction, but such a life is not a good candidate for the human good.

What, then, about lives that are cut short in the sense of ending before the person can realise many of the best and highest goods towards which their activity is orientated (e.g. a loving husband and father who dies after only a few years of marriage, while his children are still young)? MacIntyre says we should resist thinking that such lives are necessarily incomplete, precisely because there is *always* something more for someone to attain. But this is unconvincing. We should distinguish between: (1) a complete life in the sense of an ideal life, lacking in nothing that we might properly hope for in a human life; and (2) a complete life in the sense that the agent whose life it is has attained all there is to attain. Suppose we reject the idea of (2), insisting that there is always more to attain (however we spell that idea out). This is still compatible with a notion of (1), and indeed it can be a way of characterising that notion: even in an ideal life – a successful life that exemplifies the human good and can be described as complete – there will never be a moment in which the task of living well can been finished once and for all. Affirming that, however, is consistent with holding that a life cut short before the attainment of central goods is thereby incomplete. Even if there is always more to attain, it might be that a life can be considered complete only once someone has attained *enough* (however we understand that), and that someone might fail to attain enough on account of their life ending too soon.

Elsewhere in *ECM*, MacIntyre says that it was 'Aquinas's central insight about the final end of human beings' that our final end 'cannot be identified with any finite and particular end'. This insight, MacIntyre says, can be expressed by saying that 'we complete our lives by allowing them to remain incomplete. A good life is one in which an agent, although continuing to rank order particular and finite goods, treats none of these goods as necessary for the completion of her or his life, so leaving her or himself open to a final good beyond all such goods, as good desirable beyond such goods.' And on this view, 'lives cut short by inopportune and untimely deaths are not thereby imperfect. What matters is what the agent was open to at the time of her or his death, not the perhaps great, but finite goods of which the agent was deprived by that death.'[41]

---

[41] MacIntyre 2016: 230–31.

After Virtue, Narrative and the Human Good

These remarks deserve more attention than I can give them here, and I will only make two brief points. First, even if there is no particular finite good – or even a particular configuration of finite goods – that is necessary for the completion of a person's life, it could nevertheless be true that *some* configuration of finite goods is both necessary and sufficient for living a complete life. Second, if we refuse to say that 'lives cut short by inopportune and untimely deaths' are thereby lacking with respect to their final end, it becomes unclear why we should describe these deaths as *in*opportune or *un*timely. The most intuitive way of explaining their untimeliness is to say that because of *when* someone died, that person was prevented from attaining something that would have contributed to the realisation of their final end. Because of dying too soon, their life lacked something. But if an untimely death does not make a life any less perfect or complete, we can't offer this explanation.

Let's return to stories. We tell many different types of true stories about a human life. Our stories communicate how persons pursue ends of different sorts and various kinds of success or failure in achieving those ends. Out stories also communicate different *meanings* that a life can have (i.e. different dimensions of what a life amounts to, especially when viewed as a whole and in its social and historical context). For some lives, the true stories of that life will include *both* stories that depict that life as tragically cut short, with much unrealised promise and much lacking, *and* stories that depict that same life as one that was lived nobly and beautifully up to its ending.

Is there any reason to expect, or wish for, stories of human lives that convey whether or not those lives were complete overall, stories that pass a kind of summative judgement on whether the individual realised the human good? In another passage from *ECM* that echoes the passage quoted above, MacIntyre imagines a neo-Aristotelian agent who tells 'a narrative of her life as agent'. Such a narrative, MacIntyre says, will 'have a teleological structure, so that, if she was to recount it to us, we would find ourselves asking, 'Will she achieve her end? *Will her life be complete or left unfinished?*'[42] I accept MacIntyre's point about the teleological structure of narratives and of human lives. But is this last question really one that we will, or should, be asking when telling or hearing the story of a life?

I am sceptical. There is, for instance, something forced and unconvincing about MacIntyre's declaration that Vassily Grossman's commitment to his task as a writer 'completed Grossman's own life', and that

---

[42] MacIntyre 2016: 57, emphasis added.

Grossman's life was 'in fact *eudaimon*'.[43] There is too much left out of MacIntyre's narrative of Grossman's life to sustain these declarations (e.g. we hear very little about Grossman's friendships and family life and little about his personal virtues or vices). This is not to say that MacIntyre's narrative is poorly told or uninformative or otherwise defective. On the contrary, it is insightful and thought-provoking. The point, rather, is that we should not ask too much of our narratives of human lives. Our most general notion of the human good, of a perfected and completed life, is extremely abstract. We should see this notion of the human *telos* as defining a general conceptual space that needs to be filled with more specific ways of conceiving success or failure along a variety of dimensions. The stories we tell about human lives often highlight only a few aspects of how someone lived and the shape their life took, only a few dimensions of excellence or defect, only a small part of the life's meaning. Our stories rarely allow us to say with much confidence whether or not a person 'completed their life' in the most encompassing sense, or to identify precisely what was lacking that would have 'brought it to completion'. But that is fine. This is another case where we should not expect too much from narrative.

[43] MacIntyre 2016: 264.

10 *After Virtue* as a Narrative of Revolutionary Practical Reason

Christopher Stephen Lutz

Alasdair MacIntyre has passed through significant changes in his religious outlook over the course of his career. As a young man he wrote as a Christian Marxist (MacIntyre 1953), later he wrote as an atheist Marxist (MacIntyre 1978a; see also MacIntyre 1969b), then as a disillusioned ex-Marxist interested in sociology and Aristotle (MacIntyre 1977a; see also MacIntyre 1977b), then as a Christian Aristotelian indebted to Marx (MacIntyre 2007), and since 1988 he has written as a Catholic Thomistic-Aristotelian indebted to Marx (MacIntyre 1988; 1990; 1999a; 2006d; 2016). These transformations may appear to segment MacIntyre's career into distinct phases, but the main themes of MacIntyre's moral philosophy have remained remarkably constant throughout his career. *After Virtue* is the most widely celebrated milestone in MacIntyre's moral philosophy, but as I have argued elsewhere (Lutz 2004; 2012; 2014; 2018; 2020), appearing a few years after the 1977 essay 'Epistemological Crises, Dramatic Narrative and the Philosophy of Science', which marked the beginning of MacIntyre's mature work, *After Virtue* stands in the middle of a career that is unified as a pursuit of a peculiar kind of moral truth that acknowledges the role of history in that pursuit.

Jason Blakely argued in his 2020 article 'MacIntyre contra MacIntyre' that *Dependent Rational Animals* (1999) marks a break from the theory of rationality that informed the books that preceded it (Blakely 2020b: 132).[1] The first sections of Blakely's article interpret *After Virtue* as a synthesis of historicist, interpretive philosophy and Aristotelian ethics (2020b: 126), but Blakely overstates the historicism of *After Virtue* and reads MacIntyre's later work as a retreat from that exaggerated historicism: 'Beginning with *Dependent Rational Animals* MacIntyre increasingly embraced a form of Aristotelianism that returned to biological metaphysics' (2020b: 131). Blakely argues 'that MacIntyre's turn

---

[1] Blakely mentions my first book at 2020b: 132.

180 *Christopher Stephen Lutz*

toward metaphysical biology is philosophically incompatible with his development of an interpretive and historicist account of human action' (2020b: 132). Blakely rejects what he takes to be the normative role of Thomistic-Aristotelian ontology in MacIntyre's ethics:

> MacIntyre's attempt to naturalise normative theory precisely robs it of its historicity, rendering ethical and political meanings as if they were a set of facts outside of tradition. Suddenly humans are analysable in the tradition-free, ahistorical species-being of dolphins and not the rival moral communities characteristic of the debates of *After Virtue*. (2020b: 137)

Blakely's complaint is no small matter for MacIntyre's project; if it were accurate, it would mark MacIntyre's abandonment of that project.

Following Gilbert Ryle (1945–1946) MacIntyre approaches morality as a matter of 'knowing how' rather than 'knowing that'. Narratives about desire, human relationships and practical choices play the defining role in MacIntyre's ethics and politics, not abstract normative theories about knowledge of duties and obligations. For MacIntyre, modern normative theories are fictional narratives that distort practical reasoning by separating morality from human desire. This chapter will review some of MacIntyre's early work to illuminate the critical argument of *After Virtue* (chapters 1–9) and to emphasise the limitations it imposes on his approach to moral philosophy. MacIntyre's mature work observes those limitations by uniting morality and desire; he does not appeal to Thomistic ontology to support any normative theory in moral epistemology, for he rejects moral epistemology. I will defend the continuity of MacIntyre's enquiries, and particularly the continuity of his mature work, from 'Epistemological Crises' to the present. In the process, I will frame the questions about MacIntyre's moral philosophy in a way that will, I hope, allay Blakely's concern. I defend the qualified historicism of MacIntyre's theory of rationality[2] and its application to moral philosophy, even as I affirm the realism of the ontological stance that I share with MacIntyre, including our shared affirmation of Thomistic natural law.

10.1 MacIntyre's Moral Narrative

Two themes unite seventy years of MacIntyre's writings in ethics and politics: the rejection of modern normative theories and the pursuit of practical reasoning. Conventional moral philosophers and their critics debate *which* normative theory provides the true criterion of moral duties

---

[2] For a more thorough treatment of MacIntyre's theory of rationality, see Lutz 2019.

After Virtue as Narrative of Revolutionary Practical Reason   181

and obligations or *whether* philosophy can determine moral duties and obligations at all; MacIntyre takes a different course. MacIntyre asks the Aristotelian question: how can we become the kind of people who recognise what is good and best for us to do and who exercise the moral freedom to act on that judgement? He responds with an ethics of practical reasoning.

MacIntyre's moral narrative finds the human person at home in a web of relationships with others, principally with members of the communities that have raised and educated the person, but also with those to whom their communities' relationships bind their members. The naturally social members of these communities discover the practical demands of free and deliberate human agency together in their quest to recognise and attain what is truly choice-worthy. Working together, these people may discover that certain habits of judgement and action – the virtues and vices – help or hinder their pursuits of worthwhile things. If the members of communities are attentive to the nature of these habits, they may learn to define the virtues as qualities of character that enable them to succeed in practices, in life considered as a whole and in fostering the life of their community.

10.1.1 *Modern Normative Theory*

By contrast, conventional modern moral philosophers ask what rational morality obliges them to do and what behaviour it forbids, and they seek the sources of their knowledge of this kind of compulsion. Christine Korsgaard, a Kantian, writes in 'The Normative Question', the first of her Tanner Lectures:

ethical standards are normative ... They make claims on us; they command, oblige, recommend, or guide ... And it is the force of these normative claims – the right of these concepts to give laws to us – that we want to understand. (Korsgaard 1996: 8–9)

For Korsgaard, morality is a matter of obligation, not desire. In the prologue to her Tanner Lectures, Korsgaard contrasts the Platonic and Aristotelian moralities of excellence with modern moralities of obligation:

When we seek excellence, the force that value exerts on us is attractive; when we are obligated, it is compulsive. For obligation is the imposition of value on a reluctant, recalcitrant, resistant matter. Obligation is the compulsive power of form. Excellence is natural; but obligation – as Nietzsche says ... – is the work of art. (1996: 4)

Korsgaard's search for the sources of this kind of obligation leads her to Kant and his theory of autonomy: 'The ethics of autonomy is the only one

182   *Christopher Stephen Lutz*

consistent with the metaphysics of the modern world, and the ethics of autonomy is an ethics of obligation' (1996: 5). A normative theory, in Korsgaard's sense, is an epistemological theory explaining the human agent's knowledge of obligations that are contrary to that agent's desires. Is Alasdair MacIntyre's moral narrative a normative theory in this sense? It is not.

10.2   Background to the Critical Argument of *After Virtue*

MacIntyre's moral narrative has more in common with Elizabeth Anscombe's contentions that we should stop doing moral philosophy and jettison conventional moral concepts because modern normative ethics is incoherent, unreliable and, due to pervasive consequentialism, available for grave misuse (Anscombe 1958). MacIntyre's rejection of modern normative ethics is like Anscombe's but more radical, and it is inseparable from his moral outlook. The critical argument of *After Virtue* is based on positions that MacIntyre had been developing and advancing since his student days, hence we can gain a better appreciation of the critical argument by considering how it follows from his education and early writings.

10.2.1   *MacIntyre's Education*

From the very beginning of his philosophical career, MacIntyre has rejected modern normative moral theories. In the autobiographical lecture 'On Having Survived the Academic Moral Philosophy of the Twentieth Century', delivered in Dublin in 2009 (MacIntyre 2013c), MacIntyre credits his early aversion to modern normative theories to two distinct influences: A. J. Ayer and the Communist Party.

Ayer's book *Language, Truth, and Logic* was one of the first works to defend emotivism (see Ayer 1952: 102–20). Ayer argued that 'the fundamental ethical concepts are unanalyzable' because 'they are merely pseudo-concepts' (1952: 107),[3] and that 'ethical statements are expressions and excitants of feeling' (1952: 109–10). Thus, moral judgements are neither true nor false; they express only our emotional responses.

MacIntyre found his reading of Jean-Paul Sartre's lecture 'L'existentialisme est un humanisme',[4] and Ayer's response to it, to reinforce his rejection of normative theory:

---

[3] MacIntyre uses this phrase in his treatment of utilitarianism in *After Virtue*: 'the notion of the greatest happiness of the greatest number ... is indeed a pseudo-concept available for a variety of ideological uses, but no more than that' (MacIntyre 2007: 64).

[4] MacIntyre reports that he read this lecture during a trip to Paris in 1947 (2013c: 19). For a current English translation, see Sartre 2007.

After Virtue as Narrative of Revolutionary Practical Reason   183

Sartre argues that although we may have reasons for making our choices as we do, those reasons have only such weight as each of us chooses to give them ... And on this Ayer concurred, even though he and Ayer disagreed about much else. 'It is one of Sartre's merits', Ayer wrote, 'that he sees that no system of values can be binding on someone unless he chooses to make it so' (Ayer 1950: 633–4). (MacIntyre 2013c: 19)

By his own account, MacIntyre was convinced as an undergraduate that the power of moral values must be explicable in terms of the subjective determinations of the agent.

The Communist Party taught MacIntyre to criticise morality and moral philosophy in a way that paralleled the lessons he took from Ayer:

Marx and Engels had argued that every morality is the morality of some particular social and economic order and that every moral philosophy articulates and makes explicit the judgements, arguments, and presuppositions of some particular morality, either in such a way as to defend both that morality and the economic order of which it is the expression, or in such a way as to undermine them. And my acknowledgement of the truth of this thesis was reinforced by my encounters with social anthropology. (MacIntyre 2013c: 20; see also MacIntyre 1996)

Like Ayer and Sartre, the Marxists denied that conventional moral philosophy has any connection to moral truth; moreover, they taught MacIntyre to interpret modern moral philosophy as the ideology of the liberal, individualist moral and economic order.

Where Ayre and Sartre had argued that morality was either a psychological phenomenon or the outcome of personal choices, the Marxists held that moral philosophy is an ideology produced to defend or to criticise the conventional moral order, which in turn had been produced to fix and sanctify the arrangements of the underlying, arbitrary, social and economic order. These two complementary assessments of moral phenomena leave little room for normative theory.

10.2.2 *MA Thesis*, The Significance of Moral Judgements *(1951)*

The lessons MacIntyre drew from Ayer, Sartre and Marx barred the path to conventional moral philosophy and made the meaning or significance of moral judgements problematic. In his 1951 MA thesis, *The Significance of Moral Judgements*, MacIntyre weighs G. E. Moore's intuitionist normative theory against C. L. Stevenson's emotivist reduction of morality to a psychological phenomenon before proposing an account of practical reasoning that refutes Moore and supplements Stevenson.

Moore had argued that moral judgements were propositions about the presence or absence of the non-natural quality of goodness in an action

184 *Christopher Stephen Lutz*

or object. C. L. Stevenson, whose writings (Stevenson 1937: 14–31; 1944) had become standard statements of emotivist theory, argued that moral judgements are propositions expressing the emotive response of the speaker to the object in an attempt to align the attitudes of others to the speaker's own (see Stevenson 1937: 23). MacIntyre judged that both theories follow from the same presupposition: namely, that if there is knowledge in morals, it must be knowledge of moral propositions. Moore affirms the consequent, and his invalid inference cannot justify the antecedent. Stevenson denies the consequent, arguing validly that the antecedent is false. But this argument traps Stevenson in the paradox of denying 'that there are moral truths which can be known' (MacIntyre 1951b: 9).[5] MacIntyre denies the presupposition shared by Moore and Stevenson. Citing Gilbert Ryle's Presidential Address to the Aristotelian Society, MacIntyre argues that morality is not a matter of 'knowing that', but of 'knowing how' (MacIntyre 1951b: 10). Summing up, MacIntyre explains:

They hold in common that the language of moral disagreement is referential, that if one is asked what one is disagreeing about, one can always show this ostensively by pointing to some fact. Nor does either consider that moral disagreement might be neither disagreement *about* the facts or *in* the attitude but rather *how* to attack a practical problem. '(MacIntyre 1951b: 22, emphases in original)

MacIntyre criticises both Moore and Stevenson, but he credits Stevenson for the refutation of Moore's false theory (MacIntyre 1951b: 27), even as he supplements Stevenson's conclusion with his own:

This is not to deny the emotive character of the moral judgement: it is to suggest that when we have said of moral judgements that they are emotive that we have left a great deal unsaid – and even the emotive may have a logic to be mapped. Such a logic can never be enunciated in rigorous terms. This is partly because practical problems never recur in quite the same way and partly because morality is not a 'knowing that' but a 'knowing how' (MacIntyre 1951b: 89).

MacIntyre's answer to the question of the significance of moral judgements is not a normative theory, but a reconsideration of the meaning of moral judgements that supplements emotivism with a narrative of practical rationality that interprets moral judgements as solutions to practical problems, as judgements of practical reason.

MacIntyre concludes that moral judgement is an unavoidable element of ordinary human life:

For if the function of moral judgements, as we have argued, is to guide us in dealing with practical problems, then moral judgements can never be evaded.

---

[5] It is paradoxical to assert as a moral truth that there are no moral truths.

After Virtue as Narrative of Revolutionary Practical Reason   185

And if the moral as distinguished from but never perhaps to be experienced apart from the psychological constraint of obligation which has some connections with the performatory and committing nature of the moral judgement, then obligation is as inevitable in the solution to our problems. (MacIntyre 1951b: 90)

The question is not *whether* one will judge practical problems morally, but *which morality* will inform one's judgements concerning practical problems (see MacIntyre 1951b: 90–91). Nevertheless, for MacIntyre, the normativity of those obligations is purely practical, drawn from the connections between what people are trying to do and the available means to achieve it.

10.2.3 Marxism: An Interpretation *(1953)*

MacIntyre's first book, *Marxism: An Interpretation*, criticises the contemporary Christian Church and the contemporary Communist Party in the light of the Gospel and the early writings of Marx in order to highlight the lessons that Christians may take from Marxists, even as they reject Marxist atheism (see MacIntyre 1995b: 145–58). MacIntyre takes a special interest in two of Marx's works: *The Economic and Philosophic Manuscripts of 1844*[6] and *The Theses on Feuerbach*.[7] The former represents the early, 'prophetic' Marx, before his unfortunate turn to predictive social science.[8] The latter marks the path that MacIntyre would follow throughout his career, a path that Marx abandoned when he turned to predictive social science.

The Theses on Feuerbach are eleven brief statements criticising Feuerbach, whose focus on theoretical questions had robbed his philosophy of practical power. The third thesis questions the relationship between theory and practice in social progress. Observing that there is no knowledge of progress prior to progress to guide progress, Marx finds that everyone involved, whether leader or follower, must discover together what revolution will mean for their own education and for the restructuring of the social world. This kind of progress does not follow

---

[6] MacIntyre cites this book as *National Economy and Philosophy*, a direct translation of its German title, *National-Ökonomie und Philosophie*. Later it received its standard English title *The Economic and Philosophic Manuscripts of 1844* with the publication of Marx 1959.

[7] The *Theses on Feuerbach*, written in the spring of 1845, was first published as an appendix to Friedrich Engels, *Ludwig Feuerbach und der Ausgang der Klassischen Deutschen Philosophie* (Stuttgart 1888), first English translation, *Ludwig Feuerbach and the End of Classical German Philosophy* (Moscow: Progress Press 1946).

[8] See MacIntyre 1953: 68–72. This passage is heavily redacted and revised in MacIntyre 1968: 70.

186   *Christopher Stephen Lutz*

the application of theory; it is an engagement in revolutionary practice. MacIntyre asks:

> in changing the world should we start with transforming ourselves and mankind ... or should we begin with transforming our circumstances? Marx's answer is that we cannot do one without the other. To acquire a true philosophy is, of course, to transform oneself: this truth itself is only to be acquired in practice. 'The coincidence of the changing of [circumstances and of][9] human activity or self-changing can be comprehended and rationally understood only as *revolutionary practice*'. (MacIntyre 1953: 59, emphasis in original)

MacIntyre's endorsement of Marx's notion of revolutionary practice fits closely with the arguments in his MA thesis that morality is a matter of 'knowing how' rather than 'knowing that', and that moral judgements are solutions to practical problems. Solutions to practical problems are not justified by appeal to any normative theory. They are justified by their effectiveness in solving the problem at hand without creating new ones.

10.2.4   *'What Morality Is Not' (1957)*

MacIntyre's critique of R. M. Hare's theory of universal prescriptivism in the 1957 essay 'What Morality is Not' (MacIntyre 1978b) advances the themes of MacIntyre's MA thesis and first book. MacIntyre first explores a broad range of moral valuations that are not universal, not prescriptive or neither universal nor prescriptive. Next, MacIntyre returns to the lessons from Sartre and Ayer that he explained in his autobiographical Dublin lecture. Real-world moral thinking has little to do with weighing possible actions against authoritative universalisable maxims, because in real life we seldom consult any maxims, and when we do their authority depends on our own choice:

> Most of the actions discussed in moral philosophy textbooks – promise-keeping, truth-telling, and the like – are in practice carried out without any sort of conscious reference to maxims ... [T]he relevant maxims do not guide us because we do not need to be guided. We know what to do. We tell the truth and keep promises most of the time because it does not occur to us to do otherwise. When we are tempted not to do these things from some motive of self-indulgence, it would still not be true to say that if we resist temptation, the maxim guided our conduct. What guided our conduct was our decision to abide by the conduct prescribed by the maxim. (MacIntyre 1978b: 106)

---

[9] The bracketed phrase, absent from MacIntyre's quotation, follows Marx 1969, third thesis.

After Virtue as Narrative of Revolutionary Practical Reason   187

Subjective choice, not objective authority, gives the maxims their power.

MacIntyre likens real moral thinking to Huckleberry Finn's decision to abandon what he takes to be his moral obligations in order to help his friend escape slavery.[10]

> When Huckleberry Finn wrestles with the problem of whether to return Jim, Miss Watson's slave, he is not guided by the maxims of his morality, for his whole problem is whether to abide by those maxims or not ... In fact in deciding not to return Jim he feels wicked and thinks of himself as wicked ... He finds his way morally by means of an only half-articulate sympathy. But he does not find it by universalizable maxims or indeed by any maxims at all. (MacIntyre 1978b: 106–107)

Once again, MacIntyre's argument turns to practical reasoning about goods that a person judges to be worth pursuing, not moral reasoning about duties and obligations.

Huck Finn finds himself compelled by his relationship with Jim to depart from conventional morality; he does not do so because of his maxims. 'When you leave the ground of conventional morality, you leave the guidance of maxims behind' (MacIntyre 1978b: 107). For MacIntyre, the tools appropriate to the study of moral judgement are not those of 'the logician and the linguistic analyst', but 'the kind of phenomenology ... that is supplied by the novelist', particularly 'the moral philosophers of existentialism' (MacIntyre 1978b: 107), and he identifies Jean-Paul Sartre and Simone de Beauvoir in particular. For MacIntyre in 1957, as with his Existentialist contemporaries, modern moral philosophy cannot offer any criteria to govern our choices and decisions, and if we choose to adhere to moral conventions in our choosing, the authority of those conventions depends entirely upon our choice to adhere to them.

10.2.5 *Initiating a New Project: 'Notes from the Moral Wilderness' (1958)*

A year later, MacIntyre published 'Notes from the Moral Wilderness', the essay that announced the project that would become *After Virtue*. 'Notes from the Moral Wilderness' contributed to a discussion in *The New Reasoner*.[11] This journal of the New Left was a forum for people who had abandoned the Soviet-dominated Communist Party, disillusioned

---

[10] See Mark Twain, *The Adventures of Huckleberry Finn*, ch. 31: www.gutenberg.org/files/76/76-h/76-h.htm#c31, accessed 30 May 2022.

[11] All ten issues of *The New Reasoner* (1957–1959) are available online at https://banmarchive.org.uk/new-reasoner/.

188   *Christopher Stephen Lutz*

by the revelations and events of 1956.[12] Members of the New Left remained committed to Marxism, even as they repudiated the Party. MacIntyre had chosen Marxism over the Party a decade earlier, while he was still a student, presumably over the shortcomings of the Party and its orthodoxy, problems he wrote about in *Marxism: An Interpretation* (see MacIntyre 1953: 92–109).

Unlike MacIntyre, many adherents of the New Left had rejected the Communist Party on moral grounds. MacIntyre found their sentiments admirable, but he found their arguments incoherent. 'Notes from the Moral Wilderness' challenges their moral condemnation of Stalinism. 'A position we are all tempted into', MacIntyre begins, 'is that of moral critic of Stalinism' (MacIntyre 1998e: 31). It is a *temptation*, an invitation into error; for although '[t]he ex-Communist turned moral critic of Communism ... confronts the Stalinist with attitudes that in many ways deserve our respect', the Marxist commitments that govern their conversation undercut any appeal to modern secular moral standards – the only moral standards available to these ex-Communist moral critics of Stalinism and Communism.

To press his point, MacIntyre raises the following normative question: 'They repudiate Stalinist crimes in the name of moral principle ... Whence come these standards ... and why should they have authority over us?' (Knight 1998a: 32). To answer this modern normative question, MacIntyre returns to the lessons he learned from Ayer and Sartre:

the moral philosophy of [British analytical philosophers and Continental metaphysicians] can breed the notion of unconditional and arbitrary choice as a, if not the, crucial feature of the individual's moral life. In both there is a picture of the individual standing before the historical events of his time, able to pass judgement on them exactly as he pleases ... They affirm this or that 'ought'; but their morality has no basis. (Knight 1998a: 33)

Returning to the normative question, MacIntyre concludes: 'Why do the moral standards by which Stalinism is found wanting have authority over us? Simply because we choose that they should' (Knight 1998a: 34). Where scholars like Korsgaard would affirm the authority of moral principles and seek the source of their normative power, MacIntyre denies that modern moral principles carry any authority whatsoever and raises the normative question only to dismiss it. It does not follow that Stalinism and Communism are not to be condemned morally; it

---

[12] For an excellent treatment of the origins of the New Left, see Paul Blackledge and Neil Davidson, 'Introduction: The Unknown Alasdair MacIntyre' in Blackledge and Davidson 2008: xx–xxvi.

After Virtue as Narrative of Revolutionary Practical Reason 189

only follows that modern liberal individualist moral ideology[13] is unsuited to the task.

What is the alternative? Where 'Stalinism ... represented the historical process as automatic and as morally sovereign', and the moral critic of Stalinism 'substituted moral values wholly devoid of history', MacIntyre suggests 'a third alternative, ... a theory which treats what emerges in history as providing us with a basis for our standards' (Knight 1998a: 40). This third way cannot be a different way of asking the normative question; it cannot be a different kind of clever, *ex post facto* apologetic that pretends to discover what it presupposes.

MacIntyre saw that his project would demand a different approach to morals: 'we ought to re-examine some of the traditional questions about human nature and morality. What is the relation between what I am, what I can be, what I want to be and what I ought to be?' (Knight 1998a: 40). MacIntyre prescribes questions about the reality of our condition, the possibilities for our development (which we may or may not recognise), the aspirations that we can articulate and the criteria emerging from our histories that give direction to our struggles. These are not 'moral' questions, in the traditional sense, since they are not questions about duties and obligations; they are practical, calculative,[14] teleological questions about the goals that we have and pursue through free and deliberate human actions.

MacIntyre next probes the relationship between human action and moral standards: 'we make both individual deeds and social practices intelligible as human actions by showing how they connect with characteristically human desires, needs, and the like' (MacIntyre 1959, in Knight 1998a: 41). Human actions have a teleological structure; we act to pursue goals to satisfy desires. But modern moral theory specifically denies that moral actions are directed to the agent's goals or desires (Knight 1998a: 41). Hence, 'to represent morality in this light is to make it unintelligible as a form of human action' (Knight 1998a: 42).

MacIntyre briefly outlines the history of modern secular moral demands, from the eudaimonism of Aristotle, to its Christianisation in mediaeval thought, through the shift to divine command theory, to the modern secularisation of morality. He concludes:

[13] Since Marxists dismissed conventional moral philosophy as an ideological apologetic for conventional morality, which they took to be merely a sanctification of arbitrary economic and social arrangements, MacIntyre found it incoherent for Marxists to criticise Stalinism by appeal to conventional morality and moral philosophy.

[14] Cf. Anscombe 1963: §§32–5. Anscombe argues that Aristotelian practical reasoning and the Aristotelian practical syllogism are not properly 'ethical'; they take 'the form of a calculation' (§35).

190 *Christopher Stephen Lutz*

'Do this, because it will bring you to happiness'; 'Do this because God enjoins it as the way to happiness'; 'Do this because God enjoins it'; 'Do this'. These are the four stages in the development of autonomous morality. At each stage our moral concepts are silently redefined so that it soon appears self-evident that they must be used in the way that they are used. (Knight 1998a: 43)

The arbitrary commands that remain at the end of that history are rationalised by Kantian and utilitarian moral philosophy, but their arbitrary character is masked by our culture.

In the conclusion of 'Notes from the Moral Wilderness', MacIntyre proposes a new project to define a Marxist morality. This project would eventually become *After Virtue*.[15] The moral philosophy MacIntyre envisioned would have these characteristics:

As against the Stalinist it is an assertion of moral absolutes; as against the liberal critic of Stalinism it is an assertion of desire and of history ... The liberal sees himself as choosing his values. The Marxist sees himself as discovering them. He discovers them as he rediscovers fundamental human desire; this is a discovery he can only make in company with others. (Knight 1998a: 47)

The insight that understanding what it takes to fulfil fundamental human desires can illuminate real values and give direction to our choices makes the practical project MacIntyre proposes in 'Notes from the Moral Wilderness' essentially *calculative* rather than *ethical*, in the same way that Anscombe found Aristotle's practical syllogism to be calculative rather than ethical in the modern sense (Anscombe 1963: §35). All of MacIntyre's subsequent work in moral philosophy defends communal, goal-directed and goal-discovering, calculative, prudential, practical reasoning as the basis for a moral philosophy in which the criteria governing action are discovered in the pursuit of true practical wisdom, not cleverly imposed in the service of arbitrary goals.[16]

10.2.6 *The Critical Argument in Light of MacIntyre's Earlier Writings*

MacIntyre's early work informs the critical argument of *After Virtue*. In chapters 1–3, MacIntyre introduces emotivism and acknowledges its

---

[15] 'Preface' in MacIntyre 2007: xvii–xviii (1984: ix–x).

[16] Aristotle, in *Nicomachean Ethics* 6.12, distinguishes between prudence (φρόνησις) and cleverness (δεινότης); he defines cleverness as a faculty that enables a person to pursue stated goals effectively, 'to do the things that tend towards the mark we have set before ourselves, and to hit it' (trans. Ross). He warns that cleverness without prudence is 'mere knavery' (πανουργία; trans. Rackham). Nonetheless, Aristotle notes that prudence implies cleverness. To say that, in MacIntyre's view, practical reasoning is calculative rather than 'ethical' *in the modern sense* is to say that it is a deliberative activity in pursuit of true goods rather than an exercise in moral epistemology. See also Anscombe 1963: §35; Aquinas, *Summa Theologiae* II-II, q. 47, a. 13.

After Virtue as Narrative of Revolutionary Practical Reason   191

failure as a general theory of the meaning of moral judgements, but defends it as a theory of the use of moral judgements. MacIntyre calls contemporary culture the 'culture of emotivism'; it is a culture of manipulation in which individuals and organisations work to align the wills of others with their own by making apparently rational appeals to a variety of moral fictions.

Chapters 4–6 explore the history that produced the arbitrary commands rationalised by modern moral philosophy. The central event in this history is the rejection of teleology (MacIntyre 2007: 52–3). The teleological anthropology of Aristotle and of mediaeval Aristotelians defended a functional concept of the human person that 'is far older than Aristotle' (MacIntyre 2007: 58); versions of it appear in classical literature; 'according to that tradition to be a man is to fill a set of roles each of which has its own point and purpose: member of a family, citizen, soldier, philosopher, servant of God' (MacIntyre 2007: 59). '*To be a man*' – that is, to be complete as a human being – is to fulfil the demands of such relationships.

In a variety of ancient and mediaeval moral schemes, various functional concepts of the human person stood as the *telos* of human action, informing different versions of 'a moral scheme … which required three elements: untutored human nature, man-as-he-could-be-if-he-realisedhis-telos and the moral precepts that enable him to move from one state to the other'(MacIntyre 2007: 54). The rejection of Aristotelian metaphysics and the rise of voluntarist theologies in late mediaeval thought had already made the teleological moral scheme untenable and displaced it with divine command ethics. The rejection of those voluntarist theologies during the Enlightenment left educated Europeans with moral claims that needed to be defended without the authority of the Church or State, or against one or the other, if not both.

At this stage secular moral philosophers, who were as convinced of the content of their morality as they were sceptical of its traditional theological justification, began to ask the normative question. These modern secular moral philosophers felt 'a pressure to vindicate [the norms of morality] by devising some new teleology or by finding some new categorical status for them' (MacIntyre 2007: 62). Those modern moral philosophers could not see, as their post-modern critics would, that they were engaged, for the most part, in an *ex post facto* defence of culturally formed and reinforced moral opinions and practices, and that the principles they invented to defend their opinions – the categorical imperative, utility, human rights – were 'moral fictions'.[17]

---

[17] In *After Virtue*, MacIntyre characterises modern moral practices, theories and arguments (including the misuse of social science by manipulative managers) as false, deceiving and

192   *Christopher Stephen Lutz*

In the seventh and eighth chapters of *After Virtue*, MacIntyre pivots away from his critique of modern normative ethical theory to examine a putative alternative to it: namely, the management of social relations according to objective facts, provided by morally neutral social sciences. Chapter 7 calls into question two of the presuppositions of this manoeuvre. First, the philosophy of science teaches that 'facts' are interpretations of phenomena. Facts depend on theory, and inadequate theories yield inadequate 'facts'. Second, efforts to reduce 'the explanation of action' to 'a science of human behaviour ... which omits all reference to intentions, purposes, and reasons for action' (MacIntyre 2007: 82–3) are only another incoherent consequence of the rejection of teleology. Every attempt to govern society according to a determinist theory in social science repeats the errors that Marx rejected in the third thesis on Feuerbach, of exempting the free and deliberate actions of revolutionary leaders from the determinist theory that explains everyone else's behaviour and of masking the leaders' choices to imprint their will 'on nature and society' behind the notion that revolutionary events are merely the natural consequences of antecedent conditions (MacIntyre 2007: 84–5). So MacIntyre questions whether the social sciences have learned to apply 'a real technology or rather instead the deceptive and self-deceptive histrionic mimicry of such a technology' (MacIntyre 2007: 85). MacIntyre suggests that governmental and corporate economic interests in the culture of emotivism have learned to use the social sciences as another kind of moral fiction.

Chapter 8 examines the social sciences. The social sciences are not like the physical sciences; they do not produce law-like generalisations about human behaviour. The generalisations they produce lack predictive power (MacIntyre 2007: 92); 'they are not laws' (MacIntyre 2007: 91). They are a different kind of science (MacIntyre 2007: 92–3). The best insights of the social sciences co-exist with counterexamples related to 'four sources of systematic unpredictability in human affairs' (MacIntyre 2007: 93),[18] even as they develop largely reliable statistical models from four sources of predictability (MacIntyre 2007: 102–103). MacIntyre concludes that the social sciences are useful and valuable; but misusing the social sciences in a 'totalitarian project' (MacIntyre 2007: 106) or, in order to justify the authority of the bureaucratic manager, must be rejected as manipulative and fictive (MacIntyre 2007: 107).

---

fictional. He calls them 'moral fiction(s)' (70–77 and 107), part of a 'masquerade' (9, 40, 75, 107), and he asserts that 'our morality will be disclosed as a theatre of illusions' (77).

[18] MacIntyre discusses the four sources of systematic unpredictability at 93–101.

After Virtue as Narrative of Revolutionary Practical Reason   193

Chapter 9 concludes this critical argument by posing the ultimatum 'Nietzsche or Aristotle': is morality ultimately a matter of arbitrary choice and arbitrary imposition as in Nietzsche, or is it possible to discover values that may guide our choices as in Aristotle? The question hangs on the rationality of recovering something like Aristotelian teleology.

The beauty of the Aristotelian teleological moral scheme is that it excludes the normative question. MacIntyre argued in chapter 6:

> The precepts which enjoin the various virtues and prohibit the vices ... instruct us how to move from potentiality to act, how to realise our true nature and to reach our true end. To defy them will be to be frustrated and incomplete, to fail to achieve that good of rational happiness which it is peculiarly ours as a species to pursue. (MacIntyre 2007: 52)

This teleological scheme makes demands from within the structure of human action. It trades the normative question for the practical question: what is our *telos*?

The critical argument has set up the constructive argument. All MacIntyre has to do is to provide a tenable account of the human *telos*. But the critical argument makes strict demands on the constructive argument. It cannot ask the normative question in a disguised form; it cannot be a clever, *ex post facto* apologetic that pretends to discover what it presupposes. The critical argument binds MacIntyre's constructive argument and all the work that follows *After Virtue* to the same strict standards.

10.3   Revolutionary Practical Reason

Jason Blakely gives an impressive account in 'MacIntyre contra Macintyre' of MacIntyre's success in the constructive argument in proposing a moral narrative that discovers the virtues in what emerges from history without imposing arbitrary will and preference on his readers. Blakely's concerns arise from MacIntyre's subsequent work:

> Beginning with *Dependent Rational Animals* MacIntyre increasingly embraced a form of Aristotelianism that returned to biological metaphysics. This attempt to return to biology was accompanied by assurances that the synthesis with the interpretive concept of a tradition remained intact. Therefore, MacIntyre presented the entire biological turn as largely in continuity with *After Virtue* – albeit with an important correction. Specifically, MacIntyre admitted that *Dependent Rational Animals* marked a key moment of return to 'Aristotle's "metaphysical biology"' (via Thomas Aquinas's insistence on the virtues of dependency) and a rejection of his earlier assumption in *After Virtue* that an 'ethics independent of biology' was possible.[19] But all this, according to

---

[19] Blakely cites *Dependent Rational Animals* (MacIntyre 1999a: x).

194   *Christopher Stephen Lutz*

MacIntyre, simply marked a more complete and thorough embrace of the Aristotle of *After Virtue*. He discovered that his employment of historicised teleology had 'presupposed the truth' of biological metaphysics all along. (Blakely 2020b: 122–31)

Blakely calls this reading 'the continuity narrative'. It is a fair representation of MacIntyre, and many scholars, including myself, have echoed it in our treatments of MacIntyre's mature work.

Blakely rejects the continuity narrative because he holds that MacIntyre's affirmation of the role of biology in ethics is incompatible with the rationality of traditions that MacIntyre had developed in *Whose Justice? Which Rationality?* And *Three Rival Versions of Moral Enquiry*:

Thus, the problem with MacIntyre's later naturalised teleology is that it neglects the meanings, beliefs, and purposes of historically situated agents in favour of positing an ahistorical purpose or teleology resident in our biology. (Blakely 2020b: 136)

The real key to Blakely's complaint appears here:

Indeed, MacIntyre's attempt to naturalise normative theory precisely robs it of historicity, rendering ethical and political meanings as if they were a set of facts outside of tradition. Suddenly humans are analyzable in the tradition-free, ahistorical species-being of dolphins and not the rival moral communities characteristic of the debates of *After Virtue* … Indeed, the earlier MacIntyre could here be quoted contra the later MacIntyre, when he writes that 'there is no standing ground, no place for enquiry … apart from that which is provided by some particular tradition'. (Blakely 2020b: 137, quoting MacIntyre 1988: 350)

According to Blakely's discontinuity narrative, MacIntyre has abandoned the historicism of *After Virtue* to impose an untenable, ahistorical metaphysical biology in order to naturalise normative theory. If Blakely's interpretation is accurate, then MacIntyre has not only transgressed the standards imposed by the critical argument of *After Virtue*; he has abandoned practical reasoning and adopted a normative theory to justify universal moral obligations. Happily, I remain convinced that MacIntyre has not transgressed those standards, has not abandoned practical reasoning and has not adopted a normative theory. How is the continuity narrative consistent with MacIntyre's acknowledgement that our biological nature has an ineliminable role in ethics (see MacIntyre 1996: x)? In order to answer this, we need to back up and look at MacIntyre's earlier paper, 'Epistemological Crises'.

10.3.1   *Theism and Human Enquiry*

'Epistemological Crises, Dramatic Narrative and the Philosophy of Science' treats philosophical progress as a possible outcome of an

After Virtue as Narrative of Revolutionary Practical Reason   195

epistemological crisis (see MacIntyre 2006e: vii–viii). 'Epistemological Crises' concludes that making progress in philosophy may demand that we hold two apparently contradictory notions in tension: an acknowledgement of the objectivity of cosmic order and a recognition of the historically bound condition of human enquiry. On the one hand, MacIntyre admits *with discomfort* that science may presuppose theism. After musing about the attractiveness of Kuhn's fallibilistic view of the philosophy of science, MacIntyre counters:

> But it seems to be a presupposition of the way in which we do natural science that fallibilism has to be made consistent with the regulative ideal of an approach to a true account of the fundamental order of things, and not vice versa. If this is so, Kant is essentially right; the notion of an underlying order – the kind of order we would expect if the ingenious, unmalicious god of Newton and Einstein had created the universe – is a regulative ideal of physics. We do not need to understand this notion quite as Kant did, and our antitheological beliefs may make us uncomfortable in adopting it. But perhaps discomfort at this point is a sign of philosophical progress. (MacIntyre 1977a: 470)[20]

MacIntyre was already entertaining objective ontology – even theistic ontology – as a precondition of science and philosophy. On the other hand, MacIntyre emphasises the historicity of all theory: 'It is only when theories are located in history, when we view the demands for justification in highly particular contexts of a historical kind, that we are freed either from dogmatism or capitulation into skepticism' (MacIntyre 1977a: 471; 2006e: 23).

There is no contradiction between these two positions. If there is a cosmic order, then natural philosophy is a study of causality within that order, but we can attempt that study only within an historically situated tradition of enquiry that may help or hinder our progress in understanding that cosmic order. Inasmuch as 'Epistemological Crises' is the discourse on method that informs MacIntyre's mature work, this tension between ontological reality and historically bound enquiry already informs the argument of *After Virtue*, and all the more so because MacIntyre had returned to the Christian faith before it was published.[21] *After Virtue* leaves room for objective ontology, even theistic ontology,

---

[20] This essay is reprinted with minor revision to this passage in 2006e: 22, where it reads '*their* antitheological beliefs may make *some of our contemporaries* uncomfortable in adopting it' (emphases added). For more on MacIntyre's mature views on the influence of atheism and theism on the philosophical enterprise, see MacIntyre 2010c.

[21] The Gaelic phrase in the book's dedication, 'To the memory of my father and his sisters and brothers, *Gus am bris an la*', means 'Until the day break'. It is a common inscription on Scottish tombstones. It comes from *Song of Solomon* 2:17 and refers to the Christian belief in the resurrection of the dead.

196   *Christopher Stephen Lutz*

behind the order of the cosmos; nonetheless, as a matter of philosophical method, *After Virtue* embraces 'a kind of historicism which excludes all claims to absolute knowledge' (MacIntyre 2007: 270). The book prescinds from any exploration of ontology to focus on 'an historicist defence of Aristotle' (MacIntyre 2007: 277; see also 270–71).

Whose Justice? Which Rationality? and *Three Rival Versions of Moral Enquiry* examine and defend the theory of rationality that informs *After Virtue* (MacIntyre 2007: 260). MacIntyre became a Catholic and a Thomist before writing those books, and both books defend Thomism[22]; so the tension between faith in the ontological order and awareness of the historicity of enquiry is a pervasive theme in both books, yet these books do not offend Blakely's historicist sensibility because they emphasise method.

Dependent Rational Animals differs from its three predecessors because it defends a substantive narrative of practical reason from a standpoint within the Thomistic-Aristotelian intellectual tradition. Here, MacIntyre acknowledges the need to take 'human animality' into account in moral philosophy (MacIntyre 1999a: 5), and it is this move that Blakely interprets as 'MacIntyre's attempt to naturalise normative theory' (Blakely 2020b: 137).

Blakely's reading may seem plausible. For some strains in the Thomistic tradition are voluntaristic, and moralistic, and treat our *telos* as the end that the human agent *ought* to pursue, as if our *telos* were an external imposition rather than the fulfilment of our nature. Some have treated Thomistic ontology as a basis for epistemology. Still others treat Thomistic natural law as a kind of moral epistemology and normative theory. MacIntyre, however, is not any of those kinds of Thomist.

MacIntyre has gone to considerable length to distinguish himself from these and other deficient readings of Thomas Aquinas. In chapter 3 of *Three Rival Versions of Moral Enquiry*, entitled 'Too Many Thomisms', MacIntyre distances himself from early Neo-Thomists who made epistemological concerns central to their Thomism (MacIntyre 1990: 75).[23] In the essay 'Aquinas and the Extent of Moral Disagreements' (MacIntyre 2006a: 64–82), MacIntyre compares the transcendent nature of natural law to our experience of intractable disagreements about its

---

[22] See, e.g., MacIntyre 1988: 403 and MacIntyre 1990: 200.

[23] MacIntyre returned to the history of the Thomistic Renewal in *God, Philosophy, Universities*, briefly considering how the scholarly enterprise of recovering 'Aquinas's writings and thought' informed the curricular enterprise of simplifying and summarising Thomism for classroom use, and how the resulting 'textbook Thomism' shaped the reputation of Thomas Aquinas in the decades that followed (see MacIntyre 2009a: 153–4).

After Virtue as Narrative of Revolutionary Practical Reason   197

demands and concludes that 'Aquinas's account of the precepts of the natural law, far from being inconsistent with the facts of moral disagreement provides the best starting-point for the explanation of these facts' (MacIntyre 2006a: 81–2). For MacIntyre, natural law does not support a neat moral epistemology, and because of its teleological orientation it does not play the role of a modern normative theory. No normative theory is needed for Thomism, because Thomas Aquinas's moral thought studies human action as the pursuit of the good that the agent already desires; it does not investigate the agent's obligation to pursue an arbitrarily assigned end (see Lutz 2018). As Korsgaard said, 'When we seek excellence, the force that value exerts on us is attractive' (Korsgaard 1996: 4).

MacIntyre's ontological but non-epistemological Thomism has caused some controversy. Janet Coleman argued in her contribution to the 1994 volume *After MacIntyre* that MacIntyre (to his credit) was not a real Thomist because he was not an epistemological Thomist (Coleman 1994: 65–90).[24] John Haldane concluded his contribution to the same volume saying, 'I very much hope ... that we will see a future volume by MacIntyre setting out the truth in Thomism', thereby overcoming any concerns that MacIntyre's Thomism could lead to relativism (Haldane 1994: 105). A revised version of MacIntyre's essay on natural law was republished in a book with critical responses from eight noted scholars (Cunningham 2009). For MacIntyre, however, the tension between ontological realism and the situatedness of human enquiry remains fundamental to the human condition; that there is a true answer to a question does not free any human enquirer from the tradition-bound work of answering that question.

10.3.2 *Discovering the Demands of Morality through Practical Reason*

Returning to Blakely's complaint that *Dependent Rational Animals* marks a return to 'metaphysical biology' and is thus an 'attempt to naturalise normative theory', it is important to ask what role MacIntyre's 'reassertion of human animality' plays in the argument. Does it play a normative role, explaining why the moral agent should act against their private interests, or does it play a practical role, helping to define the human situation, so that we may understand our interests, including our common interests, more clearly? MacIntyre writes, 'Human identity is primarily, even if not only, bodily and therefore animal identity and it is by reference to that identity that the continuities of our relationships with

---

[24] Blakely cites Coleman 1994 in his critique of MacIntyre at 132.

198 *Christopher Stephen Lutz*

others are partially defined' (MacIntyre 1999a: 8). This starting point is a practical one, not an appeal to epistemological Thomism. The entire argument of the book is relentlessly practical, and in the conclusion to the book MacIntyre reiterates his rejection of normative theory, his commitment to practical reasoning and his insistence on the community-bound nature of moral enquiry:

> Rational enquiry about my practical beliefs, relationships, and commitments, is therefore ... something that *we* undertake within *our* shared mode of practice by asking, when *we* have good reasons to do so, what the strongest and soundest objections are to this or that particular belief or concept that we have up to this point taken for granted. (MacIntyre 1999a: 157, emphases in original)

Where modern normative theory is intended to justify individual autonomy or to silence objections and close debates, MacIntyre's approach to practical rationality illuminates connections between personal interests and common interests among people who ask and investigate practical questions together.

If *Dependent Rational Animals* had marked a real departure from the account of rationality that informed its three predecessors, if its 'reassertion of human animality' were intended 'to naturalise normativity', then we should see evidence of that departure and that naturalised normativity in *Ethics in the Conflicts of Modernity*, for that book restates the main points of the argument of *After Virtue*. But *Ethics in the Conflicts of Modernity* only reaffirms the rationality of traditions and the centrality of practical reasoning and human relationships to moral philosophy. Nowhere is this more evident than in the differences among the lives of the four virtuous people presented in chapter 5. Vassily Grossman, Sandra Day O'Connor, C. L. R. James and Father Denis Faul are far more complex than the fictional Huckleberry Finn and not at all like the victims of hagiography catalogued in Butler's *Lives of the Saints*.[25] They are four real people who lived remarkable and, in some respects, troubled lives, who discovered how to live well within the situatedness of their own conditions, who found ways to pursue goods that honoured their relationships and commitments. In the virtues that MacIntyre discerned in their lives, each exemplifies his conclusion that '[t]he perfection and completion of a life consists in an agent's having persisted in moving toward and beyond the best goods of which she or he knows' (MacIntyre 2016: 315).

---

[25] E.g. 'We are told that in his infancy [Saint Nicholas, Archbishop of Myra] observed the fasts of Wednesdays and Fridays, refusing to suck the breasts on those days, which were consecrated to fasting by the law of the church' (Butler 1903: vol. 4, 644).

Part IV

After Virtue beyond Philosophy

11 Theological Overtones in *After Virtue*

Charles R. Pinches

11.1 Prophetic Beginnings

Alasdair MacIntyre's brilliance and extraordinary philosophical breadth and depth are displayed in all his works. But forty years after its publication, *After Virtue* remains his most significant book. This is not because it is his most convincing, or even best argued. Indeed, it is for some readers decidedly his least convincing, his most controversial. But this is key to its character. For in *After Virtue* MacIntyre plays the role of the prophet, in the Old Testament sense.

This specific characteristic of *After Virtue*, its prophetic nature, also means MacIntyre's career is stamped by it. His writing before leads up to it; his writing afterwards extends and nuances its theses, sometimes including adjustment and correction.[1] Yet the fundamentally prophetic message, stated so boldly in *After Virtue*, marks out what Alasdair MacIntyre most yearns to convey to his readership, indeed to the entire Western world: we have forgotten who we are. And if we continue the path we have chosen, we shall never be able to remember. Let us return and remember.

To say that *After Virtue* functions prophetically opens the possibility that the whole of MacIntyre's writing should be read in terms of the career of the prophet. Of course there are other ways to read his extraordinary corpus. We might call him a virtue theorist, a historian of morals or an analytic philosopher critical of analytic philosophy. But if I am right that *After Virtue* is a form of prophecy, as with the Hebrew prophets, once the prophetic message breaks through it cannot but govern the career; it must take over as its primary telos.

Whether taken literally or analogically, invoking the Hebrew prophets in this context provides us with another way of speaking about how *After*

---

[1] For example, about what he said in *After Virtue* about Aristotle's metaphysical biology, MacIntyre later writes, 'I now judge that I was in error in supposing an ethics independent of biology to be possible' (MacIntyre 1999a: x).

202   *Charles R. Pinches*

Virtue functions. *After Virtue* shows us, and perhaps even MacIntyre himself, what work he was charged to do.[2] Hebrew prophets clearly had this sense of themselves: that they were sent for a purpose, to speak prophetically to their people at a particular time and place about the direction of their ethics and politics. This purpose could not be accomplished without disruption. The purpose, including the disruption, needed to organise the prophet's words and career. In a famous scene, Jeremiah the prophet recounts what he believes he was divinely charged with: 'Then the Lord put out his hand and touched my mouth; and the Lord said to me, "Now I have put my words in your mouth. See, today I appoint you over nations and over kingdoms, to pluck up and to pull down, to destroy and to overthrow, to build and to plant"' (Jer. 1: 9–10, New Revised Standard Version (NRSV)). This progression informs Jeremiah's career, beginning with words of destruction and ending with words of renewal.

We should not suppose that the words of the prophets were without risk. Michael Walzer has noted that the intensity with which the Hebrew prophets undertake their critical task can lead to disastrous political results. Reading the prophets, some can be drawn to 'attack the existing order without any concrete or practical alternative in mind, the vehemence of the attack masking their actual passivity vis-à-vis the social hierarchy or the fantasy-ridden character of their politics' (2012: 210–11). Yet, as Walzer points out, the Hebrew prophets also put certain matters into play in the age to which they speak that require that we listen and judge.

In this regard, it is crucial that the biblical prophets arise from a place outside political power. They were 'social critics, perhaps the first social critics in the recorded history of the West' (Walzer 2012: 86). As such, they were not – indeed, they are to be defined in contrast to – court and temple prophets, who spoke with the authority of the places from which the society at the time was ruled. The biblical prophets in fact had no authority except that they claimed to speak for God, which, while promising everything, could come to nothing in the minds of those to whom they spoke, since the question of 'did this prophet speak for the Lord? – was never settled and, indeed, could not have been settled' (Walzer 2012: 87).

Walzer notes that the Hebrew prophets had no alternative but to take to the streets. This was necessary because 'social criticism can never be

---

[2] I do not mean to imply that MacIntyre sees himself as occupying the prophetic office, nor that he imagines his words are God's. My intent here is simply to draw on how that office operated in ancient Israel and to use this as a helpful way to narrate MacIntyre's work.

Theological Overtones in *After Virtue*

authoritative. Once the prophet is in the streets, all we can do is listen to whatever he has to say and judge its value for ourselves' (2012: 87). What can the prophet do or say in the streets? They must speak with what Walzer calls eloquence. 'He has to use language in a way that engages the minds and touches the hearts of his listeners; he has to remind them of what they know, evoke their historical memories, play on their nerves or their commitments, their guilt, their hope for the future. Eloquence is not primarily linguistic but cultural' (2012: 87).[3]

Walzer's metaphor is helpful in understanding what happens in *After Virtue*. In it MacIntyre 'takes to the streets'. *After Virtue* is, of course, highly intellectual; as Stanley Hauerwas has said, one needs to read what MacIntyre reads in order to understand and fully engage with him.[4] But it is also, and fundamentally, about the social and political life we all share in Western societies. As such, the book teaches as it narrates the intellectual history it believes we share. Its eloquence is cultural, as it reminds and evokes shared memories and looks forward to what we might reasonably hope for. The prophet is in the streets and the question opened – and indeed remains open after forty years – of whether he speaks for the Lord.

11.2 The Bookends of *After Virtue*

The books of the Hebrew prophets are filled with striking allegories, analogies and parables: Jeremiah and the ox yoke, Isaiah and the vineyard, Amos and the plumbline, Ezekiel and the dry bones. Alasdair MacIntyre begins and ends *After Virtue* with similarly striking analogies. First, of course, comes his 'disquieting suggestion', drawn out imaginatively by the stark picture of a future society in which natural science has been splintered by a catastrophe that leaves only intellectual shards, random terms and scattered theorems that have lost any relation to one another. It is possible for people in the post-catastrophic world to speak of things like 'mass' or 'atomic weight'; in MacIntyre's narrative they do

---

[3] The notion that prophets take their case to the streets is powerfully illustrated in Jeremiah 28, where the prophet engages in a battle of words and symbols in the presence of 'all the people' with the (false) prophet Hananiah. He assured the people that the yoke of their Babylonian captors would soon be broken, whilst Jeremiah prophesied, and dramatically illustrated, that the people would soon be led, like yoked oxen, into exile.

[4] 'To understand MacIntyre takes work. Indeed, he *intends* for it to be a daunting and challenging task to understand him. I suspect he assumes most of his readers, possessed as they must be by the reading habits of modernity, cannot help but refuse to do the work necessary to understand him' (Hauerwas 2007: para. 8, emphasis in original).

204   *Charles R. Pinches*

this, even argue about them, but there is no coherence, no order. MacIntyre uses this picture to pose the book's central thesis:

The hypothesis which I wish to advance is that in the actual world which we inhabit the language of morality is in the same state of grave disorder as the language of natural science in the imaginary world which I have described. (1984: 2)

The closing lines of the book are equally jarring. They lead to the surprising invocation of Saint Benedict, the sixth-century founder of Western Christian monasticism.

What matters at this stage is the construction of local forms of community within which civility and the intellectual and moral life can be sustained through the new dark ages that are already upon us. And if the tradition of the virtues was able to survive the horrors of the last dark ages, we are not entirely without grounds for hope. This time however the barbarians are not waiting beyond the frontiers; they have already been governing us for quite some time. And it is our lack of consciousness of this that constitutes part of our predicament. We are waiting not for a Godot, but for another – doubtless very different – St. Benedict. (1984: 263)

These tropes, as Jeffrey Stout calls them, have drawn frequent comment from critics. Stout notes that the 'imagery of catastrophe' in the first bookend (as I shall call it) strives to reveal the 'energies of heart and mind that were concentrated in the practices of a previous epoch', now lost and ruined. Stout admits the rhetorical ploy is brilliant in its own way, since it 'somehow manages not to call attention to the artifice of the rhetoric. The uncanniness of these paragraphs consists in the sense that we have learned something we already knew but have kept hidden' (2004: 122). The artifice of it all, which Stout goes on to attack, is that MacIntyre leaps from his story of scientific catastrophe to our current moral debates, assuming, without evidence, that they are 'interminable', and that this is to be explained by a parallel shattering of our moral discourse.

Stout expresses similar dismay about *After Virtue*'s 'memorable conclusion', by which Macintyre 'assembles his readers once again among the sublime ruins' (2004: 124), awaiting the arrival of the new Saint Benedict. As John Horton and Susan Mendus comment, MacIntyre's

references to 'the construction of local forms of community' and the need 'for another – doubtless very different – St. Benedict' seem little more than whistling in the dark to keep the spirits up when set against his coruscating critique of modernity. (1994a: 3)

As these three critics agree, the bookends of *After Virtue* express, even accent, its dark, apocalyptic mood. Like Hananiah, who resists

Theological Overtones in *After Virtue* 205

Jeremiah's dire predictions of captivity to come, these critics hold that MacIntyre's account of the way things are in modern moral discourse is highly exaggerated. The cleverly contrived bookends of *After Virtue* amount to little more than a kind of morose revelling in the hyperbolic.

It is correct that MacIntyre's analogies, the bookends of *After Virtue*, conjure up dark images. So did the analogies used so often by the Hebrew prophets. As MacIntyre's critics seem to recognise, the question will be how accurate the analogies are in helping us describe our modern predicament. Again, using Walzer's metaphor, what MacIntyre has done in *After Virtue*'s bookends is take his case to the streets,[5] where even today it is still being debated.

Too much concern about the rhetorical power of the bookends may, however, help critics evade crucial matters of substance. In the book's opening, MacIntyre is attempting to get us to ask: how do we tell our story? – and this not only in terms of the progression from one idea or philosopher to the next, but on a grand and, in a way, personal scale. It is grand because MacIntyre has the audacity in *After Virtue* to offer what he takes to be the whole arc of philosophical history, and personal in the sense that he is forcing a self-examination: maybe we have been duped, thought ourselves into a corner. We believed it was all going so well, that after so many tries we were finally getting it right about morality and justice. But perhaps this was all self-deception.

Furthermore, too much focus on the breadth of MacIntyre's claim that springs from this opening analogy, namely that 'in the actual world which we inhabit the language of morality is in the same state of grave disorder' as the world he imaginatively describes, may hide from us a narrower target that is equally important and more easily substantiated. This is that, were such a catastrophe to happen, in science or morality, it would go undetected by most philosophies of our day.

We may notice that if in this imaginary world analytic philosophy were to flourish, it would never reveal the fact of this disorder. For the techniques of analytic philosophy are essentially descriptive, and descriptive of the language of the present at that ... Nor again would phenomenology or existentialism be able to discern anything wrong. All structures of intentionality would be what they are now. (MacIntyre 1984: 2)

I believe MacIntyre could even concede a little ground to critics like Stout, acknowledging points where his analogy is stretched as an account of our present moral predicament, while continuing to maintain that the

---

[5] While *After Virtue* is hardly a book read by the general populous, as we shall later notice, features of it have been popularised, especially its final bookend.

206   *Charles R. Pinches*

philosophies we depend on in our day have failed to help us describe where we are and who we are morally. These philosophies tell no story, they provide no context and begin today as if yesterday did not precede it. This is precisely what *After Virtue* tries to describe; in this its success is secured, since it has provoked others to engage with its story.

This incapacity to tell the story of our morality is what is most in need of correction. *After Virtue* tries to do this correcting. As I shall suggest in the next section, three-quarters of the way through *After Virtue*, in chapter 15, MacIntyre gives us an extraordinary sequence of arguments, condensed and trenchant, regarding how our moral lives and actions can (indeed, should) be fitted within larger, unified stories and traditions. The arguments are both suggestive and hopeful. Despite all the complaints about the darkness of the book, its structure can remind us of the progression laid out in the call of Jeremiah, to first pluck up and pull down (chapters 1–8), then to build and to plant (chapters 9–18). The building and planting surrounds a simple enough point nuanced in chapter 15: in order to tell such a story you will need to claim (or be claimed by) one. This is also the beginning of what it means to belong to a tradition.

Here is a point where what MacIntyre wrote in *After Virtue* in 1981 required further elucidation. What story or tradition did *he* claim? A first answer, that he claimed the 'virtue tradition', seemed sketchy, especially since, as MacIntyre's own account of Nietzsche demonstrates, virtues can be variously named and claimed. What MacIntyre does not say in *After Virtue*, perhaps because it was not yet fully true, he does say seven years later in the closest thing to its sequel, where he tells us he is an 'Augustinian Christian' (1988: 10).[6]

Perhaps this movement towards the Christian tradition is signalled by Saint Benedict's appearance on the last page of *After Virtue*. Saint Benedict, MacIntyre notes, took his place at the end of the Roman Empire when he led others in a way by which 'men and women of good

---

[6] As MacIntyre explicitly claims this tradition in *Whose Justice? Which Rationality?*, he also gestures to other traditions with which he believes ongoing conversation is essential, particularly as we tell and retell the stories that we differently embody. 'The derivation of Augustinian Christianity from its biblical sources is a story whose counterpart is the history of Judaism, within which the relationship of the devoted study of the Torah to philosophy engendered more than one tradition of enquiry. But of all the histories of enquiry this is the one which, perhaps more than any other, must be written by its own adherents; in particular for Augustinian Christians, such as myself, to try to write it, in the way I have felt able to write the history of my own tradition, would be a gross impertinence. Christians need badly to listen to Jews. The attempt to speak for them, even on behalf of that unfortunate fiction, the so-called Judaeo-Christian tradition, is always deplorable' (1988: 10–11).

Theological Overtones in *After Virtue*

will turned aside from the task of shoring up the Roman *imperium* and ceased to identify the continuation of civility and moral community with the maintenance of that *imperium*' (1984: 244).

Again, is this MacIntyre whistling in the dark, attempting to cover up the heaviness of his otherwise withering critique of modernity? Yet to think so requires assuming that what Benedict did was small and meagre in relation to the empire that crumbled around him. What Benedict did was found Western monasticism and write the Rule by which monks – the Benedictines, but many subsequent orders as well – could live together well, in a life that merged the sacred and secular and wherein thought and practice, community, civility and virtue could develop and last. To suppose this a small thing assumes that the empire is the main game, which we all must play if we are to count. Yet clearly MacIntyre does not place hope in the empire. (One wonders why anyone would, given how empires come and go and how they typically rule us.)

The invocation of Benedict perhaps borrows from Jeremiah when he writes to the Jewish exiles who have been deported from their homeland by the Babylonian Empire. 'Build houses and live in them; plant gardens and eat what they produce. Take wives and have sons and daughters; take wives for your sons, and give your daughters in marriage, that they may bear sons and daughters; multiply there, and do not decrease' (Jer. 29: 5–6, NRSV). It is possible to live well in Babylon. The captives' anger can and should recede.[7] Babylon's time will also come to an end. (When it does, perhaps things will get even better, as for the Jews when Persia arrived.) What is perhaps most essential is that the stories of peoples, and the habits and practices that form and anchor them, keep and expand the space they need to form lives well lived and communities well ordered – and, one might add, stories others than one's own well listened to, as the Jews listened to, and adapted, the Babylonians' stories, and as Augustinian Christians listened, or need to listen, to the Jews.

In his perceptive treatment of MacIntyre's thought, Peter McMylor calls attention to the fact that in the first book MacIntyre wrote, *Marxism: An Interpretation*, he based his critical observations on both Marxism and what he at that time called 'bourgeois Christianity' on an essentially theological point. 'Only a religion which is a way of living in every sphere either deserves to or can hope to survive. For the task of religion is to see the secular as sacred, the world as under God' (1953: 10). For MacIntyre at the time of this earlier writing, both Christianity and Marxism (which

---

[7] See Psalm 136: 8–9, where the psalmist cries: 'O daughter Babylon, you devastator! / Happy shall they be who pay you back / what you have done to us! / Happy shall they be who take your little ones / and dash them against the rock!' (NRSV).

208   *Charles R. Pinches*

is not strictly a religion but acts like one, since it arises, as MacIntyre argues, directly out of Christianity)[8] failed this test. One might say that both fell prey to the temptation of empire, which continues in our time and can easily capture us all – including the philosophers of the status quo and the contemporary moment – and which always finds a way to replace God with itself. Benedict and what came from him resisted this temptation. MacIntyre's use of him here is a sign of his growing recognition of whence hope for the future, which is also rooted in history, can reasonably arise.

11.3   Enacted Narratives

Coming to speak, as we have in these last pages, of living well even under such regimes as Babylon or Rome (or America) requires the capacity to tell our story, including the story of our present conditions, both hopefully and truthfully. Indeed, as we await 'another – doubtless very different – St. Benedict', we need practice telling this story; otherwise, we will lose where we are in time and history. Indeed, the fact that we are not telling it is a great part of our difficulty. As *After Virtue*'s penultimate sentence puts it, 'it is our lack of consciousness of this [who we are and by whom we are being governed] that constitutes part of our predicament' (1984: 263).

I have portrayed Alasdair MacIntyre as a kind of career prophet – by which I have meant that he has played a certain pivotal role in a larger story, primarily by naming a way of moral thought and practice, the dominant way for a whole civilisation, as untenable, and, further, by opening another way involving the reclamation of the significance of virtue, narrative and tradition. This prophetic role is capped in *After Virtue*, where MacIntyre is at his most visionary and imaginative, relying as much on images and allegories as on arguments. As I have argued, or suggested, those images and allegories are compelling and can support more than the critics suppose.

---

[8] See McMylor 1993: 5. As MacIntyre moves towards Benedict in these last pages of *After Virtue*, he references the failure of Marxism. 'When Marxism does not become Weberian social democracy or crude tyranny, it tends to become Nietzschean fantasy. One of the most admirable traits of Trotsky's cold revolution was his refusal of all such fantasies. A Marxist who took Trotsky's last writings with great seriousness would be forced into a pessimism quite alien to the Marxist tradition, and in becoming a pessimist he would in an important way have ceased to be a Marxist' (MacIntyre 1984: 262). The reference to the Marxist pessimist can be taken autobiographically. It sets the personal context for MacIntyre's invocation of Benedict, which is both genuinely Christian and hopeful. Hope, after all, is a theological virtue. For more on Christian hope, see Pinches 2014.

Theological Overtones in *After Virtue*

Calling MacIntyre a prophet has theological overtones, which I embrace. As an Augustinian Christian, he should not object to a theological reading of his work. Indeed, even in his atheological days MacIntyre saw that religious traditions are 'bent on rescuing individuals from insignificance by showing how the individual can have a role in a world-historical drama' (Hauerwas 2022: 90). For a while, MacIntyre believed that neither Marxism nor Christianity succeeded in this task. His reconversion to Christianity implies that he now thinks it is succeeding. And this means that his own life's story can be told in the context of a larger world-historical drama. I believe calling MacIntyre a prophet, especially a prophet like Jeremiah, is the way to begin such a story.[9]

It is also likely MacIntyre himself would reject it, not because he disbelieves that God speaks through prophets, but because he is already certain of his own self-description. Unquestionably, MacIntyre sees himself as a philosopher, before and after any embrace of the Christian faith. As Stanley Hauerwas has commented, as a philosopher 'MacIntyre disavows any attempt to do theology' – which means 'he seldom makes use of any particularistic theological concepts. [For instance] Jesus is seldom mentioned.' MacIntyre believes, in fact, in a strong distinction between philosophy and theology, and his work lies almost entirely on the former side.[10] He believes that 'the task of theology is a rational task, but theology is inquiry on revealed truths that can only be acknowledged by faith' (Hauerwas 2022: 82–3).[11]

I should like to say that MacIntyre is both a philosopher and a prophet, adding that this is a difficult thing, brimming with potential contradictions. Since he is declaredly not a theologian, we need not look for a theology in *After Virtue*. What we can find, however, are certain key philosophical moves that open to theology. (MacIntyre, following what he affirms as Aquinas's view, believes this is how the two should

---

[9] Stanley Hauerwas, MacIntyre's long-time friend, collaborator and theological counterpart, has written a memoir that he entitled *Hannah's Child* (2010). The reference leads to Samuel, son of the barren biblical Hannah. Hauerwas's mother claimed the story of Hannah as she prayed for Hauerwas's (an only child) conception and birth. The notion that stories of lives echo a sacred past, strange to modern secular ears, is standard fare for religious traditions, whose lives extend by remembered stories. It is a sign of how monotheistic religious traditions describe the world as under God.

[10] MacIntyre is most explicitly theological in *God, Philosophy, Universities: A Selective History of the Catholic Philosophical Tradition* (2009a), although, as its subtitle indicates, the book is primarily a history.

[11] In this recent treatment of his friend, Hauerwas gathers together something of a Christian theology of Alasdair MacIntyre from scattered writings, some yet unpublished. He signals disagreement on how strong a distinction one can find in Aquinas between theology and philosophy and on the merits of the work of Karl Barth.

210   *Charles R. Pinches*

interrelate.) The most important and fertile of these come in chapter 15, entitled 'The Virtues, the Unity of a Human Life and the Concept of a Tradition'. It anchors the 'building and planting' work of *After Virtue*.

Chapter 15 also does work that grounds *After Virtue*'s first bookend. As I have noted, the matter of concern for MacIntyre in this bookend was not simply that contemporary moral discourse lies in considerable disarray, but that the dominant philosophies of our time – he names existentialism, phenomenology and analytic philosophy (1984: 2) – do not notice this. Sociologically, these philosophies match our divided and compartmentalised lives. Taken together, they prevent us from 'envisaging each human life as a whole'. MacIntyre names two tendencies: one is 'chiefly, though not only, domesticated in analytical philosophy and one at home in both sociological theory and in existentialism'. In the former, the tendency is to 'think atomistically about human action and to analyse complex actions and transactions in terms of simple components'. In the latter, the tendency is to draw 'a sharp distinction ... between the individual and the role he or she plays', which we can see in Sartre's existentialism and also in the sociological theory of Erving Goffman, whereby the 'enactments of an individual life' come to seem 'as nothing but a series of unconnected episodes' (1984: 204).

MacIntyre believes these tendencies stand in the way of any serious return to the virtues, which he, as an Aristotelian, thinks is necessary if we are to draw the fragments of our moral language together. Both tendencies fail to provide a way to connect a particular person's actions under a virtue description, such as in the *Iliad*, where Hector's leaving his wife Andromache to go to battle and his subsequent confrontation with Achilles (in which he dies) are both acts of Hector's courage. By atomising human actions, analytic philosophy forgets about their essential connection to a whole human life. And by divorcing the human self from its roles, existentialism creates a self that is alienated from its actions. In either case, human actions lose their home, both in the story of a human person, a self, and in the social and political context, the human context, in which human selves live out their lives and in which human actions have meaning.[12]

MacIntyre's point is this: without a 'concept of a self whose unity resides in the unity of a narrative which links birth to death as narrative beginning to middle to end' (1984: 205), not only virtue descriptions but also human action descriptions end up making no sense. Human actions, which, MacIntyre later adds, are therefore meaningful only as '*intelligible*

---

[12] I have argued this point regarding what I call 'homeless behaviour' more extensively in *Theology and Action* (2002: esp. 11–28).

Theological Overtones in *After Virtue*

human actions' (that is, not simply as behaviours but as intentional and decipherable only in connection to the sorts of things human beings do with good reason), are essentially narrative-dependent. As MacIntyre puts it, 'Narrative history of a certain kind turns out to be the basic and essential genre for the characterization of human action' (1984: 208).

Narrativity enters for MacIntyre at at least two levels: the narrative of a particular human life, like Hector's, and a much larger story or stories that set the context within which Hector acts – the contexts, indeed, in which Hector's story is not only told by Homer but lived in ancient Troy. (Here we do not need Hector to be a historical figure to see the point.) MacIntyre uses the term 'enacted narratives' to capture this point. Crucially, enacted narratives precede written or told ones:

> It is because we all live out narratives in our lives and because we understand our lives in terms of the narratives that we live out that the form of narrative is appropriate for the understanding of the actions of others. Stories are lived before they are told – except in the case of fiction. (1984: 212)

It is true that we later 'tell' our lives in certain stylised ways, as we might tell MacIntyre's life in the stylised manner of a prophet, and these stories interpret our lives, grasping towards a larger vision of the whole. But *before* this, as one acts as a human person, no one can avoid living their life according to a narrative pattern. Remove narrative and you remove both human self and human action. Furthermore, the narrative that is so essential to the self is never an 'invented' narrative, as modern people might like to think. As MacIntyre puts it, 'Only in fantasy do we live what story we please.' For we are always only 'co-authors of our own narratives' (1984: 213) for any number of reasons, including that we depend on others, that their stories interlock with ours, that we always live in particular times, places and human communities. And these times, places and communities are themselves embedded within histories that contextualise our life stories.

For MacIntyre, this series of points cannot but shift how we consider our moral lives:

> [T]he key question for men [*sic*] is not about their own authorship; I can only answer the question 'What am I to do?' if I can answer the prior question 'Of what stories do I find myself a part?' We enter human society, that is, with one or more imputed characters – roles into which we have been drafted – and we have to learn what they are in order to understand how others respond to us and how our response to them is apt to be construed. It is by hearing stories about wicked stepmothers, lost children, good but misguided kings ... that children learn or mislearn both what a child and what a parent is, what the cast of characters may be in the drama into which they are born and what the ways of the world are. (1984: 216)

212   *Charles R. Pinches*

What MacIntyre is referring to here is practical wisdom, an Aristotelian virtue that we come to have only as we also come to have other virtues – that is, only as we learn all that is required to live well in human communities that teach us about what it means to be human, within the context and structures of particular places and given times. Practical wisdom is story dependent; it requires a teleological framework. It responds to questions that can be posed only in the mode of: 'Where are you going, O human being, with your life and actions? What story or stories are you living out, and why is it good for you to do so?'

Modern theories of the self, which eschew teleology, can neither ask nor answer these questions. For it is only as 'characters in enacted narratives', who live stories that are going somewhere, while they also fit within and are made meaningful in relation to larger historical narratives, that we can be held accountable for our behaviour. The unity of the life of a human person, and any successful notion of their identity as that person, can arise only in this context. On this point, once again, MacIntyre has 'a crucial disagreement with any empiricist or analytical philosophers on the one hand and with existentialists on the other' (1984: 217).

We are back to that first bookend. MacIntyre believes, and in this important section of *After Virtue* has argued, that without the context of a larger history, intelligible human action, a teleological understanding of the good for human life and virtue, and discourse about morality simply stop making sense[13] – in the manner of the would-be scientists in that future world of shards and fragments of what was once coherent scientific discourse.

There is one more turn in chapter 15 – to 'the concept of a tradition'. This is, arguably, the most important for MacIntyre's future work; he will return to it repeatedly, attempting to display what he really means by it. There is far too much to probe in so brief a space as this chapter. Yet any understanding of what MacIntyre does in chapter 15, and in the 'building and planting' section of *After Virtue* more broadly, is incomplete without it. If we return to the conclusion MacIntyre reaches about our life narratives (without which morality makes no sense), he stresses that morality cannot simply be about 'my story', as if it stood alone, but rather also is essentially about those stories of which I find myself a part. Crucial here is the importance of moral formation, which comes in the context of the languages, communities and stories into which a human self is

---

[13] MacIntyre is neither the only nor the first to argue in this way. In her seminal 'Modern Moral Philosophy' (Anscombe 1958), which MacIntyre cites in *After Virtue* (1984: 53), Elizabeth Anscombe makes similar points.

Theological Overtones in *After Virtue*   213

introduced by birth and practice. As MacIntyre notes, the fact that we are all in our different ways tethered to these particularities of history makes me, 'whether I recognize it or not, one of the bearers of a tradition' (1984: 221).

MacIntyre recognises trouble can come with the word 'tradition', since it turns quickly into 'what we always do' or what is 'traditional'; this is decidedly *not* what he wants. So he quickly qualifies it, speaking of a 'tradition that is in good order', or a *living* tradition. 'A living tradition then is an historically extended, socially embodied argument, and an argument precisely in part about the goods which constitute that tradition' (1984: 222). Living traditions, moreover, are properly lived within and extended by the requisite virtues, like justice and honesty. Like individual human lives, they too are unfolding narratives. 'Living traditions, just because they continue a not-yet-complete narrative, confront a future whose determinate and determinable character, so far as it possesses any, derives from the past' (1984: 223).

As mentioned, exactly what MacIntyre means by a tradition will take a long time for him to work out after *After Virtue*. It is perhaps fitting that he refers in this early articulation to the *concept* of a tradition. One might note that really to grasp what a *living* tradition is requires living in one. This is still possible today, even necessary. However – and surely there is a prophetic darkness in this point – MacIntyre believes that social conditions in our time do not conduce either to a healthy, unified human life of virtue or to the ready sustenance of those traditions that can support such a life.

With that culture [that is, the culture of bureaucratic individualism] conceptions of the virtues become marginal and the tradition of the virtues remains central only in the lives of social groups whose existence is on the margins of the central culture. (1984: 225)[14]

This final quotation sends us straightaway to the second (final) bookend. This is Saint Benedict, who, with others, turned aside from the task

---

[14] Stout criticises *After Virtue* for the 'tragic tone' of its declension narrative (2004: 121). I have attempted to read this tone (which one does find) as a dramatic, prophetic call, especially regarding how dominant Western culture scatters the moral life. This reading partly depends on how we understand MacIntyre's longing for Saint Benedict; I believe it rightly directs us to the margins, not desperately but hopefully. There are less dramatic but similarly honest and hopeful ways to proceed. Charles Taylor's writing is an example. As he tells us, he agrees with MacIntyre that the moral life needs an Aristotelian (teleological) form, but, unlike MacIntyre, Taylor believes that, even in modern life, 'we are far more "Aristotelian" than we allow, that hence our practice is in some significant way less based on pure disengaged freedom and atomism than we realize' (1994: 22).

214   *Charles R. Pinches*

of shoring up the Roman imperium to nurturing new forms of community, in which the moral life could be well lived. Our best hope for virtuous lives and living traditions, MacIntyre thinks, lies in the margins.

11.4   Theological Aftermaths

Some critics dislike *After Virtue*'s bookends, but I do not, especially in the context of what MacIntyre writes in chapter 15. The argumentation offered there regarding the meaning and intelligibility of human action and the relation of the human self to the roles in which it is discovered interprets the first bookend. It demonstrates the incapacity of most modern moral reflection to locate human action within a history and an individual human life as a story lived out, from birth to death, not within the flighty autonomy of individual choice, but rather in the social practices, roles and communal relations into which it fits.

I do not deny there is overstatement in this first bookend, but, together with *After Virtue*'s final paragraphs, it lifts this seminal book to the level of the prophetic, since it calls attention to the dramatic narrative that informs it throughout, moving from trouble to hope. The hope that the reference to Saint Benedict brings is located at the centre neither of current culture nor of contemporary academic or intellectual moral discussion. In this regard, MacIntyre's work, while hardly marginal, still lies somewhat off to the side; the bulk of modern moral philosophy goes on as if it had not been written. Happily, and as this collection shows, it is still being read and discussed, over forty years after its publication. For some of us, it marks a significant turning point.

How has it changed things? And where is it leading? In this regard, let me turn the final reflections of this chapter in the direction of the theological. For this we will not get much direct help from MacIntyre, since he is so much the philosopher. There is, however, indirect help. Indeed, MacIntyre's philosophical work clearly makes space for theological understandings. This is evident not only in his affirmation that something like an Aristotelian teleology is essential to moral reflection, but also in how, post-*After Virtue*, Aquinas becomes MacIntyre's beacon. So far as they can be distinguished, Aquinas's philosophy evidently supports his theology.[15]

---

[15] In his treatment of ethics, Aquinas assumes that the understanding of human action is a necessary building block for any further reflection about ethics, which is why he places it early in the *Prima Secundae* (questions 6–21), before any turn to the passions or the virtues (Aquinas 1920).

Theological Overtones in *After Virtue*

I have argued that the notion of 'enacted narratives' is among the most important in *After Virtue* and is essential if we are to understand human action. I do not think it is a theological notion per se; the arguments for it, and for its centrality to ethics, are philosophical, as MacIntyre shows.[16] But it lends itself to theological discussion since acts both arise from and further shape our characters, and our characters are unified in narratives, not only the ones we author, but also the ones we inhabit. Even if it is not necessary to answer it as such, MacIntyre's question – 'of what story do I find myself a part' – leans in a theological direction.

All the more so does the 'concept' of a tradition, especially that of a living tradition. Christians think they inhabit such a tradition and, moreover, that it needs to be both maintained and revivified if it is to guide the Christian community. Listen, for instance, to theologian David Bentley Hart:

> Any true and living tradition must be at once both the subject and object of a constant and pious hermeneutical retrieval that, guided by an awareness of the history and logic of what has gone before, seeks to discover the tradition's dialectical unity and rationality ever anew. And thus openness to an unanticipated future is no less necessary than fidelity to the past. (2022: 128)

Like MacIntyre, Hart takes pains to distinguish this proper loyalty to and care for tradition from what he labels 'traditionalism', which is rigid, protective and wistful. 'It is precisely the real depth, richness, complexity, subtlety and antiquity of the tradition that the traditionalist finds most threatening' (2022: 14).[17]

Nevertheless, and in this context, we should pay attention to Jeffrey Stout, who labels MacIntyre, primarily the MacIntyre of *After Virtue*, as the leader of 'the new traditionalism'. His two prominent followers are, for Stout, theologians: Stanley Hauerwas and John Milbank. Stout's chief complaint is that MacIntyre and those theologians who agree with him have 'undermined identification with liberal democracy'. Specifically, their broadsided criticisms of something they call 'the liberal

---

[16] One cannot help but wonder if *After Virtue*'s increased accent on the category of narrative might have theological roots. Stanley Hauerwas's *Community of Character* (1981), which brought narrative to the attention of the discipline of Christian ethics, was published in the same year and by the same press as *After Virtue*. MacIntyre and Hauerwas were friends even then, exchanging papers. Hauerwas's *Truthfulness and Tragedy* (1978), which contained the essay 'From System to Story: An Alternative Pattern for Rationality in Ethics', was published three years before. The two also worked together as co-editors of *Revisions* (1983).

[17] For his part, MacIntyre refers to what Hart here pejoratively calls 'traditionalism' as 'conservative antiquarianism' (1984: 223). Put another way, and associated with the 'conservatism' of the likes of Edmund Burke, he says 'when a tradition becomes Burkean, it is always dying or dead' (1984: 222).

216   *Charles R. Pinches*

project' or 'liberal society' have convinced a generation, especially in the seminaries, to decide that anything 'liberal' is by definition bad, anti-traditional (Stout 2004: 118). For these believers, political engagement with the institutions of a society such as the American one is folly; much better to separate and keep to one's own tradition, which they take to be the 'tradition' of Christianity.

Stout's criticism has at least two prongs. First, the term 'liberal society', used by the likes of MacIntyre, necessarily oversimplifies: 'the configuration of the social practices and institutions we in the United States and certain other countries happen to be in right now ... is too complicated to be explained as the expression of a single project' (2004: 130). Second, Stout himself claims membership in what he calls the democratic tradition, which, be believes, is without any theology per se, and which identifies and nurtures genuine and important 'democratic virtues' – virtues that we need to live together well. The 'new traditionalism' is undermining these crucial democratic virtues.

That Stout is prepared to refer to 'democracy' as a tradition demonstrates that he is not in complete disagreement with MacIntyre. And, surely, discussion in the contemporary world about our moral lives involves many traditions that have a role in morally forming us and in identifying and pursuing what we believe to be the good. MacIntyre clearly does not mean to confine us in the Christian tradition; traditions, he later shows,[18] need to be in dialogue, learning from and contending with each other.

What Stout's complaint highlights, though, is the fact that one way MacIntyre's points might be taken, especially his declension narrative of liberal society, is that the only real moral option for Christians and others is non-participation. Rod Dreher's *The Benedict Option: A Strategy for Christians in a Post-Christian Nation* (now in its eighth printing) is an example of the sort of thing Stout is concerned about. As Dreher tells us, the book takes its title and its inspiration from MacIntyre's last sentences about waiting for a Saint Benedict – what I have been referring to as *After Virtue*'s second bookend. As Dreher interprets MacIntyre, 'to live "after virtue" is to dwell in a society that not only can no longer agree on what constitutes virtuous belief and conduct but also doubts that virtue exists' (2017: 16).

As Dreher states his case, American Christians need to step back from trying to run things, being prepared to live intentionally and communally

---

[18] For instance, in *Three Rival Versions of Moral Enquiry* (1990) MacIntyre argues that, rightly understood, the university provides the context in which various traditions of moral enquiry contend with each other.

Theological Overtones in *After Virtue*

on the margins of power. He offers some direct advice to his fellow Christians like 'rediscover the trades' (2017: 190), which I suspect Stout would not object to, combined with 'pull your children out of public schools' (2017: 155), which I suspect he might. Dreher concentrates mainly on persuading American Christians that they need to embrace their minority status. Yet this advice sometimes strikes the careful reader as disingenuous, especially when we read passages like this:

> Because of florists, bakers, and photographers having been dragged through the courts by gay plaintiffs, we know that some Orthodox Christians will lose their businesses and their livelihoods if they refuse to recognize the new secular orthodoxies. (2017: 175)

Arguably, there is fear-mongering in Dreher's MacIntyre-inspired book, distinctly American fear-mongering, which can ignite an oppositional politics that, far from opening to dialogue, prepares for battle over the 'future of America'. It makes Stout's point and signals an ever-present danger for Christians.

Yet genuine prophecy should not lead to fear but rather hope. Once again, this is what comes at the end of the long career of the prophet Jeremiah. His advice to the Jewish exiles in Babylon included not only that they should settle down, build houses and raise families, but also 'seek the welfare of the city where I have sent you into exile, and pray to the LORD on its behalf, for in its welfare you will find your welfare' (Jer. 29: 7, NRSV). Among the implications of this passage is that if the Jews live well, virtuously, they can assist the Babylonians to do so as well – and that they can do this not simply as one group, one 'tradition', and then the other, but together. Something like this happened with the Benedictines too. Hope arises from the margins, but it can also migrate, penetrating inward.

This passage in Jeremiah can exist alongside his many jeremiads. I should like to say the same about MacIntyre. As Walzer rightly believes, reading the prophets can be dangerous, leading some to 'attack the existing order without any concrete or practical alternative in mind'. But it does not follow that we do not need prophets to wake us up, which they will do with flurries of rhetoric, offering such stories, metaphors and allegories as one finds in *After Virtue*, especially at its bookends. *After Virtue* remains MacIntyre's most influential work; as I have suggested, it secures his place as a kind of modern prophet. Yet what he has written since (and even before) fills out the picture. In his repeated attempts to see how traditions might engage with one another in philosophical and moral exchange, MacIntyre continues to show that there *is* an alternative to the flattened philosophical discourse that arises out of what he has called 'the Enlightenment project'.

In this way, theologians such as myself can be glad that MacIntyre has remained a philosopher, engaging in a lively and usually generous way with his colleagues who do not share his Christian convictions. Theologically, and for Christians today, one task is to probe the Christian tradition as living tradition, in the manner that Hart suggests. As he says further, in doing this,

no particular method can be trusted absolutely; one must instead simply attempt to exercise a kind of hermeneutical piety. Tacit knowledge, faithful practice, humility before the testimony of the generations, prayfulness, and any number of moral and intellectual virtues are required; and these can be cultivated only in being put into action. (2022: 141)

As the Jews learned in Babylon, as they produced the Babylonian Talmud and edited and compiled the Torah – including composing the remarkable stories of creation of Genesis 1–3 in dialogue with Babylonian mythologies – and read and listened to the prophets, we can live well together across traditions, grow in virtue, seek the truth and share our hopes, differently crafted. Continuing to read MacIntyre can help us do so in our own time.

12 Law as Social Practice
After Virtue *and Legal Theory*

Mark D. Retter

12.1 Introduction

Forty years from publication, it is surprising that the constructive insights developed by Alasdair MacIntyre in *After Virtue* have made few inroads into Anglophone legal theory. Surprising because the core constructive dimensions of that book – especially the concept of a 'social practice', its relationship to 'institutions' and its extension through time as a 'tradition' – have significant potential for application to legal practice. These conceptual resources were developed in light of MacIntyre's work on the intelligibility of human action within social contexts and given pivotal expression in *After Virtue*. Their relevance for legal theory is revealed in response to a prevailing conception of social practice, within a framework of rules that ground reasons. This understanding of social practice and theory has been influential in general jurisprudence, especially through H. L. A. Hart's work on the 'internal aspect of rules'. In contrast, MacIntyre's formulation of the relationship between reasons for action, goods and rules within 'practices' remains comparatively neglected in legal theory. Addressing that deficiency through a critique of Hart's internal perspective on the rule of recognition in Section 12.2, I then develop a constructive understanding of law as 'practice' on MacIntyre's terms in Section 12.3. However, significant obstacles confront a 'MacIntyrean jurisprudence', stemming from MacIntyre's neglect and criticism of juridical thought and practice. These problems are explored in Section 12.4.

12.2 Fragmenting Internal Points of View

12.2.1 *Social Practice and the Internal Aspect of Rules*

In the preface to *The Concept of Law*, Hart states that his book 'may also be regarded as an essay in descriptive sociology' (Hart 1994: v). That aspiration to descriptive adequacy supports his conceptual task of defining essential features of law, which make sense of legal practice across societies from a participant's internal point of view. From an observer standpoint on this internal view, Hart attempts to maintain the descriptive or objective character of his theory whilst also capturing the normative dimension of law as a peremptory reason for action (Hart 1994: 89–91, 242–3). According to Hart, legal theory should refrain from projecting moral evaluations on the general concept of law to avoid confusing what law *is*, in its essential features, with what it *ought to be*. This does not mean that moral scrutiny of law is unimportant; but he separates that evaluative task from the task of conceptualising law (Hart 1994: 185–212; 1958). Since participant motivations for compliance with law are multifarious, a general legal theory should abstract from contingent motives (moral or non-moral) and unpack the general explanatory presuppositions of the *acceptance* of law as a distinct type of peremptory rule-following activity across different societies, including unjust legal regimes. But there are problems with Hart's methodology relating to his strongly internalised conception of legal practice. MacIntyre's criticisms of Peter Winch's social science methodology can shed light on these problems.

In *The Idea of a Social Science*, Winch sought to extend Wittgenstein's reflections on the relationship between rules and language to social theory in general – the social world of meaningful behaviour. Social sciences, according to Winch, have an inherently different object of enquiry from natural sciences. They should attend to reasons for action, not causal explanations based on empirical generalisations. The latter never capture the meaningfulness of human behaviour (Winch 1990: 71–88). Just as the social meaning of language is embedded within and inseparable from rules of language, so too the meaningfulness of behaviour is embedded within and inseparable from socially established rules of language and other practices. These rules are interwoven with meaningful action through mutual interactions in social practice, as participants learn to distinguish right from wrongdoings based on rules within a form of human activity and life (Winch 1990: 38–61). Communicating reasons for action presupposes this socially established framework of rules, which measures the intelligibility of those reasons and provides the basis for mutual meaningfulness of behaviour within that form of life. In consequence, only by attending to the stock of concepts available to participants and the 'internalisation' of rule-following within such-and-such a form of social life can social scientists explicate the meaning of human activities within that form of life. Once social scientists articulate the most basic framework of rules within a culture, they cannot proceed further to interrogate the reasons for that framework. Doing so steps outside the 'language game'

Law as Social Practice: *After Virtue* and Legal Theory

of that culture, confusing the theorist's conceptual and evaluative framework for that of the participant.

Through his 'internal point of view', Hart adapts this hermeneutical internalisation of rules, as the participants' reasons for action, for legal theory (Hart 1994: 289, 297; MacCormick 1978: 278–9; Rodriguez-Blanco 2007). He distinguishes between the 'mere convergence of behaviour' observed from an external standpoint to legal practice and the 'existence of a social rule' associated with the ought-ness of a duty or obligation from the participants' internal point of view (Hart 1994: 9–10, 89). The distinction is between enquiry into human activity orientated by perception of empirical regularities and enquiry orientated by 'consciousness of those who use and operate with whatever standards of conduct may be in question' (MacCormick 1978: 284). Furthermore, Hart works with a mutually interwoven grounding of reasons with social rules within legal practice. Although highly immersive and particularist in terms of the content of a society's legal framework, the methodology itself is necessarily general – as a framework to understand the meaningfulness of human behaviour as such, applied to legal practice. It rests on an implicit concept of 'social practice' resembling that of Winch.

However, to explain the obligatory character of law across the internal points of view of different legal communities, Hart needs a general explanation of the volitional element securing the internal aspect of a rule. According to Hart, the relevant attitude is more than a matter of feelings (Hart 1994: 57):

> What is necessary is that there should be a critical reflective attitude to certain patterns of behaviour as a common standard, and that this should display itself in criticism (including self-criticism), demands for conformity, and in acknowledgments that such criticism and demands are justified, all of which find their characteristic expression in the normative terminology of 'ought', 'must', and 'should', 'right' and 'wrong'.

Within a rule-governed practice, the primary factor producing a sense of obligation, according to Hart, is whether 'general demand for conformity is insistent and the social pressure brought to bear upon those who deviate or threaten to deviate is great' (Hart 1994: 86). But the social pressure must follow from some volitional element of *acceptance* to explain how the 'critical reflective attitude' involves appraisal of conduct within the social group based on willed adoption of a common standard (Hart 1994: 255–9; 1982: 255–61; MacCormick 1978: 284–92). Not every participant in legal practice need adopt this critically reflective attitude. Legal officials necessarily do so since they are actively engaged in interpreting and applying the rules. Other subjects may adopt an

222 Mark D. Retter

attitude of passive acceptance and even acquiesce in the use of law for unjust purposes.

The volitional element secures Hart's 'rule of recognition' (RoR) – the grounding norm for unity in a legal order. Not all rules, Hart tells us, proscribe conduct (primary rules); some have an enabling function: 'specify[ing] the ways in which primary rules may be conclusively ascertained, introduced, eliminated, varied, and the fact of their violation conclusively determined' (secondary rules; Hart 1994: 94). Of these secondary rules, the RoR provides foundational criteria to authoritatively identify other valid legal rules and serves as the principle of unity for primary and secondary rules within a complete legal system. So, in contrast to Hans Kelsen, who separates his *Grundnorm* from the facticity of practice (Kelsen 1949: 1–40), Hart identifies the RoR as a presupposition of the reasoning of active participants, and particularly legal officials, from the internal point of view of legal practice (Hart 1983: 339–42; 1994: 292–3). The RoR is a 'customary rule' that exists insofar as 'accepted and practised in the law-identifying and law-applying operations' of legal officials and institutions (Hart 1994: 256), and that acceptance is often manifested implicitly through legal officials' conduct in identifying, interpreting and applying law. However, for that 'active acceptance' by officials to be effective in constituting a legal system, sufficient support is required from legal subjects, at least as passive acceptance of the practice of officials, reinforced by a habit of obedience (Hart 1994: 112–17; 1982: 262–8).

This endogenous basis for legal obligation, within legal practice, is a helpful step towards understanding legal normativity and an improvement on Kelsen's normative idealism. A practice-based approach explains how 'acceptance' of the peremptory status of legal rules, by the social group, is manifested through their 'interwoven' activities. There are, however, significant problems that suggest an alternative view of social practice and theory, set out in *After Virtue*.

12.2.2 *Teleological Sense of Practice and Rules*

In his work on social science and agency, MacIntyre was concerned with explaining how a culture's stock of action-guiding standards and descriptions is responsive to 'the thread of rational criticism in history' (MacIntyre 1962: 60). This work ultimately informed his account of traditions and epistemological crises (MacIntyre 1977a). Of relevance to the question of how transformations in a culture's evaluative framework can be intelligible was whether there are trans-cultural criteria to identify and critically reject 'fictions' in conflict with scientific evidence

Law as Social Practice: *After Virtue* and Legal Theory 223

yet operating as practical presuppositions within a culture's evaluative framework. According to Winch, the causal enquiry of the natural sciences should not have a bearing; and so, to identify a 'fiction' in another culture's evaluative framework is to project one's own evaluative paradigm and, by so doing, to misunderstand that other culture.

Studying witchcraft amongst the Azande, for instance, social scientists could not meaningfully ask about the truth of belief in witches, based on Winch's view (MacIntyre 1971: 228). That means the enquiry could not explain the transition from a society characterised by general belief in witchcraft to general disbelief, such as occurred in seventeenth-century Scotland. The capacity to recognise empirical evidence from within a culture does partly depend on the culture's linguistically structured conceptual schema and its stock of available causal generalisations to explain physical phenomena. Nevertheless, there is an invariant dimension to the empirical evidence, available to the sensible experience of agents within cultures that practise witchcraft and potentially communicable across cultures. That empirical evidence can support the conclusion that 'witches' do not exist, and, at a minimum, criteria of non-contradiction provide some inter- and intra-traditional standards for mutual intelligibility. This raises the potential for cultural belief in witches to be intelligibly thrown into 'epistemological crisis'. Dissonance can arise between what *seems* the case according to long-held beliefs and evaluative standards, and what *is* the case. The associated social rules intertwined with such beliefs can lose meaningfulness, like *taboo* rules that lack good reasons for members of that society to act in conformity with them – to act as if witches exist whilst knowing the opposite to be true (MacIntyre 2007: 111–13; 1990: 178–89). For the culture to sustain itself as an intelligible tradition, this form of dissonance may need to be overcome, with a broader narrative understanding of how the changes in belief and evaluative framework are genuine developments.

A key point is that the evaluative frameworks of social practices, including law, cannot be hermeneutically isolated from causal explanations. Indeed, as MacIntyre argues, some actions cannot be explained by reference to a framework of reasons at all. Sometimes, actions follow from brute desires – like a child saying: 'I want *x*!' (MacIntyre 1986: 73–7; 1999a: 68–70). In these cases, causal explanations in the psycho-physical domain hold sway in explaining such actions. Nevertheless, we can also describe the particular action as unintelligible by reference to a paradigm of *good reasons*.[1] This is because the capacity for reason

---

[1] E.g. an agent asking for a saucer of mud because 'she just wants it' (Anscombe 1957: para. 37).

provides a paradigm by which to evaluate human conduct, and that capacity can be reasonably inferred from human activities in which reasons for action are formulated and evaluated. In addition, as the witchcraft example suggests, causal explanations can inform whether reasons for action, based on a society's evaluative framework, are *good reasons* at any point in time, and thus they should inform social theory in understanding the intelligible development of cultural practices as traditions. This marks off an approach by which MacIntyre seeks to avoid being trapped by a hermeneutic circle within a culture's rules whilst resisting a naturalism that reduces the explanation of human action to material causes and a rationalism that dis-embeds human reason from qualitative contexts and traditions. His teleological notion of a 'practice' is crucial to that project.

According to MacIntyre, there are standards internal to a culture's practices, not reducible to rules and providing criteria to evaluate those rules. These standards are socially established ends internal to the performance of practices – what MacIntyre calls 'internal goods' (MacIntyre 2007: 187–91). Agreeing with Winch, he affirms that practical reasoning requires an 'individual to participate in the norm-governed transactions and relationships of a particular institutionalized social order' (MacIntyre 1998f: 123). However, in contrast to Winch, 'what makes practical rationality possible within each practice is the way in which the practice is directed towards the achievement of certain goods, specific to and internal to each particular practice, which provide both activity and enquiry within each practice with their *telos*'. Chess is an example given in *After Virtue* (MacIntyre 2007: 188–90). It is true that the rules of chess constitute its competitive challenges and can engender an internalised point of view on conduct within the game, as Hart describes (Hart 1994: 31, 56–7, 140–41, 157). However, the value of those rules, in enabling the competitive challenges, provides their point and purpose within a broader account of the overall good to be achieved in human life. In other words, the goods and rules of the game are mutually constitutive, but internal goods provide reasons for the rule-following and explain how participants can draw on internal standards to evaluate, refine and interpret an existing framework of rules. If, instead, the rules are abstracted from their relationship to internal goods, they become like *taboo* rules, lacking in meaning and purpose, no longer understood as contributing to the ends of human life, lived out through the community's practices.

Accordingly, MacIntyre identifies a teleological structure to practices that explains why a social practice's evaluative framework is never reducible to its rules. Although the participant perspective is internal to practice and tradition, it has an inherently forward-looking character,

Law as Social Practice: *After Virtue* and Legal Theory 225

as the perspective of the paradigmatic human agent with the capacity to consider and act on *good reasons*, all things reasonably considered within the relevant context. So, while the social theorist's standpoint may be descriptive, the perspective of the agent – the object of the enquiry – is necessarily teleological and orientated by a *focal sense* of good reasons for action from available considerations.

Applying this methodology to an explanation of legal obligation, the legal theorist needs to justify why legal subjects remain bound to act in conformity with law, in the *focal sense* of reasonable action, even though they have a volitional capacity to do otherwise. This requires a descriptive standpoint on the agent perspective. However, the intelligibility of the agent perspective can be sustained only by reference to the prospective, purposive viewpoint of whether there are good and presumptively over-riding reasons to obey the law. In contrast, Hart hermeneutically seals his internal viewpoint by reference to the concept of 'acceptance' in order to remain evaluatively neutral between the various motivations of different participants. In consequence, Hart's theory of law is normatively inert – it fails to explain why law ought to be binding for agents in a focal sense (cf. Finnis 2011b).

Indeed, Hart's critical reflective attitude with respect to the RoR captures only convergent motivations for what has been done on the basis of rules rather than what *ought* to have been done. The only generalisable element of that attitude that could provide reasons for prospective action is the consequent social pressure to conform. But the mere presence of social pressure does not establish good and pre-sumptively overriding reasons for action that explain 'duty' and 'obliga-tion'. Furthermore, if legal rules are simply identified with the peremptory content-independent reasons for action that Hart attempts to explain, then there is nothing else, apart from their socially accepted status as law and their embodiment within a characteristic institutional setting, to distinguish their obligatory character from other types of social rules. As MacIntyre points out against Winch, all rules would be identi-fied with reasons for meaningful action (MacIntyre 1971: 217–22). Effectively, this collapses reasons for legal obligation, and any normative hierarchy between obligations, into mere rule-following. The enquiry is left with an unanswerable question: why should we follow a legal rule? The fact that this rule-following has been predominant in the past, or that other agents would apply social pressure to non-conformists, does not give an obligatory reason to any agent – including legal officials – to engage in it in the future.

The focal sense of law should be understood, instead, by reference to the human capacity to act on good reasons (all things reasonably

226   *Mark D. Retter*

considered). Given that this rational capacity is exercised from an embedded perspective, through a community's various practices, the internal goods of practices provide available standards. And, if all things are 'reasonably considered', then the standards of each practice should never be isolated. The standards of one practice, like law, are evaluated by agents in relation to those of other practices and activities; and they are ordered by reference to their contribution to an overall good for personal and communal life. In the focal sense, then, legal practice should be understood in relation to other practices in a community, and particularly as embedded within political practice. Moreover, the best understanding of its standards so far should be open to rival understandings in other legal traditions.

By contrast, fragmentation in orders of practical rationality is endemic to the idea of 'social practice' deployed by Hart to understand law. Without analysing a practice in terms of *good reasons* for action confronting an agent, there are no criteria to evaluate how the rules of one practice relate to those of another, except the mere social facts of volitional 'acceptance', or an irreducible assumption that law has overriding authority. Such problems of fragmentation extend to how one form of legal practice (say, national law) is ordered in relation to others (such as international law, rebel law, *lex mercatoria*, etc.; Retter 2019) and how a legal practice intelligibly transfers from one regime to another, as a dynamic tradition. The Hartian legal theorist has difficulties maintaining the continuity of the German legal tradition, for instance, from Nazism to the post-war regime; or the integrity of the Colombian legal system, grappling with the legal force to be attributed to rules and decisions of rebel authorities, such as the *Fuerzas Armadas Revolucionarias de Colombia* (Provost 2021). Legal systems are highly institutionalised, practice-embodied traditions sustained by good reasons for obedience and subject to customary developments in 'dialogue with the past'. In this respect, *After Virtue*'s core concepts – particularly that of a 'social practice', 'institution' and 'tradition' – can help articulate a better understanding of law.

12.3   Law and Social Practice

12.3.1   *Human Sociability, Politics and Law*

What should be taken more seriously, in response to Hart, is that 'the internal attitude must standardly be based on the civic friendship that Plato, Aristotle, and Aquinas were inclined to identify as the standard motivation of law-making and law-maintenance in its central forms' (Finnis 2011a: 112). This point is effectively made by John Finnis in

Law as Social Practice: *After Virtue* and Legal Theory   227

his so-called new natural law theory.[2] The *focal sense* of law, as Finnis formulates it, rests on what is practically reasonable given conditions for human sociability and flourishing (Finnis 1980: 3–19, 276–81). In particular, Finnis justifies the socio-political foundations for law through the basic good of friendship as an irreducible aspect of human flourishing and the need for civic friendship to resolve coordination problems within human communities (Finnis 1980: 141–56). Much more should be said, however, about the social practices within which specific ends and coordination problems arise; and within which there is need for civic friendship to pursue common ends, and participating agents learn what standards of conduct sustain concord (MacIntyre 1997: 98–9). Moreover, law itself can be understood as a distinct 'practice', concerned with the institutional ordering of political community by the rule of law and extended through time as a 'tradition'.

As suggested in Section 12.2.2, the concept of a 'practice' provides a way to embed *good reasons* for action within the ends of analogous social contexts and a way to think through how different 'practices' are related, interdependent and institutionally ordered within an encompassing community. MacIntyre defines 'practice' in *After Virtue* using the following elements: (1) a sufficiently coherent and complex form of socially established cooperative activity; (2) internal goods realised through, and forming a definitive basis for, the pursuit of excellence in that activity; and (3) the pursuit of excellence in that activity involves a systematic extension of human powers to achieve and make practical judgements about such excellence (MacIntyre 2007: 187–91). Crucial to the definition are those goods that are internal to the achievements, motivations and justifications for the cooperative activity itself. Internal goods are defined in contrast to rival and excludable external goods, like power, money and honour, which are only contingently related to reasons for cooperative participation. As the ends of practices, internal goods are also more fundamental, in the order of practical rationality, than the institutional structures and rules that serve to orientate the practice to its achievements. Characteristically, however, practices also involve (4) an institutional form embodied in an administered system of rules, ordering and facilitating the common activity.

A range of different activities potentially embody the practical rationality of practices: chess, farming, architecture, medicine, physics, philosophy, friendship, family life, politics *and* – importantly – law

---

[2] New natural law theory originated in the 1960s with the work of Germain Grisez and was developed by Joseph Boyle, John Finnis and others. The theory was authoritatively articulated in Finnis 1980.

228   *Mark D. Retter*

(MacIntyre 2007: 194–5; 1978c: 29; Retter 2015; Kelly 2020). However, according to MacIntyre, there is the opposing potential for such activities to exhibit mutual-advantage rationality – the social manifestation of a Humean practical rationality. MacIntyre resists the reduction of practical rationality as such to this Humean form because it ignores a distinction, often made by persons within practices, between reasons for acting of the form: 'I desire X'; and intelligible reasons: 'I desire X because X is good to pursue in the circumstances' (MacIntyre 1986; 1998c: 147). Both forms of practical rationality are instantiated in social life and to greater or lesser degrees in different activities. They are competing rationalities with different kinds of cooperative standards (MacIntyre 2007: 190–91; 1988: 30–46).

Within practices, participating agents learn to distinguish between what *seems* good based on untutored desires and what *is* good by reference to cooperative standards and achievements internal to the practice. If those cooperative achievements are to be sustained and extended, proximate decisions should be accountable and subordinate to common ends of the group. Thus, participating agents learn to exercise practical rationality not simply *qua* autonomous individuals but *qua* self-directing participants within the group's collaborative enterprise. By acting instead on competing desires for external goods, such agents will instrumentalise and impair the cooperative achievements at stake. Hence, the notion of internal goods isolates ends of a social practice that are good for agents as collaborative participants whilst also providing individual motivation for cooperative participation. These are 'common goods' insofar as they are achieved and enjoyed together, as the end of a group's 'common action' (Retter 2022; cf. Simon 1980).

Achieving internal goods requires mutual commitment to standards of conduct and the cultivation of relevant virtues for successful performance of the activity (MacIntyre 2007: 190–91, 1990: 61–3). 'Rules of practice' serve to articulate these standards and can be given institutional form to provide authoritative direction for cooperative conduct within the group (MacIntyre 2007: 194–5). To external observers, a practice can appear to be constituted by this institutional form. But, as discussed in Section 12.2.2, the internal goods provide presupposed standards by which rules are evaluated. When a participant's motivation for engaging in a practice fixates on external goods, the authority of social rules, and the officials and institutions applying those rules, will have primary significance for directing their action in the practice (MacIntyre 2007: 190; 1978c: 28–30). This follows from that participant's inability to fully appreciate the goods of the practice as reason for conformity to the rules. If a chess player wants to quit because they unwittingly made a bad move, they are

Law as Social Practice: *After Virtue* and Legal Theory

following the rules only to win and not for the shared competitive challenges of the game. In contrast, when motivated by those internal competitive challenges, they will recognise the rules and virtues as constitutive means for collaborating to achieve those goods of excellence.

The human capacity to reason about some overall good is important to the integration of social practices within personal and communal life. Human persons are embedded within a web of interdependent social practices and activities. Confronting competing choices and demands, MacIntyre claims that human agents cannot avoid asking: 'What is my good?' and 'How is it to be achieved?'. Each person's search for answers is what he calls the 'narrative quest' – viz. a teleological character to human life extending beyond specific activities to the pursuit of some integrated idea of personal human flourishing (MacIntyre 2007: 204–205; 2016: 231–42). That quest is conditioned by the social locus for human fulfilment through heterogeneous social practices and by the capacities, dispositions and dependencies of human nature.

Since the *telos* of human life integrates the goods of various practices, the question 'What is my good?' requires an answer to 'What is our good?'. According to MacIntyre, the need to sustain concord within practices, and to integrate the different activities and practices within a political community, engenders the need for joint practical reasoning and decision-making. Practical demands for common action provide political practice and institutions with a *telos* – viz. an integrative common good for the political community that realises the social conditions for personal human flourishing (MacIntyre 1998b; 1999a: 113–46). Politics, then, is a type of 'architectonic' practice, on MacIntyre's view, which prioritises and integrates a society's ends for the sake of some unified common good (cf. Aristotle, *Nicomachean Ethics*, 1094a10–16, a27–b8, 1141b24–5; *Politics*, 1260a18–19).

Mutual commitment to the political common good is presupposed by personal commitment to human flourishing in the focal sense of rational human agency. This requires dedication to the virtues of civic friendship and justice to sustain concord in political relations. To some extent, standards of justice will be articulable as rules – a 'natural law' (MacIntyre 1988: 198–202; 1999a: 109–11). As examples, MacIntyre refers to ethical requirements against taking innocent life and lying and for respecting others' property, avoiding ignorance and cultivating understanding (MacIntyre 2009c: 5, 23). Through dedication to joint deliberation about the common good, an agent is committed to such moral precepts as practical preconditions (MacIntyre 2009c: 23). These moral precepts provide a minimal level of guidance to human agents on what the common good requires. Their violation undermines political

230   *Mark D. Retter*

concord and demonstrates a disregard for the political community as a common enterprise, constitutive of one's personal flourishing.

There is, however, significant under-determination of natural justice, and there are difficulties knowing what is required beyond a core practical understanding of moral precepts. As a result, substantial room exists for reasonable dispute about what should be done here, now, in pursuit of a common good. Given the need for timely decision-making for common action and in the absence of unanimity, natural justice requires that a political authority be delimited and recognised, with effective power to rule by law and to give determination to standards of common action in a political community (cf. Finnis 1980: 231–54; Simon 1980: 31–50). These political conditions, understood on MacIntyre's terms, provide the grounds for a legal theory. However, to develop that legal theory further, one needs to address a potential tension in MacIntyre's political thought against authoritative decision-making and the rule of law.

In my view, MacIntyre over-emphasises joint deliberation about the political common good, and this can work to marginalise the importance of institutions and authority for realising common action in conditions of disagreement, especially within large-scale and complex political societies. This stance ends up overstating the normative character of deliberative democracy as the ideal form of political practice, requiring a retreat to incomplete, localised forms of deliberative politics, where authentic joint deliberation about common goods might still be possible (MacIntyre 2007: 262–3; 1998b; 1999a: 129–46; 2016: 106–110, 124–5, 168–83). It also obscures the central role of authority and the rule of law in politics, especially within a more complete and encompassing community. In fact, it implies that the typical case of governance by law, through an authority exercised by representative political institutions and decision-makers, is somehow defective.

A key claim that MacIntyre wants to sustain is that growth in human virtue requires joint deliberation and the exercise of political prudence by plain persons – not being reserved to political elites. But given radical human dependency – as expressed in *Dependent Rational Animals* – the problems of common action cannot be limited to localised forms of politics, and MacIntyre recognises this (MacIntyre 1998b: 246–52). A more constructive approach would connect his arguments on the political participation of plain persons and local communities to a justification for subsidiarity in the delimitation of political authority and institutions. This would not exclude requirements of solidarity, as a correlative principle of the common good, when there are good reasons for authoritative and representative decision-making.

Law as Social Practice: *After Virtue* and Legal Theory 231

Much more should be said about MacIntyre's politics than is possible here. For current purposes, the central importance *and* dangers of institutionalised authority and rules should be acknowledged to make space for an adequate legal theory. Moreover, the focal sense of politics and law needs to be sufficiently general to explain the role of authority and the rule of law across different human communities in history. It should not be excessively determined by a particular form of political governance that may suit only a past era and culture, such as the Greek *polis* or the modern state. Here, as Finnis rightly underscores, the concept of *determinatio* has a significant role (Finnis 1980: 284–9; 1998: 267–72). That concept captures the creative, largely customary specification and delimitation of political institutions by reference to abstract principles of natural justice for the specific conditions of a geographically and temporally located people and culture.

With these corrections, a focal sense of legal practice can be developed that explains legal obligation by reference to good reasons for action. Within a political community committed to a common good for the personal flourishing of its members, there is a framework of natural justice supporting the presumptive authority of its political institutions and the rule of law; and there are moral obligations on legal subjects to obey legal rules as promulgated and interpreted by legal officials. In consequence, there are basic moral precepts that precondition the obligatory character of law because they protect the cooperative relations intrinsic to the purpose of political authority and law (Retter 2019). This makes more moderate sense of MacIntyre's 'subversive' claim that 'authority as to what the law is, on fundamentals at least, rests with plain persons' (MacIntyre 1995c: 50). Without mutual commitment to such ethical norms, legal subjects would not have overriding reasons to obey the law.

Nevertheless, incorporation of such moral precepts into the content of positive law requires authoritative acts of recognition. This is why we can speak intelligibly of 'unjust legal systems' (cf. Finnis 1980: 354–62). On the one hand, there is a non-focal, external standpoint on the institutional rules of a legal system, which perceives a system of intra-systemically valid rules that may or may not be just. On the other hand, there is a focal agential perspective, which perceives legal practice as a purposive social activity among various actors – law-makers, law-executors and administrators, judges, legal subjects and legal advocates – with a *telos* of making, interpreting, enforcing and following institutional rules, as a constitutive order for common action by the specific political community to achieve its common good. The former standpoint is parasitic on the latter. It needs to justify why the system of legal rules developed historically and why it should be sustained and extended as a legal tradition with ongoing reasons for obedience.

In the focal sense, then, law is subsidiary to politics and takes on an architectonic character as the constitutive means for political order, which directs legal subjects to the community's common good and sustains political concord by administering justice. This supporting role for political practice is the fundamental reason for rule by law. It also enables law to be distinguished from the rules of other social orders, such as cricket, religious groups, families, schools or mafia operations. These can resemble law, to some extent, as administered systems of rules, and they may even be integrated into a positive legal system. They nonetheless lack the architectonic quality of law for the sake of some unified common good of an encompassing political community.

12.3.2 *Law as Social Practice*

Describing law as a 'practice' entails that it is a purposive and collaborative activity, performed for the sake of internal goods that explain why the motivations and actions of legal participants are accountable to cooperative standards. How does law exhibit the practical rationality of practices? MacIntyre gives us a clue in *After Virtue*: 'if institutions have corrupting power', he says, 'the making and sustaining of forms of community – and therefore of institutions – itself has all the characteristics of a practice, and moreover of a practice which stands in a peculiarly close relationship to the exercise of virtues' (MacIntyre 2007: 194). On the one hand, the 'ability of a practice to retain its integrity will depend on the way in which the virtues can be and are exercised in sustaining the institutional forms which are the social bearers of the practice'; and, on the other, 'virtues are of course themselves in turn fostered by certain types of social institutions and endangered by others' (MacIntyre 2007: 195). By extension, then, the administration of legal rules constitutes a practice when undertaken with a practitioner rationality that is accountable to collaborative political standards. This is why, in an earlier essay, MacIntyre explicitly identifies law as a practice (MacIntyre 1978c: 29).

Administering legal rules involves a range of activities: articulating, drafting and amending legal rules; researching and identifying valid rules by reference to authoritative 'legal sources'; interpreting, extending and applying such rules based on shared principles, purposes and understandings; formulating, claiming and arguing a legal case; resolving disputes about divergent interpretations based on legal reasons; sanctioning proscribed conduct; and providing legal remedies. Some of these activities are undertaken only by identified authorities within legal practice, such as law-makers, law-executors and administrative officials, judges and other adjudicators. The authority of these roles is defined by a constitutional framework (the institutional form of legal practice), identifying who can legitimately exercise particular powers on behalf of the specific community and defining and delimiting those powers. The exercise of such powers is legitimate only if it justifiably represents the common agency of the political community, for its common good. This distinguishes the use of force involved in the exercise of power from acts of violence.

Who else forms part of this common agency? Legal rules govern the conduct of all persons within their jurisdiction. Such legal subjects are involved in interpreting and applying law to their conduct and the conduct of others, as well as claiming and arguing about legal duties and rights. Given that these activities can require distinct expertise, time and skills, there can be an important role for professional lawyers, bound by a professional ethic as fiduciaries, to represent clients in varying capacities. Lawyers also play a part in the argumentative development of legal doctrine.

Of course, legal subjects may not choose whether to be involved in legal practice because political regimes apply law with force and sanctions. But collaborative participation by legal subjects is essential to law in its focal sense for the following reasons. First, the efficacy of law – ordering the community to common ends – depends on a general belief in its legitimacy by legal subjects over time, which sustains their obedience to legal rules as binding reasons for action. Second, its efficacy depends on how well legal subjects guide their conduct by legal rules. This interdependence between the activities of legal officials and subjects, for achieving the ends of political practice, constitutes law as a *practice* in the sense that MacIntyre describes.

The need for collaboration and concord in legal practice does not stop with the formation of docile, law-abiding subjects. It has a teleological character extending to the participation of subjects in the virtues and goods of political practice, especially justice (MacIntyre 1999a: 93–4, 108–12). Laws against littering, for example, can be internalised as communal standards reaching beyond their legal ambit to promote communal cleanliness. Like the child who learns to play by the rules of chess for the game's excellence, it is possible for legal subjects to be formed through law to standards of communal excellence. Within legal practice, the ordinary legal subject can learn to distinguish between what is simply instrumentally good *qua* individual from what is good *qua* legal subject, and thus as member of the political community, pursuing the common good through law (MacIntyre 1999a: 66–7). This practical formation differentiates between those who treat law as a binding reason for action only insofar as it is likely to be enforced and those who grasp the internal goods of legal practice as reasons for being law-abiding citizens.

Judgements from the perspective of legal subjects inform what is good *qua* legal official in exercising their powers and also *qua* advocate in exercising fiduciary responsibilities. These roles are dependent on the reciprocating and justificatory relation they bear to legal subjects. If either type of agent restricts their reasons for action to what is good *qua* individual, they ignore the social dependency of their role within legal practice. When the legal official, in particular, invokes law as an authoritative reason for action, this has social significance connected to the standards for pursuing its internal goods. That authoritative reason for action is necessarily expressed as a justification to other participants, parasitic on a broader justification for the enforcement of law that can sustain mutual fidelity to law, as a specification of justice (see Rodriguez-Blanco 2014: 75–122).

The judge has a paradigmatic role. Delivering a judgement is a social act. The judge appeals implicitly to the social reasons for action embodied in rules, and their nature as 'law', to provide adequate justification for judicial decisions. This involves 'reflexivity' in the practice of law, whereby the application of law as an authoritative reason for action relies on an implicit appeal to the nature or function of law as an evaluative background to its justification (Simmonds 2007: 113–43, 156–8). Although it might be possible, as Hart allows, for an official to apply law for selfish reasons, this misses the point. The reasons given in a judgement are subject to justificatory standards embodied in legal practice. At a minimum, law is an indispensible means to achieve shared conditions for order and stability in a political community. But the reciprocity involved in legal practice is connected to political expectations that ends pursued on behalf of the community should be capable of justification by good reasons. Defective applications or interpretive developments of law can be identified by such standards, and this has potential bearing on a participant's reasons for recognising and acting on its binding authority.

In the articulation of legal reasons, practical wisdom has a crucial role. Judicial reasoning entails primary judgements about what should be done to resolve the practical problems presented in the particular dispute; and there are more reflexive judgements, in formulating and expressing a legal decision, which draw on practical insight into legal sources, their application to relevant problems and the importance/role of the institutional legal authority of such sources. This is the virtue of *phronesis* at

Law as Social Practice: *After Virtue* and Legal Theory 235

work in legal practice through the role of the judge; and the perspective of the 'wise judge' informs the rationality of other legal roles.

Given that the practical rationality of legal officials is parasitic on justificatory standards that support collaborative relations in legal practice, Finnis is right to identify a 'focal instance' of law. But this 'practical viewpoint', defining the 'focal instance', should be understood along MacIntyrean lines, as the practitioner standpoint committed to the cooperative standards of legal practice. Law is a purposive and cooperative activity involving the pursuit and extension of virtues and standards of excellence to realise a political order that aims at the community's common good, administered according to the virtue of justice. A richer account should flesh out the role of the virtues in legal practice (see Farrelly and Solum 2008; Amaya and Lai 2013). Moreover, legal practice has historical extension. Dialogue and disputation about the standards and virtues of legal practice and how they relate to governing conduct by legal rules are extended into a tradition, as a common project worked out dialogically over time (see MacIntyre 2007: 193–4; 1977a). The opinion of a judge resolving a legal dispute, for example, will be informed by the views of past judicial thought, the arguments of legal advocates and other legal scholarship on the legal issues at stake, with an eye to the interpretive development of legal doctrine in the future. Indeed, MacIntyre recognises that 'the elaboration of conceptions of liability, responsibility, and negligence' within the common law tradition was developed as a sustained common project over time, in accordance with practice-based rationality (MacIntyre 1978c: 29). Theoretical understandings of legal practice also form part of a dialogue with the understandings of contemporaries and predecessors. These theories can enhance or distort the rationality of legal practice depending on the extent to which they express good practice and influence agency. So the systematic extension and transformation of law's internal goods are connected to a dialogue between participants over time concerning the best understanding of its standards so far and how to best achieve them. In particular, the intelligibility of a legal tradition is sustained through dialogue about its legitimate authority in the given society by reference to good peremptory reasons for action.

12.4 Neglect of Legal Practice and Theory

Despite the potential for *After Virtue*'s key concepts to contribute to legal theory, there are critical questions concerning why MacIntyre pays little sustained attention to the rule of law or legal practice. It is too one-sided to say that his thought has been ignored by legal theorists. MacIntyre

236   *Mark D. Retter*

himself refrains from engaging with legal theory. One might think this 'gap' is explained by the fact that he is no lawyer or legal theorist. While there may be some truth to this, as a complete explanation it fails to appreciate the extraordinary range of his thought across disciplinary domains, eminently displayed in *After Virtue*. More is at work, and in this conclusion I point to some lines of argument and offer suggestions that hopefully shed light on the prospects for any 'MacIntyrean jurisprudence'.

An initial point is that MacIntyre's neglect of legal practice and theory is partly explained by the more fundamental role of virtue for the successful performance of practices in a political community and his use of virtue language to counteract any reduction of practical rationality to rule-following. A key line of argument throughout *After Virtue* is that morality has been corrupted by a rationalistic, rule-based ethics (cf. MacIntyre 1980). While not excluding the importance of moral and legal rules within society, MacIntyre 'tilts in the wind' against a mindset that places too much importance on formulating rules for action, and on institutional frameworks and bureaucratic reasoning, in the management of political life. Ultimately, this leads to understandings that reduce the practical rationality of social practices to rule-following. In this sense, Hart's legal theory can be seen as a symptom of a deeper crisis. An adequate response, however, should include an alternative legal theory that demonstrates how MacIntyre's criticisms of the dominant culture find a 'point of arrival' within legal practice and theory.

Taking full stock of MacIntyre's position, though, requires appreciation of how he interprets the state of politics, in which contemporary law and understandings of law are embedded. MacIntyre is staunchly critical of the bureaucratic and juridical mindset he identifies with a liberal form of politics, practically embodied in the institutional structures of the modern state and globalised economy (e.g. MacIntyre 1998b: 246–52). He perceives these structures as (perhaps) irredeemably corrupted by a mutual-advantage rationality, identified as antithetical to the practitioner rationality embodied in localised practices (see Section 12.3.1). In *Whose Justice? Which Rationality?*, for instance, MacIntyre refers to professionalised lawyers within the modern state as the 'clergy of liberalism'. Lawyers not only weaponise arguments about justice through the language of legal claims and rights, but also appropriate responsibility for resolving fundamental debates about justice in liberal society by reference to apportionments of legal entitlements (MacIntyre 1988: 5, 344). In consequence, the authority of legal frameworks becomes endowed in the liberal state with a mystical and quasi-religious dimension, which it cannot possibly shoulder as an artifice of will and consensus amongst political elites.

Law as Social Practice: *After Virtue* and Legal Theory

What prospects are there for constructive engagement between MacIntyre and contemporary legal theory in light of his sharp, systematic criticism of law and lawyers within modern liberal states? And if these criticisms rest on a commitment to an ideal deliberative democracy modelled on the Greek *polis* (see Section 12.3.2), to what extent can MacIntyre's thought provide for a general theory of law, with sufficient explanatory power across history? How can it avoid becoming a relic of the past?

Space prevents a thorough response to these questions. For present purposes, a couple of points should be borne in mind. The first is that MacIntyre's conceptions of practice-based rationality and mutual-advantage rationality are ideal conceptual types, present in social activities to varying extents and typically as an 'admixture'. Social activities are not reducible to either type. Instead, these rationalities vie for dominance through various agencies in social life. This resonates with my own experience of legal practice – both forms of rationality are present, and external goods of money, fame and power are perennial temptations for people to pursue the love-of-self in ways that are systematically destructive of human fellowship. However, one reason why mutual-advantage rationality never totally corrupts human practices *and* institutions is that the potential for moral virtues, including justice, is also perennial within the human condition. The experience of friendships and sociability in localised practices, such as family and religious life, can provide ample opportunities. MacIntyre's account of the ordinary knowledge of natural law precepts implicitly recognises this perennial potential for the pursuit of common goods to reveal the natural law, and, through that law, those virtues that perfect human agency to act for good ends in various contexts. Social structures can work to compartmentalise different aspects of our life and suppress the exercise of authentic virtues, with the imposition of a bureaucratic logic through large-scale social structures and institutions (MacIntyre 2006f; 1998f). But, as Charles Taylor suggests, 'we are far more "Aristotelian" than we allow' (Taylor 1994: 22). The articulation of understandings of well-ordered law, in a focal sense of good legal practice, is an important corrective to the influence of mutual-advantage rationality in legal and political practice.

The second point is that, while a political common good implies some institutionalised political community that can realise that overall good for a specific society, it is typically the case that existent institutionalised political communities are defective or incomplete in realising such historical ideals, especially given the challenges of human evil.[3] More

---

[3] On 'complete' and 'incomplete' communities, see MacIntyre 2008a: 262–5; Osborne 2008.

specifically, while I partly accept MacIntyre's claims that contemporary nation-states are not perfected political communities, that does not mean they do not participate in, contribute to or aim at a political common good in ways that give a presumptive obligatory weight to the authority of their institutions and laws – as a partial realisation of law in the focal sense. Moreover, the moral weight of good reasons to sustain obedience to a recognised but defective institutionalised authority is reinforced when one considers the precious character of order for human flourishing in community, the realisable alternatives in political governance and the means by which such alternatives *might* be brought about.

Bearing these in mind, and the work that remains, this chapter has sought to demonstrate how MacIntyre's thought helps to develop a general understanding of legal practice and the rule of law, even within modern states, as an intrinsic aspect of the political common good. The focal sense of law should be understood, on this view, through an account of good legal practice, which justifies the common action involved in the crafting, interpreting and applying of authoritative institutional rules by reference to good peremptory reasons for action. The type of practical rationality involved has been embodied to varying extents in different legal traditions, and especially within the common law tradition. Such legal traditions provide resources to correct more rationalistic and technocratic understandings of law in modernity.

13 *After Virtue*, Managers and Business Ethics

Paul Blackledge

13.1 Introduction

Over the last few decades Alasdair MacIntyre's *After Virtue* has become an increasingly important point of reference within the discipline of business ethics (Ferero and Sison 2014). This paradoxical turn of events seems to contradict not only what Ron Beadle calls MacIntyre's well-known and 'ongoing hostility to capitalism' (Beadle 2017: 60), but also *After Virtue*'s powerful critique of management and managerialism (Knight 2007: 160–61). Moreover, it stands in sharp contrast to MacIntyre's explicit comments on business ethics. For instance, in the preface to the 2007 edition of *After Virtue*, he wrote that twenty-first-century corporate managers combine the 'pretentions to expertise' he had discussed in the first edition of the book with a new tendency to mouth 'formulas that she or he learned in a course in business ethics' (MacIntyre 2007: xv). He extended this argument in 'The Irrelevance of Ethics' to claim that the kind of rote-learned moral frameworks taught in business schools, 'like the academic teaching of ethics in general, has little or nothing to do with the formation of moral character and is ineffective as an instrument of moral transformation, and … is a dangerous distraction from enquiry into the nature and causes of what is morally flawed in our economic institutions and activities' (MacIntyre 2015: 8). It is perhaps unsurprising that MacIntyre once reportedly justified his refusal to attend a conference on business ethics 'for the same reason that he wouldn't attend a conference on astrology' (Knight 1998a: 284). One might reasonably surmise that, for him, a belief in business ethics could be likened, as he once likened the concept of natural human rights, to a belief in 'witches and in unicorns' (MacIntyre 2007: 69).

Nonetheless, human rights do now exist, as a social if not a natural form. Can the same be said of business as an ethical practice? Writers such as

---

Thanks to Tom Angier, Ron Beadle, Kelvin Knight and Jeff Nicholas for their comments on a draft of this chapter.

240   *Paul Blackledge*

Greg Beabout and Geoff Moore, whom I take to be exemplary voices amongst a broader layer of MacIntyrean business ethicists (Akrivou and Sison 2016), think it can, and argue that we should revisit MacIntyre's concept of institutions with a view to exploring the possibility that good management might be understood as a MacIntyrean practice. These authors essentially seek to reposition MacIntyre as a critical voice within, rather than as a powerful critic of, management. To this end, they champion MacIntyre's neo-Aristotelianism as a framework for an ethical managerial alternative to Milton Friedman's claim that the only 'social responsibility of business is to increase its profits' (Friedman 1970).

Against these MacIntyrean business ethicists, I argue that one of the many reasons MacIntyre remains relevant to critical social theory is that his work illuminates the sociological conditions of, and the possibility of ethical resistance to, (capitalist) business institutions whose amoral essence was accurately captured by Friedman (Bakan 2004). This is not to suggest that MacIntyre's sociology of institutions can be accepted without qualifications. Beabout's and Moore's suggested revisions to his account of modern bureaucratic organisations may be unconvincing, but their work does illuminate vulnerabilities in MacIntyre's account of institutions. In what follows, I aim to strengthen the critical core of MacIntyre's sociology through the lens of a critique of the weaker, Weberian elements of his thought from the perspective of his comments on Marx in *Ethics in the Conflicts of Modernity*.

13.2   Business Ethics

By far the most important driver behind the rise of the discipline of business ethics is the demand from within business itself that capitalist production be represented as, and believed to be, an ethical practice. This form of ideological justification is important because the type of cynical realism associated with Friedman's model of capitalist firms doesn't easily lend itself to the sort of ethical self-image necessary to incorporate those managers who serve an essential role in reproducing capitalist social relations. Business likes to portray itself as something more than mere money grubbing, and the concept of business ethics functions to justify capitalism to business owners, managers and their academic apologists while helping to obscure capitalism's essentially alienated and exploitative character both from these groups and from their critics (Henning 2014: 482–513).

The ideological function of business ethics can usefully be understood in relation to Boltanski and Chiapello's concept of 'spirits of capitalism'. Capitalism, they argue, is a frankly 'absurd' system where 'wage-earners

After Virtue, Managers and Business Ethics   241

have lost ownership of the fruits of their labour and the possibility of pursuing a working life free of subordination', while capitalists 'find themselves yoked to an interminable, insatiable process, which is utterly abstract and dissociated from the satisfaction of consumption needs, even of a luxury kind'. At its core, capitalism is experienced as a system that 'is singularly lacking in justifications'. In part to counter this experience, capitalist societies function through ideologies aimed at securing the commitment of individual actors (Boltanski and Chiapello 2006: 7). Concretely, capitalism functions best when those managers who play a pivotal role in its reproduction have: first, an exciting model of their own potential to flourish; second, an account of how their security will be realised; and, finally, a moral justification of their position through some model of its fairness. Boltanski and Chiapello argue that capitalism has known three such spirits over its history. First, an entrepreneurial spirit characterised the period up until the Great Depression of the 1930s. Second was a spirit that took as its ideal the salaried director of the large firm and that emerged out of the crisis of the inter-war years. The third spirit of capitalism evolved as this older spirit morphed as a result of engagement with the 'artistic' critique of the far left in the 1960s and 1970s. Boltanski and Chiapello contend that the defeats suffered by radicals in the 1970s and 1980s can be explained, in part, by the ability of the new spirit of capitalism to subvert these previous critiques and disarm the left in the face of neoliberalism. From this perspective, the ideology of business ethics is best understood as a means through which managers both justify one aspect of their own self-image as incorruptible 'coaches' while immunising the capitalist system against radical critique through the argument that 'ethics pays' (Boltanski and Chiapello 2006: 69; Blackledge 2007). Good business, on this view, is not 'manipulative', but embraces a model of capitalism as the interaction of rational, autonomous moral agents in the marketplace (Boltanski and Chiapello 2006: 458).

To substantiate the claim that MacIntyre's neo-Aristotelianism offers the possibility of a powerful voice for a model of business ethics, his supporters within the business schools have attempted to unpick his insights about practices and institutions from his broader critique of managerialism.

13.3   Nietzsche and Weber: MacIntyre, Emotivism and the Critique of Management

The attempt to soften MacIntyre's critique of management poses an obvious, and major, problem for MacIntyrean business ethicists: how

242   *Paul Blackledge*

are they to address his damning evaluation of management given that the latter sits squarely within his broader critique of our modern emotivist culture? In *After Virtue*, MacIntyre argues that 'a moral philosophy ... characteristically presupposes a sociology', and emotivism and the culture that sustains it, in which evaluative judgements have been reduced to incommensurable expressions of preference, are characterised by the 'obliteration of any genuine distinction between manipulative and non-manipulative social relations' (MacIntyre 2007: 11–12, 23). Within this culture, actors typically deploy whatever means they believe to be most effective at any particular moment because they see others as a means to their ends and not as ends in themselves (MacIntyre 2007: 23–4). Following Weber, MacIntyre writes:

> bureaucratic structures which, whether in the form of private corporations or of government agencies ... [are] characteristically engaged in a competitive struggle for scarce resources to put to the service of ... predetermined ends. It is therefore a central responsibility of managers to direct and redirect their organizations' available resources, both human and non-human, as effectively as possible toward those ends. Every bureaucratic organisation embodies some explicit or implicit definition of costs and benefits from which the criteria of effectiveness are derived. Bureaucratic rationality is the rationality of matching means to ends economically and efficiently. (MacIntyre 2007: 25–6)

This form of life is reproduced by agents, including those MacIntyre calls social characters. A social character is somewhat similar to those stock characters in mediaeval morality plays who 'partially define the possibilities of plot and action' (MacIntyre 2007: 27). MacIntyre does not believe that all social roles are characters thus conceived because not all social roles are constrained in the way that characters are constrained. Specifically, 'in the case of a character the possibilities of action are defined in a more limited way than in general' (MacIntyre 2007: 28). Amongst the characters MacIntyre discusses are the Aesthete, the Therapist and the Manager. With regard to the Manager, MacIntyre writes that he represents the obliteration of the distinction between manipulative and non-manipulative means 'in his character' (MacIntyre 2007: 30). Indeed, the modern manager is best understood in Weberian terms as someone who 'treats ends as given, as outside his scope; his concern is with technique, with effectiveness in transforming raw materials into final products, unskilled labor into skilled labor, investment into profits' (MacIntyre 2007: 30). Consequently, the Manager, in his role as manager, neither does nor is 'able to engage in moral debate' (MacIntyre 2007: 30). This is not to say that managers as individuals are utterly amoral. On the contrary, because modern life is fragmented and compartmentalised, managers can and do separate their

After Virtue, Managers and Business Ethics 243

roles as managers from other social roles they play (MacIntyre 2006g: 196; Breen 2012: 159). There are two immediate consequences of this condition. First, it is typical that managers can maintain a personal morality alongside their characteristic role as manipulators at work. Second, however, as Boltanski and Chiapello suggest, the contrast between these roles can be assuaged through a worldview such as that supported by the discourse of business ethics, which attempts to reimagine managerial manipulation as itself an ethical practice.

MacIntyre's critique of this mode of thinking cuts against the common sense of our age. However, just because *After Virtue* has exposed the emperor's nudity doesn't mean that the children of an emotivist culture will recognise the power of his arguments. On the contrary, paralleling Marx's argument that religion is a manifestation of real suffering whose transcendence is possible only through the transformation of the social conditions of its existence (Blackledge 2019b: 150–52), so MacIntyre insists that a realistic, practical critique of the status quo must have a social basis in some form of practice.

In the 1950s and early 1960s MacIntyre followed Marx in believing that the solidarity exhibited through working-class struggles against capitalism could be the basis of such a critique. By the late 1960s, however, while he continued to deploy Marxist tools to criticise the work of others, he concluded that workers' struggles tended to remain trapped within the confines of an emotivist culture such that Marxist parties, when they bothered with such questions, tended to reproduce the inadequacies of liberal morality, either consequentialist or deontological (MacIntyre 1998g: 232; 2007: 262). Correspondingly, when nominally Marxist parties won or seriously challenged for power, they have tended to reproduce all the failings of mainstream capitalist parties: 'as Marxists organize and move toward power they always do and have become Weberians in substance, even if they remain Marxists in rhetoric' (MacIntyre 2007: 109).

The failure of Marxism thus conceived is but an extreme example of a broader tendency to Nietzscheanism within modern social life (MacIntyre 1973). As Knight paraphrases it, the institutional morality of management is, according to MacIntyre, the morality of Nietzsche: 'It is an ethic of the shepherd as distinct from the herd, the overman as distinct from his underlings. On this picture the manager is of a different kind to those whom he manages, possessing if not a superior kind of knowledge then a stronger kind of will' (Knight 2017: 81). But the idea that managers possess a superior, scientific understanding of the world is a myth. According to MacIntyre, the 'concept of managerial effectiveness functions as a moral fiction'. MacIntyre writes that just as Carnap and

244   *Paul Blackledge*

Ayer argued that metaphysical assertions generally and religious assertions particularly function as unjustifiable disguises for the attitudes of those that utter them, so the idea of managerial effectiveness is 'the name of a fictitious, but believed-in reality ... which disguises certain other realities' and which lacks 'rational justification' (MacIntyre 2007: 76).

This kind of division between knowers and doers is a characteristic of Stalinism, and MacIntyre's critique of managerialism is best understood as a generalisation of his early Marxist critique of Stalinist ideology (MacIntyre 2008c: 119; McMylor 1993: 137–8). A key reference point of this critique is Marx's third thesis on Feuerbach:

> The materialist doctrine that men are products of circumstances and upbringing, and that, therefore, changed men are products of other circumstances and changed upbringing forgets that it is men that change circumstances and that the educator must himself be educated. Hence this doctrine necessarily arrives at dividing society into two parts, of which one is superior to society. The coincidence of the changing of circumstances and of human activity or self-change can be conceived and rationally understood only as *revolutionary practice*. (Marx 1975a: 422, emphasis in original)

In *After Virtue*, MacIntyre returns to this argument as a critique of management through his claim that 'what Marx understood was that such an agent is forced to regard his own actions quite differently from the behavior of those whom he is manipulating. For the behavior of the manipulated is being contrived in accordance with his intentions, reasons and purposes; intentions, reasons and purposes which he is treating, at least while he is engaged in such manipulation, as exempt from the laws which govern the behavior of the manipulated' (MacIntyre 2007: 84).

If neither Marxist revolutionaries nor capitalist managers are capable of escaping the emotivist parameters of our age, is there any possibility that others might? MacIntyre believes there is a (limited) basis for hope. Despite his mature thought having a certain affinity with the pessimism of the Frankfurt School (Blackledge 2009: 877), he has long been keen to distance himself from their extreme pessimism. For instance, in his 1970 study *Marcuse* he suggested that if the major thesis of the latter's *One Dimensional Man* (1964) was true, 'then we should have to ask how the book came to have been written and we would certainly have to enquire whether it would find any readers' (MacIntyre 1970: 62). Similarly, in 2006 he wrote:

> To Adorno my inclination is to respond by quoting Dr Johnson's friend, Oliver Edwards, who said that he too had tried to be a philosopher, but 'cheerfulness was always breaking in', perhaps a philistine, but also an appropriate response. What grounds then are there for cheerfulness in any social order such as our own about which some of Adorno's central claims still hold true? Those grounds

After Virtue, Managers and Business Ethics 245

derive surely from the continuing resistance to deprivations, frustrations, and evils that informs so many everyday lives in so many parts of the world, as well as much of the best thinking about those deprivations, frustrations, and evils, including Adorno's and Geuss's. To be good, to live rightly, and to think rightly, it may be said in reply to Adorno, is to be engaged in struggle and a perfected life is one perfected in key part in and through conflicts. (MacIntyre 2006h)

It was through his search for the social basis for 'cheerfulness' that MacIntyre came to articulate his neo-Aristotelian conception of social practices as forms of cooperative activity through which internal goods of the practice are realised in such a way that the virtues and conceptions of the human telos and the common good are expanded (MacIntyre 2007: 187).

Whereas the concept of practice underpins MacIntyre's hope for our potential to resist the debilitating consequences of modernity, he balances this claim against the argument that practices are sustained within institutions that, though necessary for their reproduction, simultaneously tend to undermine them (MacIntyre 2007: 194). The reason for this tension is simple enough. Though practices are orientated towards their own internal goods as they have developed through traditions, institutions focus upon external goods such as money, power and prestige, and they tend, in focusing on these external goods, to create the necessary conditions for the reproduction of practices while simultaneously undermining these practices by reorientating them to external ends (MacIntyre 2007: 194; Beadle and Moore 2006: 333–4; Knight 2017: 84). Indeed, MacIntyre argues that the focus on external goods is 'always ... a type of activity at once alien and antagonistic to practices' (MacIntyre 1994d: 286).

Herein lies the importance of MacIntyre's understanding of the character of the manager. If managers are the custodians of institutions, and institutions are necessarily alienated formations, they will be, from the point of view of practices, at best a necessary evil. From this perspective, the discourse of business ethics is best understood as a form of ideological mystification that functions, in part, to obscure capitalism's manipulative essence. This is the conclusion that MacIntyrean business ethicists have sought to reject. Their argument is not simply that MacIntyre is wrong about the necessary social function of management, but also that his work can be interpreted as supportive of the idea that management might be a practice with its own internal goods that can underpin ethical forms of business. So while writers such as Beabout and Moore do not deny the power of MacIntyre's critique of management, they counter that not all managers act in this (historically limited)

246   Paul Blackledge

Weberian manner, and that good management can be understood partially as a MacIntyrean practice.

13.4   MacIntyrean Business Ethics

Geoff Moore extends MacIntyre's practices–institutions schema to distinguish between institutions and organisations. Whereas MacIntyre essentially conceives of institutions and organisations as synonymous (MacIntyre 2007: 25), Moore argues that organisations incorporate both institutions and practices. Consequently, just as institutions are the bearers of practices, organisations are the bearers of 'practice–institution combinations' (Moore 2017: 67). This argument allows him to reconceive organisations, by contrast with institutions, as 'essentially moral spaces' (Moore 2017: 68). It is within these moral spaces that management can act as a practice through its role in reproducing institutions: 'we should also note MacIntyre's point that even if institutions do have corrupting power, "the making and sustaining of forms of human community – *and therefore of institutions* – itself has all the characteristics of a practice, and moreover of a practice which stands in a peculiarly close relationship to the exercise of the virtues ..."' (MacIntyre 2007: 194, emphasis in original, quoted in Moore 2002: 27; 2017: 69, 107; Moore and Beadle 2006).

Moore argues that while 'the making and sustaining of institutions is a secondary practice', it is nonetheless 'still a practice and, as MacIntyre says, one which "stands in a peculiarly close relationship to the exercise of the virtues"' (Moore 2017: 69). Leaving to one side fundamental problems with Moore's interpretation of MacIntyre, which, as Beadle, Sinnicks and Nicholas have separately noted, confuses the practice of politics through which communities are reproduced with actions to sustain institutions, which cannot be a MacIntyrean practice (Beadle 2002; 2008; Sinnicks 2014: 13; Nicholas 2018), Moore makes a pertinent point. Without denying the potentially corrupting influence of institutions, he registers the positive side of maintaining them. The managers who carry out this function are defined by Moore as '"professional" organizers and coordinators' who 'spend most or all of their time organizing and coordinating activities and other people' (Moore 2017: 98). Because management is, for all its corrupting flaws, an essential good within society, Moore believes that it can be inferred that 'management could be redescribed in MacIntyrean terms as the practice of "making and sustaining the institution"' (Moore 2017: 107). A virtuous manager is, accordingly, someone who is concerned both with 'the ends the organization serves, and the extent to which both its products or services

After Virtue, Managers and Business Ethics

and the "perfection" of its members (the internal goods of the core practice but also, in the latter case, of the secondary practice of making and sustaining the institution itself) contribute to the common good' (Moore 2017: 110–14).

Clearly, if Moore's arguments are correct, the substance of MacIntyre's critique of management and institutions must be judged a failure. Rather than being a necessary evil, management becomes at worst a contingent evil and at best a potentially virtuous practice. However, to justify this claim, Moore must do more than substantiate his dubious assertion that managers can learn the common good through the practice of management. Because capitalism is a dynamic system that obeys a structural logic dominated by competitive accumulation, he must also show that those managers and institutions that orientate to the common good can escape the punishments meted out to those who stray from the path of profit maximisation.

Unfortunately, Moore's discussion of management does not address the deep structural barriers that capitalism places before the emergence of a common good. Or rather, where he does mention capitalism as a problem for management his comments are at best underdeveloped. For instance, he writes that 'there has been a long-standing argument as to whether capitalism and capitalist organizations generate or deplete virtue in individuals', but he does no more than comment that 'either way the influence of organisations on our moral lives is not something we should underestimate' (Moore 2017: 71). More substantively, he writes that MacIntyre was 'particularly concerned' about the 'capitalist forms of business organization' because the capitalist focus on external goods had 'won' over the practice and its pursuit of internal goods, such that 'much modern industrial productive and service work is organized so as to exclude the features distinctive of a practice', and in such a way that this type of activity is 'at once alien and antagonistic to practices'. Moore even notes that, for MacIntyre, '"practices are often distorted by their modes of institutionalisation, when irrelevant considerations relating to money, power and status are allowed to invade the practice"' (Moore 2017: 123, citing MacIntyre 1994d: 286, 289). Rather than explore in detail the mechanisms through which MacIntyre understands these problems to be reproduced and the consequences of these mechanisms for attempts to reposition MacIntyre as a theorist of ethical management, Moore simply dismisses MacIntyre as being too 'pessimistic' in his assessment of managers, who 'are not necessarily villains, demons, or agents in the service of power' (Moore 2017: 106).

Greg Beabout develops a similar argument in his *The Character of the Manager* (2013). Through his aim of applying virtue ethics to modern management, Beabout asks: can managers escape the parameters of MacIntyre's critique such that we might 'reconceive the manager as a virtuous character, that is, as one whose role is to act as a wise steward?' (Beabout 2013: 2). To this end, Beabout's goal is to 'engage, criticise and extend MacIntyre's work on the manager as a character' (Beabout 2013: 22). As Beabout sees it, the manager as described in *After Virtue* is 'virtually identical to the character praised by Milton Friedman' (Beabout 2013: 57). For Beabout, this model of the manager is not so much wrong as it is one-sided: yes, many managers act in this way, but many do not; and Beabout sees his project as building on MacIntyre's virtue ethics to explore the possibilities of managing 'in a responsible manner, with an eye to efficiently and effectively organising a group to accomplish a given, quantifiable purpose while comporting oneself in a manner that is honest and just with a concern for the common good ...'. To this end, his exploration of the possibilities of virtuous management is framed against what he claims is MacIntyre's tendency towards 'sweeping Hegelian moments of overstated grand-theorizing' (Beabout 2013: 2, 35).

One aspect of this supposed overstated grand-theorising is MacIntyre's Weberian arguments regarding bureaucratic authority. Beabout suggests that MacIntyre errs not in his use of Weber, but rather in his over-reliance on this one-dimensional account of bureaucracy, and in particular on Weber's 'offhand remark' about the necessity of bureaucratic structures in the modern world (Beabout 2013: 57). As with his comments on Friedman, Beabout's criticisms of MacIntyre's use of Weber refer not to the absolute falsity of these ideas, but rather to the argument that reality is more complex and nuanced than MacIntyre's grey theory allows.

Insofar as Beabout challenges MacIntyre's Weberian conceptualisation of bureaucracy he has point. MacIntyre's sweeping denunciations of management and institutions do appear to contradict our everyday experience of variation in these forms, and it seems only reasonable to suppose that we need a more fine-tuned theory both to grasp the reality of these differences and to build on the examples of best practice amongst them. Moreover, MacIntyre's Weberianism seems innocent of a mechanism through which to explain why institutions and managers are caused to function as he argues they do. Clearly, an answer to the latter question would help explain limits to the variations amongst institutions and forms of management. Conversely, there is a risk that simple descriptions of such variations might degenerate into a form of eclectic empiricism that loses sight of the rational core of MacIntyre's (or any other) theory of management. Unfortunately, Beabout's descriptive

After Virtue, Managers and Business Ethics

comments on management seem to fit this pattern: while he poses a pertinent question of MacIntyre's sociology of organisations, his response to this question tends to an empiricist retreat from the key insights of MacIntyre's theory of management. To argue that variations exist amongst institutions and forms of management, even large variations, is not evidence that management and institutions cannot be understood as general phenomena. Fortunately, MacIntyre's sociology points to a powerful answer to this problem through a model of capitalism as a structural limit to management that nonetheless allows for the existence of important variations amongst institutions and management.

In the strongest formulations of his method MacIntyre can be understood as a critical realist, for whom reality is conceived as a stratified whole in which agency is explained as an emergent property rooted in, but irreducible to, underlying social relations. This approach points to the existence of *tendencies* in reality rather than superficial Humean constant conjunctions (Blackledge 2020). Interpreted thus, MacIntyre's comments on managers are best understood as a theory of general predispositions amongst a *definite* type of historically and socially constituted men and women and not as a mechanical theory of behaviour – he is well aware, for instance, of Engels' role as a very idiosyncratic factory manager! The key to a clear theory of management as a social role from this perspective is not that it is able to describe the actions of all managers at all times, but rather that it will explain managerialism as a typical response of a particular type of individual to concrete social relations. Individual managers can obviously act beyond the limits set by this type, but business recruitment processes will militate against employing such mavericks, while managers will have learned both in business schools and through their experiences in business that to employ such types entails punishment. Concretely, punishment takes the form of financial penalties in a capitalist context, and any adequate theory of management must include a sophisticated theory of capitalist social relations as a set of constraints on the actions of managers and institutions.

Unfortunately, as with Moore, Beabout's discussion of MacIntyre's understanding of capitalism, and in particular of the influence of Marx on his understanding of capitalism, is weak. According to Beabout, Marx's influence on MacIntyre's youthful writings stemmed from the political appeal of his vision of communism (Beabout 2013: 46). As to capitalism, on Beabout's reading, MacIntyre viewed it as the 'social embodiment of liberalism in the economic sphere', with utilitarianism as 'the moral philosophy that corresponds with capitalism'. More concretely, Beabout believes that, for MacIntyre, capitalism is a system characterised by 'the endless pursuit of more and more money'.

250   *Paul Blackledge*

Moreover, MacIntyre believes the moral failings of Stalinism are best understood as variants of the moral failings of modern liberalism. Stalinism failed as a moral alternative to Western capitalism, and here Beabout follows MacIntyre's discussion of the subject in the 1968 edition of *Marxism and Christianity* not because it was a form of actually existing communism, but rather because it was a system of 'bureaucratic state capitalism'. Unfortunately, according to Beabout, MacIntyre does not 'provide a detailed explanation of this phrase', while conceding that 'on the positive characterization of bureaucracy specifically, Marxist analyses have been notably weak'. For Beabout, therefore, MacIntyre's Marxist inheritance can be dismissed as the least relevant, because most 'romantic', aspect of his thought (Beabout 2013: 46–8; cf. MacIntyre 1995d: 102, 139).

13.5   MacIntyre and Marx

These comments do not begin to do justice to the scale of MacIntyre's inheritance from Marx. Though *Marxism and Christianity* marked a key moment in his break with the Marxist left, it should be noted that the basic framework for his understanding of what he continues to label the 'exploitative structures of both free market and [Russian and Chinese] state capitalism' was forged in the 1950s and 1960s. And it is this framework, as he argues in *Ethics in the Conflicts of Modernity*, that 'make it often difficult and sometimes impossible to achieve the goods of the workplace through excellent work' (MacIntyre 2016: 237, 294). He has recently made Marx's influence on his understanding of capitalism explicit:

The Marx from whom we can learn is the Marx of the first volume of *Capital*, and what we need to learn is twofold. On the one hand, his theory of surplus value is the key to understanding capitalism as an economic system, both capitalist accumulation and capitalist exploitation. On the other, his account of how individuals must think of themselves and of their social relationships, if they are to act as capitalism requires them to act, is the key to understanding why in capitalist societies individuals systematically misunderstand themselves and their social relationships … to be undeceived we have to begin with surplus value. (MacIntyre 2016: 96)

These lines are of the first importance for an understanding both of capitalism and of the strongest elements of MacIntyre's mature thought, including his account of the role of managers within capitalist institutions. While his understanding of capitalism as outlined in *After Virtue*'s comment that '*pleonexia* … is now the driving force of modern productive work' might cohere with Beabout's argument that MacIntyre

After Virtue, Managers and Business Ethics 251

characterised capitalism as the 'endless pursuit of more and more money' (MacIntyre 2007: 227), the Marxist interpretation alluded to in *Ethics and the Conflicts of Modernity* points to a deeper and much more powerful model of 'bureaucratic authority' as an aspect of this mode of production. For Marx, capitalism is a system of alienation characterised not by greed, but by the self-expansion of value:

> Accumulate, accumulate! That is Moses and the prophets ... Accumulation for the sake of accumulation, production for the sake of production ... If, in the eyes of classical economics, the proletarian is merely a machine for the production of surplus-value, the capitalist too is merely a machine for the transformation of this surplus value into surplus capital. (Marx 1976: 742)

Marx's value theory, as detailed in *Capital*, effectively expands on and tremendously deepens the account of capitalism as a system of alienation outlined in the *Economic and Philosophical Manuscripts* of 1844 (Holloway 2010: 93). This is an important point, because amongst the many insights of *Capital*, Marx points to the alienated, capitalist essence of what Weber would later call the 'predetermined ends' of 'private corporations or of government agencies'. However, by contrast with Weber, for Marx, alienation refers to a historically specific system in which what we produce through our labours comes to stand opposed to us 'as *something alien*, as a *power independent* of the producer' (Marx 1975b: 324, 326–30, emphases in original). Marx argues that while capitalists appear to control this process and do in fact exercise 'power to command labour', the power of the capitalist is more apparent than real: 'capital ... is able to rule the capitalist himself' (Marx 1975b: 295). Capital acts as an ever-expanding power over everyone within the capitalist system, warping our very nature: 'Production does not produce man only as a commodity, the human commodity, man in the form of a commodity; it also produces him as a mentally and physically *dehumanized* being ... Immorality, malformation, stupidity of workers and capitalists ... the human commodity' (Marx 1975b: 336, emphasis in original). Marx shows how this condition, and the division between means and ends characteristic of alienated production, has roots in the way capitalist social relations give rise to the separation of facts and values and the division of social life into various contradictory spheres of existence – the moral, the economic and so forth – each with its own distinct standards (Marx 1975b: 362).

Understood in this way, Marx's value theory is not an insubstantial add-on to MacIntyre's neo-Aristotelianism. Rather, by illuminating the socio-historical kernel of modern, alienated bureaucratic institutions, it provides the explanatory mechanism for the alienated character of institutions and management that is otherwise missing from MacIntyre's

252   *Paul Blackledge*

sociology of organisations. Conversely, because Moore and Beabout's attempted corrections of MacIntyre's sociology essentially sidestep the issue of capitalism, their arguments mark a retreat from the insights he draws from Marx and the classical Marxist tradition. For instance, the concept of bureaucratic state capitalism is not an exercise in mere name-calling of Stalinism and Maoism. Rather, it represents MacIntyre's inheritance from a rich theoretical tradition, associated with the works of C. L. R. James, Cornelius Castoriadis, Raya Dunayevskaya, Tony Cliff and Michael Kidron, amongst others. The theory of state capitalism illuminates the essential similarities between Western 'capitalist' and Eastern 'communist' states. Beneath the surface differences, all these social formations are characterised by structures of alienation reproduced by military alongside economic competition and founded upon the commodification of labour power as the dominant form of surplus extraction (Blackledge 2014: 713).

The system of alienation continues to impose 'predetermined ends' across all institutions within the capitalist system irrespective of variations in their political (states) or the legal (enterprises) forms, because capitalist social relations are ubiquitous. Of course, there will be differing degrees of mediation between firms of different sizes, legal structures and levels of profitability, but the essential relationship remains. Recognising the amoral consequences of these relations is realism not pessimism.

13.6   Marx contra Weber

While the interpretation of Marxism to which MacIntyre alludes in *Ethics and the Conflicts of Modernity* locates the alienated, amoral essence of modern firms and states in relation to their capitalist form, elsewhere he frames this problem in more universal, Weberian terms. Indeed, the dominant theme of the sociological sections of *After Virtue*, where bureaucracy is understood as an ideal type, are Weberian (McMylor 1993: 134; Knight 2007: 160; Burns 2011: 51–2; Breen 2012: 2). This Weberianism is a problem for MacIntyre because the Marxist and Weberian themes in his work are not merely different, they are contradictory. According to Weber, ideal types are heuristic devices designed to make sense of the unity of a phenomenon over time despite the plethora of historical variations. Weber is clearly right to recognise the need for abstraction as part of the social scientific project. However, as he frames them, ideal-type concepts are utopias that do not exist in the real world: 'it is probably seldom if ever that a real phenomenon can be found which corresponds exactly to one of these ideally constructed pure types' (Weber 1978: 20).

After Virtue, Managers and Business Ethics 253

One consequence of this approach to concept formation is that attempts to apply models of this sort to the study of real-world phenomena tend, systematically, towards eclectic empiricism (Outhwaite 1987: 104; Clarke 1991: 248–55). Because no social form maps exactly to the ideal, the question of whether or not to include any specific instance within a category becomes an ungroundable matter of choice. This appears to be the route taken by Beabout and Moore, who find qualitative differences where others would see only minor variations. This appears to be the case also with MacIntyre himself, whose comments on Cummins Engines and W. E. Deming's Total Quality Management (TQM) in *Ethics and the Conflicts of Modernity* appear to contradict the damning critique of the essential amorality of institutions and management in *After Virtue* and elsewhere.

These comments by MacIntyre obviously give succour to the MacIntyrean business ethicists. However, in doing so, they blunt the critical edge of his work by relegating his criticisms of institutions and management to the much more limited – and much less realistic – claim that management and institutions are often, but not essentially, corrosive of practices. In effect, his critique of institutions and management is reduced to a critique of bad institutions and bad management.

Conversely, MacIntyre's comments on Marx in *Ethics in the Conflicts of Society* point beyond this superficial and eclectic empiricism to a more substantial basis for his original critique of management. As opposed to Weber's explicitly utopian ideal-type concepts, Marx's approach to concept formation is much more concrete and consequently much better able to comprehend real-world nuances. In the introduction to the *Grundrisse*, he argues that the 'only way in which thought' might 'appropriate' the 'concrete in the mind' is through the movement from the abstract to the concrete by reconstructing concepts as 'rich totalit[ies] of many determinations' (Marx 1973: 101; Blackledge 2019a). This method generates concepts that are, by contrast with Weber's ideal types, much richer because they are more historically and sociologically concrete. In relation to modern firms, whereas MacIntyre's Weberianism leads him to claim, as we noted above, that the focus on external goods is 'always … a type of activity at once alien and antagonistic to practices', Marx suggests that it is the capitalist form of modern business, not its focus on external goods per se, that gives it its amoral character.

Marx detailed his model of bureaucratic management in the third volume of *Capital*. And while this model of modern managerial bureaucracies is less well known than Weber's, it is, contra MacIntyre's disparaging comments in *Marxism and Christianity*, much more powerful. Whereas Weber understands bureaucratic management to be a product

254 *Paul Blackledge*

of modernity *in and of itself*, Marx has a clearer understanding of bureaucracy as a concrete historical form through its dual role in modern social relations (Beetham 1997: 92). According to Shlomo Avineri, in a book described by MacIntyre on its back cover as 'brilliant' and 'essential reading', Marx understood that bureaucracy must be explained in structural as well as functional terms, so that bureaucracy is to politics what commodity fetishism is to economics: they are two sides of the creation of human subjects as 'mere objects of manipulation' (Avineri 1968: 49). And manipulation is executed through and in the service of alienated social relations. As David Beetham writes, Marx insisted that 'the management structure in the capitalist enterprise serves not only to coordinate the different elements of the production process, but also as a means of class discipline and control' (Beetham 1997: 74). Specifically, Marx argued that as production becomes increasingly socialised there develops a need for an organising and coordinating role 'as with the conductor of an orchestra'. However, in a class-divided society this function becomes subsumed beneath an alienated supervisory role determined, under capitalist social relations specifically, by the need of the capitalist to actively consume the workers' labour power (Marx 1981: 507–508; Duménil and Lévy 2018: 34–9).

Accordingly, modern capitalist management and bureaucracy are not, for Marx, 'mere technical issues', as Knight suggests (Knight 2007: 87). Rather, they combine socially useful and alienated functions in a unity within which the former is subordinated to the latter. To discuss management while effectively naturalising its capitalist form, as do Beabout and Moore (and MacIntyre in the weaker aspects of his work), is to be blind to this essence. Management cannot be ethical under capitalist relations of production because its functions are not merely technical, but rather embed these technical roles within alienated relations that underpin emotivism as the dominant modern distortion of ethics (Blackledge 2012).

If these alienated relations underpin a concrete explanation of business amorality in a way that MacIntyre's ideal-type conception of institution cannot, they simultaneously act as a barrier to the sort of eclecticism evident in MacIntyre's comments on Cummins Engines and Deming's TQM – and more so in the work of the MacIntyrean business ethicists – while accepting that (non-capitalist) institutions may well escape the consequences of alienation.

This argument should not be interpreted as implying a *reductio* of Marx's method that all (capitalist) managers and all forms of (capitalist) management are equally bad. MacIntyre is obviously right to suggest that some managers are to be preferred over others. And if there is a scale of

After Virtue, Managers and Business Ethics 255

management from those most enabling of practices (MacIntyre 2016: 132) to those most institutionally destructive of them, then the former are to be favoured over the latter, and perhaps it is true that Cummins Engines is an example of such a better working practice. However, this insight should not lead us to accept the empiricist error that capitalist management can be a MacIntyrean practice. It is not simply that management has no goods internal to it; more importantly, even when the relative prosperity of a firm allows for some mediation of the imperative to short-term profit-making, the gravitational pull of the law of value will continue to act as a fundamental constraint on the freedom of management. It is for this reason that MacIntyre's claim that '[o]ver several decades [Cummins Engines] subordinated the need to achieve higher levels of profitability to the good of making excellent products, and individuals who worked for the company were expected to serve that common good' cannot withstand critical scrutiny (MacIntyre 2016: 172). As MacIntyre himself admits, whatever its strengths, Cummins Engines 'survived only because it did become profitable enough to survive in competitive markets and that the inexorable pressure to become, not just profitable, but more and more and more profitable does in fact result in most workplaces being quite other than those [whose management MacIntyre otherwise extolls]' (MacIntyre 2016: 172).

The implications of this caveat are far more damaging to MacIntyre's comments on Cummins Engines than he seems willing to admit. The negative consequences of the operation of the law of value was evident at Cummins Engines long before MacIntyre penned *Ethics in the Conflicts of Modernity*. In 1998, for instance, the American Environmental Protection Agency (EPA) found Cummins Engines guilty, alongside several other diesel engine manufacturers, 'of selling heavy duty diesel engines containing illegal "defeat devices", which allow an engine to pass the EPA emissions test, but then turn off emission controls during highway driving', resulting in the emission of 'up to three times the current level for NO_x' (Environmental Protection Agency 1998). This grotesque case of putting profits before the 'common good' severely problematises MacIntyre's claims for the ethical practices of management at this corporation. In effect, he seems not to have adequately integrated his comments on managing towards the common good with what he draws from Marx about value theory. Had he taken what he says about Marx more seriously, he would undoubtedly have been much more critical not only of Cummins Engines, but also of other business practices, such as the form of TQM proselytised by Deming.

According to MacIntyre, Deming's success came through his attempt to overcome alienation through teamworking:

When ... teams of workers co-operated in taking each car through the different stages of its production, taking responsibility as a team for the quality of the end product, things went much better both for the cars and for the workers. The ends informing the workers' activity are now those of achieving through shared deliberation and decision the making of an excellent car and of becoming excellent in making such cars. It matters that they understand what they are doing and that their standards are ones that they have made their own, not standards imposed by external managerial control. They share direction toward a common good. (MacIntyre 2016: 170–71)

Through these lines, MacIntyre argues that some managers are better than others because of their relentless focus on the common good. This is an odd argument for someone so influenced by Marx, for, as other theorists whose work is informed by a reading of Marx have pointed out, the end of production for firms practising Deming's methods is not the common good but increased profit. And the reality of working in such plants is, as Ricardo Antunes points out, that the capitalist form 'transforms "total quality", for the most part, into a *shell*, concerned with *the appearance* or refinement of the *superfluous*, since the products need to last for a short time and be easily inserted into the market' (Antunes 2012: 35, emphases in original). More concretely, according to Andy Danford, TQM and similar projects have simply become 'mechanisms of labour exploitation. Under the cloak of a benign "one team" ideology, workers become involved in securing for their employer higher levels of capital and labour utilisation, reductions in idle time, an intensification of their labour and a more sophisticated form of worker subordination ... [they] act to convert rank and file control into management control' (Danford 1998: 58; cf. Henning 2014: 493). Commenting on a specific plant in south Wales, Danford points out that TQM represented less a reversal of Taylorism and more 'strict management supervision of limited worker involvement in perfecting task routines after which workers are "returned to Taylorised jobs"' (Danford 1998: 60).

As to the Japanese birthplace of TQM, we should remember that Deming's project was predicated upon the defeat of the post-war revolutionary trade union movement at the hands of the Japanese state working alongside the American occupying forces, and the transformation of this movement after a 'red purge' into the more business-friendly 'enterprise unionism' (Moore 1983: xix). Teams, thus constructed, were under the hegemony of management, who accepted as natural the alienated ends set by the market.

These comments illuminate what should be obvious: *capitalist* firms cannot orientate to the common good because they are condemned by the logic of capitalist competition, as reproduced by capitalist states, to be amoral *loci* of alienated exploitation (Henning 2014: 509–10).

13.7 Conclusion

MacIntyre would have been spared his embarrassing comments on Deming had he taken his discussion of Marx more seriously. To have done so, however, would require developing these comments into a consistent critique of the Weberian elements of his sociology. A problem with the Weberian approach is that its ideal-type methodology is unable to address empirical differences except in an *ad hoc* and superficial manner. The MacIntyrean business ethicists have extended this *ad hoc*, descriptive method in isolation from an adequate model of capitalism to argue that managers can become MacIntyrean practitioners. And while MacIntyre's comments on Cummins Engines and Deming suggest that these arguments are not wholly out of step with his thought, they do contradict both the powerful critique of management outlined in *After Virtue* and the implications of Marx's value theory as outlined in *Ethics in the Conflicts of Modernity*.

These arguments suggest that while MacIntyre's semi-Marxist critique of management and institutions makes a substantial contribution to the extension of Marxist *Ideologiekritik*, to save his theory from its friends in the business schools his engagement with Marx should be deepened with the aim of freeing his legacy from the eclectic, empiricist implications of his inheritance from Weber.

Bibliography

Adams, R. M. 2006. *A Theory of Virtue: Excellence in Being for the Good*. Oxford: Clarendon Press.

Adkins, A. 1960. *Merit and Responsibility: A Study in Greek Values*. Chicago: University of Chicago Press.

Ahmari, S. et al. 2019. 'Against the Dead Consensus', *First Things*, 21 March. Available at: www.firstthings.com/web-exclusives/2019/03/against-the-dead-consensus.

Akrivou, K. and Sison, A. J. G. 2016. *The Challenges of Capitalism for Virtue Ethics and the Common Good*. Cheltenham: Elgar.

Albertson, D. and Blakely, J. 2021. 'From Here to Utopia: What Religion Can Teach the Left', *Commonweal* 148 (6): 20–3.

Amaya, A. and Lai, H. L. 2013. *Law, Virtue and Justice*. Oxford: Hart Publishing.

Angier, T. 2017. 'Book Review: Alasdair MacIntyre, *Ethics in the Conflicts of Modernity*', *Religious Studies* 53 (3): 419–27.

2018a. *Virtue Ethics* (4 vols). Abingdon: Routledge.

2018b. 'Aristotle and the Charge of Egoism', *Journal of Value Inquiry* 52: 457–75.

2020. 'Happiness as Subjective Well-Being: An Aristotelian Critique', *Revista Portuguesa de Filosofia* 76 (1): 59–90.

2021. *Natural Law Theory*. Cambridge: Cambridge University Press.

Annas, J. A. 2011. *Intelligent Virtue*. Oxford: Oxford University Press.

Anscombe, G. E. M. 1957. *Intention*. Oxford: Basil Blackwell.

1958. 'Modern Moral Philosophy', *Philosophy* 33 (124): 1–19.

1963. *Intention*, 2nd edition. Cambridge, MA: Harvard University Press.

1981. *Ethics, Religion and Politics: Collected Philosophical Papers*, vol. 3. Minneapolis: University of Minnesota Press.

Antunes, R. 2012. *The Meaning of Work*. Leiden: Brill

Aquinas, T. 1920. *Summa Theologiae* I–II. Available at: www.newadvent.org/summa/2.htm.

Aristotle 1984a. *Politics*. C. Lord (trans.). Chicago: University of Chicago Press.

1984b. *The Complete Works of Aristotle*. J. Barnes (ed.). Princeton, NJ: Princeton University Press.

2011. *Nicomachean Ethics*. R. Bartlett and S. Collins (trans.). Chicago: University of Chicago Press.

2014. *Nicomachean Ethics*. C. D. C. Reeve (trans.). Indianapolis, IN: Hackett Publishing.

Bibliography

Arneson, R. 2003. 'Liberal Neutrality on the Good: An Autopsy', in S. Wall and G. Klosko (eds), *Perfectionism and Neutrality*. Lanham, MD: Rowman and Littlefield, pp. 192–218.

Avineri, S. 1968. *The Social and Political Thought of Karl Marx*. Cambridge: Cambridge University Press.

Ayer, A. J. 1950. 'Jean-Paul Sartre's Doctrine of Commitment', *Listener* 44 (1135): 633–4.

1952. 'Critique of Ethics and Theology', in *Language, Truth, and Logic*. Garden City, NY: Dover Publications, pp. 102–20.

Bakan, J. 2004. *The Corporation*. London: Constable.

Baril, A. 2013. 'The Role of Welfare in Eudaimonism', *Southern Journal of Philosophy* 51 (4): 511–35.

Baron, M. 2011. 'Virtue Ethics in Relation to Kantian Ethics: An Opinionated Overview and Commentary', in L. Jost and J. Wuerth (eds), *Perfecting Virtue: New Essays on Kantian Ethics and Virtue Ethics*. Cambridge: Cambridge University Press, pp. 8–37.

Beabout, G. 2012. 'Management as a Domain-Related Practice That Requires and Develops Practical Wisdom', *Business Ethics Quarterly* 22 (2): 405–32.

2013. *The Character of the Manager*. Basingstoke: Palgrave Macmillan.

2020. 'MacIntyre and Business Ethics', in R. Beadle and G. Moore (eds), *Learning from MacIntyre*. Eugene, OR: Pickwick Publications, pp. 209–34.

Beadle, R. 2002. 'The Misappropriation of MacIntyre', *Reason in Practice* 2: 45–54.

2008. 'Why Business Cannot Be a Practice', in K. Knight and P. Blackledge (eds), *Revolutionary Aristotelianism: Ethics, Resistance and Utopia*. Stuttgart: Lucius and Lucius, pp. 229–41.

2017. 'MacIntyre's Influence on Business Ethics', in A. J. G. Sison, G. R. Beabout and I. Ferrero (eds), *Springer Handbook of Virtue in Business and Management*. New York: Springer, pp. 59–67.

Beadle, R. and Moore, G. 2006. 'MacIntyre on Virtue and Organization', *Organization Studies* 27: 323–40.

Beetham, D. 1997. *Bureaucracy*. Milton Keynes: Open University Press.

Beier, K. 2020. 'Virtue and Tradition: Alasdair MacIntyre's Thomistic–Aristotelian Naturalism', in M. Hähnel (ed.), *Aristotelian Naturalism: A Research Companion*. Berlin: Springer Nature, pp. 209–22.

Beiner, R. 2013. 'The Parochial and the Universal: MacIntyre's Idea of the University', *Revue Internationale de Philosophie* 264 (2): 169–82.

2014. *Political Philosophy: What It Is and Why It Matters*. Cambridge: Cambridge University Press.

Bellah, R. et al. 1996. *Habits of the Heart: Individualism and Commitment in American Life*, 2nd edition. Berkeley: University of California Press.

Bernstein, R. 1984. 'Nietzsche or Aristotle? Reflections on Alasdair MacIntyre's *After Virtue*', *Soundings: An Interdisciplinary Journal* 67 (1): 6–29.

Berry, W. 2012. *It All Turns on Affection: The Jefferson Lecture & Other Essays*. Berkeley, CA: Counterpoint.

Bevir, M. 2011. *The Making of British Socialism*. Princeton, NJ: Princeton University Press.

260   Bibliography

Blackledge, P. 2007. 'Review L. Boltanski and E. Chiapello "The New Spirit of Capitalism"', *Capital and Class* 92: 198–201.

2009. 'Alasdair MacIntyre: Social Practices, Marxism and Ethical Anti-capitalism', *Political Studies* 57 (4): 866–84.

2012. *Marxism and Ethics*. New York: SUNY Press.

2014. 'Alasdair MacIntyre as a Marxist and as a Critic of Marxism', *American Catholic Philosophical Quarterly* 88 (4): 705–24.

2019a. 'Historical Materialism', in M. Vidal et al. (eds), *The Oxford Handbook of Karl Marx*. Oxford: Oxford University Press, pp. 37–56.

2019b. *Friedrich Engels's Contribution to Social and Political Theory*. New York: SUNY Press.

2020. 'Alasdair MacIntyre's Aristotelianism', in A. Bielskis, E. Leontsini and K. Knight (eds), *Virtue Ethics and Contemporary Aristotelianism*. London: Bloomsbury Academic, pp. 220–35.

Blackledge, P. and Davidson, N. D. 2008. *Alasdair MacIntyre's Engagement with Marxism: Selected Writings 1953–1974*. Leiden: Brill.

Blackledge, P. and Knight, K. 2011a. *Virtue and Politics: Alasdair MacIntyre's Revolutionary Aristotelianism*. Notre Dame, IN: University of Notre Dame Press.

2011b. 'Introduction: Towards a Virtuous Politics', in P. Blackledge and K. Knight (eds), *Virtue and Politics: Alasdair MacIntyre's Revolutionary Aristotelianism*. Notre Dame, IN: University of Notre Dame Press, pp. 3–12.

Blakely, J. 2013. 'The Forgotten MacIntyre: Beyond Value Neutrality in the Social Sciences', *Polity* 45 (3): 445–63.

2016. *Alasdair MacIntyre, Charles Taylor, and the Demise of Naturalism*. Notre Dame, IN: University of Notre Dame Press.

2017. 'Does Liberalism Lack Virtue? A Critique of Alasdair MacIntyre's Reactionary Politics', *Interpretation: A Journal of Political Philosophy* 44 (1): 1–20.

2020a. *We Built Reality: How Social Science Infiltrated Politics, Culture, and Power*. Oxford: Oxford University Press.

2020b. 'MacIntyre contra MacIntyre: Interpretive Philosophy and Aristotle', *The Review of Metaphysics* 74 (1): 121–42.

Boltanski, L. and Chiapello, E. 2006. *The New Spirit of Capitalism*. London: Verso.

Breen, K. 2012. *Under Weber's Shadow: Modernity, Subjectivity, and Politics in Habermas, Arendt, and MacIntyre*. Farnham: Ashgate Publishing.

Brown, W. 2015. *Undoing the Demos: Neoliberalism's Stealth Revolution*. New York: Zone Books.

Burke, E. 1999 [1770]. *Thoughts on the Present Discontents*, in *Select Works of Edmund Burke*, vol. 1. Indianapolis, IN: Liberty Fund.

1999 [1790]. *Reflections on the Revolution in France*, in *Select Works of Edmund Burke*, vol. 2. Indianapolis, IN: Liberty Fund.

Burns, T. 2011. 'Revolutionary Aristotelianism?', in P. Blackledge and K. Knight (eds), *Virtue and Politics: Alasdair MacIntyre's Revolutionary Aristotelianism*. Notre Dame, IN: University of Notre Dame Press, pp. 35–53.

Butler, A. 1903. *The Lives of the Fathers, Martyrs, and Principal Saints* (complete and unabridged), 4 vols. New York: P. J. Kennedy.

Bibliography

Butler, J. 2017. *Fifteen Sermons and Other Writings on Ethics*. Oxford: Oxford University Press.

Callinicos, A. 2011. 'Two Cheers for Enlightenment Universalism: Or, Why It's Hard to Be an Aristotelian Revolutionary', in P. Blackledge and K. Knight (eds), *Virtue and Politics: Alasdair MacIntyre's Revolutionary Aristotelianism*. Notre Dame, IN: University of Notre Dame Press, pp. 54–78.

Cavell, S. 1971. *The World Viewed: Reflections on the Ontology of Film*. Cambridge, MA: Harvard University Press.

1981. *Pursuits of Happiness: The Hollywood Comedy of Remarriage*. Cambridge, MA: Harvard University Press.

1996. *Contesting Tears*. Chicago, IL: University of Chicago Press.

Chappell, T. 2014. *Knowing What to Do: Imagination, Virtue, and Platonism in Ethics*. Oxford: Oxford University Press.

Clarke, S. 1991. *Marx, Marginalism and Modern Sociology: From Adam Smith and Max Weber*. Basingstoke: Macmillan.

Clarke, S. G. and Simpson, E. 1989. *Anti-theory in Ethics and Moral Conservatism*. Albany, NY: SUNY Press.

Cohen, G. A. 2013. *Finding Oneself in the Other*. Princeton, NJ: Princeton University Press.

Coleman, J. 1994. 'MacIntyre and Aquinas', in J. Horton and S. Mendus (eds), *After MacIntyre: Critical Perspectives on the Work of Alasdair MacIntyre*. Cambridge: Polity Press, pp. 65–90.

Conly, S. 1988. 'Flourishing and the Failure of the Ethics of Virtue', *Midwest Studies in Philosophy* 13 (1): 83–96.

Copp, D. and Sobel, D. 2004. 'Morality and Virtue: An Assessment of Some Recent Work in Virtue Ethics', *Ethics* 114 (3): 514–54.

Cunningham, L. 2009. *Intractable Disputes about the Natural Law: Alasdair MacIntyre and His Critics*. Noter Dame, IN: University of Notre Dame Press.

D'Andrea, T. 2006. *Tradition, Rationality, and Virtue: The Thought of Alasdair MacIntyre*. Aldershot: Ashgate Publishing.

Danford, A. 1998. 'Work Organisation Inside Japanese Firms in South Wales', in P. Thompson and C. Warhurst (eds), *Workplaces of the Future*. Basingstoke: Macmillan, pp. 40–64.

Deneen, P. 2016. *Conserving America? Essays on Present Discontents*. South Bend, IN: St. Augustine's Press.

2018a. *Why Liberalism Failed*. New Haven, CT: Yale University Press.

2018b. 'Corporate Progressivism', *First Things*, 18 November. Available at: www.firstthings.com/article/2018/11/corporate-progressivism.

Dreher, R. 2017. *The Benedict Option: A Strategy for Christians in a Post-Christian Nation*. New York: Sentinel.

Driver, J. 1998. 'The Virtues and Human Nature', in R. Crisp (ed.) *How Should One Live? Essays on the Virtues*. Oxford: Oxford University Press, pp. 111–30.

2001. *Uneasy Virtue*. Cambridge: Cambridge University Press.

Duff, A. 2021. 'The Problem of Rule in MacIntyre's Politics and *Ethics in the Conflicts of Modernity*', *Politics and Poetics* 4: 23–41.

Duménil, G. and Lévy, D. 2018. *Managerial Capitalism*. London: Pluto Press.

262   Bibliography

Dupré, L. 1995. *Passage to Modernity: An Essay on the Hermeneutics of Nature and Culture*. New Haven, CT: Yale University Press.

Dworkin, R. 1994. *Life's Dominion: An Argument about Abortion, Euthanasia, and Individual Freedom*. New York: Vintage.

Emilsson, E. 2015. 'On Happiness and Time', in Ø. Rabbas, E. K. Emilsson, H. Fossheim and M. Tuominen (eds), *The Quest for the Good Life: Ancient Philosophers on Happiness*. Oxford: Oxford University Press, pp. 222–40.

Environmental Protection Agency 1998. 'Mack Trucks Diesel Engine Settlement'. Available at: www.epa.gov/enforcement/mack-trucks-diesel-engine-settlement.

Farrelly, C. and Solum, L. 2008. *Virtue Jurisprudence*. Basingstoke: Palgrave Macmillan.

Ferrero, I. and Sison, A. J. G. 2014. 'A Quantitative Analysis of Authors, Schools and Themes in Virtue Ethics Articles in Business Ethics and Management Journals', *Business Ethics Quarterly* 23 (4): 375–400.

Finnis, J. 1980. *Natural Law and Natural Rights*. Oxford: Oxford University Press.

1998. *Aquinas: Moral, Political, and Legal Theory*. Oxford: Oxford University Press.

2011a. 'Reason, Authority, and Friendship', in *Reason in Action, Collected Essays*, vol. I. Oxford: Oxford University Press, pp. 104–24.

2011b. 'On Hart's Ways: Law as Reason and as Fact', in *Philosophy of Law, Collected Essays*, vol. IV. Oxford: Oxford University Press, pp. 230–56.

Foot, P. 1978. *Virtues and Vices: And Other Essays in Moral Philosophy*. Oxford: Oxford University Press.

2001. *Natural Goodness*. Oxford: Clarendon Press.

Frazer, E. and Lacey, N. 1994. 'MacIntyre, Feminism, and the Concept of Practice', in J. Horton and S. Mendus (eds), *After MacIntyre: Critical Perspectives on the Work of Alasdair MacIntyre*. Cambridge: Polity Press, pp. 265–82.

Frey, J. A. 2018. 'How to Be an Ethical Naturalist', in J. Hacker-Wright (ed.), *Philippa Foot on Goodness and Virtue*. Basingstoke: Palgrave Macmillan, pp. 47–84.

Freytag, M. 1994. 'MacIntyre's Conservatism and Its Cure: The Formal Structure of Traditions', *Philosophy in the Contemporary World* 1 (2): 1–10.

Friedman, M. 1970. 'The Social Responsibility of Business Is to Increase Its Profits', *New York Times*, 13 September. www.nytimes.com/1970/09/13/archives/a-friedman-doctrine-the-social-responsibility-of-business-is-to.html.

Gaus, G. 2003. 'Liberal Neutrality: A Compelling and Radical Principle', in S. Wall and G. Klosko (eds), *Perfectionism and Neutrality*. Lanham, MD: Rowman and Littlefield, pp. 138–65.

Geach, P. 1977. *The Virtues*. Cambridge: Cambridge University Press.

Gerth, H. H. and Mills, C. W. 1946. 'Introduction: The Man and His Work', in H. H. Gerth and C. W. Mills (eds), *From Max Weber: Essays in Sociology* (trans. H. H. Gerth and C. W. Mills). Oxford: Oxford University Press, pp. 3–74.

Bibliography

Goldie, P. 2012. *The Mess Inside: Narrative, Emotion, and the Mind*. Oxford: Oxford University Press.

Gottfried, P. 1999. *After Liberalism: Mass Democracy in the Managerial State*. Princeton, NJ: Princeton University Press.

Gregson, J. 2019. *Marxism, Ethics and Politics: The Work of Alasdair MacIntyre*. Basingstoke: Palgrave Macmillan.

Guyer, P. 2011. 'Kantian Perfectionism', in L. Jost and J. Wuerth (eds), *Perfecting Virtue: New Essays on Kantian Ethics and Virtue Ethics*. Cambridge: Cambridge University Press, pp. 194–214.

Haldane, J. 1994. 'MacIntyre's Thomist Revival: What Next?', in J. Horton and S. Mendus (eds), *After MacIntyre: Critical Perspectives on the Work of Alasdair MacIntyre*. Cambridge: Polity Press, pp. 91–107.

Hamilton, A., Jay, J. and Madison, J. 2001 [1787–1788]. *The Federalist*, Gideon edition. Indianapolis, IN: Liberty Fund.

Hart, D. B. 2022. *Tradition and Apocalypse: An Essay on the Future of Religious Belief*. Grand Rapids, MI: Eerdmans Publishing.

Hart, H. L. A. 1958. 'Positivism and the Separation of Law and Morals', *Harvard Law Review* 71 (4): 593–629.

1982. *Essays on Bentham*. Oxford: Clarendon Press.

1983. *Essays in Jurisprudence and Philosophy*. Oxford: Clarendon Press.

1994. *The Concept of Law*, 2nd edition. Oxford: Oxford University Press.

Hauerwas, S. 1978. *Truthfulness and Tragedy*. Notre Dame, IN: University of Notre Dame Press.

1981. *Community of Character*. Notre Dame, IN: University of Notre Dame Press.

2007. 'The Virtues of Alasdair MacIntyre', *First Things*, October. Available at: www.firstthings.com/article/2007/10/the-virtues-of-alasdair-MacIntyre.

2010. *Hannah's Child: A Theologian's Memoir*. Grand Rapids, MI: Eerdmans Publishing.

2022. 'God and Alasdair MacIntyre', in *Fully Alive: The Apocalyptic Humanism of Karl Barth*. Charlottesville: University of Virginia Press, pp. 81–99.

Hauerwas, S. and MacIntyre, A. C. 1983. *Revisions: Changing Perspectives in Moral Philosophy*. Notre Dame, IN: University of Notre Dame Press.

Havelock, E. 1957. *The Liberal Temper in Greek Politics*. New Haven, CT: Yale University Press.

Henning, C. 2014. *Philosophy After Marx*. Leiden: Brill.

Herdt, J. A. 1998. 'Alasdair MacIntyre's "Rationality of Traditions" and Tradition-Transcendental Standards of Justification', *The Journal of Religion* 78: 524–46.

2018. 'Book Review: Alasdair MacIntyre, *Ethics in the Conflicts of Modernity*', *Studies in Christian Ethics* 31 (4): 488–92.

2022. *Assuming Responsibility: Ecstatic Eudaimonism and the Call to Live Well*. Oxford: Oxford University Press.

Herman, B. 2011. 'The Difference That Ends Make', in L. Jost and J. Wuerth (eds), *Perfecting Virtue: New Essays on Kantian Ethics and Virtue Ethics*. Cambridge: Cambridge University Press, pp. 92–115.

Hibbs, T. 2004. 'MacIntyre, Aquinas, and Politics', *The Review of Politics* 66 (3): 357–83.

264 Bibliography

Hittinger, R. 1989. 'After MacIntyre: Natural Law Theory, Virtue Ethics, and Eudaimonia', *International Philosophical Quarterly* 29 (4): 449–61.

Holloway, J. 2010. *Crack Capitalism*. London: Pluto Press.

Holmes, S. 1993. *The Anatomy of Antiliberalism*. Cambridge, MA: Harvard University Press.

Hörcher, F. 2020. *A Political Philosophy of Conservatism: Prudence, Moderation and Tradition*. London: Bloomsbury Academic.

Horton, J. and Mendus, S. 1994a. 'Alasdair MacIntyre: *After Virtue* and After', in J. Horton and S. Mendus (eds), *After MacIntyre: Critical Perspectives on the Work of Alasdair MacIntyre*. Notre Dame, IN: University of Notre Dame Press, pp. 1–15.

1994b. *After MacIntyre: Critical Perspectives on the Work of Alasdair MacIntyre*. Cambridge: Polity Press.

Hume, D. 1975 [1751]. *An Enquiry Concerning the Principles of Morals*, in *Enquiries Concerning Human Understanding and Concerning the Principles of Morals*, 3rd edition. Oxford: Clarendon Press.

2007. *A Treatise of Human Nature: A Critical Edition*, vol. 1. Oxford: Clarendon Press.

Hurka, T. 1987. '"Good" and "Good for"', *Mind* 96 (381): 71–3.

2001. *Virtue, Vice, and Value*. Oxford: Oxford University Press.

Hurley, P. 2009. *Beyond Consequentialism*. Oxford: Oxford University Press.

Hursthouse, R. 1999. *On Virtue Ethics*. Oxford: Oxford University Press.

2012. 'Human Nature and Virtue Ethics', *Royal Institute of Philosophy Supplement* 70: 169–88.

Irwin, T. H. 1989. 'Tradition and Reason in the History of Ethics', *Social Philosophy and Policy* 7 (1): 45–68.

2007–2009. *The Development of Ethics*, 3 vols. Oxford: Oxford University Press.

Jameson, F. 2016. 'An American Utopia', in S. Zizek (ed.), *An American Utopia: Dual Power and the Universal Army*. London: Verso, pp. 1–96.

Kant, I. 2017. *The Metaphysics of Morals* (revised edition, trans. M. Gregor). Cambridge: Cambridge University Press.

Kaufmann, W. 1967. 'Editor's Introduction', in F. Nietzsche, *On the Genealogy of Morals and Ecce Homo*. New York: Random House, pp. 3–12.

1974. *Nietzsche: Philosopher, Psychologist, Antichrist*, 4th edition. Princeton, NJ: Princeton University Press.

Kekes, J. 1998. *A Case for Conservatism*. Ithaca, NY: Cornell University Press.

Kelly Jr, J. J. 2020. 'MacIntyre and Law', in R. Beadle and G. Moore (eds), *Learning from MacIntyre*. Eugene, OR: Pickwick Publications, pp. 280–303.

Kelsen, H. 1949. *General Theory of Law and State* (trans. A. Wedberg). Cambridge, MA: Harvard University Press.

Klein, J. 2012. 'The Stoics', in T. Angier (ed.), *Ethics: The Key Thinkers*. London: Bloomsbury Academic, pp. 57–82.

Knight, K. 1998a. *The MacIntyre Reader*. Cambridge: Polity Press.

1998b. 'Introduction', in K. Knight (ed.), *The MacIntyre Reader*. Cambridge: Polity Press, pp. 1–28.

2007. *Aristotelian Philosophy: Ethics and Politics from Aristotle to MacIntyre*. Cambridge: Polity Press.

Bibliography

2008. 'Practices: The Aristotelian Concept', *Analyse & Kritik* 30 (2): 317–29.

2011a. 'What's the Good of Post-Analytic Philosophy?', *History of European Ideas* 37 (3): 304–14.

2011b. 'Revolutionary Aristotelianism', in P. Blackledge and K. Knight (eds), *Virtue and Politics: Alasdair MacIntyre's Revolutionary Aristotelianism*. Notre Dame, IN: University of Notre Dame Press, pp. 20–34.

2013. 'Alasdair MacIntyre's Revisionary Aristotelianism: Pragmatism Opposed, Marxism Outmoded, Thomism Transformed', in F. O'Rourke (ed.), *What Happened in and to Moral Philosophy in the Twentieth Century? Philosophical Essays in Honor of Alasdair MacIntyre*. Notre Dame, IN: University of Notre Dame Press, pp. 83–121.

2017. 'MacIntyre's Critique of Management', in A. J. G. Sison, G. R. Beabout and I. Ferrero (eds), *Springer Handbook of Virtue in Business and Management*. New York: Springer, pp. 79–87.

2019. 'Alasdair MacIntyre's Revolutionary Peripateticism', in L. Trepanier and G. Havers (eds.), *Walk Away: When the Political Left Turns Right*. Lanham, MD: Rowman and Littlefield.

Kolakowski, L. 1978. *Main Currents in Marxism*, vol. 3 (trans. P. S. Falla). Oxford: Oxford University Press.

Kolozi, P. 2017. *Conservatives against Capitalism: From the Industrial Revolution to Globalization*. New York: Columbia University Press.

Korsgaard, C. 1996. *The Sources of Normativity* (Tanner Lectures 1992). Cambridge: Cambridge University Press.

Larmore, C. 1987. *Patterns of Moral Complexity*. Cambridge: Cambridge University Press.

Lear, G. R. 2015. 'Aristotle on Happiness and Long Life', in Ø. Rabbas, E. K. Emilsson, H. Fossheim and M. Tuominen (eds), *The Quest for the Good Life: Ancient Philosophers on Happiness*. Oxford: Oxford University Press, pp. 127–45.

LeBar, M. 2013. *The Value of Living Well*. Oxford: Oxford University Press.

Lemos, J. 1997. 'Virtue, Happiness, and Intelligibility', *Journal of Philosophical Research* 22: 307–20.

Lewis, C. S. 1944. *The Abolition of Man*. New York: HarperCollins.

Lilla, M. 2016. *The Shipwrecked Mind: On Political Reaction*. New York: New York Review of Books.

2018. 'Two Roads for the New French Right', *The New York Review of Books*, 65 (20): 42.

Lipscomb, B. J. B. 2022. *The Women Are Up to Something: How Elizabeth Anscombe, Philippa Foot, Mary Midgley, and Iris Murdoch Revolutionized Ethics*. Oxford: Oxford University Press.

Lomasky, L. 2002. 'Classical Liberalism and Civil Society', in S. Chambers and W. Kymlicka (eds), *Alternative Conceptions of Civil Society*. Princeton, NJ: Princeton University Press, pp. 50–70.

Lott, M. 2012. 'Moral Virtue as Knowledge of Human Form', *Social Theory and Practice* 38 (3): 407–31.

2016. 'Constructing a Good Life', *Journal of Moral Philosophy* 13 (3): 363–75.

Lutz, C. S. 2004. *Tradition in the Ethics of Alasdair MacIntyre: Relativism, Thomism, and Philosophy*. Lanham, MD: Lexington Books.

266   Bibliography

2012. *Reading Alasdair MacIntyre's After Virtue*. London: Continuum Publishing.

2014. 'MacIntyre Overview', *Internet Encyclopedia of Philosophy*, 30 April. Available at: https://iep.utm.edu/mac-over/.

2018. 'Alasdair MacIntyre's Ethics of Practical Reasoning', *Politics and Poetics* 4: 349640.

2019. 'Narrative and the Rationality of Traditions: MacIntyre's Epistemological Stance', *Acta Philosophica* 28 (2): 205–24.

2020. 'Alasdair MacIntyre: An Intellectual Biography', in R. Beadle and G. Moore (eds), *Learning from MacIntyre*. Eugene, OR: Pickwick Publications, pp. 1–33.

MacCormick, N. 1978. *Legal Reasoning and Legal Theory*. Oxford: Oxford University Press.

MacIntyre, A. C. 1951a. 'Analogy in Metaphysics', *Downside Review* 69 [1] (215): 45–61.

1951b. *The Significance of Moral Judgements. Being a Thesis presented for the Degree of M. A. in the University of Manchester under Ordinance II (A) in April 1951*. Unpublished.

1953. *Marxism: An Interpretation*. London: SCM Press.

1962. 'A Mistake about Causality in Social Science', in P. Laslett and W. G. Runciman (eds), *Philosophy, Politics and Society*, 2nd series. Oxford: Basil Blackwell, pp. 48–70.

1965a. 'Pleasure as a Reason for Action', *The Monist* 49 (2): 215–33.

1965b. 'Imperatives, Reasons for Action, and Morals', *Journal of Philosophy* 62 (19): 513–14.

1966. *A Short History of Ethics: A History of Moral Philosophy from the Homeric Age to the Twentieth Century*. London: Macmillan.

1968. *Marxism and Christianity*. New York: Shocken Books.

1969a. 'Philosophy and Sanity: Nietzsche's Titanism', *Encounter* 32 (4): 79–82.

1969b. 'Atheism and Morals', in A. MacIntyre and P. Ricoeur (eds), *The Religious Significance of Atheism*. New York: Columbia University Press, pp. 31–55.

1970. *Marcuse*. London: Fontana Press.

1971. 'The Idea of a Social Science', in *Against the Self-Images of the Age*. London: Duckworth, pp. 211–29.

1972. 'Modern German Thought', in M. Pasley (ed.), *Germany: A Companion to German Studies*. London: Methuen.

1973. 'Ideology, Social Science, and Revolution', *Comparative Politics* 5 (3): 321–42.

1977a. 'Epistemological Crises, Dramatic Narrative and the Philosophy of Science', *The Monist* 60: 453–72.

1977b. 'Can Medicine Dispense with a Theological Perspective on Human Nature?', in H. T. Engelhardt and D. Callahan (eds), *Knowledge, Value and Belief*. Hastings-on-Hudson, NY: Hastings Center, pp. 25–43.

1978a. *Against the Self-Images of the Age: Essays on Ideology and Philosophy*. Notre Dame, IN: University of Notre Dame Press.

Bibliography

1978b. 'What Morality Is Not', *Philosophy* 32: 325–35. Reprinted in *Against the Self-Images of the Age: Essays on Ideology and Philosophy*. Notre Dame, IN: University of Notre Dame Press, pp. 96–108.

1978c. 'Objectivity in Morality and Objectivity in Science', in H. T. Engelhardt and D. Callahan (eds), *Morals, Science and Sociality*. Hastings-on-Hudson, NY: Hastings Center, pp. 21–39.

1980. 'Regulation: A Substitute for Morality', *The Hastings Center Report* 10 (1): 31–3.

1981. *After Virtue: A Study in Moral Theory*. London: Duckworth Press.

1984. *After Virtue*, 2nd edition. Notre Dame, IN: University of Notre Dame Press.

1986. 'The Intelligibility of Action', in J. Margolis, M. Krausz and R. M. Burian (eds), *Rationality, Relativism and the Human Sciences*. Dordrecht: Martinus Nijhoff, pp. 63–80.

1988. *Whose Justice? Which Rationality?* London: Duckworth.

1990. *Three Rival Versions of Moral Enquiry: Encyclopaedia, Genealogy, and Tradition*. London: Duckworth.

1991. 'An Interview for *Cogito*', in K. Knight (ed.), *The MacIntyre Reader*. Cambridge: Polity Press, pp. 267–75.

1994a. 'An Interview with Giovanna Borrado', in K. Knight (ed.), *The MacIntyre Reader*. Cambridge: Polity Press, pp. 253–66.

1994b. 'The *Theses on Feuerbach*: A Road Not Taken', in K. Knight (ed.), *The MacIntyre Reader*. Cambridge: Polity Press, pp. 221–34.

1994c. 'My Station and Its Virtues', *Journal of Philosophical Research* 19: 1–8.

1994d. 'A Partial Response to My Critics', in J. Horton and S. Mendus (eds), *After MacIntyre: Critical Perspectives on the Work of Alasdair MacIntyre*. Cambridge: Polity Press, pp. 283–304.

1995a. 'Some Enlightenment Projects Reconsidered', in *Ethics and Politics: Selected Essays*, vol. 2. Cambridge: Cambridge University Press [2006], pp. 172–85.

1995b. 'Three Perspectives on Marxism: 1953, 1968, 1995', in *Ethics and Politics: Selected Essays*, vol. 2. Cambridge: Cambridge University Press [2006], pp. 145–58.

1995c. 'Natural Law as Subversive: The Case of Aquinas', in *Ethics and Politics: Selected Essays*, vol. 2. Cambridge: Cambridge University Press [2006], pp. 41–63.

1995d. *Marxism and Christianity*. London: Duckworth.

1996. 'An Interview with Alasdair MacIntyre' [Interview with Thomas D. Pearson], *Kinesis* 20: 34–47. Reprinted in *Kinesis* 23: 40–50.

1997. 'Natural Law Reconsidered', *International Philosophical Quarterly* 37 (1): 95–9.

1998a. 'Social Science Methodology as the Ideology of Bureaucratic Authority', in K. Knight (ed.), *The MacIntyre Reader*. Cambridge: Polity Press, pp. 53–68.

1998b. 'Politics, Philosophy and Common Good', in K. Knight (ed.), *The MacIntyre Reader*. Cambridge: Polity Press, pp. 235–52.

268 Bibliography

1998c. 'Plain Persons and Moral Philosophy: Rules, Virtues and Goods', in K. Knight (ed.), *The MacIntyre Reader*. Cambridge: Polity Press, pp. 136–52.

1998d. 'Moral Relativism, Truth, and Justification', in K. Knight (ed.), *The MacIntyre Reader*. Cambridge: Polity Press, pp. 202–22.

1998e. 'Notes from the Moral Wilderness', in K. Knight (ed.), *The MacIntyre Reader*. Cambridge: Polity Press, pp. 31–52.

1998f. 'Practical Rationalities as Forms of Social Structure', in K. Knight (ed.), *The MacIntyre Reader*. Cambridge: Polity Press, pp. 120–35.

1998g. 'The Theses on Feuerbach', in K. Knight (ed.), *The MacIntyre Reader*. Cambridge: Polity Press, pp. 223–34.

1999a. *Dependent Rational Animals: Why Human Beings Need the Virtues*. London: Duckworth.

1999b. 'Toleration and the Goods of Conflict', in *Ethics and Politics: Selected Essays*, vol. 2. Cambridge: Cambridge University Press [2006], pp. 205–223.

2004. 'Questions for Confucians', in K. Shun and D. Wong (eds), *Confucian Ethics: A Comparative Study of Self, Autonomy and Community*. Cambridge: Cambridge University Press, pp. 203–18.

2006a. *Ethics and Politics: Selected Essays*, vol. 2. Cambridge: Cambridge University Press.

2006b. 'Preface', in *Ethics and Politics: Selected Essays*, vol. 2. Cambridge: Cambridge University Press, pp. vii–xi.

2006c. 'Epistemological Crises, Dramatic Narrative and the Philosophy of Science', in *The Tasks of Philosophy: Selected Essays*, vol. 1. Cambridge: Cambridge University Press, pp. 3–23.

2006d. *First Principles, Final Ends, and Contemporary Moral Issues* (The Aquinas Lecture 1990). Marquette, WI: Marquette University Press. Reprinted in *The Tasks of Philosophy: Selected Essays*, vol. 1. Cambridge: Cambridge University Press, pp. 143–78.

2006e. *The Tasks of Philosophy: Selected Essays*, vol. 1. Cambridge: Cambridge University Press.

2006f. 'Moral Philosophy and Contemporary Social Practice', in *Tasks of Philosophy: Selected Essays*, vol. 1. Cambridge: Cambridge University Press, pp. 104–22.

2006g. 'Social Structures and Their Threats to Moral Agency', in *Ethics and Politics: Selected Essays*, vol. 2. Cambridge: Cambridge University Press, pp. 186–204.

2006h. 'Outside Ethics', *Notre Dame Philosophical Reviews*, 5 March. Available at: https://ndpr.nd.edu/reviews/outside-ethics.

2007. *After Virtue*, 3rd edition. Notre Dame, IN: University of Notre Dame Press.

2008a. 'What More Needs to Be Said? A Beginning, although Only a Beginning, at Saying It', *Analyse & Kritik* 30: 261–76.

2008b. 'Prediction and Politics', in P. Blackledge and N. D. Davidson (eds), *Alasdair MacIntyre's Engagement with Marxism: Selected Writings 1953–1974*. Leiden: Brill, pp. 249–61.

2008c. 'Communism and British Intellectuals', in P. Blackledge and N. D. Davidson (eds), *Alasdair MacIntyre's Engagement with Marxism: Selected Writings 1953–1974*. Leiden: Brill, pp. 115–22.

Bibliography

2009a. *God, Philosophy, Universities: A Selective History of the Catholic Philosophical Tradition*. Lanham, MD: Rowman and Littlefield.

2009b. 'Common Goods and Political Reasoning', unpublished document, CASEP, London Metropolitan University.

2009c. 'Intractable Moral Disagreements', in L. Cunningham (ed.), *Intractable Disputes about the Natural Law: Alasdair MacIntyre and His Critics*. Notre Dame, IN: University of Notre Dame Press, pp. 1–52.

2010a. 'Five Answers to Two Questions', unpublished document, CASEP, London Metropolitan University.

2010b. 'Review of: G. A. Cohen, *Why Not Socialism?*', *Ethics* 120 (2): 393–4.

2010c. 'On Being a Theistic Philosopher in a Secularized Culture', *Proceedings of the American Catholic Philosophical Association* 84: 23–32.

2011a. 'How Aristotelianism Can Become Revolutionary: Ethics, Resistance, and Utopia', in P. Blackledge and K. Knight (eds), *Virtue and Politics: Alasdair MacIntyre's Revolutionary Aristotelianism*. Notre Dame, IN: University of Notre Dame Press, pp. 11–19.

2011b. 'Where We Were, Where We Are, Where We Need to Be', in P. Blackledge and K. Knight (eds), *Virtue and Politics: Alasdair MacIntyre's Revolutionary Aristotelianism*. Notre Dame, IN: University of Notre Dame Press, pp. 307–34.

2012. 'Practical Rationality and Irrationality and Their Social Settings', unpublished paper presented to CASEP, London Metropolitan University.

2013a. 'Epilogue: What Next?', in F. O'Rourke (ed.), *What Happened in and To Moral Philosophy in the Twentieth Century? Philosophical Essays in Honor of Alasdair MacIntyre*. Notre Dame, IN: University of Notre Dame Press, pp. 474–8.

2013b. 'Replies', *Revue Internationale de Philosophie* 264 (2): 201–20.

2013c. 'On Having Survived the Academic Moral Philosophy of the Twentieth Century', in F. O'Rourke (ed.), *What Happened in and To Moral Philosophy in the Twentieth Century? Philosophical Essays in Honor of Alasdair MacIntyre*. Notre Dame, IN: University of Notre Dame Press, pp. 17–34.

2014. 'Ends and Endings', *American Catholic Philosophical Quarterly* 88 (4): 807–21.

2015. 'The Irrelevance of Ethics', in A. Bielskis and K. Knight (eds), *Virtue and Economy: Essays on Morality and Markets*. Farnham: Ashgate Publishing, pp. 7–22.

2016. *Ethics in the Conflicts of Modernity: An Essay on Desire, Practical Reasoning, and Narrative*. Cambridge: Cambridge University Press.

2020. 'Four – or More? – Political Aristotles', in A. Bielskis, E. Leontsini and K. Knight (eds), *Virtue Ethics and Contemporary Aristotelianism: Modernity, Conflict and Politics*. London: Bloomsbury Academic, pp. 11–24.

2021. 'Human Dignity: A Puzzling and Possibly Dangerous Idea?' Available at: www.youtube.com/watch?v=V727AcOoogQ.

Mansfield, H. 2010. *Tocqueville: A Very Short Introduction*. Oxford: Oxford University Press.

Maritain, J. 1970. *Three Reformers: Luther, Descartes, Rousseau*. Port Washington, NY: Kennikat Press.

270 Bibliography

Marx, K. 1959. *The Economic and Philosophic Manuscripts of 1844* (trans. M. Milligan). Moscow: Progress Press.

1969. The Theses on Feuerbach (trans. W. Lough), in *Marx/Engels Selected Works*, vol. 1. Moscow: Progress Publishers, pp. 13–15. Available at: www.marxists.org/archive/marx/works/1845/theses/theses.htm.

1973. *Grundrisse*. London: Penguin Books.

1975a. 'Theses on Feuerbach', in *Early Writings*. London: Penguin Books, pp. 421–3.

1975b. 'Economic and Philosophical Manuscripts', in *Early Writings*. London: Penguin Books, pp. 279–400.

1976. *Capital*, vol. 1. London: Penguin Books.

1981. *Capital*, vol. 3. London: Penguin Books.

Marx, K. and Engels, F. 1975. 'The Holy Family', in *Marx and Engels Collected Works*, vol. 4. London: Lawrence and Wishart, pp. 3–211.

1978. 'Manifesto of the Communist Party', in R. Tucker (ed.), *The Marx–Engels Reader*. New York: W. W. Norton & Company, pp. 469–500.

2000 [1848]. *The Communist Manifesto*, in D. McLellan (ed.), *Karl Marx: Selected Writings*, 2nd edition. Oxford: Oxford University Press.

McAdams, D. 2013. 'The Psychological Self as Actor, Agent, and Author', *Perspectives on Psychological Science* 8 (3): 272–95.

McMylor, P. M. 1993. *Alasdair MacIntyre: Critic of Modernity*. Abingdon: Routledge.

2011. 'Compartmentalisation and Social Roles: MacIntyre's Critical Theory of Modernity', in P. Blackledge and K. Knight (eds), *Virtue and Politics: Alasdair MacIntyre's Revolutionary Aristotelianism*. Notre Dame, IN: University of Notre Dame Press, pp. 228–40.

McPherson, D. 2017. 'Traditional Morality and Sacred Values', *Analyse & Kritik* 39 (1): 41–62.

2019. 'Existential Conservatism', *Philosophy* 94 (3): 383–407.

2020. *Virtue and Meaning: A Neo-Aristotelian Perspective*. Cambridge: Cambridge University Press.

2022. *The Virtues of Limits*. Oxford: Oxford University Press.

Mendham, M. 2007. 'Eudaimonia and Agape in MacIntyre and Kierkegaard's "Works of Love": Beginning Unpolemical Inquiry', *Journal of Religious Ethics* 35 (4): 591–625.

Michéa, J.-C. 2007. *L'Empire du Moindre Mal: Essai sur la Civilisation Libérale*. Paris: Climats.

Milbank, J. 2006. *Theology and Social Theory: Beyond Secular Reason*, 2nd edition. Oxford: Blackwell Publishing.

Milbank, J. and Pabst, A. 2016. *The Politics of Virtue*. Lanham, MD: Rowman and Littlefield.

Mill, J. S. 1989. *On Liberty and Other Writings* (ed. S. Collini). Cambridge: Cambridge University Press.

2018. *Autobiography*. Oxford: Oxford University Press.

Misak, C. 2000. *Truth, Politics, Morality: Pragmatism and Deliberation*. Abingdon: Routledge.

Moore, G. 2002. 'On the Implications of the Practice–Institution Distinction', *Business Ethics Quarterly* 12: 19–32.

Bibliography

2017. *Virtue at Work*. Oxford: Oxford University Press.

Moore, G. and Beadle, R. 2006. 'In Search of Organizational Virtue in Business', *Organization Studies* 27: 369–89.

Moore, G. E. 1993. *Principia Ethica*, revised edition. Cambridge: Cambridge University Press.

Moore, J. 1983. *Japanese Workers and the Struggle for Power*. Madison: University of Wisconsin Press.

Moran, R. 2015. *The Story of My Life: Narrative and Self-Understanding*. Marquette, WI: Marquette University Press.

Mulhall, S. 2013. *The Self and Its Shadows: A Book of Essays on Individuality as Negation in Philosophy and the Arts*. Oxford: Oxford University Press.

2021. *The Ascetic Ideal: Genealogies of Life-Denial in Religion, Morality, Art, Science and Philosophy*. Oxford: Oxford University Press.

Mulhall, S. and Swift, A. 1996. *Liberals and Communitarians*, 2nd edition. Oxford: Blackwell.

Müller, J. 2018. 'Practical and Productive Thinking in Aristotle', *Phronesis* 63 (2): 148–75.

Murdoch, I. 2014 [1970]. *The Sovereignty of Good*. Abingdon: Routledge.

Murphy, J. 2020. *Your Whole Life: Beyond Childhood and Adulthood*. Philadelphia: University of Pennsylvania Press.

Murphy, M. C. 2003a. *Alasdair MacIntyre*. Cambridge: Cambridge University Press.

2003b. 'MacIntyre's Political Philosophy', in M. C. Murphy (ed.), *Alasdair MacIntyre*. Cambridge: Cambridge University Press, pp. 152–75.

Nicholas, J. 2018. 'Geoff Moore, Virtue at Work', *Philosophy of Management* 17 (2): 257–9.

Nicholas, J. L. 2021. *Love and Politics: Persistent Human Desires as a Foundation for Liberation*. Abingdon: Routledge.

Nietzsche, F. 1967a. 'On the Genealogy of Morals' (trans. W. Kaufman and R. J. Hollingdale), in W. Kaufman (ed.), *On the Genealogy of Morals and Ecce Homo*. New York: Random House, pp. 24–166.

1967b. '*Ecce Homo*' (trans. W. Kaufmann), in W. Kaufman (ed.), *On the Genealogy of Morals and Ecce Homo*. New York: Random House, pp. 223–338.

1973. *Beyond Good and Evil: Prelude to a Philosophy of the Future* (trans. R. J. Hollingdale). Harmondsworth: Penguin.

1994. *The Birth of Tragedy and Other Writings* (ed. and trans. R. Geuss and R. Speirs). Cambridge: Cambridge University Press.

Nussbaum, M. C. 1989. 'Recoiling from Reason', *New York Review of Books*, 7 December. Available at: www.nybooks.com/articles/1989/12/07/recoiling-from-reason/.

2001 [1986]. *The Fragility of Goodness: Luck and Ethics in Greek Tragedy and Philosophy*. Cambridge: Cambridge University Press.

O'Donovan, O. 1994. *Resurrection and Moral Order*, 2nd edition. Grand Rapids, MI: Eerdmans Publishing.

Oakeshott, M. 1991 [1962]. *Rationalism in Politics and other Essays*, new and expanded edition. Indianapolis, IN: Liberty Fund.

Bibliography

Osborne, T. 2008. 'MacIntyre, Thomism and the Contemporary Common Good', *Analyse & Kritik* 30: 75–90.

Outhwaite, W. 1987. *New Philosophies of Social Science*. London: Macmillan.

Parsons, T. 1947. 'Introduction', in M. Weber, *The Theory of Social and Economic Organization* (trans. M. Henderson and T. Parsons, ed. T. Parsons). Oxford: Oxford University Press.

Perreau-Saussine, É. 2005. *Alasdair MacIntyre: Une Biographie Intellectuelle*. Paris: Presses Universitaires de France.

Pettigrove, G. 2011. 'Is Virtue Ethics Self-Effacing?', *The Journal of Ethics* 15 (3): 191–207.

Pinches, C. R. 2002. *Theology and Action: After Theory in Christian Ethics*. Grand Rapids, MI: Eerdmans Publishing.

2014. 'On Hope', in K. Timpe and C. Boyd (eds), *Virtues and Their Vices*. Oxford: Oxford University Press, pp. 349–68.

Pinkoski, N. 2019. 'Why Alasdair MacIntyre Is Not a Conservative Post-Liberal', *The Political Science Review* 43 (2): 531–63.

Polanyi, K. 2001. *The Great Transformation*. Boston: Beacon Press.

Pozo, I. S. del 2022. '¿Por Qué Necesitamos Virtudes?: MacIntyre Tras Weber', in F. J. de la Torre, M. Loria and L. Nontol (eds), *Cuarenta Años de After Virtue de Alasdair MacIntyre: Relecturas Iberoamericanas*. Madrid: Dykinson.

Provost, R. 2021. *Rebel Courts*. Oxford: Oxford University Press.

Quinton, A. 1978. *The Politics of Imperfection: The Religious and Secular Traditions of Conservative Thought in England from Hooker to Oakeshott*. London: Faber and Faber.

Rawls, J. 1955. 'Two Concepts of Rules', *The Philosophical Review* 64 (1): 3–32.

1958. 'Justice as Fairness', *The Philosophical Review* 67 (2): 164–94.

1971. *A Theory of Justice*. Cambridge, MA: Harvard University Press.

1993. *Political Liberalism*. New York: Columbia University Press.

1999. *Collected Papers* (ed. S. Freeman). Cambridge, MA: Harvard University Press.

Raz, J. 2002. 'The Central Conflict: Morality and Self-Interest', in *Engaging Reason: On the Theory of Value and Action*. Oxford: Oxford University Press, pp. 303–32.

Retter, M. D. 2015. 'Internal Goods to Legal Practice: Reclaiming Fuller with MacIntyre', *UCL Journal of Law and Jurisprudence* 4 (1): 1–31.

2019. 'Before and After Legal Positivity: Peremptory Norms from Global and Transnational Social Practice', in L. Siliquini-Cinelli (ed.), *Legal Positivism in a Global and Transnational Age*. Dordecht: Springer, pp. 179–212.

2022. 'Common Goods, Group Rights, and Human Rights', in T. Angier, I. Benson and M. D. Retter (eds), *The Cambridge Handbook on Natural Law and Human Rights*. Cambridge: Cambridge University Press, pp. 291–307.

Revel, J.-F. 1970. *Ni Marx, Ni Jésus: La Nouvelle Révolution Mondiale est Commencée aux Etats-Unis*. Paris: Robert Laffont.

Roberts, R. C. 2015. 'How Virtue Contributes to Flourishing', in M. Alfano (ed.), *Current Controversies in Virtue Theory*. Abingdon: Routledge, pp. 36–49.

Rodriguez-Blanco, V. 2007. 'Peter Winch and H. L. A. Hart: Two Concepts of the Internal Point of View', *Canadian Journal of Law and Jurisprudence* 20 (2): 453–73.

Bibliography

2014. *Law and Authority under the Guise of the Good*. Oxford: Hart Publishing.

Rondel, D. 2007. 'Equality, Luck, and Pragmatism', *Journal of Speculative Philosophy* 21 (2): 115–23.

2018. *Pragmatist Egalitarianism*. Oxford: Oxford University Press.

Rorty, R. 1991. *Objectivity, Relativism, and Truth: Philosophical Papers*, vol. 1. Cambridge: Cambridge University Press.

Rowland, T. 2003. *Culture and the Thomist Tradition: After Vatican II*. Abingdon: Routledge.

Rudd, A. 2012. *Self, Value, and Narrative: A Kierkegaardian Approach*. Oxford: Oxford University Press.

Russell, D. C. 2012. *Happiness for Humans*. Oxford: Oxford University Press.

2013. 'Virtue Ethics, Happiness, and the Good Life', in D. C. Russell (ed.), *The Cambridge Companion to Virtue Ethics*. Cambridge: Cambridge University Press, pp. 7–28.

Ryle, G. 1945–1946. 'Knowing How and Knowing That: The Presidential Address', *Proceedings of the Aristotelian Society*, New Series 46: 1–16.

Sandel, M. J. 1982. *Liberalism and the Limits of Justice*. Cambridge: Cambridge University Press.

1984. 'The Procedural Republic and the Unencumbered Self', *Political Theory* 12 (1): 81–96.

Sartre, J.-P. 2007. *Existentialism Is a Humanism* (trans. C. Macomber). New Haven, CT: Yale University Press.

Sayers, S. P. 2011. 'MacIntyre and Modernity', in P. Blackledge and K. Knight (eds), *Virtue and Politics: Alasdair MacIntyre's Revolutionary Aristotelianism*. Notre Dame, IN: University of Notre Dame Press, pp. 79–96.

Scheffler, S. 1992. *Human Morality*. Oxford: Oxford University Press.

1994. *The Rejection of Consequentialism*. Oxford: Oxford University Press.

Schmidtz, D. 2006. *The Elements of Justice*. Cambridge: Cambridge University Press.

Schumpeter, J. A. 2008 [1942]. *Capitalism, Socialism and Democracy*, 3rd edition. New York: HarperPerennial.

Scruton, R. 2006. 'Hayek and Conservatism', in E. Feser (ed.), *The Cambridge Companion to Hayek*. Cambridge: Cambridge University Press, pp. 208–31.

2010. *The Uses of Pessimism: And the Dangers of False Hope*. Oxford: Oxford University Press.

2014. *How to Be a Conservative*. London: Bloomsbury Publishing.

Simmonds, N. 2007. *Law as a Moral Idea*. Oxford: Oxford University Press.

Simon, Y. 1980. *A General Theory of Authority*. Notre Dame, IN: University of Notre Dame Press.

Singer, P. 1995. *Rethinking Life and Death: The Collapse of Our Traditional Ethics*. New York: St. Martin's Press.

Sinnicks, M. 2014. 'Mastery of One's Domain Is Not the Essence of Management', *Business Ethics Journal Review* 2 (2): 8–14.

Slote, M. 2001. *Morality from Motives*. Oxford: Oxford University Press.

2010. *Moral Sentimentalism*. Oxford: Oxford University Press.

Solomon, D. 1999. 'Keeping Virtue in Its Place: A Critique of Subordinating Strategies', in J. Hibbs and J. O'Callaghan (eds), *Recovering Nature: Essays in*

274 Bibliography

Natural Philosophy, Ethics, and Metaphysics in Honor of Ralph McInerny. Notre Dame, IN: University of Notre Dame Press, pp. 83–104.

Stevenson, C. L. 1937. 'The Emotive Meaning of Ethical Terms', *Mind*, New Series 46 (181): 14–31.

1944. *Language and Ethics*. New Haven, CT: Yale University Press.

Stout, J. 2004. *Democracy and Tradition*. Princeton, NJ: Princeton University Press.

Strauss, L. 1953. *The Political Philosophy of Hobbes: Its Basis and Genesis*. Chicago, IL: University of Chicago Press.

1958. *Thoughts on Machiavelli*. Chicago, IL: University of Chicago Press.

1995. *Liberalism Ancient and Modern*. Chicago, IL: University of Chicago Press.

Swanton, C. 2003. *Virtue Ethics: A Pluralistic View*. Oxford: Oxford University Press.

Taylor, C. 1989. *Sources of the Self: The Making of the Modern Identity*. Cambridge, MA: Harvard University Press.

1994. 'Justice after Virtue', in J. Horton and S. Mendus (eds), *After MacIntyre: Critical Perspectives on the Work of Alasdair MacIntyre*. Cambridge: Polity Press, pp. 16–43.

Thompson, M. 2008. *Life and Action: Elementary Structures of Practice and Practical Thought*. Cambridge, MA: Harvard University Press.

Thomson, J. J. 2008. *Normativity*. Chicago, IL: Open Court Publishing.

Tocqueville, A. 2004. *Democracy in America*. New York: Library of America.

Toner, C. H. 2010. 'Virtue Ethics and the Nature and Forms of Egoism', *Journal of Philosophical Research* 35: 275–303.

Tosi, J. and Warmke, B. 2022. 'Conservative Critiques', in M. Zwolinski and B. Benjamin (eds), *The Routledge Companion to Libertarianism*. Abingdon: Routledge, pp. 579–92.

Trilling, L. 1978. *The Liberal Imagination: Essays on Literature and Society*. New York: New York Review Books.

Velleman, D. 2000. *The Possibility of Practical Reason*. Oxford: Oxford University Press.

Vermeule, A. 2018. 'Integration from Within', *American Affairs* 2 (1). Available at: https://americanaffairsjournal.org/2018/02/integration-from-within/.

2019. 'All Human Conflict Is Ultimately Theological', *Church Life Journal*, 26 July. Available at: https://churchlifejournal.nd.edu/articles/all-human-con flict-is-ultimately-theological/.

2022. *Common Good Constitutionalism*. Cambridge: Polity Press.

Walzer, M. 2012. *In God's Shadow: Politics in the Hebrew Bible*. New Haven, CT: Yale University Press.

Weber, M. 1978. *Economy and Society: An Outline of Interpretive Sociology*. Berkeley, CA: University of California Press.

1994. 'Parliament and Government in Germany under a New Political Order' (trans. R. Speirs), in P. Lassman and R. Speirs (eds), *Weber: Political Writings*. Cambridge: Cambridge University Press, pp. 130–271.

2004. 'Politics as a Vocation' (trans. R. Livingstone), in D. Owen and T. B. Strong (eds), *Max Weber: The Vocation Lectures*. Indianapolis, IN: Hackett, pp. 32–94.

Bibliography

2016. *Die Protestantische Ethik und der Geist des Kapitalismus / Die Protestantischen Sekten und der Geist des Kapitalismus* (Max Weber Gesamtausgabe, Teil 1, Vol. 18; ed. W. Schluchter. Tübingen: Mohr Siebeck.

Whiting, J. 2002. 'Eudaimonia, External Results, and Choosing Virtuous Actions for Themselves', *Philosophy and Phenomenological Research* 65 (2): 270–90.

Williams, B. A. O. 1985. *Ethics and the Limits of Philosophy*. London: Fontana Press.

2009. 'Life as Narrative', *The European Journal of Philosophy* 17 (2): 305–14.

Winch, P. 1990. *The Idea of a Social Science and Its Relation to Philosophy*, 2nd edition. Abingdon: Routledge.

Wood, A. 2000. 'Kant vs. Eudaimonism', in P. Cicovacki (ed.), *Kant's Legacy: Essays Dedicated to Lewis White Beck*. Rochester, NY: University of Rochester Press, pp. 261–82.

2011. 'Kant and Agent-Oriented Ethics', in L. Jost and J. Wuerth (eds), *Perfecting Virtue: New Essays on Kantian Ethics and Virtue Ethics*. Cambridge: Cambridge University Press, pp. 58–91.

Woodcock, S. 2015. 'Neo-Aristotelian Naturalism and the Indeterminacy Objection', *International Journal of Philosophical Studies* 23 (1): 23–41.

Wright, E. O. 2010. *Envisioning Real Utopias*. London: Verso.

Zagzebski, L. T. 2017. *Exemplarist Moral Theory*. Oxford: Oxford University Press.

Index

administrative state, 99, 105
Ahmari, Sohrab, 132
alienation, 6, 114–15, 122, 146–7, 171,
  250–6
analytic philosophy, 7, 165, 201, 205, 210
antiliberalism, 83, 86, 126
Austen, Jane, 14, 151, 154, 158

Beabout, Greg, 239–46
Benedict Option, The, 126, 131, 216
Benedict, Saint, 2, 204–7, 213–16
Bentham, Jeremy, 1, 32–6, 40, 136
British New Left, 133
bureaucracy, 5, 9, 52–3, 76, 98, 104,
  247–57
bureaucratic manager, 50, 58, 76–7, 84, 89,
  192
bureaucratic state, 93, 99, 250, 252
business, 9, 239–57
Butler, Joseph, 21, 43

capitalism, 9, 31, 48, 51–3, 82, 92, 94, 97,
  105, 112, 121, 124, 133–40, 239–57
  post-capitalism, 133–9
  spirits of capitalism, 240
  state capitalism, 249–52
Cavell, Stanley, 146, 147, 154, 156
characters, 7, 50, 76, 155–8, 211, 212, 215,
  242
Christianity, 2, 50, 138, 153, 155, 216,
  249–50, 253
  Augustinian, 103–4, 206–9
complete life, 161, 172–7
Cummins Engines, 253–7

deliberation, 8, 13, 20, 22–3, 27, 80, 130,
  170, 229–31, 256
Deming, W. E., 253–7
Deneen, Patrick, 72, 95, 112, 126–7, 132–3
determinatio, 231
Dreher, Rod, 6–8, 126, 131

egoism, 40, 43–5
emotivism, 6, 34, 57, 71–3, 76, 89, 127–30,
  151, 182, 184, 190, 192, 242, 254
enacted narrative, 161, 167–9, 208–15
epistemology, 132
  epistemological crisis, 145, 150, 179–82,
    194–8, 222
eudaimonia, 14, 18–24, 31, 36, 38–46, 189
  goodness-prior, 32, 39–46
  welfare-prior, 32, 39–46
existentialism, 165, 182, 187, 205, 210

final end, 41, 64, 100, 159–69, 172–7
Finnis, John, 225, 226, 231, 235
flourishing, 19–21, 29, 31–42, 74, 77, 84,
  90, 127, 150, 151

Geuss, Raymond, 132, 245
good life, 7, 22–4, 26, 35–9, 46, 59, 73–5,
  77–9, 111, 119, 124, 128, 160, 163,
  168–9, 173–7
goods
  common, 3, 5, 8, 42, 57–66, 89–101,
    105–6, 112, 121, 228–38, 245–8,
    254–7
  external to a practice, 3, 20, 56–66, 91,
    127–8, 137, 162, 227–9, 237, 245,
    247, 253
  internal to a practice, 3, 5, 8–9, 14, 55–9,
    66, 91, 118–19, 127–9, 135, 162,
    171–2, 224–35, 255
  shared, 14, 30, 135
  social, 4, 14, 17, 30

Hamlet, 145
happiness, 4, 7, 14, 18–46, 155, 190, 193
Hart, H. L. A, 219–27, 234, 236
Holmes, Stephen, 70, 83, 87, 93, 125–6
human action, intelligible, 35–6, 42, 82,
  150, 161–6, 180, 189–93, 197,
  210–15, 219, 224

276

Index

277

human good, 36–40, 59, 69, 74, 77, 81, 89–91, 102, 112, 117, 159–62, 168, 175–8
humanism, 105, 125, 133, 137–40, 182

Ideologiekritik, 257
illiberalism, 125
institutions, 1–5, 47–66, 91–3, 97–8, 104–6, 127–31, 215–16, 219, 222, 228–38, 239
integration, 7, 166–70

James, Henry, 154–8
Judaism, 138, 207, 217–18

law
  juridical, 8, 65, 74–6, 78, 81, 97, 99–101, 105, 219–38
  moral, 181
  natural, 94, 97, 105, 123, 180, 196–7
left, the political, 6, 71, 82, 92–6, 104–6, 125, 135–40, 187, 241, 250
legal officials, 221–2, 225, 231, 233–5
legal subjects, 222, 225, 231–4
legal theory, 219–21, 230–1, 235–7
legal tradition, 226, 232, 235
Leo XIII, Pope, 104
liberalism, 2–9, 49, 69–106, 121–2, 125–31, 133, 215–16, 236–7, 249
  individualism, liberal, 4, 52, 70, 73, 76–8, 82, 84, 86, 92, 96, 121–2, 183, 189
  neutrality, liberal, 70, 97, 99–101

management, 9, 51, 65, 90, 192, 236, 239
manipulation, 9, 57, 64, 90, 148, 191, 243, 244, 254
markets, 50, 74, 128, 255
Marxism, 2, 52–3, 90, 122, 126, 133–9, 185–8, 207–9, 243, 249–54
melodrama, 145–6, 154
Milbank, John, 5, 95–101, 215
Mill, John Stuart, 1, 19, 35, 83, 148
Moore, Geoff, 9, 28, 147, 183–4, 240, 246–57
moral formation, 212

narrative, 1–8, 64–5, 70–3, 118–20, 143–58, 159, 179–85, 193–6, 208–15
  quest, 118, 165, 167–9, 229
  self, 119, 120, 165–8, 212
  unity, 7, 14, 155, 159, 163, 168–9
nation-state, 99

Nietzsche, Friedrich, 4–7, 19, 47–65, 87, 101–3, 130–2, 138, 147–58, 181, 193, 206–7, 243

O'Donovan, Oliver, 42, 45
obligation, 117, 119, 180–2, 185, 187, 189, 194, 197, 221–5, 231
ontology, 180, 195–6

Pabst, Adrian, 5, 95–101
phenomenology, 18, 20, 144, 187, 205, 210
pleasure, 4, 24–9, 31–6, 42–5
political community, 63, 93, 135, 226–38
postliberalism, 5, 85–6, 94–106, 135
power, 47–66, 77–9, 90–2, 97–105, 185, 233, 247
  as domination, 50, 53, 90, 94
  labour, 250–4
  will to, 49, 55, 57, 62–6, 138
practical wisdom, 162, 190, 212, 234
prophet(s), Hebrew, 201–5

Rawls, John, 57, 71, 75, 78, 82
reactionary, 85, 93–4, 105, 125–35
right, the political, 6, 71, 82, 95–7, 126, 133
Rorty, Richard, 81–2
rule of law, 64, 121, 226–38

science fiction, 143
social criticism, 202
social sciences, 51–2, 54–6, 129, 134, 185, 192–3, 220, 222
social theory, 89, 220, 224, 240
socialism, 6, 98, 121, 125, 133–40
stories. *See* narrative

telos, 7, 14, 18, 21, 24, 28, 34–8, 43, 54, 82, 128, 135, 150–1, 155, 159, 162, 166, 169, 173–8, 191, 193, 196, 201, 224, 229, 231, 245
theology, 1, 8, 65, 87, 99, 191, 195, 209, 214–16
theory of rationality, 179–80

utopianism, 6, 109, 122–4, 125, 133–40

Vermeule, Adrian, 5, 82, 95–101

Weber, Max, 4, 9, 48–65, 89, 239–41
well-being, 21, 24, 29, 40–4, 108
Winch, Peter, 219–26

Printed in the United States
by Baker & Taylor Publisher Services